State of India's Livelihoods Report 2016

Thank you for choosing a SAGE product!
If you have any comment, observation or feedback,
I would like to personally hear from you.
Please write to me at **contactceo@sagepub.in**

Vivek Mehra, Managing Director and CEO, SAGE India.

Bulk Sales

SAGE India offers special discounts
for purchase of books in bulk.
We also make available special imprints
and excerpts from our books on demand.

For orders and enquiries, write to us at

Marketing Department
SAGE Publications India Pvt Ltd
B1/I-1, Mohan Cooperative Industrial Area
Mathura Road, Post Bag 7
New Delhi 110044, India

E-mail us at **marketing@sagepub.in**

Get to know more about SAGE

Be invited to SAGE events, get on our mailing list.
Write today to **marketing@sagepub.in**

State of India's Livelihoods Report 2016

Girija Srinivasan
Narasimhan Srinivasan

Los Angeles | London | New Delhi
Singapore | Washington DC | Melbourne

Jointly published in 2017 by

SAGE Publications India Pvt Ltd
B1/I-1 Mohan Cooperative Industrial Area
Mathura Road, New Delhi 110 044, India
www.sagepub.in

SAGE Publications Inc
2455 Teller Road
Thousand Oaks, California 91320, USA

SAGE Publications Ltd
1 Oliver's Yard, 55 City Road
London EC1Y 1SP, United Kingdom

SAGE Publications Asia-Pacific Pte Ltd
3 Church Street
#10-04 Samsung Hub
Singapore 049483

ACCESS Development Services
28, Hauz Khas Village
New Delhi 110 016
www.accessdev.org

Published by Vivek Mehra for SAGE Publications India Pvt Ltd, Phototypeset in 10/13 pt Minion by Diligent Typesetter India Pvt Ltd, Delhi, and printed at Sai Print-o-Pack, New Delhi.

Library of Congress Cataloging-in-Publication Data Available

ISBN: 978-93-860-6223-9 (PB)

SAGE Team: Rajesh Dey, Guneet Kaur Gulati, Madhurima Thapa and Rajinder Kaur

Contents

Contents

List of Tables

List of Figures

List of Boxes

List of Annexures

List of Abbreviations

AAP	Annual Action Plan
AAS	Agromet Advisory Services
ADB	Asian Development Bank
ADS	Area Development Society
ADWDR	Agriculture Debt Waiver and Debt Relief
AIBP	Accelerated Irrigation Benefits Programme
AIGF	Auto Ikat Group Former
AMFU	Agrometeorological Field Units
APCO	Andhra Pradesh State Handloom Weavers' Cooperative Society
APDAI	Andhra Pradesh Drought Adaptation Initiatives
APFAMGS	Andhra Pradesh Farmers Managed Groundwater System
ASDP	Aajeevika Skills Development Programme
AWCS	Apex Weavers' Cooperative Societies
BAIF	Bharatia Agro-Industries Foundation
BAPU	Biometrically Authenticated Physical Uptake
BC	Business Correspondent
BE	Budget Estimates
BPL	Below Poverty Line
BSE	Bombay Stock Exchange
CACP	Commission for Agriculture Costs and Prices
CAMPA	Compensatory Afforestation Fund Management and Planning Authority
CBGA	Centre for Budget and Governance Accountability
CBO	Community-based Organization
CCA	Climate Change Adaptation
CCD	Covenant Centre for Development
CCEA	Cabinet Committee on Economic Affairs
CDS	Current Daily Status
CDS	Community Development Society
CEDRA	Climate change and Environmental Degradation Risk and Adaptation
CEO	Chief Executive Officer
CET	Commissionerate of Employment and Training
CGTMSE	Credit Guarantee Fund Trust for Micro and Small Enterprises
CHC	Custom Hiring Centers
CHI	Channels of High Impact
CIG	Common Interest Group
CII	Confederation of Indian Industry

CIP	Central Issue Price
CMIE	Centre for Monitoring Indian Economy
CMRC	Community Managed Resource Centers
CMSA	Community Managed Sustainable Agriculture
CoDriVE	Community Driven Vulnerability Evaluation
CPI	Consumer Price Index
CPRs	Common Pool Resources
CREDA	Chhattisgarh State Renewable Energy Development Agency
CRIDA	Central Research Institute for Dryland Agriculture
CSF	Classic Swine Fever
CSO	Central Statistical Office
CSR	Corporate Social Responsibility
CSS	Central Sector Schemes
CWS	Centre for World Solidarity
DAY	Deen Dayal Antyodaya Yojana
DBT	Direct Benefit Transfer
DCCB	District Central Cooperative Bank
DDU-GKY	Deen Dayal Upadhyaya Grameen Kaushalya Yojana
DGET	Directorate General of Employment and Training
Discom	Distribution Company
DPIP	District Poverty Initiative Project
DSC	Development Support Center
EDP	Entrepreneurship Development Programme
e-NAM	Electronic National Agricultural Market
FAO	Food and Agriculture Organisation
FC	Farmers Collective
FCI	Food Corporation of India
FICCI	Federation of Indian Chambers of Commerce and Industry
FIG	Farmer Interest Group
FPC	Farmer Producer Company
FPO	Farmers' Producers Organization
FPS	Fair Price Shop
FSA	Food Security Act, 2013
FWWB	Friends of Womens World Banking
FY	Financial Year
GCF	Green Climate Fund
GDP	Gross Domestic Product
GER	Gross Enrolment Ratio
GHG	Greenhouse Gases
GI	Galvanized Iron
GIZ	Gesellschaft für Internationale Zusammenarbeit
GNDI	Gross National Disposable Income
GoI	Government of India
GST	Goods and Services Tax

GVA	Gross Value Added
HDI	Human Development Index
HDR	Human Development Report
HHs	Households
HIH	Hand in Hand
HR	Human Resource
HRA	Handloom Reservation Act, 1985
HYPN	Hank Yarn Packing Notification
IARI	Indian Agricultural Research Institute
IAY	Indira Awaas Yojana
ICAR	Indian Council of Agricultural Research
ICDS	Integrated Child Development Services
ICSI	International Chamber for Service Industry
IDS	Institute for Development Studies
IEG	Independent Evaluation Group
IFAD	International Fund for Agricultural Development
IFFCO	Indian Farmers Fertiliser Cooperative Limited
IFMR	Institute for Financial Management and Research
IFMR-LEAD	Institute for Financial Management and Research - Leveraging Evidence for Access and Development
IGA	Income-generating Activity
IHDS	India Human Development Survey
IHHL	Individual Household Latrine
IIBM	Indian Institute of Bank Management
IIE	Indian Institute of Entrepreneurship
ILO	International Labour Organization
IMD	India Meteorological Department
IMR	Infant Mortality Rate
INCCA	Indian Network of Climate Change Assessment
INDC	Intended Nationally Determined Contribution
IPPE	Intensive Participatory Planning Exercise
IRDP	Integrated Rural Development Program
IRMA	Institute for Rural Management Anand
IRR	Internal Rate of Return
ITES	Information Technology Enabled Services
ITI	Industrial Training Institute
IWDP	Integrated Watershed Development Program
IWMI	International Water Management Institute
JAM	Jan Dhan, Aadhaar and Mobile
JLGs	Joint Liability Groups
JPC	Joint Parliamentary Committee
KCC	Kisan Credit Card
KGFS	The Kshetriya Gramin Financial Services
KVIB	Khadi and Village Industry Board

KVIV	Khadi and Village Industry Commission
KVK	Kaushalya Vardhan Kendras
KVKs	Krishi Vigyan Kendras
LAMP	Livelihood and Microfinance Promotion Fund
LEISA	Low External Input Sustainable Agriculture
MAVIM	Mahila Arthik Vikas Nigam
MDM	Midday Meal Scheme
MFI	Microfinance Institution
MGNREGA	Mahatma Gandhi National Rural Employment Guarantee Act
MGNREGS	Mahatma Gandhi National Rural Employment Guarantee Scheme
MGVCL	Madhya Gujarat Vij Company Ltd
MI	Microirrigation
MIS	Management Information System
MKSP	Mahila Kisan Sashaktikaran Pariyojana
MMR	Maternal Mortality Ratio
MNCs	Multinational Companies
MNRE	Ministry of New and Renewable Energy
MOF	Ministry of Finance
MORD	Ministry of Rural Development
MOSPI	Ministry of Statistics and Programme Implementation
MoU	Memorandum of Understanding
MRDS	Meghalaya Rural Development Society
MSME	Medium Small and Micro Enterprises
MSP	Minimum Support Price
MT	Metric Tons
MUDRA	Micro Units Development and Refinance Agency
NABARD	National Bank for Agriculture and Rural Development
NABFINS	NABARD Financial Services Ltd.
NAFCC	National Adaptation Fund for Climate Change
NAPCC	National Action Plan on Climate Change
NBFCs	Nonbanking Financial Companies
NCAER	National Council of Applied Economic Research
NCGTC	National Credit Guarantee Trustee Company Ltd
NCVT	National Council for Vocational Training
NDDB	National Dairy Development Board
NDP	National Dairy Plan
NDRI	National Dairy Research Institute
NDSP	National Dairy Support Project
NER	Northeastern Region
NFSA	National Food Security Act
NFSM	National Food Security Mission
NGO	Nongovernmental organization
NHDC	National Handloom Development Corporation

NHG	Neighborhood Groups
NICRA	National Initiative on Climate Resilient Agriculture
NIDA	NABARD Infrastructure Development Assistance
NITI	National Institution for Transforming India
NLM	National Livestock Mission
NMMI	National Mission on Micro Irrigation
NMSA	National Mission for Sustainable Agriculture
NOS	National Occupational Standards
NPMSH&F	National Project on Management of Soil Health & Fertility
NPOF	National Project on Organic Farming
NPS	National Pension Scheme
NPV	Net Present Value
NREGA	National Rural Employment Guarantee Act
NREGS	National Rural Employment Guarantee Scheme
NRHM	National Rural Health Mission
NRLM	National Rural Livelihood Mission
NRLP	National Rural Livelihoods Programme
NSAP	National Social Assistance Programme
NSDA	National Skills Development Agency
NSDC	National Skills Development Corporation
NSDF	National Skill Development Fund
NSDM	National Skills Development Mission
NSQC	National Skills Qualification Committee
NSQF	National Skills Qualification Framework
NSSO	National Sample Survey Organization
NTFP	Nontimber forest produce
NULM	National Urban Livelihood Mission
NVIUC	National Vegetable Initiative around Urban Clusters
NYP	National Youth Policy
OROP	One Rank One Pension
PACS	Poorest Areas Civil Society
PACS	Primary Agricultural Credit Society
PAT	Profit After Tax
PDS	Public Distribution System
PHI	Points of High Impact
PIAs	Project-implementing Agencies
PMEGP	Prime Ministers Employment Generation Programme
PMFBY	Pradhan Mantri Fasal Bima Yojana
PMGSY	Pradhan Mantri Gram Sadak Yojana
PMJDY	Pradhan Mantri Jan-Dhan Yojana
PMKSY	Pradhan Mantri Krishi Sinchai Yojana
PMKVY	Pradhan Mantri Kaushal Vikas Yojana
PMMY	Pradhan Mantri Mudra Yojana
PMO	Prime Minister's Office

POP	Poorest of the Poor
POPIs	Producer Organisation Promoting Institutions
POS	Point of Sale
PPA	Power Purchase Agreement
PPP	Public Private Partnership
PR	Public Relations
PRADAN	Professional Assistance for Development Action
PRC	Performance Review Committee
PRRS	Porcine Reproductive and Respiratory Syndrome
PS	Principal Status
PSLCs	Priority Sector Lending Certificates
PSU	Public Sector Unit
PWCS	Primary Weavers Cooperative Society
RADP	Rainfed Area Development Programme
RBI	Reserve Bank of India
RE	Revised Estimates
RIDF	Rural Infrastructure Development Fund
RKVY	Rashtriya Krishi Vikas Yojana
RRB	Regional Rural Bank
RSETI	Rural Self Employment Training Institutes
RTE	Right to Education Act, 2009
RTI	Right to Information Act, 2005
RUDSETI	Rural Development and Self Employment Training Institute
SAPCC	State Action Plan on Climate Change
Sasha	Sarba Shanti Ayog
SAUs	State Agricultural Universities
SC/ST	Scheduled Caste/Scheduled Tribe
SCB	State Co-operative Bank
SCI	System of Crop Intensification
SDG	Sustainable Development Goals
SDIS	Skills Development Initiative Scheme
SECC	Socio-Economic Caste Census
SEDI	Skills and Entrepreneurship Development Institutes
SERP	Society for Elimination of Rural Poverty
SETU	Self-Employment and Talent Utilization
SF/MF	Small Farmers/Marginal Farmers
SFAC	Small Farmers' Agri-business Consortium
SFB	Small Finance Bank
SFDA	Small Farmers Development Agency
SGSY	Swarnajayanti Gram Swarozgar Yojana
SHG	Self-Help Group
SI	Sum Insured
SIA	Social Impact Assessment
SIDBI	Small Industries Development Bank of India

SJSRY	Swarna Jayanti Shahari Rozgar Yojana
SL	Sustainable Livelihood
SLI	Sustainable Livelihood Initiative
SLUSI	Soil and Land Use Survey of India
SME	Small and Medium-sized enterprise
SMP	Skimmed Milk Powder
SNF	Solids Not Fat
SoRs	Schedule of Rates
SPICE	Solar Pump Irrigators' Cooperative Enterprise
SRI	System of Rice Intensification
SRLM	State Rural Livelihood Mission
SRWM	Social Regulations in Water Management
SS	Subsidiary Status
SSA	Sarva Shiksha Abhiyan
SSC	Sector Skill Council
STAR	Standards Training Assessment and Reward
STEPUP	Skill Training for Employment Protection amongst Urban Poor
SVEP	Start-up Village Entrepreneurship Program
TDF	Tribal Development Fund
TOT	Terms of Trade
TRIBAC	Tripura Bamboo and Cane Development Centre
UIDAI	Unique Identification Authority of India
UNDP	United Nations Development Programme
UNFCC	United Nations Framework Convention on Climate Change
UPNRM	Umbrella Programme on Natural Resource Management
UPSS	Usual Principal and Subsidiary Status
VAT	Value Added Tax
VC	Vigilance Committee
VO	Village Organization
WASSAN	Watershed Support Services and Activities Network
WBCIS	Weather Based Crop Insurance Scheme
WCS	Weavers' Cooperative Society
WEF	World Economic Forum
WEST	Wheelbox Employability Skill Test
WOTR	Watershed Organisation Trust
WPI	Wholesale Price Index

Foreword

The inception of the State of India's Livelihoods (SOIL) report dates back to the year 2008, when ACCESS envisaged the laborious task of putting together a publication that would track the progress and trends relating to the livelihoods of the poor in India as well as address contemporary issues emerging in the livelihoods sector in a comprehensive manner. Given the complexity and diversity of the sector, the nature and number of initiatives, the variety of stakeholders engaged as well as the national and international trends influencing the lives of the poor, the task of bringing together the State of India's Livelihoods report was indeed daunting and arduous. A group of authors, among the most knowledgeable experts in the field, was brought together to write the report. To bring focus to the initiative, the document outline was developed along a 4-P framework focusing on the poor, the policy environment, the potential, and promoters.

Over the years, the SOIL report has evolved and emerged as a significant reference document that attempts to aggregate the diverse experiences of different stakeholders; comprehend current trends, collate dispersed data, and string together the state of livelihoods of India's poor. Views, opinions, and perspectives of various institutions and experts are sought to track the dynamics within the livelihood sector to strengthen the content and analysis of the report. From 2015 onwards, to better unify and intertwine the flow of the report, N. Srinivasan and Girija Srinivasan were requested to bring together the full report. The two of them have been authoring the report since then, which has perceptibly helped in improving its flow. The SOIL report is released annually at the Livelihoods Asia Summit and has received widespread appreciation.

The State of India's Livelihoods report explores critical issues and themes concerning the livelihoods sector in India. In the 2016 report, the "Overview" chapter covers a wide sweep of issues reflecting the complexities that have come to characterize the livelihood environment and the vulnerability of the poor households. Starting with an overview of the macroeconomic trends in the last one year that have a bearing on the livelihoods of the poor, it looks at the employment situation while analyzing the quality and equity in growth. It also looks at trends in the agriculture sector which is the major livelihood option of the poor. Chapter 2 on the "Policy and Fiscal Framework" analyzes the Budget 2016–17 for positive and adverse impacts that allocations may have on the livelihoods of the poor while taking stock of the ongoing and emerging policy initiatives of Government of India that are in various stages of formulation and adoption. Chapter 3 takes a stock of "Important Government Programs and Schemes," covering some of the ongoing poverty reduction and livelihoods promotion programs and schemes such as National Rural Livelihoods Mission, National Food Security Act, Prime Ministers Crop Insurance Scheme (PMFBY), and National Skills Development Mission. In the subsequent chapter, "A Decade of Rural Employment Guarantee," the authors examine insightfully, the impact and outcomes of Mahatma Gandhi National Rural Employment Guarantee Scheme (MGNREGS), one of the flagship social protection programs of the government and assess how it has fared in achieving its objectives in providing employment guarantee and creation of durable assets.

Climate change impairing livelihoods is not a future scenario, but a compelling current conundrum. Few countries in the world are as vulnerable to the effects of climate change as India is with its large population dependent upon climate-sensitive sectors such as agriculture, forestry, and livestock for its livelihoods. Chapter 5 on "Climate Change—Farming in a Hotspot?" looks at the likely effects of climate change in India with a focus on agriculture sector. Government policies and programs in combating climate change are also covered in the chapter. Chapter 6 "Handlooms" is a deep dive on the handloom sector, given that it is the second largest employer in the informal sector after agriculture. The chapter looks at the production and employment trends in the sector, the current government's initiatives and challenges for marketing of handloom products, and the role of apex handloom marketing societies therein. Livelihoods of people at the bottom of the pyramid in the Northeast have always been vulnerable since income opportunities in this part of the country is lower than those available in the rest of the country. Chapter 7 on "Livelihoods in Northeast" analyzes the current opportunities and challenges for the people in the Northeast in various sectors such as agriculture, sericulture, livestock, forestry, arts and crafts, and tourism. Chapter 8 looks at access to finance for livelihoods and concludes that flow of finance to agriculture continues to be a matter of concern despite all the progress made in financial inclusion space. Chapter 9 summarizes the insights of the practitioners involved in designing, implementing, and funding livelihoods at macro, meso and micro levels, captured based on a free-wheeling Round Table organized for the purpose of the report. The concluding Chapter 10 summarizes the continuing concerns and generates a wish list for the near future scenario relating to the livelihoods of the poor.

I deeply appreciate the incredible efforts made by both Srini and Girija for committing their valuable time in bringing together this complex report; meeting with several stakeholders, visiting various organizations, and organizing Round Tables and consultations to enrich the analysis and insights for the report. I am well aware of the time stretch for them, and for them to agree to anchor this complex task for the second consecutive year has been of immense value for the report.

I also take this opportunity to thank the Livelihoods Asia Group of Advisors for their guidance and suggestions. Importantly, I am grateful for the continued support to the report by National Bank for Agriculture and Rural Development (NABARD), particularly M.V. Ashok, and Rabobank Foundation, particularly to Arindom. Both institutions have been steadfast in their support to the report on an ongoing basis, and perhaps see value in its continuation.

Lastly, I would like to acknowledge the effort put in by the Livelihoods Asia team in providing support to the authors in putting together the SOIL 2016 Report in the designated time frame. Both Puja and Ila put in tremendous efforts in their support to the authors. I would also like to thank my program support team, particularly Lalitha for handling the logistics and making necessary arrangements.

Each year, I feel proud that our efforts at ACCESS have contributed in creating this annual knowledge product. We owe it to the overwhelming support received from diverse stakeholders within the sector that has encouraged us to bring out yet another edition of the SOIL report. Our vision each year is to do our bit in creating a resource book for those in the sector and to contribute to a better understanding of the livelihoods space for all interested stakeholders working to realize and impact the livelihoods of the poor. I hope the SOIL 2016 Report will add value in better appreciating the complex ecosystem within which the poor strive to sustain their livelihoods.

Vipin Sharma
CEO
ACCESS Development Services

Preface

We are in the second year of authoring the SOIL report and we realize that our learning of the first year about complexity and diversity of livelihoods is yet to be complete. We have continued to receive support from all parts of the sector and its stakeholders. We had visited several states (Andhra Pradesh, Odisha, Tamil Nadu, Karnataka, Madhya Pradesh, West Bengal, Assam, Telangana) and met institutions and key persons to get insights in to the livelihood situation and its challenges. We met officials in state governments and the center. While there are significant improvements in some vocations, there are continuing problems in some locations and vocations. We see aspirational changes in young people and high expectations. While the policy and strategy side of livelihood development seems to be changing radically, the implementation machinery is struggling to keep pace. The task of improving livelihoods of the vulnerable is not going to be less challenging in near future.

We have many organizations and people to thank for easing our burden (but at times they also set us additional tasks by setting us out on investigation of new ideas and projects). The authors are extremely grateful to Dr C. Rangarajan, Former Chairman of Prime Minister's Economic Advisory Council, who spared time to provide insights on the macroeconomic issues in livelihoods. NABARD, Bharatia Agro-Industries Foundation (BAIF), Watershed Organisation Trust (WOTR), Indian Institute of Bank Management (IIBM), Guwahati, Action Aid, Handloom Directorates of Odisha, West Bengal, Andhra Pradesh, Directorates of Rural Development (MGNREGS) in Odisha, Telangana, and Tamil Nadu are some agencies which deserve our utmost gratitude. Our thanks are due to a number of institutions and practitioners from the Northeastern states which participated in the consultation meet held in IIBM, Guwahati—Mrinal Gohain of Action Aid and Abhijit Sharma of IIBM in particular for organizing the meet. A listing of the participant contributors to the discussions is provided in the annexure to the report. We thank Santosh Mathew, Joint Secretary, National Rural Livelihood Mission (NRLM), Ministry of Rural Development (MORD), Benugopal Mukhopadhyay of NABARD, Bharat Kakade of BAIF, Marcella and Crispino Lobo of WOTR, for holding exclusive discussions with us for the purpose of the report. Managing directors of Boyonika, Serifed, Utkalika, Tantuja, Co-optex, Apco and Lepakshi, weavers' societies and weavers in the states of Odisha, West Bengal, Andhra Pradesh, and Tamil Nadu and Sasha, marketing agency provided us deep insights into the handloom-based livelihoods. Our heartfelt thanks to veteran practitioners Deep Joshi and Brij Mohan for their contributions to the report. Jeyaseelan, Hand In Hand, Narender Rathore, Venkatesh Tagat, P. Satish, Muthu Velayutham, and Aloysius Fernandes helped us in many ways. We were fortunate to get some of the leading practitioners in this space for half a day Round Table on key aspects of livelihoods in the country, which is carried verbatim in a separate chapter. This chapter is rich with more than 350 years of combined practitioner wisdom in livelihood development. We thank Harsh Kumar Bhanwala, Chairman, NABARD, Narendranath, Professional Assistance for Development Action (PRADAN), Vijay Mahajan, BASIX, Girish Sohani, BAIF, Arindom Datta, Rabobank, Rajiv Williams, Jindal Steel CSR, Meera Mishra, International Fund for Agricultural Development (IFAD), Madhu Sharan, Hand in Hand, Jaydeep Shrivastav, NABARD and Vipin Sharma, ACCESS for their contributions in the expert Round Table held in Delhi. Pravin Shende, as in the past years, met tough deadlines to complete the preparation of draft document in time. The ACCESS team of Puja Gour and Ila Bose put up with our demands and managed the several events and meetings. Lalitha Sridharan has always remained our anchor making seamless arrangements for our visits to different parts of the country. We also thank the group of advisors of Livelihoods Asia in ACCESS for their understanding and unstinting support. We express our heartfelt thanks to the sponsors of the report and the summit.

While we have continued some core chapters in order to provide stability to the structure of the report we have also covered interesting new themes. An overview of the situation from the macro viewpoint and a concluding chapter summarizing key challenges in future are carried as in the last year. Apart from continuing to report on policies, legal and fiscal framework for livelihoods, important government programs, we have covered climate change and a deep dive into handloom livelihoods. The report also devotes space for a topical issue, the challenge of climate change. The decade long employment guarantee program National Rural Employment Guarantee Scheme (NREGS) has been taken up for a separate detailed review. A chapter on livelihoods in Northeast and another on financing of livelihoods make up the rest of the report. As always, authors of the report feel that more could have been done. But limitations of time and resources always impose limits on ambitions and aspirations. We hope the readership will enjoy reading this. We look forward to your insights and comments on the report. We are responsible for the comments and conclusions drawn in the report. The sponsors and ACCESS do not necessarily subscribe to the views of the authors.

N. Srinivasan   **Girija Srinivasan**

Overview: Changing Context of Livelihoods

In the last year's report, it was hoped that having done the spadework on several fronts the government will get down to the task of delivering results on the ground. In the year that had passed since then, there have been several developments. The economy as such has improved in terms of growth as also in enabling conditions. The RBI's annual report 2015–16 noted that despite intensified global risks and shocks faced by global financial markets post-Brexit referendum, underlying conditions have been improving in India for scaling up the growth momentum. There had been increasing progress toward greater macroeconomic stability as the former Governor Dr Rajan, in the preface to the RBI annual report 2015–16, observed that

> Expectations of a good monsoon … coupled with more money in the hands of government servants (as a result of the implementation of the 7th Pay Commission recommendations) should boost consumer demand. With final demand picking up, capacity utilization is likely to increase, and so will investment. A virtuous cycle of growth is possible, reinforced by anticipation of the coming benefits from reforms like the recently passed Goods and Services Tax legislation ….

There are three areas in macroeconomic consolidation that continued to be important according to him.

First, economic growth, while showing signs of picking up is still below levels that the country is capable of. The key weakness is in investment, with private corporate investment subdued because of low capacity utilization and public investment slow in rolling out in some sectors. Second, inflation projections are still at the upper limits of RBI's inflation objective. Third, the willingness of banks to cut lending rates is muted. Not only does weak corporate investment reduce the volume of new profitable loans, their impaired assets have tightened capital positions which will prevent them from lending freely.

However, the prospects for the economy seem to have improved with a good monsoon and a continuing moderate crude oil price situation. The 23% increase in remuneration recommended for Central Government employees by the Seventh Pay Commission will no doubt increase public expenditure but will also boost customer demand with beneficial downstream effects on capacity utilization and investments. The reforms that are being put through such as implementing the unified goods and services tax, liberalizing foreign direct investment, and easing up of running small enterprises under Startup India are likely to change business sentiments and improve willingness to invest. The last year's GDP growth (2015–16) has been estimated at 7.6%, which is an increase over the previous year's growth rate of 7.2%. While the growth rate is higher than the previous year's, the same does not fully reflect the growth potential in the country. The Economic Survey 2015–16 predicted that the GDP would be of the order of 8% to 8.5% but the achieved growth rate fell short of the same. The growth rate, however, was higher than the RBI estimate of 7.2%. The assumptions underlying the last year's projection in the economic survey were that reforms were being introduced, crude oil prices were declining, and input cost reduction would increase profits of business and hence improve investment sentiments. Furthermore, the declining rate of inflation was assumed to result in boosting household spending and borrowing.

The Economic Survey 2016–17 has been more sober in its assessment of growth prospects by saying "Assessment of India's performance over the coming year will therefore need to be conditional. This is not an advance apology for likely future performance, but the sobering reality of India becoming so entwined with the world." As for prospects of improving conditions of the economy specific to livelihoods, the survey points out implementation of major public investment program in infrastructure, instituting the new crop insurance scheme for farmers, the financial inclusion mission through Jan Dhan Yojana, the game-changing Jan Dhan, Aadhaar and Mobile (JAM) payments platform, and also the comprehensive reforms in the power sector. The economic survey still maintains that the long-run potential growth rate of the country is around 8% to 10%. The three key aspects of further work to realize the high growth potential have been identified as moving toward genuinely procompetition policies for creating a competitive environment; divesting the remainder of the legacy of licenses, exemptions, and subsidies; and making the state lean to play only the essential governance roles.

The RBI had projected a GDP growth of 7.6% (in gross value added terms) for the year 2016–17. According to the RBI,[1]

Looking ahead, the momentum of growth is expected to be quickened by the normal monsoon raising agricultural growth and rural demand, as well as by the stimulus to consumption spending that can be expected from the disbursement of pay, pension and arrears following the implementation of the 7th CPC's award. The passage of the Goods and Services Tax (GST) Bill augurs well for the growing political consensus for economic reforms. While timely implementation of GST will be challenging, there is no doubt that it should raise returns to investment across much of the economy, even while strengthening government finances over the medium-term. This should boost business sentiment and eventually investment. The current accommodative stance of monetary policy and comfortable liquidity conditions should also provide a congenial environment for the reinvigoration of aggregate demand conditions. However, successive downgrades of global growth projections by multilateral agencies and the continuing sluggishness in world trade points to further slackening of external demand going forward. Accordingly, the growth projection for 2016–17 is retained at 7.6 per cent, with risks facing the economy at this juncture evenly balanced around it.

The savings rate in the economy (Table 1.1) had been declining over a period of time. Between 2011–12 and 2014–15, the gross domestic savings rate had declined by about 1.6%. Whether the persistent consumer inflation[2] had an influence on the declining savings rate requires a deeper

Table 1.1: Savings and Capital Formation Rates

(2011–12 Constant Prices)	2012–13	2013–14	2014–15	2015–16
Gross savings rate as % of GNDI*	33.0	32.3	32.3	–
Gross fixed capital formation as % of GDP	31.9	33.0	32.3	31.2
GDP growth rate %	5.1	6.6	7.2	7.6

Source: RBI Annual Report 2014–15 and 2015–16—Appendix Tables 1 and 2.
Note: * Gross National Disposable Income.

---

[1] Third bimonthly Monetary Policy statement (August 10, 2016) sourced from RBI website.

[2] Measured through movements in consumer price index (CPI).

study. The decline in savings rate will have an impact on the overall credit levels, investments, and also capital formation rates. The capital formation rate in the economy has also been declining from 33% in 2013–14 to 31.2% in 2015–16. These are aspects that have to be attended to in order to ensure that economic activity and growth rate necessary are at appropriate levels to cause the trickle down to the poorest people in the country and sustain their livelihoods. The RBI on its part holds the view that the economy requires to create an environment for savers and ensure that they are fully protected through low inflation rates and as a result pave the way for a low interest environment leading to competitive funding costs for businesses.

On the inflation front, there were some encouraging developments during the year that seemed to be turning adverse in the last few months. By July–August 2015, inflation had declined to a low of 3.7% but subsequently it went on increasing up to 5.7% in January 2016 (Figure 1.1). In March 2016, it had again declined to 4.8%. Since March

2016, inflation has been rising and crossed the threshold of 6% set by the RBI in July 2016. For the year 2015–16 as a whole, the inflation average was 4.9% which was less than the 5.8% level of the previous year. The rising prices of pulses, vegetables, and fruits during the year did impact the food consumption basket of vulnerable people. The wholesale price inflation, which was in the negative territory till March 2016 on account of falling international commodity prices, has rapidly climbed up to 3.5% by July 2016. The RBI had assessed that the inflation target of 5% for March 2017 may not be achieved and inflation might end up above this level. The RBI has stated in its bimonthly monetary policy (August 2016) statement that the impact of the Seventh Pay Commission award on inflation, especially relating to house rent allowances, need to be looked through and its effect on inflation expectations will have to be carefully monitored. In terms of immediate inflation outcomes, much will depend on the benign effects of the monsoon on food prices according to the RBI.

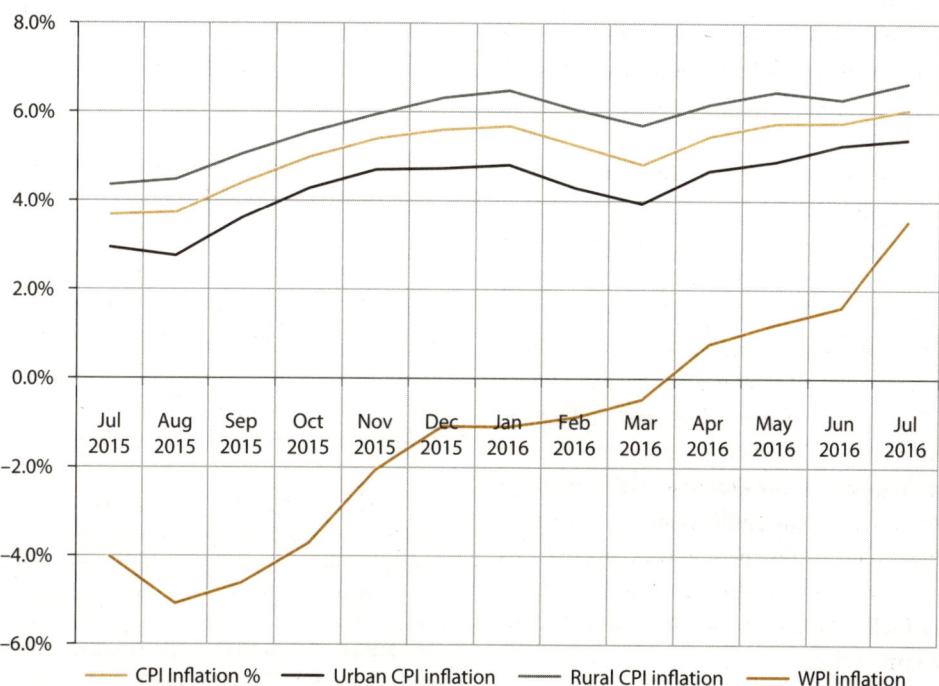

Figure 1.1: Inflation Trends

Source: Data from RBI web-based database (DBIE). Graph by the authors.

Employment Created (Lakhs)

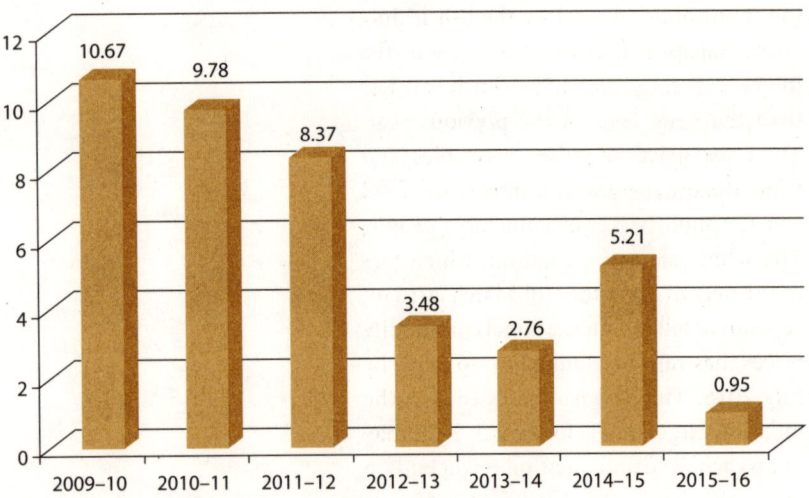

Figure 1.2: Employment Generated in Select Industries

Source: Quarterly Report on Changes in Employment in Selected Sectors (October 2015 to December 2015), Labour Bureau, Ministry of Labour and Employment, GOI. The data available for first three quarters of 2015–16 has been annualized for the chart.

1.1 The Employment Situation

The increased growth rate in GDP did not seem to impact the employment front very positively. Last year's report dealt with the phenomenon of jobless growth and the declining employment elasticity. During the year 2015–16 in the first three quarters additional employment had been created to the extent of 0.071 million as per the data compiled by the Labour Bureau. This is the lowest level of employment creation since 2009–10 (Figure 1.2).

According to data on unemployment and consumer sentiments gathered by the Bombay Stock Exchange (BSE) and Centre for Monitoring Indian Economy (CMIE), unemployment rate rose to 9.84% in August 2016, against 8.65% in July 2016 and 8.84% in June 2016. The increase in unemployment in August was spread across urban and rural regions. Urban India continued to face higher unemployment rates compared to rural regions, perhaps owing to a slowdown in hiring in key sectors, including IT and e-commerce.

As was pointed out in the last year's report, it had been difficult to fully explain why the high GDP numbers did not translate to high levels of employment growth. Whether the growth strategies chosen by the country are aiming toward jobless growth, that is, using less of manpower and more of other means to fulfil the different tasks and processes involved, requires deeper analysis. Shweta Punj and MG Arun[3] in an article point out that weak industrial growth, a struggling agriculture sector, cost rationalizations in manufacturing and service sectors, and the knock-on effect of a global slowdown have impacted employment creation. The traditionally labor-intensive industries are beginning to increasingly mechanize their operations in a bid to become more productive and profitable. The comparatively slow progress in infrastructure projects as also in mining has had its impact on new job creation. As pointed out in the last year's report, the employment elasticity had been declining all over the country and across sectors. The informal sector accounts for a large proportion of jobs that are created; unorganized sector creates 15 times more jobs than are created in the organized sector. As long as an overwhelming part of the labor is in the unorganized sector subject to uncertain conditions of work, not only employment rates cannot be reliably improved but also the quality of employment cannot be assured.

Mahesh Vyas[4] points out that the youth are likely to be disproportionately impacted in the search for jobs. The population in the age bracket of 15–20 years is at the beginning of the transformation from dependents to grown-ups and ready to join the workforce. It is this age bracket that has the largest share in India's total population. While many in this age bracket are employed, the bulk is ready to enter the workforce in the next five years.

---

[3] Shweta Punj and M.G. Arun, "Where are the Jobs," *India Today* (April 20, 2016), http://indiatoday.intoday.in/story/employment-scenario-job-crunch-jobless-growth-economy/1/647573.html, accessed on July 30, 2016.

[4] Mahesh Vyas is CEO of CMIE; excerpted from Mahesh Vyas, *264 Million is India's Demographic Dividend.* CMIE website. https://www.cmie.com/kommon/bin/sr.php?kall=warticle&dt=2016-07-07%2018:53:26&msec=276, accessed on July 31, 2016.

Over 11% of India's population is therefore in a state of readiness to look for jobs. This translates to about 147 million young Indians. With an average labor participation rate of 20.9% in this age bracket, it implies that 30.7 million young Indians are seeking jobs today. Some of them get it, but most of them are likely to take some time. The 20–25 years age bracket contributes the most to the addition to the labor force. This age bracket accounts for about 9% of India's population. Thus, the age bracket that adds the greatest to the labor force—15 to 25 years—accounts for 20% of India's population. Thus, keeping a five-year perspective in mind, India's demographic dividend or challenge comes from the 264 million people who are in the age bracket of 15–25 years today or would be in this bracket in the coming five years. These are the ones who, given the right jobs, can propel India's growth through additional production and consumption demand. Without a job this large group could potentially pose serious social problems.

While the problems relating to employment and unemployment are old, the changes in the economic and business environment driven by changing nature of demand and technology of operations make it difficult to deal with the demand and supply side issues with certainty. The World Economic Forum (WEF) in its report on employment[5] points out

> Together, technological, socio-economic, geopolitical and demographic developments and the interactions between them will generate new categories of jobs and occupations while partly or wholly displacing others. They will change the skill sets required in both old and new occupations in most industries and transform how and where people work, leading to new management and regulatory challenges. Given the rapid pace of change, business model disruptions are resulting in a near-simultaneous impact on employment

and need for new skill sets, requiring an urgent and concerted effort for adjustment.

Based on a survey carried out in India (among other countries) the report has brought out the top trends in labor that impact industries as also the strategies needed to deal with the disruptions (Table 1.2). Climate change and the changing nature of work and technology in different dimensions are impacting the employment scenario in industries. Reskilling of employees, supporting mobility, job rotation, and collaboration with educational institutions for better skilled manpower are the top strategies that HR managers and CEOs are willing to adopt. The barriers to managing change and making organizations future ready are (a) insufficient understanding of the disruptive changes and (b) resource constraints. Short-term outlook on profits by shareholders and a mismatch between available staff skills and required competencies are also impeding planning for change management.

The expected impact of the disruptions on the employment outlook in India

Table 1.2: Top Trends in Labor

Top Trends Impacting Industries	% Reporting*	Strategies	% Reporting*
Changing Nature of Work, Flexible Work	43	Invest in Reskilling Current Employees	48
Climate Change, Natural Resources	40	Support Mobility and Job Rotation	48
Processing Power, Big Data	33	Collaborate, Educational Institutions	28
Mobile Internet, Cloud Technology	27	Target Female Talent	24
Middle Class in Emerging Markets	27	Attract Foreign Talent	12
New Energy Supplies and Technologies	23	Target Minorities' Talent	12
Young Demographics in Emerging Markets	17	Offer Apprenticeships	8
Women's Economic Power, Aspirations	17	Collaborate with Other Companies Across Industries	8

Source: The Future of Jobs—Employment, Skills and Workforce Strategy for the Fourth Industrial Revolution—Global Challenge Insight Report—World Economic Forum January 2016.
Note: *The percentages in the case of trends indicate the share of survey respondents from the industry in question who selected the stated trend or disruption as one of the top three drivers of change affecting business models in their industry. In the case of strategies, the percentages indicate the share of survey respondents from the industry in question who selected the stated measure as one of the top three future workforce and change management strategies they expect to undertake in their company.

---

[5] World Economic Forum, The Future of Jobs—Employment, Skills and Workforce Strategy for the Fourth Industrial Revolution (January 2016), Global Challenge Insight Report.

is positive according to the WEF report. International Labour Organization (ILO) in its Labour Market Report[6] concurs

> The fundamentals to sustain high rates of growth in the longer term are in place in India: favourable demographics, high savings and investment rates, and increased resources for infrastructure and skills development. The challenge is to ensure that these drivers of growth are associated with the creation of more decent jobs that are accessible to youth, women and social groups across the country, particularly in rural areas.

The sixth economic census report had been released. The census was carried out in 2013–14 on enterprises and employment in the country (except those engaged in crop production). The highlights of the census are as follows: 58.5 million establishments were found to be in operation, 34.8 million establishments (59.48%) were found in rural areas, and nearly 23.7 million establishments (40.52%) were found to be located in urban areas. About 77.6% establishments (45.36 million) were engaged in nonagricultural activities and 22.4% establishments (13.13 million) were engaged in agricultural activities (excluding crop production and plantation). Over an 8-year period between Fifth Economic Census and Sixth Economic Census (Table 1.3), the total number of

establishments in the country increased by 41.8% (from 41.25 million in 2005 to 58.5 million in 2013). During the period between the two economic censuses (2005 and 2013), nonagricultural establishments grew at the rate of 28.97%, while agricultural establishments grew at the rate of 115.98%. Despite the high migration rates reported from rural to urban areas, more agricultural establishments had come up and 93% of all establishments were perennial in nature. UP, Maharashtra, Tamil Nadu, Karnataka, and AP accounted for more than 50% of the establishments in the country. Livestock was the major activity in agriculture (86%); retail trade (35%) and manufacturing (22.7%) were the major activities in nonagricultural space. A total of 131.29 million persons were employed in these establishments, with 67.89 million persons (51.71%) employed in rural areas and 63.4 million (48.29%) employed in urban areas. The employment growth from 2005 was 30%.

The sixth census findings show that a greater proportion of establishments being set up were agricultural and rural. In the context of finding employment in the wage labor space, this is a welcome development. An important reflection from the data is that more women in greater proportion are being employed compared to 2005. The average employment growth is about 4 million jobs per annum at a growth rate of 3.8%. When compared with the prospective accretion to the labor force each year of about 30 million as pointed out by Mahesh Vyas of CMIE the employment generated seems small. The census provides disaggregated data at state and subsector level that would be extremely useful in planning.

The employment situation seems grim, despite all the efforts being made in skill development and enterprise creation. The questions are whether there are takers for all the skill trained persons that different government and corporate social responsibility (CSR) programs are turning out. Is the assumption that 'high unemployment rates are a function of lack of skills' valid? There

Table 1.3: Economic Census—A Comparison

	V Census 2005	VI Census 2013	Growth Rate
No. of establishments	41.83	58.5	39.9%
Agricultural	6.08	13.13	116.0%
Nonagricultural	35.75	45.36	26.9%
Urban	16.29	23.7	45.5%
Rural	25.54	38.4	50.4%
Number employed	100.9	131.29	30.1%
Men employed	78.3	98.25	25.5%
Women % children employed	22.6	33.04	46.2%
Numbers in Million			

Source: All India report of sixth Economic census, 2014, Ministry of Statistics and Programme Implementation—March 2016.

[6] International Labour Organization, India Labour Market Update (July 2016), India Country Office.

are fundamental problems with the enabling conditions and incentives for labor-intensive economic growth at the enterprise level. A thorough reexamination of fiscal, credit, and labor policies is needed to reverse the propensity to choose high automation and low formal employment over labor-intensive manufacturing processes. Subsidizing labor costs to ensure that businesses do not shift to labor-reducing technologies (with other aspects such as quality, reliability, and timeliness remaining unaffected) may be an option to be pursued. The subsidy can be in the form of tax waivers.

As Vijay Mahajan pointed during the exclusive roundtable[7] a massive national campaign to change cropping practises and profitability of dry land areas is needed to create more employment and better local economic growth that can absorb labor. Skill building in this context will have a different connotation—one of making rural people deal with vagaries of weather and adopt cultural practices and resource saving input technologies. A new paradigm in skilling agricultural laborers, with focus on women (recognizing the increasing feminization of agriculture in the field) is required. A further point made during the roundtable was that we need to develop a few thousand smart towns in addition to 100 smart cities as a way of ensuring more jobs are created and the pressure of migration is lessened.

While employment situation has not been rosy in the recent past, the rural wages situation is also showing signs of stress. The growth rates in rural wage rates have been consistently falling except for a brief period of stabilization during December 2015 to June 2016 (Figure 1.3). The inflation rates based on consumer price index (CPI) did not decline as much as the wages growth rate with the result that the real wage growth is marginal in the last 18 months. While the minimum wages guaranteed under National Rural Employment Guarantee Scheme

---

[7] Please refer to Chapter 9 for the roundtable proceedings.

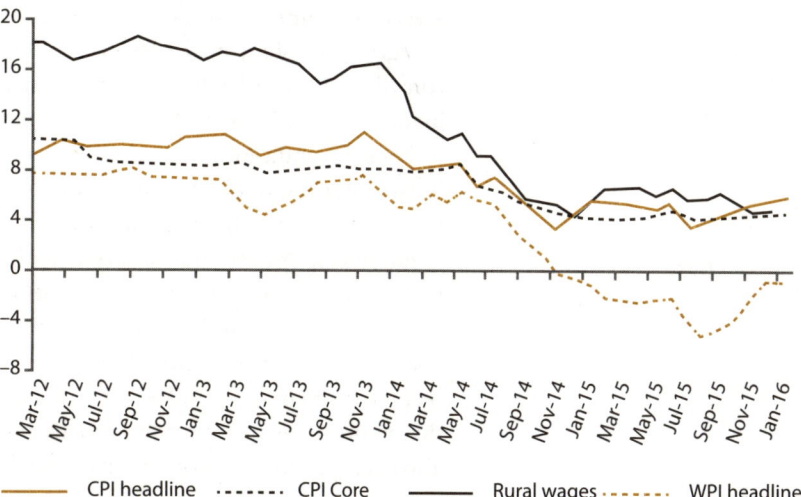

Figure 1.3: Rural Wage Growth and Inflation

Source: Excerpted from the Economic Survey 2016, Ministry of Finance Government of India February 2016.

(NREGS) have an impact on wage rates, the states did not act diligently in notifying the minimum wages. Apart from monitoring employment there is a need to monitor wage levels too to ensure that the real wages do not become negative.

1.2 Quality and Equity in Growth

Dr Rangarajan, former Governor, RBI and Chairman of the Prime Minister's Economic Advisory Council during an exclusive interview for this report stated that for growth to percolate down to the vulnerable livelihoods as a positive benefit there are two aspects that have to be considered. One is the rate of growth and whether it is high enough to flow to the tail end to create an impact. The other is the composition of growth. A low rate of growth on a high rate of population growth will have no great impact at the per capita net income level. However, talking about the trickle-down theory he was of the view that 'a rising ride lifts all boats', including those of the vulnerable people. Disaggregated analysis of data shows that the rate of increase in incomes is higher at the bottom than at the top percentile of the economy. But one of the issues is that a very large number of people dependent on agriculture share only 18% of the GDP contributed. In order for the 60% people involved in agriculture-related activities to benefit significantly the rate of growth in agriculture should be high. Hence, bias toward high growth in agriculture is a requirement. The resources available to the government for investment in agriculture should be increased. The second aspect relates to the fiscal capacity of the government to invest in social and welfare schemes that improve the quality of livelihoods and also support people who do not have viable access to incomes. The capacity to invest in such schemes will increase only when the overall economic growth is high and as a proportion of GDP the government can then raise higher volume of resources.

However, a high growth rate will not automatically reach all sections of people. The skills, the capacities, and access to different livelihoods are variable in different geographies and in different sections of people. This is why targeted schemes that look after vulnerable people and specific subsectors and geographies are necessary. Indian policy making has been working on these tracks. In designing the antipoverty programs while cognizance is taken of the poverty count, the depth of poverty is also an issue that needs to be considered. Dr Rangarajan and Prof. Mahendra Dev[8] have concluded that the poor are bunched around the poverty line and hence efforts to deal with vulnerable people on or around the poverty line would significantly bring a large number of people out of poverty.

On the perceived importance of a bank account in the livelihoods of the vulnerable Dr Rangarajan pointed out that while savings and payments services are necessary, credit is the more critical driver in livelihoods whether of service enterprises or producing enterprises. Savings and payment instruments alone cannot drive economic activity. Overall the direction that the economy should take according to Dr Rangrajan is that planning should prioritize those sectors that take care of very large number of people and at the same time economic reforms that will induce larger investments in the economy. While high growth rate might benefit the vulnerable it may not do so in an equitable manner. Targeted programs that improve livelihood conditions and access to resources for vulnerable people should be prepared and implemented. National Food Security Act (NFSA) and the employment guarantee scheme under Mahatma Gandhi National Rural Employment Guarantee Scheme (MGNREGS) were cited as good examples of ensuring equitable dispersion effects through public spending.

Narendranath, Pradan, during the roundtable discussions, reacting to the theory of high growth trickling down to vulnerable sections questioned metaphorically, "The rising water can only lift boats. What if the people in the water did not have boats?" High economic growth may not necessarily benefit all the vulnerable and the growth strategies have to be tuned to target the vulnerable in the form of employment, welfare, and social safety net programs.

1.3 Agriculture—The Poor, Major Livelihood Option

The current year's union budget has prioritized agriculture. A number of initiatives had been announced besides consolidating and refining the existing ones. A snapshot of the agriculture-related initiatives announced in the budget is indicated in the Box 1.1.

National Institution for Transforming India (NITI) Aayog has prepared an occasional paper[9] based on the work of the

[8] Dr C. Rangarajan and S. Mahendra Dev, "How deep is Indian Poverty," *Indian Express*, December 15, 2015, p. 11.

[9] NITI Aayog, "Raising Agricultural Productivity and Making Farming Remunerative for Farmers" (Occasional Paper, December 2015).

Box 1.1: *Prioritization of Agriculture in Union Budget*

Agriculture in Union Budget 2016–17

- Reorient government interventions in the farm and nonfarm sectors to double the income of farmers by 2022.
- Pradhan Mantri Krishi Sinchai Yojana (PMKSY) is to be implemented in mission mode and 2.85 million hectares brought under irrigation.
- Implementation of 89 irrigation projects under the Accelerated Irrigation Benefits Programme (AIBP), which are delayed for a long time, will be fast tracked.
- A dedicated long-term irrigation fund to be created in National Bank for Agriculture and Rural Development (NABARD) with an initial corpus of ₹200 billion.
- Program for sustainable management of groundwater resources with an estimated cost of ₹60 billion to be implemented with multilateral funding
- In rainfed areas, 0.5 million farm ponds and dug wells and 1 million compost pits for production of organic manure under the MGNREGS.
- Soil Health Card scheme to cover all 140 million farm holdings by March 2017.
- 2,000 model retail outlets of fertilizer companies will be provided with soil and seed testing facilities during the next three years.
- Promote organic farming through 'Paramparagat Krishi Vikas Yojana' and 'Organic Value Chain Development in North East Region'.
- Unified Agricultural Marketing e-Platform to provide a common e-market platform for wholesale markets.
- Ensure that the benefit of minimum support price (MSP) reaches farmers in all parts of the country, through the following initiatives:
  - The remaining states will be encouraged to take up decentralized procurement.
  - An online procurement system will be undertaken through the Food Corporation of India (FCI).
  - Effective arrangements have been made for pulses procurement.
- To make dairying more remunerative to the farmers, four new projects to be taken up:
  - 'Pashudhan Sanjivani', an animal wellness program and provision of animal health cards (Nakul Swasthya Patra)
  - An advanced breeding technology
  - Creation of 'E-Pashudhan Haat', an e-market portal for connecting breeders and farmers
  - National Genomic Centre for indigenous breeds

Source: Prepared by author based on Union budget 2016–17 documents.

Task Force on Agricultural Development constituted by the NITI Aayog, in March 2015. The paper has come up with several findings and recommendations. The paper emphasizes that raising agricultural productivity and making farming remunerative for farmers should be the core objectives of the government. This, according to the report, is possible by improving irrigation efficiency through better agronomic practices, accelerating seed replacement rates, optimizing fertilizer use through better farmer awareness, opening up selectively to genetically modified seeds, introducing high technology means of farming, making agricultural research more focused and effective, diversifying toward high value products in horticulture and livestock subsectors, liberalizing land leasing and tenancy markets, reforming marketing laws and judicious use of essential commodities act, investing in farmer producer collectives that can aggregate demand and drive cost reductions, creating a price deficiency payment mechanism that can compensate farmers who fail to achieve the MSP in open markets, promoting organic farming especially in East and Northeastern region (NER), and providing for natural disaster relief in a transparent manner as a social welfare measure. It has been suggested that the government should evolve a mechanism for the provision of a diversified set of crop insurance products

> **Box 1.2:** *Price Deficiency Payment for Farmers*[10]
>
> There is a need for reorientation of price policy if it is to serve the basic goal of remunerative prices for farmers. This goal cannot be achieved through procurement backed MSP since it is neither feasible nor desirable for the government to buy each commodity in each market in all regions. One possible way to keep a check on prices falling below threshold level is to adopt system of "price deficiency payment." While MSP may still be used for need-based procurement, the remainder of the produce may be covered under "price deficiency payment." This approach would help prevent unwanted stocks and spread price incentives to producers in all the regions and all crops. To assess the viability of deficiency price payment system, cotton may be adopted as a test crop for pilot in selected districts of leading states.

by a diverse set of insurer firms. Farmers with less than 2 ha of area inclusive of all crops may be provided a substantial subsidy on the premium while larger farmers are required to pay commercial rates for coverage.

Agriculture-based livelihoods seem to be under severe stress. Successive droughts and market volatilities combined with rising cost of cultivation has put the farming community under stress. The rising trend of farmer suicides is symptomatic of the pressures faced in farm-based livelihoods. In a 20-year period (1995 to 2015) about 300,000 farmers have committed suicide. The causes are many, but economic causes have mostly been at the root. The Commission for Agricultural Costs and Prices (CACP) has calculated net returns to farmers from different crops at prevailing MSP (See Annexure 1.1 at the end of this chapter). The conclusion is that out of 14 major kharif crops 7 provide a negative

net return, and 3 others offer a net return of less than 5%. *Sesamum* and Arhar seem to be the only crops that provide a decent return. The resetting of MSP year after year is intended to ensure that farmers get an increase in support prices that are positive. An analysis of last five years of movements in CPI Rural and MSP fixed for seven major crops (paddy, wheat, maize, Arhar, soybean, cotton, and sugarcane) shows that MSP increases lagged the inflation rates. The percentage increase in MSP was lower than the inflation as reflected in CPI for three crops in 2011–12, one crop in 2012–13, four crops in 2013–14, all seven crops in 2014–15, and five crops in 2015–16. If MSP, despite being an annual exercise lags inflation rates and profitability calculations show that returns can be negative or just marginal at the fixed MSP, the very premise for the MSP exercise becomes questionable. ***The effort and expenditure on a national commission is not justified if the recommended prices fail to secure a fair return to farmers.***

Figure 1.4 reveals that from 2013–14 MSP increases of at least five to seven crops in different years were below inflation rates of the respective years. While a case is made out that MSP is the minimum price and the farmers might be able to achieve higher prices prevailing in the market, the ground reality suggests otherwise. NITI Aayog study[11] found that wholesale prices were lower than MSP in different parts of the states. Distance from procurement centers, delay in payments, and exploitative practises compelled farmers to sell crops through other means. In the survey, 79% of farmers were not satisfied with the MSP arrangements and wanted an overhaul of the same. The Situation Assessment Survey of Farmers clearly brought out that barring paddy and sugarcane crops the sale through procurement at MSP was not significant

---

[10] Reproduced from NITI Aayog, "Raising Agricultural Productivity and Making Farming Remunerative for Farmers".

[11] NITI Aayog, Evaluation Report on Efficacy of MSP on farmers (January 2016), PEO report no 231, GOI.

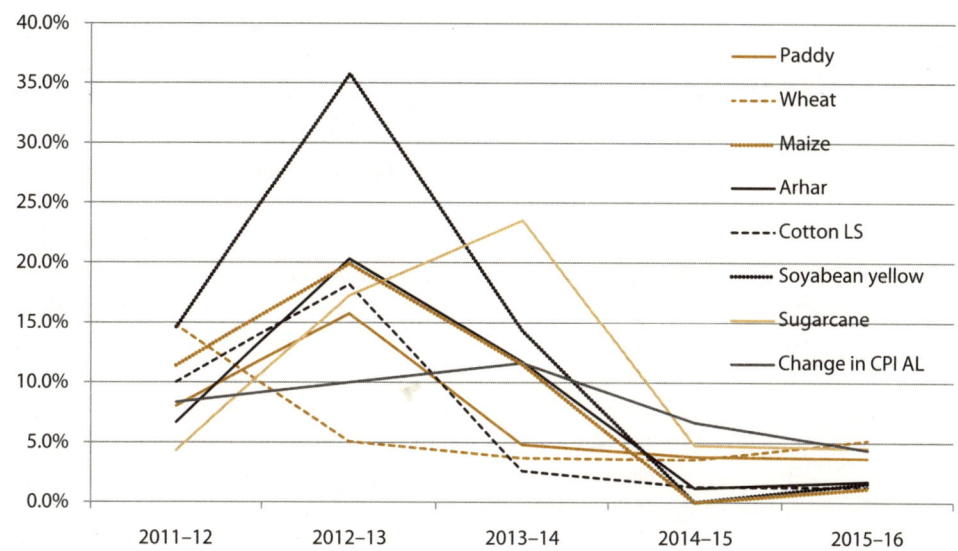

Figure 1.4: Comparison of Changes in MSP of Key Crops with Inflation

Source: Pocket book of Agricultural Statistics 2015, Ministry of Agriculture, Government of India—graph by authors.

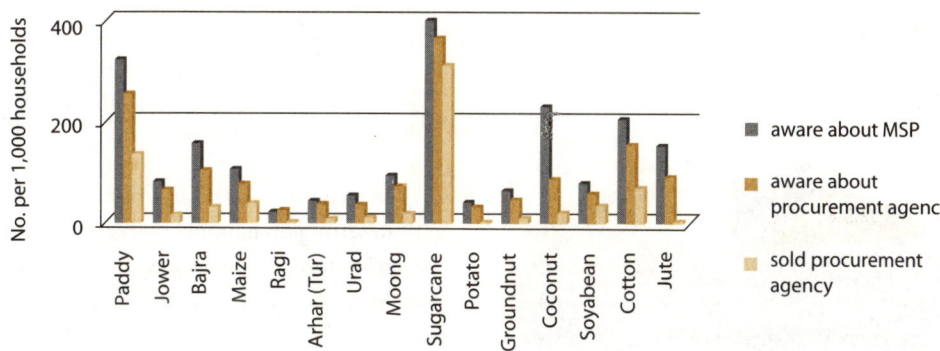

Figure 1.5: MSP Awareness and Utilization

Source: Reproduced from Key indicators of situation of agricultural households in India—NSSO survey 70th Round—2014, Ministry of Statistics and Programme Implementation, GOI.

(Figure 1.5). Awareness of MSP was low and knowledge of procurement agency was lower. Actual sale to procurement agency was made by less than 10% households!

The trends in acreage under cultivation of different crops show that cropping follows profitability and the feasibility of growing the crop. Paddy, pulses, and oilseed acreage has been declining over the last seven years. Other crops have seen an increase in planting (Figure 1.6). Unless price response from the market is adequate, diversion of land for nonfood crops (area under cotton is increasing year after year) that are remunerative is likely.

The government therefore rightly emphasizes doubling of farmers' incomes over the next six years. While the objective is valid, is it feasible to achieve? Dr C. Rangarajan[12] said while it is a legitimate objective, it might not be easily achieved. "When the best growth in agricultural GDP is only 4% and it is shared by very large number of farm households there are difficulties in achieving a doubling of farm income unless much larger investments in agriculture targeting much higher

---

[12] Former Governor RBI and Chairman, PMs Economic Advisory Council, in an exclusive interview with the author for this report.

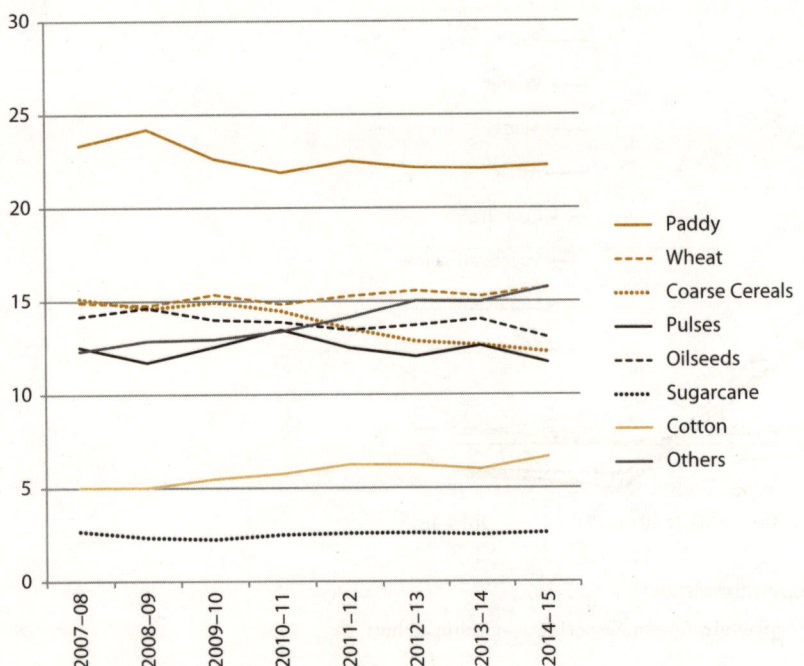

Figure 1.6: Trends in Acreage Under Different Crops

Source: Price policy for Kharif—Marketing Season 2016–17, Commission on Agricultural Costs and Prices, Ministry of Agriculture, Government of India.

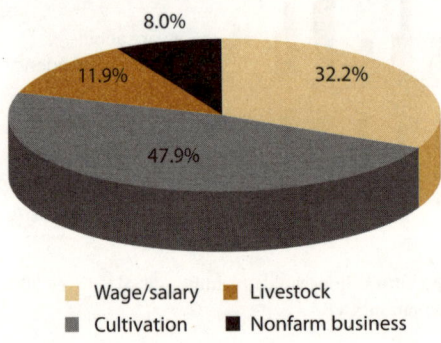

Figure 1.7: Distribution of Average Monthly Agricultural Household Income by Sources

Source: Key indicators of situation of agricultural households in India—NSSO survey 70th Round—2014, Ministry of Statistics and Programme Implementation, GOI.

profitability are made." The NSSO survey[13] brought out that farm incomes account for less than 50% of household income in agricultural households (Figure 1.7). The percentage of agricultural income is inversely

proportional to the extent of landholding by households. Doubling of incomes will be a key benefit for small farmers with small pieces of land. The investments required in these farms to make them productive and more importantly to improve their access to markets could be heavy. The risks faced by these farmers are very high, with the result that one poor season might plunge them from above poverty line to deeply below the line. Concerted action is required in several areas to improve income of such households and the actions should not be restricted to farming alone. S. Chandrasekhar and Nirupam Mehrotra[14] conclude that

> Focusing only on income from cultivation for facilitating doubling of income will prove to be inadequate. Policy measures aimed at increasing net income of households from animal farming will be the key driver of incomes in agricultural households. We also need to improve our understanding of what constrains income growth from non-farm business at the households.

The recent initiatives in improving irrigation, setting up national market platform for agricultural produce, and an improved crop insurance scheme should improve the condition of farm livelihoods. Last year we had referred to the adverse terms of trade (TOT) in agriculture. Despite higher prices for agricultural produce the terms of trade between farmers and nonfarmers has not improved. The terms have turned more adverse in 2014–15 compared to the previous year. The TOT between agriculture sector and nonagriculture sectors has however shown improvement. While a mixed picture emerges from the two different TOTs calculated (Figure 1.8), the overall picture of the last decade is that farmers have prolonged periods of adversity compared to other occupations or other sectors. Under such circumstances it is understandable that

---

[13] Ministry of Statistics and Programme Implementation, Key Indicators of Situation of Agricultural Households in India (2014), NSSO survey 70th Round, GOI.

[14] S. Chandrasekhar and Nirupam Mehrotra, "Doubling of Farmer's Income by 2022—What Would It Take," *Economic and Political Weekly*, no. 18 (April 30, 2016).

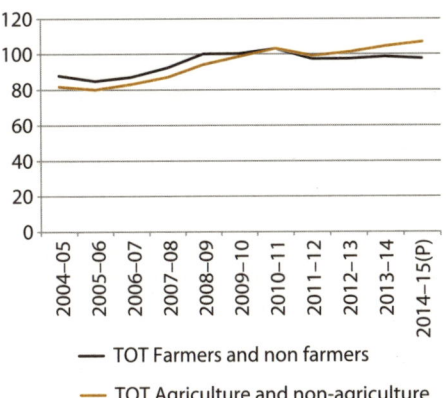

Figure 1.8: Terms of Trade for Farmers and Agriculture Sector

Source: Chart by the author based on data from Pocketbook of Agricultural Statistics, 2016; Directorate of Economics and Statistics, Department of Agriculture, Cooperation and Farmers Welfare, GOI.

a large number of farmers want to leave farming and migrate—not just geographically, but across sectors too.

The economic survey rightly points to need for making irrigation efficient and use scarce water for improving crop output. According to the Impact Evaluation of the National Mission on Micro Irrigation[15] carried out by the Ministry of Agriculture in 64 districts, there were significant reductions in irrigation costs and savings on electricity and fertilizers. This was on account of water being efficiently supplied and pumps being used for a limited time. Moreover, water soluble fertilizers are supplied directly to the roots of the plant and hence there is less wastage. Yields of crops also went up—up to 45% in wheat, 20% in gram, and 40% in soybean. The resulting improvement in net farm incomes is substantial. Until now, microirrigation techniques, owing to high fixed costs of adoption, have mostly been used for high value crops. However, recent research has shown its feasibility even in wheat and rice. While water today might not cost heavily, in the near future scarcity will drive up the costs making drip and microirrigation a cost-effective option.

---

[15] As reported in the *Economic Survey 2016*, p. 75.

1.4 Social Sector and Human Development

The government has chosen to place heavy reliance on direct benefit transfer (DBT) as a means of making delivery of social welfare benefits in a leakage-free and efficient manner. The Economic Survey 2016–17 (as also in 2015–16) dwells at great length on how the cost of the government had been drastically reduced especially in adopting DBT for domestic gas. However, the Comptroller and Auditor General's report which came out recently pointed out that the claimed ₹240 billion reduction in subsidy burden was not achieved entirely by the decrease in offtake of subsidized cylinder. The lower subsidy rates actually came from the sharp fall in global crude prices which in effect reduced the price of cooking gas.

> The subsidy burden over the period from April 2015 to December 2015 was lower than that for comparable period in 2014 by ₹233.1621 billion. However, this was a combined effect of decrease in off take of subsidised cylinders by consumers (₹17.6393 billion) and lower subsidy rates arising from sharp fall in oil prices (₹215.5228 billion) in 2015–16. While implementation of Pahal scheme coupled with a 'give it up' campaign has resulted in reduction of off take of domestic subsidised LPG cylinders, the resultant subsidy savings was not as significant as that of generated through fall of subsidy rates. ("Savings in Subsidy in Pahal (DBTL) scheme" no.[16]

The evidence of DBT leading to significant subsidy optimization in cooking gas is mixed.

Similarly, the estimated reduction on food subsidy might not entirely come from digitization of ration cards, but from missing members in ration cards and missing (but eligible) families from Public Distribution System (PDS). The estimates of missing members from cards can be as high as 12.5% as per sample surveys carried out in six

---

[16] CAG. Savings in Subsidy in Pahal (DBTL) scheme. Report no. 25 of 2016, Chapter 9. Available at http://www.cag.gov.in/sites/default/files/audit_report_files/Union_Commercial_Compliance_Report_25_2016_Chapter-9.pdf (accessed on July 31, 2016).

Table 1.4:   Conceptual Differences in Funds Flow Systems

Characteristic	Old system	New system	Effect
When are funds allocated?	Before spending occurs, based on forecasts	When spending occurs, in real-time	Reduced float (26%)
How do funds flow?	Level by level: Centre → State → District → Block → Panchayat;	Directly from fund pool to spender: Centre/State → Panchayat	Reduced payment delays and uncertainty
When does expenditure documentation occur?	Aggregated and ex-post: For multiple beneficiaries at a time, and after funds have been disbursed	Individually and in real-time: For every individual beneficiary's payment and in order to secure fund release	Reduced leakages (14%) and funds disbursed by 38%

Source: Reproduced from Ministry of Finance, GOI, Economic Survey 2016.

states. There is no estimate of families that have not been admitted to the new ration cards as they do not have Aadhaar numbers. There have been complaints of households that are very poor having been issued with above poverty line cards. All these missing people and mistakes will tend to reduce the quantum of PDS sales and extent of subsidization. The savings in such a case will come not from smart technology-based design, but from deficiency in service that impacts livelihoods of vulnerable people adversely.

The Economic Survey 2016 continues to underline the importance of JAM as game changing combination for direct delivery of benefits from government and also others who have to make payments to a large number of people. The reasoning in the economic survey (Table 1.4) is that the cash floats required to run government programs can be lower with accompanying lower costs and reduced tiers through which funds have to flow and reduced leakages on account of payment direct to bank accounts of intended beneficiaries.

Even while making persuasive arguments for utilizing JAM framework, the survey observes that the readiness in most states to implement JAM-based payments is low. Taking this lack of readiness into account the survey concludes that a modified digital system can be introduced till the readiness of states for JAM improves. The survey calls such a system as Biometrically Authenticated Physical Uptake (BAPU). Beneficiaries identify themselves through biometric information authentication and take delivery of their entitlements physically. While banks might be able to make payments using technology and ensure delivery to intended beneficiaries accounts without problems, it should be remembered that there are other public goods and services that are delivered by small people and tiny organizations on the ground that cannot make investments required to establish real-time connections and fault-free identification of people. The PDS shops, cooperative societies, schools, and a number of other places where benefits to people are being passed on do not have the best of facilities consistent with their current tasks and activities. The new infrastructure and skills required to make JAM or BAPU work is likely to be beyond their means. The government should support in setting up the infrastructure and connectivity as also training of staff.

1.5 Human Development

The country is ranked 130 based on the human development index (HDI) scores. For a country that is growing rapidly with a large number of social safety nets and welfare programs, the HDI ranking as part of medium level of human development group is not acceptable.

While the country had acute problems of poverty, health care, and access to basic services, economic growth over the last two decades had been vigorous enough to attend

Table 1.5: HDI Ranks and Scores—A Cross Country Comparison

Country	1990	2000	2010	2011	2012	2013	2014	Rank 2014
India	0.428	0.496	0.586	0.597	0.600	0.604	0.609	130
Sri Lanka	0.620	0.679	0.738	0.743	0.749	0.752	0.757	73
Brazil	0.608	0.683	0.737	0.742	0.746	0.752	0.755	75
China	0.501	0.588	0.699	0.707	0.718	0.723	0.727	90
Indonesia	0.531	0.606	0.665	0.671	0.678	0.681	0.684	110

Source: HDI database maintained by UNDP. http://hdr.undp.org/en/data# Downloaded on September 15, 2016.

to the problems that aggravate human suffering. A look at the progress of India in the HDI scores shows that the decade 2000–10 was perhaps the best and that significant gains were made. The four years that followed have seen subdued progress with indices inching up by a measly 3.9% over four years averaging less than 1% per annum improvement in the HDI score. Countries at a similar stage of development have done far better than India in dealing with issues of poverty, health, and livelihoods. With renewed attention on economic growth, there should also be concern for access to basic services in education and health and a focus on those aspects that improve quality of life. Measurement of progress on social and welfare issues is an essential ingredient for driving positive changes in human development. It is in this context the move on the part of Central Statistical Office (CSO) to evolve a National Statistical Reporting Mechanism for Social Progress in the Country is timely and laudable. A draft report[17] issued on the proposed mechanism states that "social indicators covered under the Millennium Development Goal and the proposed Sustainable Development Goals (Box 1.3) will be reported upon.

The draft report has identified the indicators, data to be collected, and the sources of data. The report is expected to be a useful

> **Box 1.3:** *Coverage by National Statistical Reporting Mechanism for Social Progress*
>
> Goal 1: Abolish poverty in all its forms
> Goal 2: Universal education up to secondary level for both the genders
> Goal 3: Empowerment and safety of women
> Goal 4: Conducive environment for children
> Goal 5: Prenatal and antenatal care for mother and infants
> Goal 6: Skill development amongst youth
> Goal 7: Eradication of HIV/AIDS, malaria, TB, and other fatal diseases
> Goal 8: Accessibility to basic infrastructure
> Goal 9: Universal financial inclusion
> Goal 10: New technology in agriculture and allied sectors
> Goal 11: Cleanliness and safe drinking water
> Goal 12: Welfare of deprived classes including minorities, disabled, aged, and SC/ST
> Goal 13: Sustainable environment
> Goal 14: Comprehensive e-governance
>
> *Source:* Revised Draft Report on Evolving a National Statistical Reporting Mechanism for Social Progress in the Country—Social Statistics Division, CSO, MOSPI, GOI. mospi.nic.in/mospi_new/upload/Social_Development_in_India_22dec15.pdf

planning and monitoring tool that can help the center, states, and public institutions.

1.6 Other Matters

The higher growth rate in 2015–16 and projected growth rate in 2016–17 have provided expanded fiscal space to the government. The ongoing subsidy rationalization should make it possible for making better decisions on expenditure. How will the additional fiscal space be used? The flagship livelihood

---

[17] Social Statistics Division, CSO, MOSPI, GOI, Revised Draft Report on Evolving a National Statistical Reporting Mechanism for Social Progress in the Country, mospi.nic.in/mospi_new/upload/Social_Development_in_India_22dec15.pdf, accessed on October 1, 2016.

Box 1.4: *Stand-Up India*

"Stand-Up India Scheme" is intended to promote entrepreneurship among SC/ST and women entrepreneurs. The scheme will facilitate at least two such projects per bank branch, on an average one for each category of entrepreneur. It is expected to benefit at least 2.5 lakh borrowers. The scheme is expected to reach a target of at least 2.5 lakh approvals within 36 months from the launch of the scheme in April 2016.

Source: http://www.pradhanmantriyojana. co.in/stand-up-india-loan-scheme-sc-st-women-sbi-hindi-pdf/ Accessed on August 1, 2016.

program (National Rural Livelihoods Mission [NRLM]) should be tweaked to actually deliver livelihoods. The support to NRLM is less than 40% of what was planned during the XII plan. The allocation for NREGS has been increased in the current year after reductions in the previous three years. The increased devolution of funds in favor of states and reduced influence of the center on states expenditure might reduce development spending by states. The proposed hike in infrastructure spending will have significant short term and long impact on employment and economic growth. The Make in India, Startup, Stand-up India campaigns, when accompanied by proemployment strategies can make a difference.

The climate change issues already have an impact on livelihoods especially those that depend on natural resources—land, water, and forests. While the intended national commitments on emission reduction have to be targeted, mitigating risks of farm and allied livelihoods from adverse impacts of climate change has become a priority. The ongoing organic farming campaigns and low input agriculture programs are very closely aligned to climate resilient cultivation practises. The linking of rivers is another idea being floated. While there are positive spin-offs, the negative outcomes of river linking have to be thought through. The problems caused by inundation, increasing salinity,

loss of arable land, and displacement of people have to be balanced with gains from access to irrigation in parched lands, better management of flood waters, and making larger part of the country water secure. The smart city initiative and the plan to provide more of urban facilities in smaller towns will no doubt increase jobs in local areas, and also arrest migration to larger cities. A key constraint to growth of smaller towns is the lack of entrepreneurial spirit as also lack of investments in small, microenterprises. Bank finance will hopefully now flow to such enterprises, on account of the new small finance banks (SFBs) and the clear focus of Micro Units Development and Refinance Agency Bank (MUDRA) on such customer segments. The farmer aggregation models in which considerable investments have been made in farmer producer organizations (FPOs) are yet to yield results on a larger scale. While isolated successes are reported, there are continuing policy infirmities in the approach to collectivizing farmers. The FPOs face difficulties of finances apart from governance shortfalls. Institutions such as NABARD and SFAC should realize that the time taken for stabilizing an FPO can be as high as six years as pointed out in last year's report.

On the corporate front, the pace of spending on CSR projects has improved significantly. A study by NextGen of 91 companies out of the top 100 listed in National Stock Exchange revealed that CSR spending increased to ₹60.33 billion in 2015–16 from ₹47.6 billion;[18] 43 companies had failed to spend the prescribed amount on CSR in 2015–16 compared to the 51 in 2014–15. An analysis of corporate spends in 2014–15 showed that only 12% of funds were committed to rural development. Poverty reduction projects and skill development projects were also popular with the corporates. CSR spending was hampered by lack of good

---

[18] NextGen is a CSR management entity that helps corporate to manage their CSR spending. The information is based on an article in *Live Mint* on September 21, 2016.

ideas, credible and competent voluntary sector partners, and also limited availability of skilled CSR personnel. There was an increasing tendency toward outsourcing the management of CSR investments as seen from emergence of NGOs, voluntary networks, and social enterprise firms that offer to intermediate between companies and CSR project implementers.

The year past has seen several positive developments. The overall livelihood situation is assessed to have marginally improved in rural areas. The moderating inflation, the higher minimum wages set under MNREGS, and availability of skill building programs have made employment situation better. The slew of schemes and programs has to result in ground level action and produce desired impacts. The ambitious programs announced by the government, apart from funding, also need quality technical expertise, robust implementation arrangements, and timely monitoring. Even as the growth potential of 8% is being targeted, the aspirations of the vulnerable for an equitable share in growth has to be brought to the center of the development strategies. Let us hope that the year brings livelihoods concerns to the center of political and economic discourse.

ANNEXURE 1.1
Net Returns from Cropping

₹/ha., Percent

Sl. No.	Crop	Cost A$_2$	Cost A$_2$ +FL	Cost C$_2$	GVO	Gross Returns over A$_2$		Gross Returns over A$_2$ +FL		Net Returns	
		₹/ha.				₹/ha. (Col.6– Col.3)	Percent (Col.7/ Col.3*100)	₹/ha. (Col.6– Col.4)	Percent (Col.9/ Col.4*100)	₹/ha. (Col.6– Col.5)	Percent (Col.11/ Col.5*100)
(1)	(2)	(3)	(4)	(5)	(6)	(7)	(8)	(9)	(10)	(11)	(12)
A. Cereals											
1	Paddy	25,179	33,631	47,547	53,242	28,063	111	19,611	58	5,696	12
2	Maize	18,989	26,462	36,659	37,958	18,969	100	11,497	43	1,299	4
3	Jowar	17,330	21,657	30,546	29,659	12,329	71	8,002	37	–887	–3
4	Bajra	10,399	17,219	23,166	22,605	12,206	117	5,386	31	–561	–2
5	Ragi	19,340	27,575	36,188	29,616	10,276	53	2,041	7	–6572	–18
B. Pulses											
6	Arhar (Tur)	19,508	25,902	38,593	46,505	26,997	138	20,602	80	7,912	21
7	Moong	10,882	15,381	20,598	21,321	10,440	96	5,940	39	723	4
8	Urad	11,901	15,950	22,716	23,850	11,949	100	7,901	50	1,134	5
C. Oilseeds											
9	Groundnut	33,257	40,935	56,913	63,119	29,862	90	22,183	54	6,206	11
10	Soybean	17,299	20,762	29,818	36,078	18,779	109	15,317	74	6,261	21
11	Sunflower	14,415	17,579	23,958	23,579	9,165	64	6,000	34	–379	–2
12	Sesamum	9,647	15,048	21,880	28,273	18,626	193	13,225	88	6,393	29
13	Nigerseed	5,483	11,311	15,815	14,460	8,977	164	3,149	28	–1,355	–9
D. Commercial Crop											
14	Cotton	37,266	46,208	64,931	74,519	37,253	100	28,311	61	9,588	15

Source: Ministry of Agriculture, GOI, Price Policy for Kharif Crops, Marketing Season 2016–17 (March 2016), Commission on Agricultural Costs and Prices.

Policy and Fiscal Framework

The Union Budget 2016–17 came in the aftermath of overwhelmingly positive and optimistic statements with regard to the future enunciated in the budget 2015–16. The 13 major goals focusing on a clean, green, and poverty-free India that has skilled manpower required to be followed up in the 2016–17 budget. The current year's budget recognized the need for macrostability, boosting domestic demand, economic reforms, focus on vulnerable sections, and increasing expenditure on priority areas. The budget also tried to underline the importance of improving farm profitability. Doubling farm incomes by 2022 has been the government's one of the stated objectives. The government's thrust to reorient its interventions to double the income of the farmers by 2022 seems very appealing. However, questions around the timeline and whether the government intends to double the farmers' income from the present level need to be resolved. Whether it is possible to double farmers' income within the next six years is a question that is making rounds in academic and practitioner circles. The budget while coming under reasonably good GDP growth conditions had also to factor in a hike in expenditure arising from the pay commission awards representing a 23% increase in the salary package of government staff as also the expenditure resulting from introduction of the one rank one pension (OROP) scheme for defense services personnel. While the positive side of this expenditure by the government is an increase in customer demand, the potential adverse long-term fiscal impact cannot be ignored.

The redeeming feature of the current year's budget is the stepping up of the expenditure outlay for agriculture and irrigation, which has crossed the expenditure levels reached in 2013–14 (Table 2.1). However, the allocation for agriculture and farmer's welfare of ₹359.84 billion mentioned in the budget speech is not in the sectoral allocations—the key difference being the ₹150 billion interest subvention on farm loans, which is accounted for under the Ministry of Finance and not Agriculture. Significant programs related to irrigation have been announced, which will be supported through three Central Government schemes (PMKSY, AIBP, and MGNREGS), and a long-term irrigation fund will be set up NABARD with a corpus of ₹200 billion. A program for the sustainable management of groundwater at a cost of ₹60 billion had also been announced. Agriculture found a number of new schemes and continuation of support to old schemes such as organic value chain development in the Northeast, traditional agricultural development program, unified agricultural marketing e-platform (e-NAM), four dairy projects, and soil health card scheme. Further, the government also announced the provision

Table 2.1:   Sector-wise Central Plan Outlays (₹ Crores)

Sector	2013–14 Actuals	2014–15 Actuals	2015–16 Budgeted Estimates (BE)	2015–16 Revised Estimates (RE)	2016–17 BE
Agriculture and Allied Activities	17,788	9,795	11,657	10,942	19,394
Rural Development	51,757	1231	3,131	3,027	2,751
Irrigation and Flood Control	441	910	772	1,105	1,024
Energy	182,388	170,812	167,342	171,519	205,878
Industry and Minerals	33,433	44,006	43,113	45,512	49,372
Transport	103,959	100,520	193,417	178,502	229,874
Communications	16,209	6,437	12,032	13,451	13,806
Science Technology and Environment	13,535	14,382	19,023	17,965	20,926
General Economic Services	26,064	16,766	20,333	38,596	46,685
Social Services	150,736	50,858	81,003	83,535	100,291
General Services	7,263	5,164	26,559	18,553	16,247
Grand Total	**603,573**	**420,881**	**578,382**	**582,707**	**706,248**

Source: Budget documents, Union Budget 2016–17 MOF website, http://indiabudget.nic.in/ accessed on August 3–5, 2016.

of ₹55 billion for operating the new Pradhan Mantri Crop Insurance Scheme (PMFBY).

The Union Government expenditure budgeted for 2016–17 is at 13.1% of GDP. In fact, this is the lowest level so far since 2012–13 when it was at 14.2% of GDP. In the last year, based on the XIV Finance Commission's report, the center provided a higher devolution to states. The devolution to states from the Union Government in 2015–16 was at 6.1% of the GDP as compared to 5.4% in 2014–15. The budget for devolution to states in 2016–17 is at 6.1% of the GDP, reflecting the same level of funding. The devolution during 2016–17

proposed in absolute terms is higher than 2015–16 by about ₹1000 billion on account of GDP growth. The increased devolution of resources from the center to states was expected to make available increased funds for development schemes entrusted to them. An analysis of the transfer of resources to states in 2015–16 shows that the overall increase in funds flow has been marginal. While the net transfer of resources to the states have increased since the last year because of higher tax devolution, central assistance to state plans has also been cut down significantly. The states' share of taxes increased by 1.02% of GDP in 2015–16 over the previous year, but at the same time, central grants and loans to states declined by 0.40% of GDP.

The budget is continuing to rationalize subsidies and reduce the outgo on this score (Table 2.2). There has been a continuing attempt over the last three years to keep the fiscal deficit under check. The fiscal deficit has been brought down from 4.1% of GDP in 2014–15 to 3.9% in 2015–16 and further down to a targeted 3.5% in 2016–17.

As far as the sectoral allocation and the priorities are concerned, most of the ministries that deal with livelihoods such as agriculture, rural development, urban development, labor and employment, environment and forest, and so on have seen a higher allocation compared to the last year. Overall, as per an analysis carried out by the Centre for Budget and Governance Accountability (CBGA),[1] 17 ministries with a development agenda have been allocated ₹510 billion more than the amount allocated the previous year. The share of these 17 ministries in the total budget expenditure was 24%, which is much higher than the 21.5% share they had in 2012–13. In terms of allocation of resources for social sector activities and livelihood-related programs, the performance of the current budget has been better than in the previous years.

Table 2.2:   Subsidies as a Proportion of GDP

	2014–15 (Actuals)	% of GDP	2015–16 (RE)	% of GDP	2016–17 (BE)	% of GDP
Subsidies	258,258	2.07	257,801	1.90	250,433	1.66
Of which (i) Food Subsidy	117,671	0.94	139,419	1.03	134,835	0.90
(ii) Fertilizer Subsidy	71,075	0.57	72,437	0.53	70,000	0.46
(iii) Petroleum Subsidy	60,269	0.48	30,000	0.22	26,947	0.18
Defence Spending	218,694	1.75	224,636	1.66	249,099	1.65

Source: CSO National Income Statistics (http://www.cso.ie/en/statistics/nationalaccounts/), RBI Annual Report 2015–16.

[1] Centre for Budget and Governance Accountability, Connecting the Dots, An Analysis of the Union Budget 2016–17 (March 2016), New Delhi.

The Ministry of Rural Development (MORD) got an increased allocation of ₹85 billion compared to the previous year (revised estimates for 2015–16 ₹729.22 billion, raised to ₹797.76 billion in Union Budget 2016–17). A bulk of this, that is, ₹385 billion was for the MGNREGA which has now started receiving full attention of the government after some initial reluctance in the previous years. However, as some experts point out, the center has to pay out the arrears of expenditure of the past year to many states. When arrears in payment are adjusted, the net fresh allocation available for the current year's program will be less by about ₹65 billion. As such, the claimed higher allocation may not result in a higher number of days of employment. The NRLM, which had not been getting adequate support in the past, has been provided ₹30 billion, the highest so far in the last five years.[2] Indira Awaas Yojana and Prime Minister Rural Road Scheme (PMGSY) have also been provided a much higher outlay compared to the previous years. Both these schemes, apart from improving housing availability and connectivity for villages, also have a livelihood impact in terms of employment opportunities for skilled and unskilled wage labor.

In agriculture, a special allocation for the development of pulse production under the National Food Security Mission (NFSM) has been made. While pulse production in the country got renewed focus, Krishi Unnati Yojana witnessed decreased allocation under the NFSM from ₹18.73 billion to ₹17.06 billion. The ₹5 billion incentive for enhancement in pulses production under the NFSM is only a reprioritization of budgetary allocation within different missions of NFSM. In absolute terms spending for NFSM got reduced to the tune of ₹1.67 billion. A cess for farmer welfare at 0.5% of all taxable services has also been proposed. For the new insurance scheme (PMFBY), ₹55 billion have been allocated. Already there

are indications that the allocation might be insufficient.

The benefit of interest subvention and the newly announced crop insurance scheme might have some positive impact on farmers. However, both the schemes will tend to benefit those who are able to access bank loans, virtually excluding the others from the government's development spending. The CBGA[3] has commented that "the present level of budget allocation for the sector might only be able to address the symptoms and not the root causes of distress." The ministry of agriculture had a share of 2% of the total government expenditure last year from which it has been stepped up to 2.25%. However, the agriculture ministry's budget as a percentage of GDP is 0.3% in the current year. At these levels of low expenditure, transforming the lives of millions of people employed in agriculture is very difficult. When an estimated 40% to 60% of population and workforce depend on agriculture, the allocations for agriculture should be much higher than 0.3% of the GDP.

Recognizing the importance of climate change, some major proposals have been made in the union budget. A clean energy cess levied on coal has been increased, and an increased allocation for production of clean energy through nuclear power has also been made. To reduce pollution and traffic congestion, an infrastructure cess of 1% has been announced on different types of personal transportation. One of the ministries that did not get a significant step-up in the budget is that of women and child development. In fact, the current year's allocation of ₹174 billion is less than the allocations made in 2013–14 and 2014–15. The allocation made for the Integrated Child Development Scheme has been reduced by ₹7 billion compared to the last year. However, the general budget statement indicates that

---

[2] A detailed review of NRLM is carried in Chapter 3.

[3] Centre for Budget and Governance Accountability, "Connecting the Dots, An analysis of the Union Budget 2016–17."

despite reduced allocation to the Ministry of Women and Child Development, the overall expenditure on women and related aspects is of the order of ₹906.25 billion. While school education has been provided a small increase in the budget, the University Grants Commission budget has been slashed by almost half—from ₹93.15 billion 2015–16 to ₹44.92 billion in 2016–17, which can have an adverse impact on higher education in the country.

The priority for skill development for employment has been reflected in the move to set up 1,500 multiskill training centers. The budget has also proposed the setting up of National Board for Skill Development Certification on the lines of existing boards for secondary and higher secondary education. The board will approve the curriculum, the mode of examination, and certification at different levels of skill training to bring about uniformity across the country and institutions. The board will ensure that curriculum is benchmarked against international standards for skill training to improve employability of skilled workers abroad.

The budget also recognized the special problems of children pursuing education through madrassas. It announced the Nai Manzil program that will offer integrated education and livelihood skills to students of minority community studying in Madrassas. The program will aim to modernize education and introduce skills as an integrated package, so that students can take up employment on completing their education. The center has allocated ₹37.38 billion for Nai Manzil to the Ministry of Minorities, the implementing ministry. The Maulana Azad Education Foundation will support the ministry in implementing the program.

A matter of concern is that of allocations for the social sector not being able to reach the levels achieved in 2013–14 by a large margin of more than ₹500 billion. An important social welfare scheme announced was the health insurance scheme. To quote from the Union Budget

Serious illness of family members cause severe stress on the financial circumstances of poor and economically weak families, shaking the foundation of their economic security. In order to help such families, the Government will launch a new health protection scheme which will provide health cover up to ₹0.1 million per family. For senior citizens of age 60 years and above belonging to this category, an additional top-up package up to ₹30,000 will be provided.

Apart from the central plan outlays, the budget also makes allocations to support state and union territory plan expenditure. A comparison shows that the allocation to states has not registered the same level of growth as the central plan assistance (Table 2.3). The allocation made for state plans in 2016–17 is less than the actual expenditure in 2014–15. Hopefully, the increased devolution of resources will fill in the gaps.

The combined expenditure of the center and states on agriculture, irrigation, and rural development initiatives shows that after a decline in expenditure as a proportion of GDP from the levels achieved in 2006–2009, in the last two years (2013–14, 2014–15) there is a healthy increase (Table 2.4). However, the effect of proposed change in funding pattern for central schemes, which affect almost all agriculture and rural development schemes, remains to be seen. (See Annexure 2.1 for detailed data on expenditure relating to agriculture, irrigation, and rural development.)

The expenditure on agriculture and irrigation as a proportion of GDP has been

Table 2.3: Plan Expenditure—A Comparison Between the Center and States

	2014–15 Actuals	2015–16 BE	2015–16 RE	2016–17 BE
Central Plan Outlay	420,881	578,382	582,707	706,248
State/UT Plan Outlay	270,829	204,784	216,108	241,900

Source: Budget Documents, Union Budget 2016–17 MOF website.

Table 2.4: Combined Current and Capital Expenditure of the Center and States

Expenditure on	1990–91	2000–01	2005–06	2006–07	2007–08	2008–09	2009–10	2010–11	2011–12	2012–13	2013–14	2014–15
Agriculture, allied areas as % of total exp.	4.30	2.95	2.33	2.67	3.21	3.13	2.92	2.90	2.81	3.17	3.26	3.52
Rural Dev as % of total exp	3.37	2.70	3.96	3.87	3.68	4.87	4.10	3.97	3.62	3.74	3.48	4.13
Agri, irri, and RD as % of total exp	10.80	8.40	9.54	10.09	9.91	10.68	9.49	9.09	8.53	9.12	8.87	9.54
Agriculture as % of Agri GDP	3.91	3.18	3.40	4.01	4.75	5.00	4.89	4.63	4.40	5.26	5.37	6.33
Agriculture rural development as % of total GDP	3.10	2.29	2.61	2.77	2.68	3.03	2.81	2.64	2.39	2.65	2.66	2.91
Agri and irri as % of agri GDP	6.74	6.13	8.13	9.33	9.23	9.27	9.01	8.17	7.69	8.91	8.86	9.73

Source: Indian Public Finance Statistics 2014–15, Ministry of Finance, Department of Economic Affairs, Economic Division July 2015.

growing over the last 3 years and is at the highest level in the last 25 years (Figure 2.1). However, the expenditure on rural development has been declining from 2008–09 onwards till 2013–14. Only in 2014–15 it registered a marginal increase.

An important aspect of the budget is also the manner in which different development programs will be supported when they are undertaken at the state level. After the XIV finance commission award, the states are to be provided with 42% of tax revenues by the center. The center altered the funding of central plan schemes to states last year. The states had reservations on the impact of such unilateral move by the center. As a result a committee of chief ministers of states was set up to examine the issue of how the Central Government will fund the state budgets. The committee came out with classification of the major schemes into a core of core schemes and noncore schemes (Box 2.1). Six schemes are considered as core of core schemes and another eighteen are considered to be just core schemes. Furthermore, there are three optional schemes that are

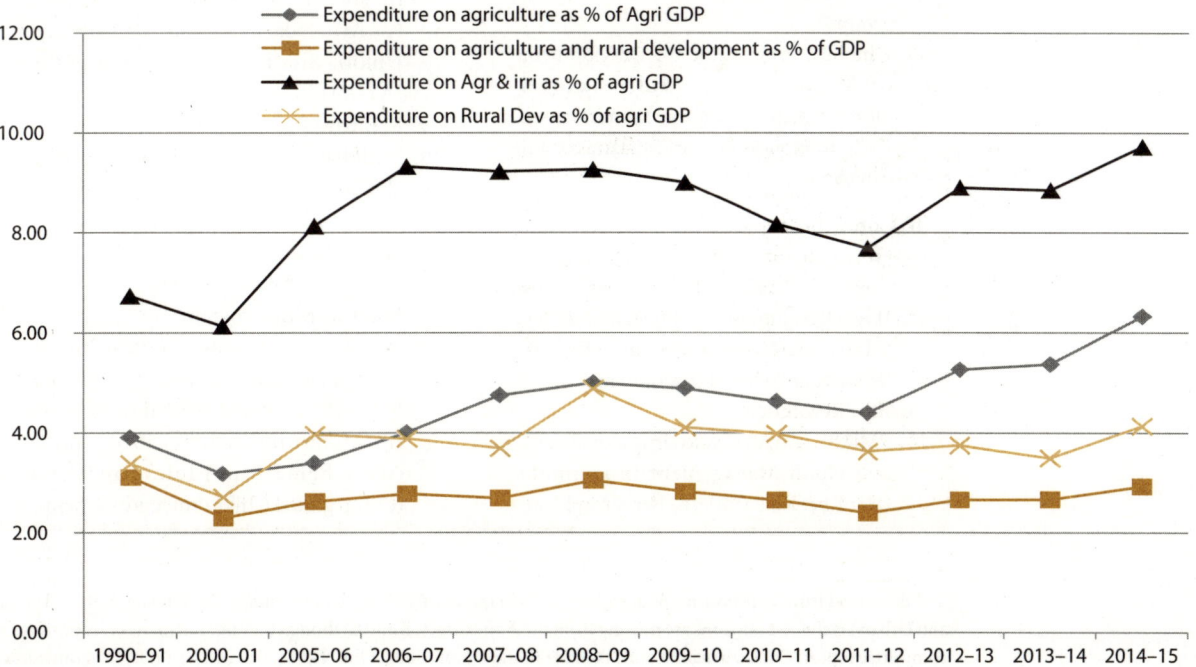

Figure 2.1: Budget Expenditure on Agriculture and Rural Development

Box 2.1:   *Core and Noncore Schemes—Basis of Funding State Budgets*[4]

As per the decision of the government, schemes defined as 'core of the core' schemes would be fully funded by the center, continuing the existing pattern. The funding pattern of 'core' schemes, which form part of the National Development Agenda, will be shared 60:40 between the center and the states (90:10 for the eight Northeastern and three Himalayan states). A list of these schemes is attached under Annexure B. In the case a scheme/subscheme in the above list has a central funding pattern less than 60:40, the existing funding pattern will continue. The other optional schemes listed in Annexure 'B' will be optional for the state governments and their fund sharing pattern will be 50:50 between the center and the states (80:20 for the eight Northeastern states and three Himalayan states.

Table 2.5:   Proposed Funding Pattern for CSS (Ratio of Center: States Funding)[4]

States	Core Schemes	Optional Schemes
Northeastern States[5]	90:10	80:20
Himalayan States[6]	90:10	80:20
All Other States	60:40	50:50
Union Territories	Funded entirely by the center	Funded entirely by the center

(A) Core of the Core Schemes

1. MGNREGA
2. National Social Assistance Programme
3. Umbrella Scheme for the Development of Scheduled Castes
4. Umbrella Programme for Development of Scheduled Tribes (tribal education and Vanbandhu Kalyan Yojana)
5. Umbrella Programme for Development of Backward Classes and other vulnerable groups
6. Umbrella Programme for Development of Minorities (a) Multi-sectoral Development Programme for minorities. (b) Education Scheme for Madarassas and minorities.

(B) Core Schemes

1. Green Revolution (a) Krishi Unnati Yojana (b) Rashtriya Krishi Vikas Yojana
2. White Revolution—Rashtriya Pashudhan Vikas Yojna (Livestock Mission, Veterinary Services, and Dairy Development)
3. Blue Revolution
4. PMKSY—(a) Accelerated Irrigation Benefit and Flood Management Programme (Har Khet Ko Paani), (b) Per Drop More Crop, and (c) Integrated Watershed Development Programme
5. PMGSY
6. National Rural Drinking Water Mission
7. Swachh Bharat Abhiyan (a) Swachh Bharat Abhiyan—Rural (b) Swachh Bharat Abhiyan—Urban
8. National Health Mission (a) Rural and Urban Mission (b) Human Resources in Health and Medical Education (c) Ayurveda, Yoga and Naturopathy, Unani, Siddha, and Homoeopathy (AYUSH)
9. Rashtriya Swasthya Suraksha Yojana
10. National Education Mission (a) Sarva Shiksha Abhiyan (b) Rashtriya Madhyamik Shiksha Abhiyan (c) Teachers Training and Adult Education (d) Rashtriya Uchchatar Shiksha Abhiyan
11. Mid Day Meal Program
12. Integrated Child Development Services (Umbrella ICDS) (a) Core ICDS (b) National Nutrition Mission (c) Maternity Benefits Programme (d) Scheme for Adolescent Girls (e) Integrated Child Protection Scheme

---

[4] Excerpted from Expenditure Budget, Part III Plan outlay 2016–17—Union Budget Documents. National rural and Urban Livelihood missions are missing from the Annexure A, B and C, though they figured in the chief minister's committee report. Considering the outlays made in the Union Budget for NRLM, this can be a mistaken omission.

[5] Northeastern states include Arunachal Pradesh, Assam, Meghalaya, Manipur, Mizoram, Nagaland, Sikkim, and Tripura.

[6] Himalayan states include Himachal Pradesh, Jammu and Kashmir, and Uttarakhand.

13. Pradhan Mantri Awas Yojna (a) Rural (b) Urban
14. Forestry and Wild Life (a) National Mission for Green India (b) Integrated Development of Wildlife Habitats (c) Conservation of Natural Resources and Ecosystems
15. Urban Rejuvenation Mission—Smart Cities and Atal Mission for Rejuvenation and Urban Transformation (AMRUT)
16. Modernization of Police Forces
17. Infrastructure Facilities for Judiciary
18. Member of Parliament Local Area Development Scheme

(C) Optional Schemes
1. Border Area Development Programme
2. National River Conservation Plan
3. Shyama Prasad Mukherjee Rurban Mission

also available for support from the center. With this revised funding ratios and also a clear classification of which schemes will get a higher level of central support, the problems that arose last year in the matter of the center's support to state budget had been resolved. It can be seen that a number of schemes having direct impact on livelihoods are now part of core schemes and they will find the center's support only if the state governments prioritize the same by spending 40% of the requirements.

The devolution pattern provides for allocation of nearly ₹3 trillion to gram panchayats. There are 250,000 panchayats in the country that will now get almost ₹0.01 billion every year. This is a key departure from existing funding pattern and has the potential to pave the way for democratization of public spending in India.

As in the past, the Union Budgets made announcements on expenditures and investments that were not provided for in the budget but which are meant to be done by other institutions. A long-term irrigation fund of ₹200 billion and MUDRA loans of ₹1800 billion are to be provided from out of priority sector lending shortfalls. ₹313 billion are to be raised by five public sector entities (for roads, renewable energy, rural development, and power supply) through bond issuance.

2.1 Legislation

The big ticket legislation that had been on the wish list of every corporate and business in the country is the goods and services tax (GST), which was finally passed by Rajya Sabha, 13 years from the first initiative in this regard. While different political parties were convinced of the economic logic of GST, procedural and other considerations had delayed the passage of the bill. Considerable benefits from the bill have been predicted for the ultimate customer, businesses, and the government (Box 2.2) through reduction in number of indirect taxes at the center and states, simplification of procedures, easier interstate movement of goods, and overall lower incidence of taxes on goods and services.

Box 2.2: *Good and Services Tax—Predicted Benefits*

For Businesses
Uniformity of taxes, as GST subsumes several other state and central taxes
Avoidance of cascading
Ease of compliance on account of a single tax authority and regulations, lower cost of compliance
Improved competitiveness on account of lower taxes and ease of movement of goods

For the Consumers
Single transparent indirect tax with certain rates
Overall lower tax burden, without the cascading effect of multiple taxes

For Center and State Governments
Easy to administer and collect
High revenue efficiency on account of lower cost of collection
Better control over leakages

Source: Compiled by the authors from a reading of available literature on GST.

However, with the states imposing their own state goods and service tax (SGST) and the Integrated GST being applicable on interstate transactions, there are still issues of coordination, information, and revenue sharing between states and accounting complexities for the taxpayer in claiming tax credits on applicable transactions. But with five central taxes and possibly six state taxes being subsumed[7] in to GST, the difficulties faced by taxpayers will be much less. However there are concerns about GST and its effect on business, especially those that have multistate operations. An analysis of the working modalities of GST reveals that the businesses operating in several states have to register in each state separately. Each registration will be treated as an independent entity even where these are branches of one company from which goods or services are being supplied. While at present a typical entity with a pan-India operation files 2 semiannual returns and 12 monthly returns, this will go up by many multiples under GST, depending on how many states it has operations in. This could create an overwhelming overload for tax compliance and will have a very negative effect on the costs of compliance and worsen the business environment. There are also apprehensions that the GST could adversely affect the livelihoods of those in the unorganized sector. According to Professor Arun Kumar[8]

> The unorganised sector in India employs 93 percent of the workforce. The small and tiny units producing and selling locally would lose from a unified market, which will benefit large-scale producers. This will aggravate under-employment, distress in the farm sector and adversely impact the poorer states. No wonder, GST is being strongly backed by large businesses—foreign and Indian. Just because VAT exists in more than a hundred nations is no reason that it would uniformly benefit all in India.

According to some critics of GST, the small and microindustrial and service units might face adverse consequences of the new tax regime. Small and Medium-sized enterprises (SME) manufacturers, presently exempt (if annual taxable turnover is up to ₹1.5 crores) from paying excise duty, would be liable to pay full rate of GST. The small units might find it difficult to compete with large and more organized industry leaders in terms of costs. Small scale service sector is likely to face an increase in tax rate under GST as against the present effective rate of 15%. The cost of compliance with GST for small units and business which were so far spared of the tax regulations could be high.

The Aadhaar bill had been passed by the Lok Sabha as a money bill, giving the statutory basis for a unique identification number introduced a few years back on a voluntary basis. The bill is more to resolve the issues raised by the Supreme Court's decision that the requirement of Aadhaar cannot be binding. Aadhaar bill is interestingly titled "The Aadhaar (Targeted Delivery of Financial and Other Subsidies, Benefits and Services) Bill, 2016" and its objective is described as to provide for targeted delivery of subsidies and services to individuals residing in India by assigning them unique identity numbers called Aadhaar numbers. The use of biometric identifiers that are unique to target subsidies and government benefits is intended to prevent leakage, promote efficiency, and reduce transaction costs of government in implementing social and welfare programs. Information privacy issues and technology failures blocking benefits flow, dominate discussions on the negative features of Aadhaar. In Chapter 3, some of the problems arising from Aadhaar-based PDS under the NFSA

---

[7] Central Excise, Additional Excise, Additional Customs Duty (countervailing), Special Additional customs Duty and service tax of center, Sales tax/VAT, Entertainment Tax, Octroi and Entry Tax, Luxury Tax, Purchase tax and Tax on lottery, racing or betting of states are subsumed in to GST.

[8] Prof. Kumar is former Sukhamoy Chakravarty Chair Professor at the Centre for Economic Studies and Planning, Jawaharlal Nehru University. Excerpted from http://www.firstpost.com/politics/why-some-economists-think-gst-is-over-hyped-it-wont-help-you-or-me-2920016.html

have been dealt with. A more fundamental question is on the uniqueness of the biometric identifiers—fingerprint and iris scan. Hans Varghese Mathews[9] has argued in an article that two persons with matching biometric identifiers are probable and has estimated—using data generated in the early testing stages of Unique Identification Authority of India (UIDAI)—that one out of every 121 people can be a duplicand. This renders the uniqueness questionable. He concludes

> We have considered the biometric identification programme of the UIDAI, and for varying levels of population estimated the proportion of duplicands: persons whose biometric identifiers match that of some other person. These proportions are too high: and indicate that the programme would badly fail to uniquely identify individuals. The estimation depends on the results of one experiment conducted by the UIDAI itself, and requires the elementary knowledge of the differential calculus …. The experiment was performed in the very early stages of the programme, and the UIDAI should have been able even then to estimate the proportions of duplicands as we have here.

The Child Labour (Prohibition and Regulation) Act 1986 has been amended to ensure that children below 14 do not get employed in any kind of industry and those between 14 and 18 do not get employed in hazardous industries. The long title of the Act has been amended as "An Act to prohibit the engagement of children in all occupations and to prohibit the engagement of adolescents in hazardous occupations and processes and the matters connected therewith or incidental thereto" conveying the apparent intent of eliminating child labor. However an exception made in Section 5 of the amendment Act provides for the child to

help his family or family enterprise, which is other than any hazardous occupations or processes set forth in the schedule, after his school hours or during vacations as long as the work does not affect the school education of the child. The children of up to 14 years can end up working in the family enterprise at home, in fields, or in a forest. While the Act now covers adolescent children, all it does is protect a small number of children engaged in certain specific forms of child labor especially in mines, inflammable material, explosives, or hazardous processes. By failing to define family work sharply, the Act legitimizes the different jobs that millions of children render in home-based units such as *bidi*, *bindi* and bangle production, food processing units, embroidery, *zari* (silver thread craft), *chikankari* (needlework) and other handicraft work, packing and sticking labels, leather bags and chappal making, and the manufacturing of several other products.

The family work permitted is of the type that requires the entire family to participate to meet the demands of bulk buyers who procure the finished product on a piece rate basis. The arrangements in such cases is exploitative and shifts production to poor homes with unregulated labor conditions in which numerous children from deprived and marginalized communities are engaged. By allowing children to work after school hours 'in the family' the law ends up rationalizing child labor by law. Nobel Laureate Kailash Satyarthi has said that the changes would lead to further 'victimization of children' in their poverty.[10] Most of the work done by the children in such family enterprises are jobs that do not reach the market in which millions are unemployed. The low/no payment to children in family work keeps costs at exploitative low levels

---

[9] Hans Varghese Mathews does mathematical and statistical modelling for the Centre for Internet and Society, Bengaluru, where he is a Fellow. This is excerpted from Hans Varghese Mathews, "Flaws in the UIDAI Process," *Economic and Political Weekly*, 9 (February 27, 2016).

[10] *Times of India*, "Child labour bill passed, Unicef voices concern", July 27 2016, http://timesofindia.indiatimes.com/india/Child-labour-bill-passed-Unicef-voices-concern/articleshow/53406863.cms, accessed on July 29, 2016.

leading to suppressed demand for labor and wage rates.

In an important initiative, the Compensatory Afforestation Fund Act 2015 has been passed by parliament. The Act establishes the National Compensatory Afforestation Fund under the Public Account of India, and a State Compensatory Afforestation Fund under the Public Account of each state. This paves the way for transfer of 90% of the accumulated amounts, which presently is of the order of ₹400 billion, to the states. The funds have to be utilized for creation and maintenance of compensatory afforestation and other activities for conservation, protection, improvement, and expansion of forest and wildlife resources of the country. All fresh amounts to be realized by the states in lieu of forest land to be diverted for nonforest purpose will be deposited directly into the funds to be created under public account of the respective state. These funds will receive all future payments for: (a) compensatory afforestation, (b) net present value of forest (NPV), and (c) other project-specific payments. The National Fund will receive 10% of these funds, and the state funds will receive the remaining 90%. The 10% amounts to be retained at the national level will be used for monitoring and evaluation of activities to be undertaken by the states/UTs and Central Government and for providing, research and technical support to the states so as to ensure that these amounts are used in the technically best possible manner. The Act establishes a funding mechanism for compensating of diversion of forest lands and improving forest cover through afforestation, protection, and conservation measures.

The Fund might not be able to carry out compensatory afforestation in the absence of land in some states. The Parliamentary Standing Committee, in its 277th report[11]

had stated that there might be a situation where not enough land may be available for afforestation purposes. To address this contingency, it recommended a specific provision in the bill "for encouraging densification and revitalization of available forest closest to areas where deforestation is considered unavoidable on account of critically important national projects." However, the final Act does not contain any such provision. There are also concerns that the Act might harm the interests of tribals and forest dwelling communities, erode their hard-won rights over forests making their livelihoods even more vulnerable. Under the Act, the Compensatory Afforestation Fund Management and Planning Authority (CAMPA) fund authorities are dominated by the forest bureaucracy, who will almost unilaterally decide how this multicrore outlay will be spent, and administer it. (As a concession, the bill provides for one 'tribal expert' or tribal representative in the authority.) The Act, according to the practitioners, centralizes the afforestation efforts and completely ignores the Forest Rights Act, which vests rights of forest management with tribal and forest dwelling communities, recognizing that their livelihoods depend on the same. According to activists, the law will enable bureaucracy to seize control over CAMPA funds and administer with a governance structure that has little democratization or accountability.

Paris agreement on climate change was agreed upon by different countries under the United Nations Framework Convention on Climate Change (UNFCCC). The agreement has the objectives of (a) holding the increase in the global average temperature to well below 2 °C above preindustrial levels and to pursue efforts to limit the temperature increase to 1.5 °C above preindustrial levels, recognizing that this would significantly reduce the risks and impacts of climate change; (b) increasing the ability to adapt to the adverse impacts of climate change and foster climate resilience and low greenhouse gas emissions development, in a manner that

---

[11] Parliamentary Standing Committee, Report of the Department related parliamentary Standing Committee on science & technology, environment & forests placed in parliament on February 26, 2016.

does not threaten food production; (c) making finance flows consistent with a pathway towards low greenhouse gas emissions and climate-resilient development."

India had submitted its Intended Nationally Determined Contributions (INDCs) to the UNFCC in October 2015. India's INDCs include achieving the following targets by 2030:

- Reducing greenhouse gas emissions per unit of GDP by 33%–35% from 2005 levels;
- Achieving 40% of installed electric power capacity from nonfuel-based energy sources (such as solar, wind, hydropower);
- Creating additional carbon storage and absorption capacity for 2.5–3 billion tons of carbon dioxide by increasing forest and tree cover.

The Indian position that climate change mitigation action requires common, but differentiated, responses from countries consistent with their specific development requirements has been accepted. The obligations taken up by India will impact livelihoods that use high energy and depend on processes and technologies contributed higher emissions. On the other hand the investment in nonconventional sources of energy, carbon sequestration through afforestation, and biomass are likely to increase both skilled and unskilled employment. A detailed account of climate change and its impact on livelihoods is discussed in a later chapter.

The Land Acquisition bill,[12] which has been hanging fire for a long time, is before the Joint Parliamentary Committee (JPC). An ordinance was promulgated to give effect to the amended provisions of Land Acquisition bill and was repromulgated in May 2015. After its validity the ordinance lapsed and the government did not pursue

the same. The JPC had asked for more time which was granted. But contrary to hopes, the JPC has not come out with its report. The bill enables the government to exempt five categories of projects from the requirements of carrying out a Social Impact Assessment, restrictions on acquisition of multicropped land, and consent level for PPPs and private projects from 80 of landowners. The five categories of exempt projects are: (a) defense, (b) rural infrastructure, (c) affordable housing, (d) industrial corridors, and (e) infrastructure including PPPs where the government owns the land. The amendments can erode the rights of landowners and disenfranchise them without a transparent due process. The inclusion of commercial purposes for easier land acquisition processes is criticized by several commentators.

A Draft Labour Code comprising the different pieces of legislation relating to employment and labor has been prepared. The aim of the code is to consolidate and amend the law relating to registration of trade unions, conditions of employment, investigation and settlement of disputes, and the matters related therewith or incidental thereto. This move at consolidation is expected to ease the problems of employers in complying with different labor regulations and make way for increased formal employment.

Amendment of Ministry of Micro, Small and Medium Enterprises (MSME) Act: The MSME amendment bill had been introduced in the parliament to increase the investment limits for defining the enterprise. A comparison of existing norms and the norms proposed in the amendment bill are shown in Table 2.6.

The changed limits will enable a larger number of units to get the benefits intended for MSMEs and also enable a large number of Start-up India units to come under the MSME banner. The livelihood impact of the amendments to MSME Act is beneficial.

A draft National Water Framework Bill, 2016 was released by the Ministry of Water Resources, River Development & Ganga

---

[12] Land Acquisition (Second Amendment) Bill, 2015.

Table 2.6: Comparison of Investment Limits for Enterprises Manufacturing/Producing Goods

Manufacturing Units	Existing limits ₹ Million	Proposed limits ₹ Million
Micro	2.5	5
Small	2.5 to 50	5 to 100
Medium	50 to 100	100 to 300
Service Units		
Micro	1	2
Small	1 to 20	2 to 50
Medium	20 to 50	50 to 150

Source: By the authors based on a reading of the draft MSME (amendment) Bill 2015 and http://pib.nic.in/newsite/PrintRelease.aspx?relid=133655 (seen on June 1, 2016).

Rejuvenation in June 2016. The bill seeks to introduce a national legal framework for protection, conservation, regulation, and management of water. Key features of the bill include:

- Right to water for life, with responsibility cast on the state governments to ensure this for all citizens regardless of caste, creed, or color.
- Standards for water quality: national water quality standards shall be binding on all types of water use.
- Integrated River Basin Development and Management: A river basin, with its associated aquifers should be considered as the basic hydrological unit for planning. A river basin authority will be established, which will prepare master plans for river basins under its jurisdiction.
- Water security: the appropriate state government will prepare and oversee the implementation of a water security plan to ensure sufficient quantity of safe water for every person. These plans will include: incentives for switching from water-intensive crops, adoption of water-conserving methods, and setting up groundwater recharge structures.
- Water pricing: pricing of water shall be based on a differential pricing system in accordance with the fact that water is put to multiple uses.

This proposal to introduce a national legal framework on water is a landmark effort. A systematic attempt is sought to be made to understand aquifer level water resources and plan on that basis to ensure water security for people and for agriculture. While considerable debate expected on the different aspects of the framework on account of conflict of interests between groups of users, it would recognize water as a valuable resource the use of which needs to be regulated. For agriculture-based livelihoods, especially in low rain fall areas there would be benefits while in areas where irrigation dependence is high, changes to cropping pattern toward water-efficient crops might cause some distress. Overall this is a welcome measure that needs support from all livelihood development practitioners.

The Ministry of Water Resources, River Development & Ganga Rejuvenation also released a model Bill for the conservation, protection, regulation, and management of groundwater, 2016 in June 2016. This bill will be a part of the national water framework referred to in the previous paragraph. The groundwater exploitation in many districts has been at very high levels, leading to mining for water. Failure of wells on account of repeated boring and deepening of existing tube and bore wells has resulted in infructuous investments and raised farmer debt levels in some parts of the country. The norms of depth, interwell distance, and discharge used by NABARD to ensure safe exploitation of groundwater have been ignored by financing banks. Those who do not borrow from a bank for groundwater structures were not under any regulation. This bill will, for the first time, bring groundwater under national regulation and hopefully create enforcement capacity in states. The Act has the potential to safeguard the interests of small farmers, reduce failure of investments, and ensure equitable use of water. It is likely to have a positive effect on agricultural livelihoods dependent on groundwater.

The Expert Committee on Land Leasing chaired by Dr T. Haque submitted its report and a draft model law on land leasing. The findings were that most states restricted or banned leasing of agricultural land. The land reform laws did not meet their objectives. Leasing market had to go underground and operate informally, placing small tenant farmers at a disadvantage. Legalizing leasing of land will embolden owners lease out larger area, secure interests of tenant farmers, and enable them to make investments on leased land on account of security of tenure. The committee suggested a model leasing law the key aspects of which are as follows.

Permit and facilitate leasing of agricultural land to improve access to land by the landless and marginal farmers. It also provides for recognition to farmers cultivating on leased land to enable them to access loans through institutional credit and insurance. Important provisions of the model Act include: (a) legalizing land tenancy to provide complete security of land ownership rights for land owners and security of tenure for tenants for the lease period, (b) mutual determination of terms and conditions of lease by the land owner and the tenant, and so on. The act if passed and implemented will make the lives of tenant farmers better. In the absence of legal tenancy agreements and short duration arrangements, tenant farmers do not have many enforceable rights against the landlords. With legitimized tenancy, longer duration leases become possible, which will encourage the farmers to make long-term investments on the farm to improve productivity.

Under the NFSA the cash transfer for food subsidy rules 2015 have been notified (Box 2.3). These rules provide for direct cash transfers to beneficiaries in certain identified areas in the states and union territory. While food grains will continue to be available under the existing PDS, the state governments will be allowed to implement cash transfer of food subsidy in those areas where complete digitization of ration cards

---

Box 2.3: *Features of Food Subsidy—Cash Transfer Rules*

State governments may implement cash transfer of food subsidy in areas which have fulfilled the following conditions: (a) completed digitization and de-duplication of the beneficiary database, (b) merged bank account details with the Aadhaar numbers, (c) ensured adequate availability of food grains in the open market, and (d) identified a state agency which will receive funds from the central government and transfer them to accounts of beneficiaries.

State governments will prepare summary proposals for funds required as food subsidy. The central government will transfer the food subsidy funds to state accounts. State governments will then transfer these funds to individual bank accounts of entitled households which are on the digital beneficiaries' database.

State governments will submit utilization certificates to the central government, for the funds transferred by it to states.

Under the PDS, each beneficiary household is entitled to 5 kilograms of food grains per person per month. The food subsidy payable to each entitled household will be calculated as: the entitled quantity of food grains per household, multiplied by (1.25 * MSP) - CIP.

MSP is the price at which the government purchases grains from farmers and central issue price (CIP) is the price at which the state government sells grains to beneficiaries.

Source: Compiled by authors based on Gazette Notification no 522 dated August 21, 2015 of Ministry of Consumer Affairs, Food and Public Distribution, http://dfpd.nic.in/writereaddata/Portal/News/32_1_cash.pdf, accessed on July 15, 2016.

---

has taken place and de-duplication of beneficiary database has been carried out. The cash transfer can take place only through those bank accounts that are seeded with Aadhaar numbers. The states have to ensure that adequate food grains are available in the open market. Chapter 3 covers NFSA in detail.

2.2 Other Developments

The Union Cabinet approved the Interest Subvention Scheme 2016–17 for farmers in July, 2016. The government has allocated ₹182.76 billion for this scheme in the budget for the year 2016–17. Key features of the scheme are: farmers will be provided with an interest subvention of 5%. This would be applicable on short-term crop loans of one year, of up to Rupees 0.3 million, taken during 2016–17. Farmers will have to pay only 4% interest, out of the 9% interest rate if the repayment is made on time as per loan agreement. In the case a farmer does not repay the loan on time, he would be eligible for a 2% interest subvention as opposed to 5% (in such a case the rate of interest would be 7%). Small and marginal farmers (with land holdings of less than two hectares) who borrow money for postharvest storage would be eligible for a 2% interest subvention on loans of up to six months. In the case of a national calamity, banks would be provided an interest subvention of 2% on the loaned amount, for the first year.

Union Cabinet had decided in January 2016 not to move a bill to establish MUDRA as an independent financial institution. The decision is contrary to the announcement made last year when MUDRA was established. It has now been decided to make MUDRA function as a wholly owned subsidiary of Small Industries Development Bank of India (SIDBI). The decision is a welcome one as the viability of niche financial institutions at the apex level without own resources is doubtful.

A credit guarantee fund for MUDRA loans was announced by the Finance Minister, Mr Arun Jaitley, in his budget speech for Union Budget 2015–16. The fund is aimed at reducing the credit risk faced by lending institutions such as banks and microfinance institutions (MFIs). The fund is expected to guarantee more than ₹1000 billion worth of loans. Key features of the fund include:

- Loans sanctioned under the Pradhan Mantri Mudra Yojana (PMMY) from April 8, 2015 onwards will be guaranteed by the fund.
- The National Credit Guarantee Trustee Company Ltd. (NCGTC) will be the trustee of the fund. The NCGTC was established in 2014 to act as a trustee for credit guarantee funds set up by the government.

Based on the loan portfolio of the MUDRA Bank, a maximum guarantee of 50% of the defaulted amount will be provided. The guarantee facility will enthuse the banks to provide loans to small, micro, and tiny enterprises covered by MUDRA. The adequacy of underlying guarantee fund for meeting liabilities that might arise should be ensured.

RBI had released the report of the **Committee on Medium-term Path on Financial Inclusion**, chaired by Deepak Mohanty, Executive Director. Among other suggestions relating to financial inclusion and literacy, the committee recommended, "Phasing out the interest subvention scheme which was introduced to make agriculture credit available at a reasonable cost. The subsidy amount must be utilised for a universal crop insurance scheme, aimed at small and marginal farmers." This is an important suggestion that will go a long way in improving flow of institutional credit and preventing diversion of low cost credit to other than intended purpose. Livelihood risk mitigation is a better welfare measure for farmers than reduction in cost of credit.

Union Cabinet approved the PMFBY in January 2016. The scheme provides insurance coverage to farmers against crop failure and thereby encourages modern cultivation practises. Farmers will have the option to insure the value of outputs by paying proportionately premium, which will be at a subsidized rate. The Department of Agriculture and Cooperation will be the primary implementing agency. The state governments, banks, and insurance companies will be involved extensively in implementation. All farmers with banks loans will be compulsorily covered while it is open to all farmers. More details about the operationalization of the scheme are provided in Chapter 3.

The Cabinet Committee on Economic Affairs (CCEA) approved a central sector scheme for the promotion of a National Agricultural Market (NAM) through the Agri-Tech Infrastructure Fund in July 2015. The Small Farmers Agribusiness Consortium is the implementing agency for creating a common electronic market platform for farmers. The scheme intends to: (a) promote reform in the agriculture marketing sector, (b) promote the free flow of agricultural commodities across the country, (c) improve access to market-related information and better price discovery through a more efficient and competitive marketing platform, and (d) increase access to markets through warehouse-based sales. A budget allocation of ₹2 billion has been made for implementation.

Following up on the decision of CCEA, an e-NAM was launched on April 14, 2016. e-NAM is a national level e-trading portal that will electronically link 585 regulated wholesale markets across the country by March, 2018. To be able to participate in e-NAM, the states are required to undertake reforms in their market regulations on the following lines: (a) a single license should be valid across the state, (b) levy of market fee should be at one single point, and (c) electronic auction as a mode for price discovery should be provided for. The regulated markets require electronic price discovery mechanisms to join the e-NAM portal, which is a virtual market. Under the scheme, Department of Agriculture and Cooperation, GOI, will provide a one-time grant of ₹3 million per *mandi* (market) for equipment and infrastructure under the scheme. Big private *mandis* will also be allowed to participate in the scheme, but will not be eligible for any grants. The agricultural market initiative will be effective in boosting incomes of small farmers if effective linkages between small farmers and higher level organizations dealing with markets are established. As long as farmers dispose of produce at the farm gate, they will not receive benefits of improved markets. The practise of traders providing an advance to the farmers for procurement of produce at harvest time also works against the interest of small farmers. Institutional finance through farmer collectives for part of the crop output value alone can prevent capture of produce by traders at less than market prices. Apart from creating national market platforms, designing means of making small farmers participate in such markets through

their collective organizations and appropriate funding mechanisms is necessary.

The Parliamentary Standing Committee on Water Resources submitted its report on the repair, renovation, and restoration of water bodies. The Committee examined, among other things issues such as the state of water bodies in the country, encroachment on water bodies, and its impact. The Committee recommended that a national database of waterbodies should be created. A census of waterbodies across the country should be carried out with a timeline so that national database can come up quickly. A suggestion for uniform classification of water across the country has been made. If adopted this will avoid the problems arising from the interstate differences in planning for water requirements for different uses and monitoring the use of water. A far-reaching recommendation was to replace multiple schemes in restoration, rejuvenation, or conservation of water bodies in to one national scheme, cutting across ministries and states. Inclusion of all waterbodies in land records so that local bodies and state governments can monitor their use and check encroachment and attempts to change land use. Maintenance of water bodies, prevention of change of use of these waterbodies (especially encroachment), and rejuvenation of waterbodies are livelihood impacting issues. The recommendations of the committee merit serious consideration from a livelihood sustenance perspective.

Ministry of Water Resources launched a nationwide water campaign in June 2015 with the objectives of

- enhancing livelihood security through reliable availability of acceptable quantity and quality of water in rural areas;
- strengthening involvement of all stakeholders including panchayats and local bodies in the water security and development schemes;
- utilizing sector expertise from different levels in government, nongovernmental organizations, and citizen groups; and

- encouraging the adoption and utilization of traditional knowledge in water resources conservation and its management.

The campaign expenditure will be met from existing schemes of central or state governments. This initiative, taken along with the proposed national water legal framework and the proposed groundwater legislation, will go a long way in promoting good practises in water use as also enforcement of discipline on all stakeholders. While regulation provides a legal basis for punishing improper use of water, campaigns like this will promote voluntary compliance as also build necessary skills in the community.

2.3 Startup India

The action plan for the Startup India initiative was released by the prime minister in January 2016. The initiative seeks to encourage startups in India, with the aim of promoting sustainable economic growth and generating employment. The action plan defines a startup as a business, which is less than five years old, and has an annual turnover of less than ₹0.25 billion.

Key points of action plan:

- Startups will be allowed to self-certify their compliance with six labor laws (such as the Contract Labour [Regulation and Abolition] Act, 1970, the Payment of Gratuity Act, 1972) and three environmental laws (such as the Air [Prevention & Control of Pollution] Act, 1981 and the Water [Prevention & Control of Pollution] Act, 1974).
- A mobile application for registering startups with government agencies will be launched.
- No inspections will be conducted for three years in respect of labor laws, unless there is a complaint. In the case of environmental laws, random checks would be carried out.
- Applications for registering patents will be fast-tracked. In addition, a panel of facilitators to assist filling of patents will be set up, with costs being borne by the government. The scheme will also provide startups with a rebate on costs for filing patents.
- A swift and simple process for winding up operations of a company will be in place, as per the Insolvency and Bankruptcy Code, 2015.
- Startups will not be subject to income tax for the first three years.
- A startup hub will be set up to act as a single window contact point for businesses. The hub will facilitate obtaining finances, improving marketing skills, business plans, and so on.

The Startup India is a key initiative in the livelihoods space on account of the employment potential. By easing entry conditions and reducing the regulatory rigor at the teething stages, the Startup India plan can spawn a number of new enterprises with favorable effects in the market for skilled labor. The Union Cabinet also approved the creation of a fund of funds for startups which was announced in the Startup India Action Plan. The fund would be established under the SIDBI and is expected to address the challenges faced by startups in obtaining funds from domestic investors. The fund is expected to build a corpus of ₹100 billion over the next nine years. An initial allocation of ₹5 billion has been made to the fund for 2015–16, followed up by ₹6 billion for 2016–17. A further scheme announced to improved credit flow to SC/ST entrepreneurs and women is the Stand-up India program. Each bank branch is required to make two loans to such entrepreneurs. Over a three year period about 0.25 million entrepreneurs are expected to be provided loans across the country.

2.4 Institutions

In the last year, the report referred to the creation of new institutions such as NITI Aayog and MUDRA. NITI Aayog has been active in facilitating policy papers and dialogue on fiscal and development issues of the country. It has developed policy approaches, among other things, on agriculture, crop insurance, land leasing laws, restructuring of public sector units (PSUs) and their strategic sale and improving quality of education, especially medical education. The Aayog is also preparing a fifteen year vision for the country as whole at the behest of the government. However it came under severe criticism from the Parliamentary committee on MSME for very slow progress on Self-Employment and Talent Utilization (SETU) scheme for which it was allocated ₹20 billion in the last year's budget. The commission has only three full-time members apart from the vice chairman. In a country with diverse development issues, there seems to be a scarcity of senior level personnel to provide direction to the work of the commission. Whether the NITI Aayog will grow in to a full-fledged independent think tank and strategy powerhouse will depend on the autonomy and quality of human resources. The question is will the NITI Aayog allow itself to become independent and voice its opinions in a forthright manner designed to serve national interests?

MUDRA, as stated earlier, will not become an independent entity in the financial sector as originally envisaged. After a review of its work and the ground realities of apex financial institutions, the Cabinet has decided to convert MUDRA Ltd in to a development finance organization, which will be a wholly owned subsidiary of SIDBI. MUDRA has been able to influence credit flow toward micro and tiny customers from banks and MFIs. During 2015–16, the first year of its operations it has reported that 12.7 million new customers in this segment have been provided with ₹589 billion in loans.[13] Overall MUDRA loans disbursed during 2015–16 amounted about ₹1330 billion and for 2016–17 a target of ₹1800 billion has been fixed.

Of the 11 licensees for payments banks three have withdrawn from the race and have decided not to set up the banks. There is debate on whether the applicants did not appraise the business prospects or whether the policy on payments banks is flawed. The blame seems to lie on both policy and the business model prepared by the applicants. In the case of SFBs, 2 out of 10 licensees have commenced operations. One was a local area bank,[14] which could easily transform in to SFB. Another is an MFI[15] which had transformed in to a bank in early September 2016. The other licensees are in different stages of transformation in to a bank. The SFBs are required to focus on small loans and achieve priority sector lending to the extent of 75% of their loan portfolio (compared with 40% required of commercial banks). Given their current operations and the regulatory mandate, SFBS are a welcome development for livelihoods of vulnerable people and tiny, microenterprises. The SFBs, with their ability to generate priority sector portfolio and sell it to other banks through priority sector lending certificates, will direct more of banking system resources in to loans—which otherwise went in to Rural Infrastructure Development Fund (RIDF) and other such facilities. On the whole SFBs are expected to cater to millions of livelihoods in the bottom half of the pyramid.

The past year has been full of action in the sphere of legislation and policy making. The budget while seeking to walk the path of fiscal consolidation, has tried to attend to needy sectors and segments of people. A number of policy and strategy papers had been released and a number of draft papers are in various stages of consultation. However the attention to agriculture and rural development seems suboptimal compared to the weighty problems posed by large numbers, large geographical distribution, and high

---

[13] Source: Review of performance of Pradhan Mantri Mudra Yojana, MUDRA Bank 2016.

[14] Capital Small Finance Bank Limited, Jalandhar, Punjab commenced operations in April 2016.

[15] Equitas Small Finance Bank Limited, Chennai, Tamil Nadu commenced operations in September 2016.

expectations. The gradual transition toward a low subsidy, low leakage regime of public funding of development is visible and needs to be accelerated. At the same time populist schemes that do not have sound economic logic such as interest subvention for crop and self-help group (SHG) loans need to be reviewed and closed. Creating favorable conditions for businesses is critical for economic growth and employment generation. But the requirement of enabling conditions for business should be balanced carefully against the considerations of equity, environment, and social costs of creating such enabling conditions. While technology adoption is inevitable to cut down transaction costs, the core objective in development programs should be hassle-free delivery of intended outcomes to people. The unanimity and sense of purpose in passing the GST is commendable. A similar spirit in coming to a consensus in respect of other important bills such as Amendment to Land Acquisition Act will go a long way in improving the investment climate and hasten the pace of investments.

ANNEXURE 2.1
Combined Current and Capital Expenditure of Center and States (₹ Billion)

	1990–91	2000–01	2005–06	2006–07	2007–08	2008–09	2009–10	2010–11	2011–12	2012–13	2013–14	2014–15
Allocation for Agri allied sectors	117.14	308.21	584.27	709.66	853.63	1205.82	1270.91	1446.43	1509.11	1886.62	2115.83	2699.14
Of which rural dev	51.47	147.28	367.67	419.89	456.35	734.37	741.58	835.98	850.15	1021.24	1092.61	1455.88
Net agri, allied	65.67	160.93	216.6	289.77	397.28	471.45	529.33	610.45	658.96	865.38	1023.22	1243.26
Irrigation major	32.78	120.71	248.64	300.02	307.92	326.84	346.05	346.7	363.27	430.34	469.99	478.65
Minor	14.82	28.88	53.44	84.69	66.95	76.34	100.93	121.26	130.45	170.36	195.26	188.77
Net irrigation	47.6	149.59	302.08	384.71	374.87	403.18	446.98	467.96	493.72	600.7	665.25	667.42
Capital exp on agri	6.67	37.11	55.42	71.15	90.74	124.31	164.24	126.06	173.41	195.42	213.17	380.78
Agri + irri	113.27	310.52	518.68	674.48	772.15	874.63	976.31	1078.41	1152.68	1466.08	1688.47	1910.68
Total exp	1526.01	5448.32	9292.06	10842.24	12392.26	15071.1	18103.75	21060.41	23478.32	27284.07	31352	35276.94
Agri + irri + rural dev	164.74	457.8	886.35	1094.37	1228.5	1609	1717.89	1914.39	2002.83	2487.32	2781.08	3366.56
Agri, allied as % of total	4.30	2.95	2.33	2.67	3.21	3.13	2.92	2.90	2.81	3.17	3.26	3.52
agri + irri i as % of total	7.42	5.70	5.58	6.22	6.23	5.80	5.39	5.12	4.91	5.37	5.39	5.42
Rural Dev as % of total	3.37	2.70	3.96	3.87	3.68	4.87	4.10	3.97	3.62	3.74	3.48	4.13
GDP	5318.14	20007.43	33905.03	39532.76	45820.86	53035.67	61089.03	72488.6	839.1691	93888.76	104728.07	115502.4
Agri GDP	1681.66	5464.76	6377.72	7229.84	8365.18	9432.04	10835.14	13196.86	14990.98	16449.26	19063.48	19645.07
Expenditure on Agr, irri and RD as % of total exp	10.80	8.40	9.54	10.09	9.91	10.68	9.49	9.09	8.53	9.12	8.87	9.54
Expenditure on agriculture as % of Agri GDP	3.91	3.18	3.40	4.01	4.75	5.00	4.89	4.63	4.40	5.26	5.37	6.33
Expenditure on Agriculture rural development as % of total GDP	3.10	2.29	2.61	2.77	2.68	3.03	2.81	2.64	2.39	2.65	2.66	2.91
Expenditure on Agr & irri as % of agri GDP	6.74	6.13	8.13	9.33	9.23	9.27	9.01	8.17	7.69	8.91	8.86	9.73

Important Government Programmes and Schemes

The major programs covered in this chapter this year are the National Rural Livelihoods Mission (NRLM) (now named differently as Deen Dayal Antyodaya Yojana and National Livelihoods Mission—rural in different government documents), National Food Security Act (NFSA), Prime Ministers Crop Insurance Scheme (PMFBY), and National Skills Development Mission (NSDM).

3.1 National Rural Livelihoods Mission

In last year's report we had pointed out the need for NRLM to become more active in the livelihoods space, rather than in community mobilization and financial linkages. During the current year some new thrusts toward livelihoods strengthening and support are visible. The macropicture of NRLM is that by end March 2016, it is under implementation in 449 districts in all 29 states covering 3092 blocks (Table 3.1). The program today covers 32.1 million households formed into 2.71 million SHGs. NRLM has also set up 0.14 million village organizations across the country comprising SHGs as its constituents. The community investment fund provided by the project was to the tune of ₹17.13 billion and in the last three years SHGs have been able to cumulatively access bank credit of ₹711.13 billion.

The funding pattern of NRLM underwent a change in the last year. In the light of recommendations of Committee of Chief Ministers, the changes made to the pattern of funding of several development schemes has impacted NRLM as well. NRLM has been listed as a 'core' scheme in Annexure B of list of core schemes that qualify for central assistance.[1] Core schemes receive assistance from the center to the extent of 60% of expenditure with the remaining 40% being brought in by the states (Northeastern and Himalayan states receive 90% from the center). NRLM prior to 2015–16, used to get central support to the extent of 75% with states bearing the balance of 25%. With the higher resource burden being placed on states whether they will continue to enthusiastically support this mission is doubtful. In the current year, allocation for NRLM has been stepped up to ₹30 billion from ₹25.05 billion (BE) in 2015–16.

The allocations made for NRLM have been low compared to the XII five year plan projections (Table 3.2). The allocations amount to 60% of what was envisaged. Actual utilization of the budget for NRLM has been less than the budget projections in three out of last four years. Even if we assume that the entire budget expenditure

---

[1] NRLM figures in the annex to Committee of Chief Ministers report on pattern of funding for central plan schemes. Strangely in the Union Budget Document explaining central assistance (Expenditure Budget—part III, Plan outlay), NRLM does not figure in any list. This seems to be a mistaken omission.

Table 3.1:   NRLM: A Snapshot

Aspect	Cumulative Achievement (March 31, 2016)
No. of Districts Covered	449
No. of Blocks Covered	3,092
No. of SHGs Promoted (million)	2.63
No. of Participating Households (million)	30.519
No. of Village Organizations Promoted	34,790
No. of Cluster Federations Formed	2,335
Amount of Revolving Fund Released (₹ billion)	2.2371
Amount of CIF Released (₹ billion)	4.6587
No. of SHGs Credit Linked (million)	1.283
Amount of Credit Linkage (₹ billion)	303.72

Source: From NRLM MIS website—Report R22 for 2015–16 http://59.177.80.38/nrlmdemo/KeyPerformance IndicatorsAction.do?methodName=showDetail, accessed on July 25, 2016.

Table 3.2:   Budget Outlays for NRLM during XII Plan Period (₹ Billion)

	2012–13 Actuals	2013–14 Actuals	2014–15 Actuals	2015–16 (Revised Estimates)	2016–17 (Budget Estimates)	Achievement as % of 12th Plan Allocation (₹290.06 Billion)
Allocation	39.15	40	40	25.05	30	0.6
Utilization	21.95	20.22	14.13	26.72	30	0.389
Utilization %	56	51	35	106	–	–

of the current year will be fully utilized, the final expenditure during the 12th plan period is unlikely to exceed 40% of the outlay of ₹290 billion envisaged.

The budget outlays for NRLM during the 12th plan period and the actual expenditure so far indicate that the original enthusiasm has waned. The reasons why the mission is receiving a lukewarm response under successive governments is not very clear. The livelihoods aspects of the program possibly have not been delivered in a satisfactory manner. The community mobilization and financial inclusion component have dominated the missions work and diverted the attention from livelihood-related issues. Even the progress reports contain aspects of financial inclusion rather than livelihood-related aspects.

The Union Cabinet, based on a review of progress and implementation issues, approved some changes to NRLM in December 2015.

The key features of the Cabinet decision are:

- NRLM should target reduction of poverty and to achieve this it should prepare plans using Socio-Economic Caste Census (SECC) database. Rural households in poverty should be identified with parameters such as income level and asset ownership.

- Interest subvention is to be extended to 100 more districts from current financial year. All women SHGs are eligible for interest subvention on loans up to Rupees 0.3 million to enable them avail loans at the interest rate of 7% per annum. An additional subvention of 3% for prompt repayment will also be available which will bring the effective rate to 4%.

- NRLM should emphasize skill development under Deen Dayal Upadhyaya Grameen Kaushalya Yojana (DDU-GKY). The existing restriction on budgets which limits the allocation to this scheme to 25% of NRLM funds has been removed. The Ministry will be able to include courses of longer duration with better placement prospects for rural youth.

- Administrative expenses: The existing ceiling for administrative expenses is enhanced to 6% of the NRLM allocation.

- Need-based financial allocation of Himayat program: The existing cap of ₹2.35 billion on the total outlay for Himayat (a training-cum placement scheme for unemployed youth in Jammu & Kashmir) will be replaced with a demand-based allocation and target within the overall budget provision of NRLM, to be funded entirely by the Central Government.

The changes are a combination of financial inclusion and livelihoods aspects in NRLM. The focus on poverty reduction should drive larger and specific initiatives on livelihoods. The interest subvention dispensation favors only those groups that are credit linked. Of the 2.63 million SHGs formed, less than 50%, that is, 1.28 million groups have a loan. The amount spent on subvention (₹6.43 billion in 2015–16) could have been gainfully utilized for market access and value addition infrastructure which has a better, nondiscriminatory distribution effect among the SHGs.

During the year 2015–16 the program covered 362 additional blocks and promoted 0.33 million SHGs. Community investment fund support of ₹7.15 billion was made available and 0.43 million candidates were trained in vocational skills by Rural Self Employment Training Institutes (RSETIs). Bank credit access to the tune of ₹303.73 billion was facilitated by the program. Across the states barring West Bengal, Orissa, Jharkhand, and Chhattisgarh, other all mainstream states had achieved the yearly target for the promotion of SHGs. The all India achievement stood at 110% of the target. However, provision of community investment support target was met only by six states with Madhya Pradesh achieving 210% of its target. At the country level the achievement of the target was to the extent of 86%. The progress in SHG bank linkage was satisfactory with an all India target achievement of 108%. Among the mainstream states, Uttarakhand, UP, Telangana, and Madhya Pradesh had fallen short of the linkage targets. Southern states had a dominant share of 77% of the SHG bank linkage facilitation. However, their share had registered decline in 2015–16 compared to 83% in the previous year. Seen in terms of numbers NRLM has done significantly well compared to the previous year. The skew toward southern states continues in bank linkage as well. Against total bank credit of ₹139.71 billion facilitated under NRLM, 75%, that is, ₹104.82 billion went to AP, Telangana, Tamil Nadu, and Karnataka. Even if mobilization of people in other states proceeds well, finance for livelihoods does not seem to flow to the extent of need.

However, the point to note is that the program is positioned as a solution for livelihoods in the rural areas. Livelihoods under the program are supported by four different broad initiatives—women farmers skill upgradation through Mahila Kisan Sashaktikaran Pariyojana (MKSP), improving agriculture-based livelihoods through Community Managed Sustainable Agriculture (CMSA), vocational Skill training and placement for rural youth through RSETIs, and setting up of enterprises in rural areas through Start-up Village Entrepreneurship Program (SVEP). The achievements under these livelihood interventions are furnished in Table 3.3.

Table 3.3: Progress Under Livelihood Initiatives

Initiative	Coverage	
	Till 2015–16	Remarks
MKSP	3.4 million women farmers, 4.48 million ha—During 2015–16 against target 0.517 million, 0.239 million women farmers trained.	Most of the trained women in the past are from two states—AP and Telangana. The skew should be remedied.
Skill training through RSETI (Placement %)	1.846 million (60.5%).	Target for 2015–16 was 0.375 million candidates. Placement rate needs to improve.
CMSA	350 villages (53,000 farmers/SHG members with land).	Has a small footprint when compared with millions that have been mobilized (0.17% of participating households).
SVEP	8 states, 24 blocks—757 group and 267 individual enterprises.	Against a target of 12,000 enterprises, 1,020 were set up.

Source: Compiled from Agenda for the Performance Review Committee Meeting of Department of Rural Development July 14, 15, 2016 and Presentation made to PRC meeting on 14, 15 July in New Delhi by Department of Rural Development; http://ruraldiksha.nic.in/writereaddata/Circulars_Rural/82_Latest_PRC_FINAL_DRAFT_AGENDA_NOTES.pdf, accessed on August 1, 2016.

The share of AP and Telangana in the cumulative achievements continues to be high on account of the fact that they had an early start to the program. But the slow progress in other states and the inability to rapidly implement livelihood initiatives is a matter of concern.

Under the skill component, with the support of 583 RSETIs, nearly 1.8 million candidates have been trained in different vocational skills of which 1.2 million candidates have been settled. As a part of improving the skill sets, 3.4 million women farmers across the country have been trained. The focus on women farmers recognizes the increasing feminization of agriculture. In a bid to diversify livelihood bases under MKSP the states have been asked to propose annual action plans to focus on cultivation of medicinal plants, and value chain interventions. The SVEP is to be implemented in 24 blocks covering 20 districts in 8 states. Overall 36,000 enterprises are to be set up. During 2015–16, 1,020 enterprises were set up against a target of 12,000, possibly because of the late start to the program and the fact it is the first year in which the implementation processes had to stabilize. Guidelines on submission of draft project reports under SVEP were issued only in June 2016. The guidelines limit the enterprises to be supported to 2,400 per block of which not more than 25% can be existing enterprises. Skill sets required for enterprise creation and nurturing are very different and it is not clear that State Rural Livelihood Missions (SRLMs) have the required competencies. In the incubation stage, enterprises require business and commercial guidance which is very different from advice on finances and production techniques with which a number of SRLM staff are familiar. Success of SVEP will depend on finding persons with enterprise incubation expertise and utilize their skills to best advantage.

Under the CMSA program 350 villages in 27 blocks are being covered. About 53,000 persons in all are reported to be covered—farmers and SHG members with land. The coverage is negligible compared with the more than 30 million households that had been mobilized. CMSA has been training farmers for adoption of water harvesting and conservation, soil conservation, improved agriculture practises, Integrated Pest Management practises that reduce pesticide use, improve natural pest control material and techniques, and make farming more sustainable in terms of costs and environment. One of the aspects in sustainability is that of farm incomes. Value chain activities and market access at an aggregated level can improve farm sustainability—and contribute to achieving the vision of doubling of farm incomes by 2022. There are signs that NRLM will move toward these objectives through a range of measures. During the year 2016–17 CMSA will endeavor to cover additional 750 villages. There is a move to focus on livestock initiatives under CMSA. MORD has entered in to a partnership with National Dairy Development Board (NDDB) dairy services to promote the dairy value chain. Furthermore, state level livelihoods resource persons are being engaged in the areas of sustainable agriculture, nontimber forest produce, and livestock.

MORD also reports that the prime minister's office (PMO) has provided a few action points for improving the efficacy and delivery efficiency of NRLM. These are (a) identification of 5 to 10 commodities or products in each block to provide additional source of income for women, (b) identification in training of SHG women on a range of services and events where they can become service providers, (c) promotion of medicinal plants in areas with high potential as an additional livelihoods resource, (d) promoting livelihood diversification through commodity value chains, (e) training of 15 to 20 master trainers in each block, and (f) development of 1 or 2 business correspondent agents per gram panchayat (GP). The suggestions from PMO are a combination of livelihood-related aspects as also financial inclusion-related aspects.

The geographical skew in the program is yet to be remedied in any significant manner. As stated earlier southern states account for a very large proportion of households, SHGs, village organizations and support in the form of revolving funds and community investment funds. Even in the case of training and support under MKSP for women farmers a lion's share has been that of southern states. The relatively late starters and vulnerable states in the north have not been able to gain the kind of support that southern states had been able to achieve. It might be worth considering whether in future the support available to southern states needs to be continued. The program might do well to focus on the northern states with higher levels of poverty and provide solutions for the vulnerable sections of society languishing for want of better livelihoods. The second issue is that of introduction of interest subvention to the SHGs. Bank credit at 7% to members of SHGs discriminates between those who are not part of NRLM and those groups which, though a part of NRLM, are unable to access bank credit. Furthermore, the lower rate of interest distorts delivery of financial services in the hands of financial institutions. Despite the rebate in interest available for prompt repayment defaults in bank loans have not declined. According to NABARD, the non perform assets (NPAs) arising from loans extended to SHG under NRLM was of the order of 6.23% as on March 31, 2016. However, it must be added that the loans given by banks to SHGs as a whole including those under NRLM was higher at 6.45% indicating that the NRLM groups performed marginally better than other groups in repayment performance.

The NRLM skills component was renamed as DDU-GKY and focused on training rural youth in different trades for placement in suitable employments. Two supplementary initiatives for Jammu & Kashmir named Himayat and Left Wing Extremism affected districts named Roshni were also launched with specific budgets and targets.

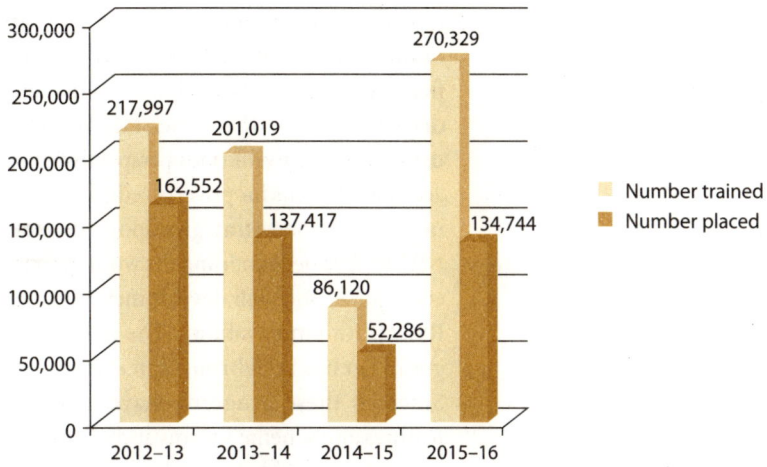

Figure 3.1: DDU-GKY Performance

Source: Graph by the author based on information in MORD website, http://rural.nic.in/netrural/rural/sites/downloads/right-information-act/rti_ddugky.pdf, accessed on October 12, 2016.

During 2014–15 the number of candidates trained fell drastically compared to the previous two years (Figure 3.1). During 2015–16 the scheme put up its best performance in terms of skills training, but placements were below par. The placement rate continued to fall over the 12th plan period from 75% in 2012–13 declined to 50% in 2015–16. The target for placement is 75% as provided in the scheme objectives, but has not been achieved except in the first year. Merely meeting training targets without meeting placement targets results in wastage of resources as also frustration among the youth who enroll for skill training on the promise of a job.

When NRLM was launched, the Government of India explained as to why this is being implemented in a mission mode. The explanation said that a mission mode implementation enables (a) shift from present allocation-based strategy to a demand driven strategy enabling states to formulate their own livelihoods-based poverty reduction action plans, (b) focus on targets of outcomes and time bound delivery, (c) continuous capacity building imparting requisite skills and creating linkages with livelihood opportunities for the poor including those emerging in the organized sector, and (d) monitoring against targets of poverty outcomes. After five years of implementation of NRLM it is very difficult to conclude that it follows a demand driven strategy[2] where the states develop demand-based livelihoods perspective plans and annual plans for poverty reduction. The major livelihood strategies adopted under NRLM have been training the women farmers, CMSA, and skill development through RSETIs for employability. The recent program that has been brought in is the SVEP. Since all these programs have common features and scheme's terms and conditions are centrally decided there seems little scope for the flexible demand-based livelihood opportunities creation. The CMSA is more an intervention in farming practises than in livelihoods. The weakest part of NRLM has been its lack of focus on value chains and linking the project households to viable markets. The recent focus on producer companies is a move in the right direction. Developing rural markets and linking people with marketing institutions and marketing networks should have been a priority given that the focus was on improving livelihoods. Instead the mission has focused exclusively on community mobilization and training of people to improve access to financial services without any effective linkage of finance to livelihood activities. In fact there was little to connect the bank loans with the plans that the households might have for livelihood activities. The aggregation of the livelihood activity outputs with a view to facilitating market linkages has not yet been attempted on scale. Localized experiments in linking people to markets have been undertaken with success. But a mission of this scale should have prioritized access to

markets and linkage to market networks as its initial intervention. The moneys provided for interest subvention could have been gainfully utilized in providing better market access which then would have benefitted members of SHGs as also nonmembers without a bias in favor of those who manage to access bank credit.

A continuing issue with the program has been that there have been no livelihood-related deliverables on the ground that is verifiable. The monitoring and evaluation function of NRLM has been weak. To rectify the deficiencies in monitoring and review, a comprehensive baseline survey was launched last year in most of the states. The surveys have been completed; reports are under finalization and should be in public domain shortly. A comprehensive monitoring and impact measurement system is required to ensure that livelihood outcomes are identified with quantitative and qualitative parameters and a measurement methodology designed.

The states have not been able to mobilize as rapidly as was expected in the initial stages of NRLM. There are states in which even now staffing at the block and district levels is not complete. Formation of groups is still an ongoing process and it is difficult to hazard a guess as to when livelihoods activities for recently promoted groups would commence. Without significant investments on markets and value chains the households enrolling under the program may not see great improvements in their livelihoods. The capture of the program by the cadre of quasi government staff is a matter for concern.[3] There have been reported issues in some states of the rural development societies that were formed to

---

[2] NRLM requires that SHGs prepare their own plan which is to be basis for support. The FAQs clarify "Micro planning is a process where members are encouraged to recognize, understand and evaluate their resources; analyse challenges they face; identify needs and make future plans to overcome vulnerabilities by making optimum utilization of resources and fostering convergences. The SHGs receive their CIF only on developing their micro plans or microcredit plans."

[3] A total of 4,174 employees are working in Society for Elimination of Rural Poverty (SERP), Telangana, including 767 as Mandal Samakhya Cluster Coordinators. The monthly salary of Cluster Coordinators was raised from the existing ₹6,150 to ₹12,000 and that of other employees in SERP by 30% on the orders of Chief Minister, Telangana. *The Hindu*, "Salary hike to SERP, MGNREGS staff," August 3, 2016.

implement the program wanting to become government employees and supervisors of the mission. If this happens the original intention of a demand-based project that will flexibly attend to the livelihoods aspirations of people of the ground might be forever lost. NRLM has to strategize the acquisition and contracting of human resources in a manner that recognizes the need for flexibility in delivery of services without vested interests of staff blocking meaningful progress.

3.2 National Food Security Act

After the enactment of the NFSA in 2013, the government has been trying hard to implement the same in the field to benefit the promised 0.81 billion people in the country. The states had been asked by the center to ensure that the appropriate target households for support under NFSA are identified and issued with new digitized ration cards. Furthermore, the states were to make the appropriate de-duplication exercise to weed out ghost ration cards that clogged the PDS. The state governments have been taking action in this regard both on eliminating the duplicate ration cards and also digitizing the data. Thirty-five states are reportedly implementing the NFSA driven PDS that supplies food grains to each household to an extent of 35 kg at a price of ₹1, 2, or 3 per kg depending on the level of poverty and also nature of food grain that is supplied. Chandigarh and Puducherry are implementing the NFSA in the DBT mode, that is, they provide cash to the households directly. The preparatory work by the states had taken a pretty long time and even at the extended dead line as of September 2015, some states were unable to complete the work of identifying suitable households and issuing ration cards. However, most of these issues have now been sorted out. In an answer to parliamentary question the Ministry of Food had stated that currently 0.73 billion persons are covered under the NFSA provisions.

The Comptroller and Auditor General carried out a quick audit to assess the preparedness of states for implementation of NFSA. The report indicated that only 51% of qualifying households had been identified in the different states. Only three states had issued new ration cards to the identified families. In others, the old ration cards were stamped to indicate that they qualify for food grains under NFSA. Though the act provisions mandate that the ration card should be issued in the names of the women in the household the same had not been adhered to, in violation of the act provisions. The infrastructure and logistics arrangements were found to be deficient. The shortage in railway rakes' availability for moving food grains was estimated at 13% to 18% over the previous 4-year period. Storage for food grains that are moved from other centers before release to the fair price shops (FPSs) was also reported to be inadequate. The door step delivery services envisaged in the scheme to the FPSs was not in vogue in most of the states. Only Bihar and tribal districts of Maharashtra were ensuring that the quantity of the food grain required for the PDS actually reached the doorsteps of the FPSs.

The outlay by the government of India had been gradually increasing from 2013–14 to 2015–16 (Table 3.4). However, in the current year's budget the outlay had been reduced by about ₹45 billion compared to the previous year. In 2016–17, ₹25 billion has been additionally allocated to support states in implementation of NFSA. It is not clear whether the reduced subsidy allocation is on account of government's plan to

Table 3.4: Expenditure on Food Subsidy (₹ Billion)

2012–13 Actuals	2013–14 Actuals	2014–15 Actuals	2015–16 (RE)	2016–17 (BE)
850	920	1176.71	1394.19	1348.35

Source: Compiled from Notes on demands for grants—Department of Food and Public Distribution—from Union Budget Documents of various years, http://indiabudget.nic.in/, accessed on July 16, 2016.

Table 3.5: Income Gains at Household Levels on Account of PDS[4]

States	Effective income gain per BPL household (in ₹)	Total number of BPL ration cardholders in the state (in lakh)	Effective income gain at state level for BPL households (in crore)	Effective income gain per AAY households (in ₹)
Assam	443.80	12.02	53.34	523.71
Bihar	458.35	142.11	651.36	611.78
Chhattisgarh	622.16	48.72	303.12	589.00
Karnataka	594.12	96.61	573.98	679.53
Uttar Pradesh	404.43	65.85	266.32	536.33
West Bengal	329.11	13.14	43.25	390.83
Total			1891.37	

withhold part of the subsidies payable to FCI (this had been happening for a number of years) or actually the government believes that there will be a net reduction in the subsidy burden. The economic survey 2016 has estimated that as much as ₹250 billion in subsidy payments can be saved by introduction of a DBT scheme for people receiving ration through PDS if they are paid cash instead of food grains being supplied.

National Council of Applied Economic Research (NCAER), in a study commissioned by the Department of Food and Public Distribution found that PDS, with its subsidized food grains had a positive income effect (Table 3.5) among poor families on account of avoided expenditure on food.

After the study and survey of PDS, NCAER[4] came up with following suggestions for implementation of NFSA.

Identification of Target Households

- The identification process needs to be state or region-specific since state priorities are different across the country. However, the criteria adopted should help in easily identifying the target group.

[4] National Council of Applied Economic Research, Evaluation Study of Targeted Public Distribution System in Selected States (September 2015), Sponsored by Ministry of Food and Consumer Affairs.

Improving Efficiency in PDS Functioning

- Adoption of modern techniques to improve the functioning of the PDS, (some of which have been adopted in the better performing states) will help.
- Distribution of food coupons should be adopted to stop leakages at the FPS level.
- Digitization of ration cards: (although many of the states claim to have completed the process of digitization, these cards had not yet been circulated at the time of our survey).
- Introduction of electronic weighing machines in place of conventional ones.
- One important step in plugging leakages is to authenticate whether the food grain distributed through the PDS is received by an eligible household. Collecting biometric information on all members of a cardholder's family or of all cardholders where the entitlement is on an individual basis, linking it with their Aadhaar number and storing it in the electronic weighing machine may solve the problem.
- Display boards containing the correct information about entitlement, availability of food grain, and the issue price should be maintained at all FPSs in the local language.

  This would have to be supplemented by awareness campaigns conducted by NGOs and government officials in villages.
- The introduction of an SMS alert to the beneficiary at the beginning of the month regarding their entitlement and the exact price to be paid at the FPS. Even if all beneficiaries do not have mobile phones, they could get this information from their peers or neighbors.

Introducing an Effective Monitoring Mechanism

- Unbiased inspection of FPSs by the state department of food and civil supply should be arranged on a regular basis. At present, inspectors visit FPSs only occasionally and they do not always check all the registers in the FPS. The process is characterized by corruption.

- Introducing a corruption-free monitoring mechanism will be crucial to the success of the food security program.
- GP members should be made aware of their role in the PDS in states like Karnataka. Such awareness may be increased through the involvement of civil society and local NGOs.
- Representatives from state food departments should meet beneficiaries in villages or urban wards to hear their complaints and address their concerns at regular intervals.
- The grievance redressal mechanism in all six states needs to be revamped immediately. Awareness campaigns about the grievance redressal mechanism should be conducted with the help of local NGOs and civil society.
- The details of delegated officials and functional help lines should be made available to beneficiaries through display boards at FPSs.
- The Department of Food and Public Distribution in each state should open a special cell on grievance redressal and appoint a grievance redressal officer as the nodal person. Although the appointment of a grievance redressal officer was proposed, it never happened. There should be a small grievance redressal cell in each district supply office as well.
- State governments should take initiatives to reconstitute the vigilance committee (VC) in all villages and urban wards. Awareness of the existence of the committee should be increased among beneficiaries. Members of the VCs should also take part in the grievance redressal process and awareness campaigns.

In accordance with its earlier decision, the government created an enabling framework for payment of cash subsidies instead of supplying food grains through PDS. The government had notified the rules for cash transfer of food subsidy in August 2015. The cash transfer of food subsidy rules provide for direct cash transfers to beneficiaries in identified areas in states and union territories. State government may implement cash transfer scheme if they met the following conditions.

1. Completing digitization and de-duplication of beneficiary database;
2. Merge bank account details with Aadhaar numbers seeded to the bank accounts;
3. Ensure adequate availability of food grains in the open market; and
4. Identify the state agency which will receive funds from Central Government and transfer the same to the beneficiaries.

Based on the rules which enable states to take up cash transfers, two union territories (Chandigarh and Puducherry) have introduced the DBT schemes under NFSA. The experiments will be watched with interest.

It remains to be seen whether instead of handling such a large volume of food grains and distributing the same through the FPSs, the government can enable the private trade to sell the required food grains to people directly. However, there are a number of concerns expressed in this regard by several

---

Box 3.1: *DBT in FSA—How it Works*[5]

Depending on the number of persons, the quantity of PDS entitlement of food grains is worked out. The economic cost of the food grains is computed for the entire family and this is directly credited to the account of the cardholder. In Chandigarh the economic costs of rice and wheat are taken at ₹23.12 and ₹16.12, respectively. The PDS entitlement per person is 3 kg of wheat and 2 kg of rice per month. For a family of five, the amount transferred to the account will be ₹473 every month.

---

[5] Sandip Das, "Union Territories script Success Story of Cash Food Subsidy", *Financial Express*, October 18, 2015, http://www.financialexpress.com/economy/union-territories-script-success-story-of-cash-food-subsidy/152915/, accessed October 19, 2016.

institutions. The first being diversion of cash from food to other more emergent requirements by poor households leading to increased hunger and lower nutrition levels among vulnerable people. The second is that of market price fluctuations of food grains making it difficult for poor households to manage purchase of food during periods of inflation with the fixed cash that is transferred every month. The third issue relates to procurement of food grains becoming redundant making the MSPs less influential in ensuring fairer price realizations by farmers. The NFSA offers a statutory backing to the entitlement of people to access food from the government systems at reasonable prices; providing cash transfer in place of food may not really meet the intended objectives of the NFSA. The nutritional security and health of masses of vulnerable people depend on a well-functioning food distribution system. The government by withdrawing from the scene might jeopardize the food security of people which it had sought to secure through legislation. However as stated earlier the economic argument that the subsidy bill can be slashed by about ₹250 billion has considerable merit.

The center's push for digitizing almost all processes relating to purchase of food grains through the PDS can derail the NFSA objectives and make it difficult, if not impossible for people to access their entitlement to food grains. The state is required to issue digitized ration cards that are machine readable. At the entry level it requires the people to acquire Aadhaar numbers (for all members in the family, including children), then seed their ration cards with the same. At the PDS outlet level a point of sale (POS) machine is required that can read digitized ration cards and can authenticate the biometrics of the buyer through access to the Aadhaar database. These processes require electricity, access to the Internet, and connectivity to enable authentication of biometrics. There are a number of households in which no member has been able to acquire Aadhaar numbers. Typically children, the very old

and infirm are those who are unable to get registered for Aadhaar. According to a survey finding[6]

> Missing persons on the ration cards was a problem encountered across villages. Approximately, every 1 person in 8 is left out of the ration card. This is in addition to the households which are completely excluded. This matters, since NFSA entitlements are defined in per-capita terms (5 kg of grain per person per month). It was also observed, that for most households which have been recently included as AAY, there is just one person's name on the card (usually the head of the household). Though, this doesn't affect the ration entitlements, since it is 35 kg/household but it undermines the coverage done in the state.

Box 3.2:   *Is the Technology Push Increasing Food Insecurity[7]*

Recent progress is in danger of being undone soon due to the Central Government's counterproductive push for Aadhaar-based biometric authentication in the PDS. This involves installing POS machines at PDS shops, and verifying the identity of cardholders by matching their fingerprints against the Aadhaar database over the Internet. This system requires multiple fragile technologies to work at the same time: the POS machine, the biometrics, the Internet connection, remote servers, and often other elements like the local mobile network. Furthermore, it requires at least some household members to have an Aadhaar number, correctly seeded in the PDS database. This is a wholly inappropriate technology for rural India, especially in the poorest

---

[6] House-to-house survey in 3 villages, each of Verno Block (Gumla District) and Ramgarh Block (Dumka District), Jharkhand in June 2016. Excerpted from South Asia Citizens Web, *National Food Security Act (NFSA) Makes Headway in Poorest States, Bihar and Jharkhand Lag Behind*. http://www.sacw.net/article12824.html, accessed on October 1, 2016.

[7] Reproduced from the article by Prof Jean Drèze, "Dark Clouds Over the PDS," *The Hindu*, September 10, 2016, http://www.thehindu.com/opinion/lead/aadhaarbased-biometric-authenticationdark-clouds-over-the-pds/article9091334.ece?utm, accessed on October 1, 2016.

states. Even in state capitals, network failures and other glitches routinely disable this sort of technology. In villages with poor connectivity, it is a recipe for chaos. Note that the Internet dependence is inherent to Aadhaar since there is no question of downloading the biometrics.

The people left out for want of Aadhaar numbers will be counted as evidence of elimination of ghost ration cards and benefits of de-duplication. At the PDS outlet, the Internet connectivity is an issue in the remoter parts of the country. Without connectivity, the shops refuse to issue the rations in some states. In others a manual system of registers is introduced to issue the rations, but this lends itself to leakages which the new dispensation is supposed to prevent.

The online systems increase the problems of both the dealer and the ration cardholder. The POS machines fail to recognize or authenticate the fingers of the buyer in about 50% cases according to a field observation in Jharkhand. The additional issues of connectivity and transaction time in authentication over the network results in fewer people being served by the dealer. Ration distribution takes many days in a month, rendering leakages and frauds possible. There are effective alternatives available which can achieve the same goals of reducing leakages, targeting the rations to those who are really entitled and at the same reducing costs of transaction and delivery. Madhya Pradesh has introduced an offline solution (Box 3.3) that downloads and stores relevant information on the ration card which then can be compared with the buyer details at the time of sales of rations. This does not depend on connectivity, Internet traffic, and the response time of UIDAI servers. The transaction data can be uploaded whenever Internet connection is established.

A survey of NFSA was conducted using student volunteers in six of India's poorest states in early June 2016. Early survey findings suggest that four of these six states (Chhattisgarh, Madhya Pradesh, Odisha, and West Bengal) are making good progress toward food security for all: the PDS is working quite well and most people are covered. Bihar and Jharkhand, however, are yet to complete essential PDS reforms. Chhattisgarh emerged as the leading state in food security matters. Chhattisgarh enacted its own Food Security Act in December 2012. The state has a well-functioning, near-universal PDS which guarantees 7 kg of food grains (more than the NFSA's 5 kg norm) per person per month to rural households. Most of the sample households were receiving their full entitlements without

---

Box 3.3: *The Offline System in Madhya Pradesh*

The beneficiary will be bound to a particular FPS. Offline mode is to be adopted in FPS where connectivity is not available at present.

Following are the steps involved in this mode:

1. The POS machine will download the list of eligible families and their eligibility from the central server in the beginning of the month.
2. Ration will be distributed on the basis of SAMAGRA ID verification (issued by the state government).
3. The sale transaction and receipt thereof will be generated through the POS device.
4. The machine database will be updated as per the sales on real-time basis.
5. The FPS shopkeeper will come to an area on a designated day every week with the POS device where he can connect with the server and the data will be uploaded to the central server.
6. The POS device will also generate the receipt of material received at the FPS and such receipt is recorded on central server on the next designated day.

Source: Department of Food and Public Distribution, http://dfpd.nic.in/writereaddata/images/FPS_Automation_in_MP.pdf, accessed on October 3, 2016.

Table 3.6:   NFSA Survey 2016—Some Findings

	Proportion of sample households (hhs) with a ration card (%)		Proportion of "missing names" in the ration cards[a] (%)	Average purchase of PDS food grains, as % of entitlements[b]		Proportion of hhs who felt quality of PDS grain is "good" or "fair" (%)
	Before NFSA (BPL or AAY)	After NFSA (Priority of AAY)		May 2016	"Normal month"	
Chhattisgarh	81	95	15	96	97	99
Odisha	62	88	8	96	99	86
Madhya Pradesh	55	84	6	100	98	72
West Bengal	51	86	13	95	95	57
Jharkhand	50	76	12	55	84	91
Bihar	64	83	17	15	84	58
SIX STATES	58	85	13	71	92	69

Source: "Poorest States Make Headway Towards Food Security But Bihar and Jharkhand Lag Behind", press release on survey, https://www.countercurrents.org/nfsa140616.pdf, accessed on July 1, 2016.

fail. The PDS reforms in Chhattisgarh have inspired similar reforms in Odisha, and more recently in Madhya Pradesh. The survey suggests and consolidates earlier evidence that the reach and effectiveness of the PDS has dramatically improved in both states during the last few years (Table 3.6).

The survey data indicates that the coverage of PDS has increased after implementation of NFSA in terms of ration card issuance. NFSA implementation has been an inclusive exercise that will secure livelihoods through food entitlement. However the missing names, lower quantity of rations issued, and the low quality of grains are matters for attention at the state levels. Overall, it is clear that the NFSA, despite its initial problems, is having a beneficial impact on most of the households. The objectives of lowering the costs of delivery, targeting the needy and reducing leakages are achievable, but reliance on high technology as the sole means of doing the same, in the short run, will reduce the quality of implementation. Prof. Jean Drèze, having travelled across some of the states rightly observes: "There are better ways of plugging last-mile leakages, including the use of simpler technologies not dependent on the Internet. Imposing a technology that does not work on people who depend on it for their survival is a grave injustice."

3.3 National Skills Development Mission

The mission was launched in July 2015 to rapidly scale up skill development efforts in India, by creating an end to end, outcome-focused implementation framework, which aligns demands of the employers for a well-trained skilled workforce with aspirations of Indian citizens for sustainable livelihoods. The overall target for the mission is to skill train 400 million people by 2022. This, as explained in the last year's report is through a combination of training courses through different ministries, state governments, and training partners. On the rather steep targets, there have been reservations. Santosh Mehrotra[8] makes the point

> Given the limited progress since 2007, the number needing Technical, Vocational Education and Training is, we have estimated, at least 20 million per year, but the system is barely churning out 5 million per year. The number to be trained is nowhere as high as the previous Government policy believed (500 million between 2012 and 2022, as stated

---

[8] Santosh Mehrotra, Professor, JNU, "The Private Sector's Commitment to the National Skill Development Programme is Shaky," *The Wire*, May 31, 2016, http://thewire.in/39280/the-private-sectors-commitment-to-the-national-skill-development-programme-is-shaky, accessed on October 3, 2016.

in the National Skills Policy 2009). Nor is the number even as high as 400 million (by 2025), as stated in the current National Skills Policy, 2015. Nor is the number joining the labour force (for whom employment has to be found) anywhere close to the 12 million per annum that is repeated ad nauseum by policy-makers, industry and the media; it is no more than 7 million per annum.

The first meeting of the governing council of NSDM (with PM chairing the meeting) was held in June 2016 and the following were the important decisions taken.

- Skill training to be scaled up to cover at least 15 million people during 2016–2017.
- The Central Board for Skills Certification will be set up by September 2016 to infuse quality into India's skill development ecosystem.
- Unutilized infrastructure in existing engineering colleges will be leveraged for skill training courses.
- Profit-making PSUs will be mandated to scale up apprenticeships, up to 10% of total manpower, over the course of this year. Private corporations are also expected to follow suit.
- Five hundred Pradhan Mantri Kaushal Kendras will be opened this year to provide free skill training.
- Fifty overseas employment skill training centers to be opened this year, in migration pockets of the country.
- Five hundred Rozgar Utsavs will be held across industrial training institutes (ITIs), central training institutes, Pradhan Mantri Kaushal Vikas Yojana (PMKVY) training centers, toolrooms, and so on, to make skill training aspirational amongst youth.
- A national skills competition, known as 'India Skills' will be launched during 2016–2017, to recognize the skills of India's youth. This will be an annual event.
- Over the next one year, the capacity of ITIs to be further enhanced from 1.85

million to 2.5 million and over 5,000 new ITIs will be created.

- Traditional skills will be recognized, nurtured, and promoted through informal apprenticeships, under various programs.

A budget allocation of ₹18.0428 billion has been made for the skill development initiatives in 2016–17. In 2015–16 the allocation was ₹15.43 billion of which the likely expenditure as per revised estimates is ₹10.38 billion. The budget provisions include expenditure on apprenticeship training as well to the tune of ₹2.3 billion.

The physical achievements against targets in skill training over the last five years show a mixed picture (Table 3.7).

The progress in the first seven months of the year 2015–16 has been slow and it seems unlikely that the full target would have been achieved by March 2016. No data is available in the public domain on achievements in 2015–16 even after five months from the end of the year.

National Skills Development Corporation (NSDC) has been the principal actor in skill development working with guidance from National Skills Development Agency (NSDA). The key scheme operated by NSDC is the PMKVY. NSDC has been successful in conduct of skills training through various government departments and its own partner agencies and meeting the targets for number of candidates to be trained. But the

Table 3.7: Targets and Achievements in Skill Development

| Year (No. of Ministries) | Number of Persons Millions | | % of Annual Target |
	Target	Achievement	
2011–12 (13)	4.65	4.57	98
2012–13 (19)	7.25	5.19	72
2013–14 (21)	7.34	7.64	104
2014–15 (21)	10.51	7.61	72
2015–16 (21)	12.20	(Till Oct 2015) 2.88	24

placement rates for the trained candidates has been low and raised questions about the quality, relevance and acceptability of the outputs from such courses.

The coverage of candidates in training was in accordance with the targets from 2010–11 till 2014–15. In 2015–16 the target for candidates was achieved 37%.

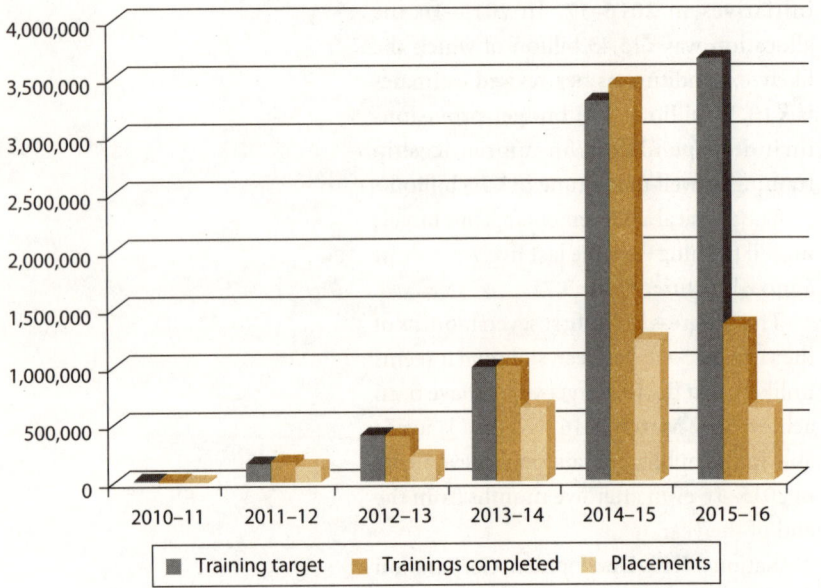

Figure 3.2:　Year-wise Break-up of Annual Skilling Targets and Achievements of NSDC

Source: Graphs by authors based on Reply to Loksabha question no 2787 on May 11, 2016. http://164.100.47.190/loksabhaquestions/annex/8/AU2787.pdf, accessed on October 19, 2016.

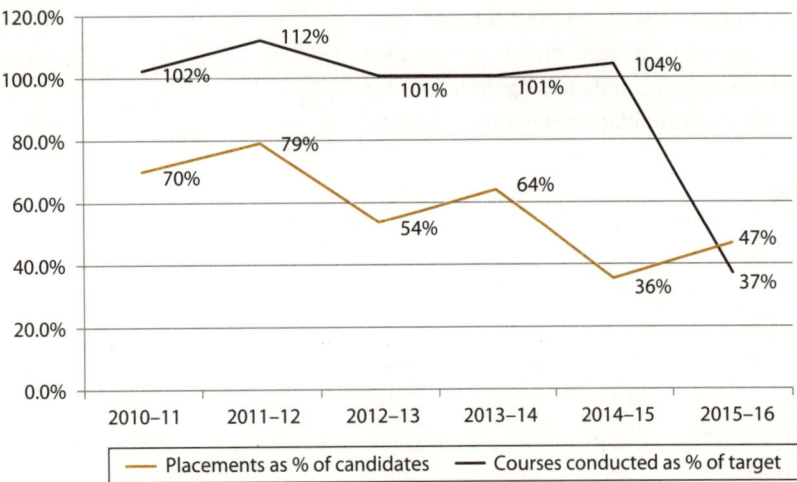

Figure 3.3:　Skills Training by NSDC—Achievement Levels

Source: Graphs by authors based on Reply to Loksabha question no 2787 on May 11, 2016. http://164.100.47.190/loksabhaquestions/annex/8/AU2787.pdf, accessed on October 19, 2016.

Given the ambitious targets for training and placement, the underachievement, especially in placements, is a cause for alarm. The government is betting on skill building and gap filling in several sectors as a means of providing gainful employment opportunities. If the skills provided to people do not result in employment the credibility of skills training would be eroded. Perhaps more homework on employer readiness for accepting the trained persons has to be done. Similarly, the trades and skill sets in which requirements are low should be either discontinued or given low priority.

NSDC had carried out a number of skill development courses through its partners. The detailed data relating to 2014–15 shows some interesting trends that need to be factored into strategies and implementation aspects in future initiatives (Table 3.8). Though there were 44 broad sectors in which training was available, 5 sectors accounted for 60% of the trainees and 58% of placements. Overall placements were around 55%. Of the top 12 sectors that accounted for 90% of all trainees, 5 had more than 75% placement rates. Three sectors had very poor placement rates, that is, 25% or lower. Training in IT and information technology enabled services (ITES) with a focus on informal employment which took up the maximum number of people (0.216 million) fared badly in placement with just 23% candidates being placed. Again, training for informal sector jobs in beautician, facility management, and domestic help resulted in placement for just 11% of candidates. There is a clear need to figure out likely placements before deciding on the sectors for training of candidates. Courses that do not lead to employment (near the benchmark 70% adopted by the NSDA) should be discouraged.

Only a few states were able to benefit significantly from NSDC initiatives (Table 3.9). Five out of thirty-six states accounted for 55% of trainees and 61% of all placements. Some states had not made much progress,

Table 3.8: Sectoral Comparisons in Skill Training and Placement

NSDC Partners Performance 2014–15			
Sector	Number Trained	Number Placed	Placement Rate (%)
IT and ITES (Informal Employment)	216,221	48,947	23
IT and ITES (Formal Employment)	137,064	107,669	79
Telecom	146,454	138,567	95
Organized Retail	133,789	33,848	25
Banking and Finance	104,107	65,747	63
Construction, Real Estate	71,607	39,556	55
Automobile, Components	63,145	51,334	81
Healthcare	58,591	47,945	82
Electronics, IT Hardware	51,095	33,560	66
Tourism, Hospitality	42,271	22,176	52
Informal Sector (Domestic Help, Beauticians, Facility Management)	35,787	4,114	11
Agriculture	28,457	21,754	76
All 44 Sectors	1,233,346	675,255	55
Top 5 Sectors as % to total	60	58	

Source: Derived by authors from data presented in NSDC Annual Update 2015–16, http://www.nsdcindia.org/sites/default/files/files/NSDC_Annual_Update_2014-15.pdf, accessed on July 15, 2016.

Table 3.9: Skill Training—Comparison Across States

State	Number Trained	Number Placed	Placement Rate (%)
Maharashtra	184,881	122,754	66
West Bengal	173,025	107,135	62
Karnataka	117,441	55,099	47
Tamil Nadu	101,277	72,406	71
Uttar Pradesh	95,792	57,524	60
Top 5 States	672,416	414,918	62
All 36 States	1,233,346	675,255	55
Top 5 States as % of all States	55	61	

Source: Derived by authors from data presented in NSDC Annual Update 2015–16, http://www.nsdcindia.org/sites/default/files/files/NSDC_Annual_Update_2014-15.pdf, accessed on July 15, 2016.

with number of candidates confined to a few hundred. All eight Northeastern states together had 23,200 candidates trained of which about 53% were placed in jobs. The share of NER in the total national effort was 2%, about half their share in population of the country. With establishment of a comprehensive implementation framework and a matching organizational structure it is hoped that the all the states get an equitable share of skill development benefits.

The PMKVY was launched in July 2015 with the objective of enabling Indian youth to take up industry-relevant skill training and help them secure a better livelihood. The Union Cabinet approved the new framework of PMKVY in July 2016 for a period of four years 2016–2020. PMKVY aims at skilling 0.01 billion people over the next four years (April 2016 to March 2020) with an outlay of ₹120 billion. The scheme will impart fresh skill training to certify 6 million individuals and certify skills of 4 million individuals who have already acquired the skills informally. The major features of revised PMKVY include the following:

- Training centers under the scheme will be categorized on the basis of their infrastructure, training capacity, past performance, and other relevant parameters, to improve the quality of training imparted by them. In addition, targets assigned to these training centers will be on a long-term basis along with a review mechanism.

- The scheme will be aligned to common norms (these norms outline the base cost of training per candidate for different sectors in various job roles). The scheme will be based on a grant-based model where the training and assessment cost will be directly reimbursed to training providers and assessment bodies, in accordance with the common norms.
- Special projects will be promoted for sector-specific skilling initiatives, such as Swachh Bharat, Digital India and Smart Cities. Of the respective schemes' budgets, 10%–15% will be made available for these special projects.
- Under the scheme, training partners will be required to ensure the validation of the Aadhaar number when enrolling a candidate.
- Respective state governments will be made responsible for 25% of the total training targets under the scheme.

As per the Union Cabinet's decision, state governments would be involved through a project-based approach under the PMKVY with 25% of the total training targets. The financial budget for achieving 25% of the total training targets would be allocated to the states by the center. In another major change, PMKVY would directly reimburse the training and assessment cost to training providers and assessment bodies. The earlier system of providing monetary reward to students for successful completion has been discontinued. However financial support to trainees in the form of travel allowance, boarding and lodging costs will continue. Post placement support would be given to the beneficiaries through DBT. PMKVY will also focus on overseas employment in Gulf countries, Europe, and other overseas destinations and align the skill training to international standards.

There are several state level initiatives in skill development which are aligned to the NDSMs schemes. Corporate India has also been collaborating with the different ministries in skill development. However, corporate involvement has been limited compared to the scope available. According to Santosh Mehrotra,

> Industry needs to get directly involved in the assessment of trainees and students of vocational education, which should be a deliverable for SSCs and industry associations, which industry chambers should facilitate on a much larger scale than currently happening. But assessors themselves must be trained to be assessors by industry and educators.

The Wheebox Employability Skill Test, 2016 found that only 38% of a sample of 0.52 million students were readily employable. (Box 3.4).

The India Skills Report[9] concludes

> [C]reating a platform for the supply and demand side of talent to come together and bridge the demand as well as expectation is a pressing need. The demand for matchmaking skills and jobs has also been heard by the Government with initiatives like National Career Service and Model Career Centers being launched. This is one of the crucial moves made by the Government that will surely make

---

Box 3.4: *Employability Test*

Out of about 520,000 candidates who appeared for Wheebox Employability Skill Test across domains 38.12% were found employable. Though this number is an improvement from the number of past two years—37.22% (2015) and 33.95% (2014)—it clearly shows the need for the initiatives taken up by government toward skill development. However these initiatives need to be immediate and impactful, if the gap between the supply and the demand side is to be diminished.

Source: India Skills Report 2016, by Wheebox, an online talent assessment Company in partnership with People Strong, CII, Linked in and Association of Indian Universities.

---

[9] India Skills Report 2016, by Wheel Box, an online talent assessment Company in partnership with People Strong, CII, Linked in and Association of Indian Universities.

a huge impact in resolving the Great Indian Talent Conundrum. As the new platforms like NCS and MCCs evolve it can play a larger role in overall implementation by providing the necessary insights to the decision makers.

It is still early days in skill development under the new ministry. The new policy and organizational structure will take some time to stabilize. The implementation arrangements and training partners will also have to be tested for producing robust results. The Ministry and the NSDA are leading the effort, but the strength of partners and willing cooperation of potential employers and enterprise incubators is yet to be proven. The concerns are that many training service providers that partner the NSDC lack the commitment, passion, and the effort required to fulfil placement targets which are critical to achieve the promise of dignified and remunerative jobs. Some rethinking of the numbers as also the strategies seem warranted at the center and state levels.

3.4 Prime Ministers Crop Insurance Scheme (PMFBY)

The PMFBY was announced in January 2016 as a solution to the weather and pest-related risks for farmers. The prime minister, in an open letters to the farmers, listed the new features as well benefits of the scheme (See Annexure 3.1 at the end of this chapter). The scheme sought to rectify some of the shortcomings of both Weather Based Crop Insurance Scheme (WBCIS) and modified agricultural insurance schemes. Following up on the PM's announcement, the Union Budget 2016–17 allocated ₹55 billion for implementation of the scheme. PMFBY differs from the existing MNAIS in the following aspects:

- While the scheme follows an area approach, the area is defined as a village or GP, thus flexible enough to respond to localized weather events.
- Scheme will cover losses arising from prevented sowing, postharvest damage, and localized calamities including unseasonal rain, cyclones, and inundation.
- The sum insured will be the scale of finance for loanee farmers. However, farmers can opt for higher cover up to the extent of the value of threshold yield of the crop (if it is higher than crop loan), by paying the higher premium.
- The premium rates payable by farmers are fixed as 2% of insured value for Kharif crops, 1.5% for Rabi, and 5% for horticultural/commercial crops. The difference between premium charged by insurance companies and that paid by farmers will be borne by the government.
- The liability of the insurers is capped at 350% of total premium collected (farmer share plus government subsidy) or 35% of total sum insured (SI), of all the insurance companies combined, whichever is higher. The losses at the national level in a crop season beyond this ceiling shall be met by equal contribution (i.e., on 50:50 basis) from the Central Government and the concerned state governments.

This scheme will be compulsory for all farmers borrowing from banks for cropping (including those having Kisan Credit Cards). Other farmers should enroll in the scheme and pay the premium. About 10 insurers have been identified and district notifications of which insurers will operate have been issued by the state governments.

State governments have responded enthusiastically to the scheme, especially in the aftermath of acute drought situation faced in many states. Just the 10 states which declared a drought last year have together budgeted ₹67.17 billion for crop insurance in 2016–17, surpassing the center's allocation for the year.[10] Drought-hit Maharashtra leads the pack with a budget of ₹18.55 billion (see first

---

[10] Sayantan Bera, "States pitch in heavily for Narendra Modi's crop insurance scheme," *The Mint*, March 31, 2016. http://www.livemint.com/Politics/NrDn1VtJLFWGmDop5TTqjJ/States-pitch-in-heavily-for-Narendra-Modis-crop-insurance-s.html, accessed on October 19, 2016.

Table 3.10: Statewise Coverage of Villages Under PMFBY—Kharif 2016

State	No. of Villages
Andhra Pradesh	17,160
Bihar	45,073
Chhattisgarh	10,857
Goa	404
Gujarat	18,221
Haryana	6,615
Himachal Pradesh	18,919
Jharkhand	32,584
Karnataka	8,099
Madhya Pradesh	8,053
Maharashtra	24,400
Odisha	51,427
Rajasthan	6,671
Tamil Nadu	17,075
Telangana	11,156
Uttar Pradesh	21,208
Uttarakhand	16,833
West Bengal	41,112
Total	355,867

10 states listed in Table 3.10). Furthermore, the amount budgeted by these 10 drought-hit states—AP, Telangana, Madhya Pradesh, Chhattisgarh, Rajasthan, Maharashtra, Karnataka, Uttar Pradesh, Odisha, and Jharkhand—is 82% higher than what they spent during the previous year (2015–16).

The state budgets also show that all drought-hit states have increased funding for PMFBY manifold. While Maharashtra more than doubled funds for PMFBY—from ₹7.25 billion in 2015–16 (revised estimates) to ₹18.55 billion in 2016–17—Karnataka and Odisha increased allocations more than sixfold and tenfold, respectively. Even Haryana, where 90% of the crop area is irrigated, has allocated ₹3 billion in its budget for 2016–17, a first for the state which budgeted a paltry ₹0.8 million for crop insurance in 2015–16. But then Haryana had its fair share of trouble due to the white fly pest damaging the cotton crop last Kharif season and unseasonal rains damaging the wheat crop just ahead of harvest last year.

For Kharif, state governments have notified crops for coverage. The number of notified crops range from 2 to 41 and from food grains to horticultural crops. Karnataka has notified the maximum number of 41 crops including 14 horticultural crops.

The proportion of villages covered is more than 50% of villages in the country. The overall coverage in Kharif is estimated to go beyond 40 million farmers compared to 30 million farmers last year.

Despite the new features and promised low premium rates, many states are also continuing with the WBCIS, as they are familiar with the same (See Annexure 3.3 for state-wise details for notified crops and ongoing work on engaging insurance companies). Some states are yet to notify the crops, areas, and the scheme that would be applicable during this Kharif. There are many challenges that arise from the features built in to improve the support available to farmers. The risk cover is not capped leaving the government open-ended on claim settlements in excess of 350% of premium collected. The crop cutting experiments at the GP level require manpower and adequate technical supervision both of which are in short supply in most states. Verification of localized weather events will be another area where attention is needed to prevent moral hazards exploiting the scheme. But the scheme is a clear departure from the normal risk aversion in government schemes that limit the scope to contain the potential costs to the exchequer. Foolproof arrangements on identification of farmers, cropping, and the damages should make it possible for insurers and government to have necessary financial disciplines. The scheme has the potential of becoming a game changer in mitigating risks of the farming community and rendering agricultural livelihoods more sustainable.

ANNEXURE 3.1
Skill India Targets and Achievements

Ministry/Organization	Tentative Targets 2015–16 (Persons)	Targets Accepted by Ministry/ Department	Cumulative Achievement for 2015–16 Reported till Oct 2015	
			Number	% of Annual Target
1	2	3	4	5
Ministry of Skill Development and Entrepreneurship	2,400,000	2,400,000	394,763	16.44
	1,250,000	1,250,000	427,000	34.16
Ministry of Agriculture	2,775,000	1,600,000	569,214	35.5
National Skill Development Corporation	3,700,000	3,660,000	480,083	13.11
Ministry of Rural Development	750,000	528,000	301,992	57.1
Ministry of Micro, Small & Medium Enterprises	600,000	557,000	–	–
Department of Higher Education	125,000	488,060	162,213	33.23
Department of Electronics & Info Technology	1,425,000	360,000	142,153	39.48
Ministry of Housing & Urban Poverty Alleviation	450,000	300,622	108,987	36.25
Ministry of Women & Child Development	225,000	33,020	4,094	12.39
Ministry of Textiles	100,000	400,000	84,598	21.11
Ministry of Social Justice & Empowerment	275,000	86,800	31,050	35.77
Ministry of Tourism	100,000	100,000	53,463	53.46
Ministry of Minority Affairs	175,000	57,000	30,480	53.47
Ministry of Tribal Affairs	55,000	86,000	–	–
Ministry of Home Affairs	12,000	7,000	3,564	50.59
Ministry of Road Transport and Highways	17,500	17,500	–	–
Ministry of Chemicals & Fertilizers	100,000	80,000	31,903	39.87
Ministry of Commerce and Industry	75,000	144,000	44,594	30.96
Department of Heavy Industry	40,000	40,000	12,671	31.67
Ministry of Development of North-eastern Region	6,000	4,000	1,437	35.92
Ministry of Food Processing Industries	500	1,108	823	74.27
Total	14,656,000	12,200,110	2,885,082	23.64

ANNEXURE 3.2
Prime Minister's Letter to Farmers on PMFBY

My dear farmer brothers and sisters,

The news of the **'Pradhanmantri Fasal Bima Yojana'** must have already reached you. Farmers in our country have often felt at risk—at times from crop losses due to natural disasters, at times by falling market prices. Over the last eighteen months, we have taken several steps to help those of you who faced such difficulties.

(Continued)

(Continued)

There have been insurance schemes for farmers in the past as well. However, they were unsuccessful because of various reasons—ranging from high premium rates to low claim value and non-coverage of localised crop-loss. As a result, not more than 20 percent of farmers opted for crop insurance; and those who did faced many difficulties to get their due. Eventually, farmer's faith in insurance schemes eroded over time.

It was against this backdrop that we engaged in detailed consultations with States, farmers and insurance companies; following which I now place before my farmer brothers and sisters, the farmer-friendly Pradhanmantri Fasal Bima Yojana.

This Pradhanmantri Fasal Bima Yojana has the following highlights:

- **This is the biggest-ever government contribution to crop insurance**
- As a result, farmers will have to pay the **lowest-ever premium rate**
- Government will bear the remaining financial burden—even if the Government's share exceeds 90%
- There will be only **one premium rate for each season** for all food grains, oilseeds and pulses—removing all variation in rates across crops and districts within a season—Kharif: 2% only—Rabi: 1.5% only
- Farmers will get **full insurance cover**—there will be no 'capping' of the sum insured, and consequently, claim amounts will not be cut or reduced
- For the first time, **inundation** has been included under localised risk cover
- For the first time, **postharvest losses arising out of cyclones and unseasonal rain** have been covered nationally
- For the first time, emphasis has been given to mobile and satellite **technology** to facilitate accurate assessment and quick settlement of claims

This scheme will be implemented from the forthcoming Kharif season. It is simple to join and offers maximum security. **I welcome your wholehearted participation.**

Yours sincerely

Narendra Modi

Source: PMO website.

ANNEXURE 3.3
Progress of Crop Insurance Kharif 2016 Across States[11]

State	Scheme	No. of Clusters	Unit Area	Crops Selected	L1[a] Premium Rate (%)	L1[b] Companies
Assam	WBCIS	3		Paddy (*Ahu* & *Sali*), Black Gram, Green Gram, Ginger, Turmeric	(1) 3.09, (2) 2.45, & (3) 4.77	(1) HDFC ERGO, (2) & (3) Reliance GIC
Bihar	PMFBY	6	GP	Paddy & Maize		
Chhattisgarh	PMFBY	5	GP/Mandal	Paddy, Maize, Ground Nut, Soybean, Arhar, Urad, Mung	(1) 4.43, (2) 5.24, (3) 3.83, (4) 2.59, & (5) 3.87	(1), (3), (4) & (5)—IFFCO (2) Reliance
Jharkhand	PMFBY	4	GP & Block	Paddy, Maize	(1) 16.45, (2) 17.03, (3) 11.45, & (4) 10.34	All 4 clusters to AIC

---

[11] From Ministry of Agriculture website, http://agri-insurance.gov.in/StateWiseNotifyUnit.aspx, accessed on September 15, 2016.

State	Scheme	No. of Clusters	Unit Area	Crops Selected	L1[a] Premium Rate (%)	L1[b] Companies
Odisha	PMFBY	6	GP & Block	Paddy, Ground Nut, Cotton, Ginger, Turmeric	(1) 8.04 (2) 7.25, (3) 7.59, (4) 5.84, (5) 5.82, & (6) 11.12	(1) Reliance, (2) HDFC ERGO (3) & (4) Future Generali (5) ICICI Lombard, & (6) SBI GIC
West Bengal	PMFBY	4	GP & Block		(1) 2.23, (2) 2.56, (3) 1.32, & (4) 6.9	(1) & (2)—Cholamandalam, (3)—Future & (4) AIC
	WBCIS	4				
Mizoram	PMFBY	3		Selected 5 Crops		
Tripura		1		Aus Paddy & Aman Paddy	1.49	Reliance
Himachal Pradesh	PMFBY	2	Subdivision	Paddy, Maize	(1) 0.95 & (2) 1.60	(1)—AIC & (2)—IFFCO
	WBCIS			Tomato, Potato, Pea, Ginger	Bilaspur—6.02, Chamba—6.21, Kangra —10.76, Kinnaur—1.77, Kullu—11.28, Lahaul & Spiti—2.50, Mandi—4.79, Shimla—9, Sirmaur—6.79, & Solan—9.00	**IFFICO**—Bilaspur, Sirmaur, & Solan, **SBI**—Chamba, Kangra, & Shimla **CHOLA**—Kinnaur, Lahaul & Spiti, **ICICI**—Kullu, **Bajaj**—Mandi
J&K (Jammu region)	WBCIS	–		Paddy & Maize		
Haryana	PMFBY & WBCIS	3		Cotton, Paddy, Bajara maize during Kharif and Wheat, Barley, Mustard, Gram in Rabi	(1) 2.69, (2) 3.73, (3) 2.43	(1) Reliance (2) Bajaj, & (3) ICICI Lombard
Uttarakhand	PMFBY	2	Village Panchayat & Naiya Panchayat	Rice & Ragi	(1) 0.95 & (2) 1.21	AIC
	WBCIS	–		Ginger, Tomato, Potato, French Bean, Chili	(1) 10.52, (2) 5.54, (3) 19.25, & (4) 14.70	(1) & (4)—Chola, (2) HDFC, & (3) AIC
Uttar Pradesh	PMFBY	12	Village Panchayat	11 crops in Kharif 6 crops in Rabi (Paddy, Sugarcane, Pea, Potato, Wheat, Mustard)	(1) 6.91, (2) 3.97, (3) 4.34, (4) 3.93, (5) 3.16, (6) 2.97, (7) 5.35, (8) 5, (9) 3.74, (10) 4.10, (11) 2.46, & (12) 2.91	Cluster 1 to ICICI Lombard & remaining 11 clusters to AIC
	WBCIS	4	Village Panchayat & Block		18	ICICI (all four districts)
Karnataka	PMFBY	3	GP & Firka	41 crops including 14 Hort. Crops (paddy, Ragi, Onion, Chili, Tomato, Jowar)	11.39, 10.43, & 9.4	Universal Sompo—2 Tata AIG—1 cluster
	WBCIS			17 Horticulture Crops including grapes		
Kerala	PMFBY	1 (14 districts)		Paddy (3 districts), Papaya & Banana (14 districts)	3.81	Reliance
	WBCIS	1		Paddy (12 districts)	7.99	AIC
Andaman & Nicobar	PMFBY	–	Tehsil	Paddy, Green Gram & Black Gram *Lobiya*, Bhindi and Tomato	5.45	Reliance
Andhra Pradesh	PMFBY	2	Revenue Village/ Mandal	Paddy, Sugarcane	(1) 9.83 & (2) 7.20	(1)—AIC, (2)—ICICI GIC
	WBCIS	1		Cotton, Ground Nut, Red Chili, Tomato, Palm Oil, White lime	8.50	Bajaj

(Continued)

(Continued)

State	Scheme	No. of Clusters	Unit Area	Crops Selected	L1ᵃ Premium Rate (%)	L1ᵇ Companies
Telangana	PMFBY	3		Paddy, Red Gram, Jowar, Chili	(1) 2.83, (2) 7.71 & (3) 3.26	(1) & (3)—AIC & (2) Bajaj
	WBCIS	3		Cotton, Sweet Lime, Oil Palm	(1) 9.72, (2) 16.89 & (3) 12.12	(1) Reliance (2), & (3) SBI GIC
Tamil Nadu	PMFBY	–		Paddy, Sugarcane	Issue tender within 7 days	issued the tender
Gujarat	PMFBY	3	GP & Block	16 crops	(1) 14.10, (2) 13.30, & (3) 9.40	(1) —Bajaj Alliance, (2), & (3) —HDFC—ERGO
Madhya Pradesh	PMFBY	5	Patwari Halka & Taluka	Paddy, Soybean, Bajra, Maize, Ground Nut, Jowar, Arhar, Til, cotton, Wheat, gram, Mustard, Moong,	(1) 13.23, (2) 7.58, (3) 7.22, (4) 9.74, & (5) 9.97	(1) ICICI Lombard (3) — HDFC ERGO and (2), (4), & (5) —AIC
	WBCIS	5		Banana, Chili, Coriander, Green Pea, Garlic, Mango, Orange, Papaya, Potato, Vegetable		
Maharashtra	PMFBY	6	Revenue Village & Mandal	15 Crops	(1) 29.37, (2) 27.02, (3) 13.46, (4) 12.96, (5) 12.58, & (6) 27.7	(1) IFFCO, (2) & (3) AIC, (4) & (5) Reliance (6) Bajaj
	WBCIS	5	.	8 Horticulture Crops	(1) 33.98, (2) 50.11, (3) 10.47, (4) 42.13, & (5) 23.38	(1) & (2) IFFCO, (3), (4), & (5) Reliance
Rajasthan	PMFBY	8	GP level	Paddy, Maize, Guar, Moong, Bajra, Cotton, Month	Issue tender within 7 days. Last date July 8, 2016	
	WBCIS			Castor, horticulture crops, Oranges, Cow Pea, *kinnu*, vegetable		

Note: L1ᵃ refers to the lowest premium rate quoted, L1ᵇ: refers to the name of the company that quoted the lowest rate.

A Decade of Rural Employment Guarantee

4.1 Introduction

MGNREGS, that guarantees rural households 100 days of unskilled manual work on demand, has completed 10 years of implementation. In 2005, the Central Government formulated the National Rural Employment Guarantee Act (NREGA), reportedly the first ever law internationally, that created a rights-based framework by conferring legal entitlements and the right to demand employment upon the workers. The law makes the government accountable for providing employment in a time-bound manner.

Apart from guaranteeing 100 days of work per household, which is the core objective, the program emphasizes on creation of durable productive assets that can strengthen the livelihood resource base of the poor and vulnerable. Finally, its operational design built around strong decentralization and lateral accountability to local community offers a new way of doing business anchored on the principles of transparency and grassroot democracy. In this way, the potential of NREGA spans a range from basic wage security and recharging rural economy to a transformative empowerment process of democracy.[1] This chapter examines how the program has fared in achieving its objectives of providing employment and creation of durable assets since these directly impact livelihoods.

Box 4.1: *Salient Features of the Act[2]*

Rights-based Framework

Any rural household is entitled to 100 days of employment in a financial year at a minimum wage rate as notified by the state government. Work can be split among household members, but workers must be at least 18 years old.

Adult members of a rural household who are willing to do unskilled manual work can apply for registration to the local GP, in writing, or orally.

The GP after due verification will issue a job card. The job card will bear the photograph of all adult members of the household and is free of cost.

A job card holding household can submit a written application for employment to the GP, stating the time and duration for which work is sought.

Time-bound Guarantee

The GP will issue a dated receipt of the written application for employment, against which the guarantee of providing employment within 15 days operates. If employment is not provided within 15 days, daily unemployment allowance,

---

[1] GOI, Annual report of 2007–08 (2008), Ministry of Rural Development, Government of India.

[2] Adapted from GOI, Annual report of 2007–08.

in cash has to be paid. Liability of payment of unemployment allowance is of the states.

Work should ordinarily be provided within 5 km radius of the village or else extra wages of 10% are payable.

Wages are to be paid according to minimum wages. Disbursement of wages has to be done on weekly basis and not beyond a fortnight.

Women Employment

At least one-third of persons to whom work is allotted work have to be women.

Work Site Facilities

Work site facilities such as crèche, drinking water, and shade have to be provided.

Decentralized Planning

The shelf of projects has to be prepared by gram sabha. At least 50% of works have to be allotted to GPs for execution. Panchayat Raj Institutions have a principal role in planning and implementation.

Labor-intensive Works

A 60:40 wage and material ratio has to be maintained. Contractors and use of labor-displacing machinery is prohibited.

Public Accountability

Social audit has to be done by the gram sabha.

Grievance redressal mechanisms have to be put in place for ensuring a responsive implementation process

Transparency

All accounts and records relating to the scheme are to be made available to any person desirous of obtaining a copy of such records, on demand and after paying a specified fee.

4.1.1 The Design Draws on Lessons from Earlier Rural Wage Employment Programs

The rights-based design of Mahatma Gandhi National Rural Employment Guarantee Act (MGNREGA) has a genesis in the preceding wage employment programs of the government. The need to evolve a mechanism to supplement existing livelihood sources in rural areas was recognized early in development planning in India. State governments with central assistance have implemented a number of wage employment programs[3] that were self-targeting,

offered wage employment on public works on minimum wages for those dependent on casual manual labor. The forerunner to MGNREGS is the Act formulated by the Government of Maharashtra—Maharashtra Employment Guarantee Scheme and Maharashtra Employment Guarantee Act, 1977—to provide wage employment to those who demanded it.

Though the rights-based framework was inherited from Maharashtra Employment Guarantee Act, MGNREGA made a departure in that the Panchayati Raj Institutions have been vested with the responsibility of planning, implementation and monitoring of activities taken up under the scheme. Financial obligations both of the center and the state are part of the legal framework. The MGNREGA guidelines address the limitations of the earlier wage employment programs, placing greater emphasis, on planning processes, and MIS for improving data management.

---

[3] The wage employment programs started as pilot projects in the form of Rural Manpower Programme (1960–61), Crash Scheme for Rural Employment (1971–72). Drought Prone Area Programme was started as Rural work Programme (1972), Small Farmers Development Agency (SFDA), Marginal Farmers and Agricultural Labour Scheme (MF&AL) to the poorest of the poor. These experiments were translated into a full-fledged wage-employment program in 1977 in the form of Food for Work Programme. In 1980s this program was further streamlined into the National Rural Employment Programme and Rural Landless Employment Guarantee Programme, Jawahar Rozgar Yojana (1993–94), and Employment Assurance Scheme (EAS). The Jawahar Rozgar Yojana was merged with Jawahar Gram Samridhi Yojana (JGSY)

---

from 1999–2000 and was made a rural infrastructure program. The program was merged with Sampoorna Grameen Rozgar Yojana during the year 2001–02 and National Food for Work (2005).

4.1.2 Important Milestones in the Implementation of MGNREGS

February 2, 2006	NREGS launched in 200 selected districts; the first phase districts were chosen on the basis of Scheduled Caste/Scheduled Tribe (SC/ST) population, inverse of agricultural productivity per worker and inverse of agricultural wage rate.
2007–08	Extended to 130 more districts; A significant amendment was made for provision of irrigation facility, horticulture plantation, and land development facilities on land owned by households belonging to SC and ST, below the poverty line (BPL) families, beneficiaries of land reforms, and the beneficiaries under Indira Awaas Yojana (IAY).
2008–09	As against the original target of five years, within three years of its launch extended to all the districts. Based on convergence task force report, joint guidelines on convergence of NREGS with Indian Council of Agricultural Research (ICAR), schemes of Ministry of Environment, Forest and Climate Change, schemes of the Ministry of Water Resources, River Development & Ganga Rejuvenation, and within the MORD—PMGSY and Swarnajayanti Gram Swarozgar Yojana (SGSY), and watershed development programs. Since demand driven program, NREGA exempted for earmarking of 10% allocation for Northeast regions.
2009–10	Renamed as the MGNREGA. MGNREGA workers identified as a category for Janashree Bima Yojana of LIC for insurance cover Convergence extends to schemes of Ministry of Agriculture and Fisheries. 115 pilot districts identified in 22 states to carry forward the convergence initiatives.
2010–11	Wages under MGNREGS indexed to CPI for agricultural labor and rates revised on the basis of minimum of ₹100 or price indexed rate whichever is higher; 17% to 30% enhancement in wages in different states. Partnership with UIDAI for providing unique identification number to MGNREGS workers based on biometrics for preventing leakages.
2011–12	Scope of MGNREGS expanded for improving access to sanitation under Total Sanitation Campaign. Convergence with other schemes gains momentum with several states reporting good models. MORD commences reporting of statewise outcomes on MGNREGS in its annual report.
2012–13	List of permissible works expanded substantially for agriculture-related durable quality assets and flexibility provided to states for meeting location specific demand. Comprehensive revision to operational guidelines to address implementation challenges of accurate capturing of demand, delays in wage payment, issues of transparency, and accountability. Habitation level as the unit of planning, clear time line for approval of works at each level of governance, registering of demand through mobile devices, dedicated program officers in blocks with high concentration of SC/ST/landless laborers are a few key improvements. Standard operating procedures for grievance redressal formulated. Operational guidelines made for providing employment to disabled.
2013–14	Substantially revised the Schedules I and II of the Act; list of works further expanded and classified into four categories—public assets, assets of poor, and vulnerable households, works in relation to livelihood plans for SHG members, and rural infrastructure. Introduction of concurrent social audit. All states to draw up convergence plans. Cluster facilitation teams placed in 250 Blocks in 10 states with poor human development indicators and high SC/ST population.
2014–15	For improving participation and scientific method of planning of works, Intensive Participatory Planning Exercise (IPPE) started in 2,500 backward blocks using Participatory Rural Appraisal Techniques (PRA) techniques. This will enable the labor budget for 2015–16. 60% of the works to be directly related to agriculture. 21 state convergence plans have been prepared. Every state has designated senior officer for such convergence. Provision of barefoot technical staff for every 2,500 job cards and their costs to be covered under materials component.
2015–16	House construction included as a permissible activity. IPPE—II being carried out in 2,569 blocks in convergence with other major rural development programs. Project Livelihood in Full Employment (LIFE) launched for skilling youth aged up to 35 years. Households completing 100 days of employment will be targeted.

4.2 Financial and Physical Performance of the Program

The program has made considerable achievements in the last 10 years;[4]

While overall the program's outreach and financial performance looks impressive, the yearwise performance given in Table 4.1 shows some weak trends;

The program has had a peak performance in 2009–10 where the number of households that demanded work, households that were provided employment, and person days of employment were the highest. The year 2014–15 is the worst year of performance since 2008 when the program was rolled out in all the districts. The major concern is the decline in absolute levels of MGNREGA employment and also the decline in the number of households benefiting from it. The number of households receiving employment dropped from 54.94 million in FY 2010–11 to as low as 41.39 million in 2014–15. The last three years from 2013 to 2016 witnessed lower proportion of households provided with employment. Since this decline coincided with a relatively slow period of growth in the Indian economy, particularly in agricultural sector[7] it would be difficult to argue that other increased

Box 4.2: *MGNREGS Scorecard for 10 Years[5]*

Job cards issued—130,673,183 households.

Average number of households demanded employment in a year—46,407,977.

Average number of households provided employment in a year—44,556,833.

Total person days of employment—20,623 million

% of share of SCs—25.7

% share of STs—21

% share of women—49.5

Total wages disbursed—₹2,105.55 billions.[6]

Total expenditure—₹3,245.28 billions.

Table 4.1: Employment Performance

Year	Households Issued Job Cards	Households Demanded Employment	Households Provided Employment	Households Provided Jobs %	Total Person Days in Lakhs
2006–07	37,850,390	21,188,894	21,016,099	99	9,051
2007–08	64,740,595	34,326,563	33,909,132	99	14,368
2008–09	100,145,950	45,516,341	45,112,792	99	21,632
2009–10	112,548,976	52,920,154	52,585,999	99	28,359
2010–11	119,824,434	55,756,087	54,947,068	99	25,715
2011–12	125,025,265	51,128,994	50,645,132	99	21,876
2012–13	130,630,164	51,458,981	49,887,675	97	23,048
2013–14	128,162,177	51,797,601	47,930,454	93	22,036
2014–15	127,755,269	46,503,201	41,397,121	89	16,629
2015–16	130,673,183	53,482,952	48,136,862	90	23,523

Source: MIS of NREGS with Department of Rural Development, http://164.100.129.6/Netnrega/nrega-reportdashboard/index.html#/

[4] Please see Annexure 4.1 for more data on the scheme.

[5] for the years 2006–07 to 2015–16.

[6] As per annual report of 2012–13, ₹129,000 crores disbursed as wages since the inception. As per the dash board, wages disbursed in the years 2013–14, 2014–15, and 2015–16 are ₹26,491.21 crores, ₹24,187.26 crores, and ₹30,876.39 crores, respectively. GOI, 2013, Annual Report of Ministry of Rural Development, Government of India, 2012–13, http://mnregaweb4.nic.in/netnrega/all_lvl_details_dashboard_new.aspx, accessed on October 4, 2016.

[7] According to Economic Survey 2016, MOF, GOI Agricultural Sector growth which was 4.2% in 2013–14 declined to negative growth of -0.2% in 2014–15 and estimated to recover to 1.1% in 2015–16.

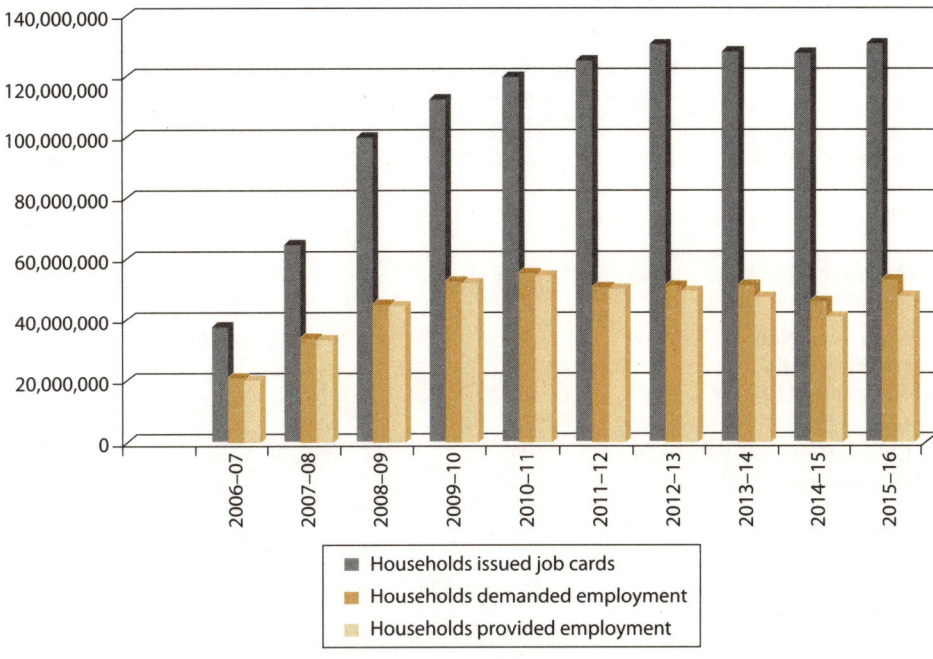

Figure 4.1: Job Cards Issued, Employment Demanded and Provided

Source: MIS Data from the website of Ministry of Rural Development.

employment opportunities elsewhere reduced demand for MGNREGS work.[8]

While there are over 130 million job cardholders, annually only about 50 million households demand jobs (Figure 4.1). The percentage of households that demanded jobs and provided employment, which was high at 99% in the initial years, has been declining steadily.

4.2.1 Statewise Performance

As per the data from the management information system (MIS) of the government, those who applied for job cards got them and almost all those who demanded were provided employment. However, some national studies provide a different picture. Dhanya,[9] analyzing NSSO (68th Round)

data pertaining to the time period July 2011 to June 2012 on statewise performance on issue of job cards and job provision for job cardholders who demanded job has categorized the states (Table 4.2).

Maharashtra ranks top in terms of percentage share of individuals who have sought but did not get work. Among the households with MGNREGS job card, 57% have sought work under MGNREGS and were not able to get work in Maharashtra. On the other hand, Northeastern states and Southern states such as Kerala and Tamil Nadu were more effective in providing work for those having job card and demanding work.

Northeastern states and Chhattisgarh are found to be the most effective in implementing MGNREGS in both counts. States such as Tamil Nadu, Kerala, and Jammu and Kashmir also performed well in terms of providing jobs for the job cardholders, though in coverage their performance is low. Haryana, on the other hand, though came in the top group in terms of work provided, performed dismally when the coverage was considered. Out of the total

---

[8] Sonalde Desai, Prem Vashishtha, and Omkar Joshi, MGNREGA A Catalyst for Rural Transformation (2015), National Council for Applied Economic Research, New Delhi.

[9] V. Dhanya, "Implications of MGNREGS on Labour Market, Wages and Consumption Expenditure in Kerala" (RBI Working Paper Series, Department of Economic and Policy Research, Reserve Bank of India, Mumbai, 2016).

Table 4.2: Performance-based Classification of States

Share of job cardholders among rural household excluding regular salaried/wage earners (%)	States	Share of individuals who have sought work but not provided work among the job cardholders (%)	States
More than 80	Mizoram, Nagaland, Tripura, Sikkim, Manipur, Meghalaya, Chhattisgarh	1–10	Manipur, Mizoram, Tripura, Nagaland, Sikkim, Kerala, Meghalaya, Tamil Nadu, Arunachal Pradesh, Jammu and Kashmir, Haryana, Chhattisgarh
60–80	Rajasthan, Madhya Pradesh, West Bengal, Himachal Pradesh	10–20	Uttaranchal, Himachal Pradesh, Uttar Pradesh, Andhra Pradesh, Rajasthan
40–60	Andhra Pradesh, Tamil Nadu, Arunachal Pradesh, Odisha, Uttaranchal, Jammu and Kashmir, Assam	20–30	West Bengal, Assam, Jharkhand, Punjab
20–40	Jharkhand, Kerala, Uttar Pradesh, Gujarat, Bihar, Karnataka, Maharashtra	30–40	Odisha, Karnataka, Madhya Pradesh
Less than 20	Punjab, Haryana	40–60	Bihar, Gujarat, Maharashtra

Source: V. Dhanya, 2016, Implications of MGNREGS on Labour Market, Wages and Consumption Expenditure in Kerala, RBI Working Paper Series, Department of Economic and Policy Research, Reserve Bank of India, Mumbai.

rural household with land below 5 hectares and also excluding the regular salaried and wage class, Haryana could provide job card only for a meager 7%. Hence, even though it came top in terms of job provided, it cannot be considered as a high performer. On the other hand, Maharashtra, Bihar, Gujarat, and Karnataka were poor performers on both counts.

4.2.2 Average Days of Employment

Average employment days for each participating household reached a peak at 54 in 2009–10 and declined to 40 in 2014–15 and have improved to 49 days in 2015–16. During 2015–16 large parts of the peninsular India was hit by severe drought and the number of days of employment was increased to 150 in 10 states including Andhra Pradesh, Uttar Pradesh, Maharashtra, and so on. Given this background, the average number of days of employment is not showing a satisfactory trend (Figure 4.2).

4.2.3 The Promise of 100 Days

One of the clear outcomes promised by the scheme is 100 days of wage employment for those who seek it. The percentage of households that completed 100 days have been very low and has never crossed 15%.

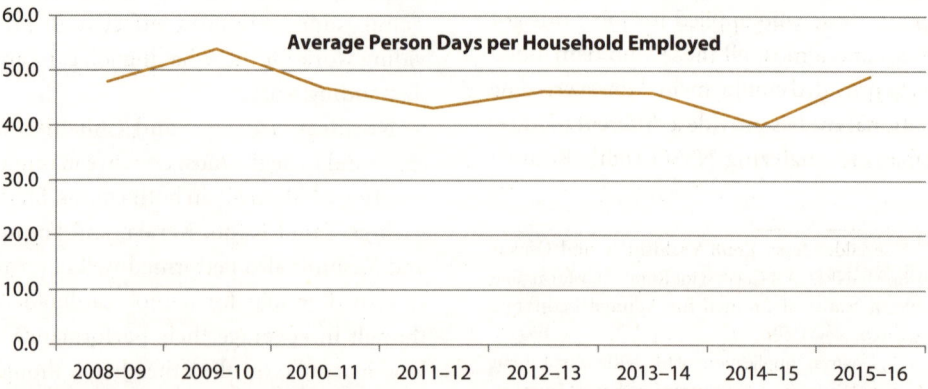

Figure 4.2: Average Employment Days per Participating Household

Source: MIS Data from the website of Ministry of Rural Development.

Table 4.3: Households Provided 100 Days Employment

Year	% of Households with 100 Days Employment
2008–09	14.46
2009–10	13.47
2010–11	10.12
2011–12	8.23
2012–13	10.37
2013–14	9.72
2014–15	6.02
2015–16	10.07

Source: Website of Ministry of Rural Development.

While it touched the lowest level of 6% in the year 2014–15, the average performance has been about 10% (Table 4.3).

Looking at statewise performance, Tripura has been ranking high consistently in providing 100 days of work for 45% of households in the last five years. Among other states, Kerala (17%), Tamil Nadu, Maharashtra, and Andhra Pradesh (14% each) performed relatively better than others.

While it is understood that the nature of employment is seasonal and that the duration of employment sought varies according to the prevailing job opportunities in agriculture and other alternative forms of employment, there are considerable interstate and interdistrict variations in workforce participation under NREGA. Moreover, all job cardholding families may not necessarily request for the full 100 days of employment;[10] however, only such low percentage of families getting the promised 100 days of wage employment is an aspect to be examined especially in poorer districts. In each state there are districts known for migration for extended periods in search of employment. In such districts, one would expect the prospect of 100 days of local employment would curb migration. The expected decline in migration does not

seem to have happened. This leads us to the phenomenon of work rationing which is discussed further.

4.3 Social Equity

MGNREGS is a self-targeting demand-based program open to all rural households; thus there are no quotas or targets for coverage of poor or marginalized communities of SC/ST. By insisting that participants do physically demand manual work at a low wage rate, schemes such as MGNREGS aim to be self-targeted, in that nonpoor people without a dire need will not want to participate. It is worthwhile to analyze the employment provided to these communities since these sections of the population are more vulnerable than others and need livelihood security.

4.3.1 Participation of Poor

As per 2011 Census, the poor households are concentrated in the states of Uttar Pradesh, Bihar followed by Madhya Pradesh and Maharashtra. The state's share of population living BPL is compared with the state's share in the all India expenditure under MGNREGS for last five years (Figure 4.3)

From Figure 4.3 it is clear that the three southern states of Andhra Pradesh (including Telangana), Tamil Nadu, and Kerala have been drawing lion's share of the MGNREGS expenditure of 26.64% whereas their share of population living BPL are much lower at 6.30%. Rajasthan and West Bengal are the other two states that are able to draw larger share of expenditure as compared to their share of poor. Uttar Pradesh and Bihar where 36.91% of the country's poor live, have incurred only 13% of total MGNREGS expenditure for the past five years. The other two states of Madhya Pradesh and Maharashtra also are incurring lesser expenditure vis-à-vis their share of poor population.

Although the poor are far more likely than the rich to work in MGNREGA, nearly 70% of the poor remain outside its

---

[10] GOI, Annual report, 2008–09 (2008), Ministry of Rural Development, Government of India.

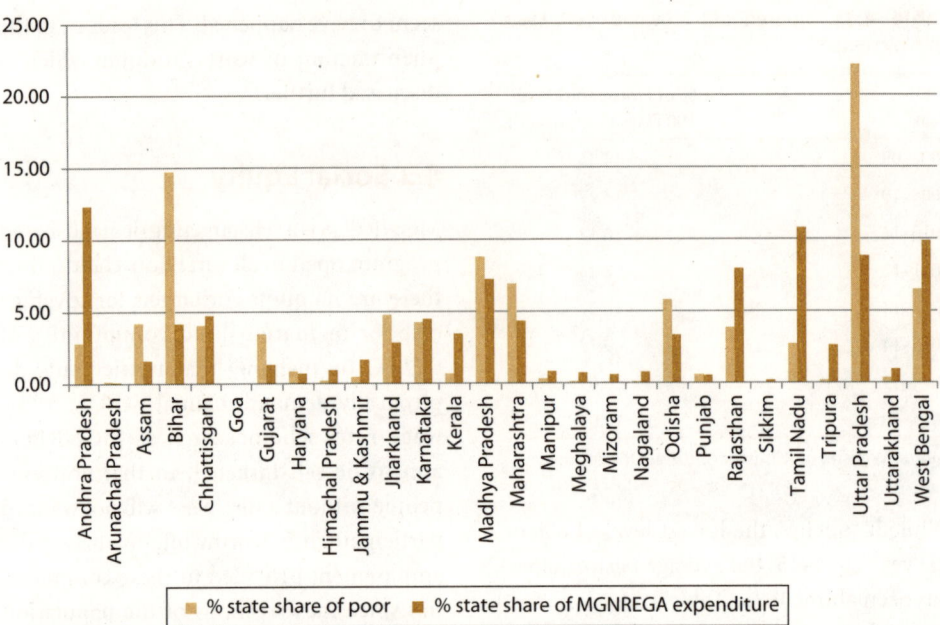

Figure 4.3: Skew in MGNREGA Expenditure Across States

Source: Calculated from Census report 2011 for numbers of poor and website of the Ministry of Rural Development on state wise expenditure from 2011–12.

purview.[11] Why do the remaining 70% of the poor not participate in MGNREGA? NCAER[12] study mentions that one major explanation is that work is not easily available. More than 70% of rural households in India Human Development Survey (IHDS) claim that they did not participate in MGNREGA because not enough work was available. In states with a stronger program, 60% of poor households participate, while in low-prevalence states barely 11% of poor households participate. Improving state-level implementation could thus have a tremendous impact on the ability of poor households to obtain MGNREGA work.

Overall, weak governance in the poorer states coupled with ignorance of the rural population about the scheme and vested interest of land owners and local elites to limit the choices for the poor seem to be contributing to the skewed expenditure in the states.

4.3.2 Employment of Scheduled Castes and Scheduled Tribes

Though separate earmarking of employment and resources for SCs/STs has not been provided, the government has been monitoring and reporting on their participation in the scheme, creating a positive bias in favor of SC/ST households (Figure 4.4).

The slow and steady rise in the share of others vis-à-vis SCs and STs is a cause of concern. Since the program was launched initially in the districts where ST population was high, in terms of their share of employment, it was highest in 2006–07 at 36%. When the program was launched in all the districts in 2008, their share was 21% till 2011. However, there has been a steady decline since then to 18%. Similarly, the trend for SC participation shows that the highest level of participation was in 2011–12 at 31% and it has fallen to 22% since then.

Studies[13] show that for SCs, MGNREGA is an important livelihood opportunity

[11] Sonalde Desai, Prem Vashishtha, and Omkar Joshi, MGNREGA. A Catalyst for Rural Transformation.

[12] Sonalde Desai, Prem Vashishtha, and Omkar Joshi, MGNREGA. A Catalyst for Rural Transformation.

[13] IDS, "Employment Guarantee as Social Protection: Lessons from Tamil Nadu, India" (Global Insights, Policy Brief No. 6, IDS Sussex, July 2013).

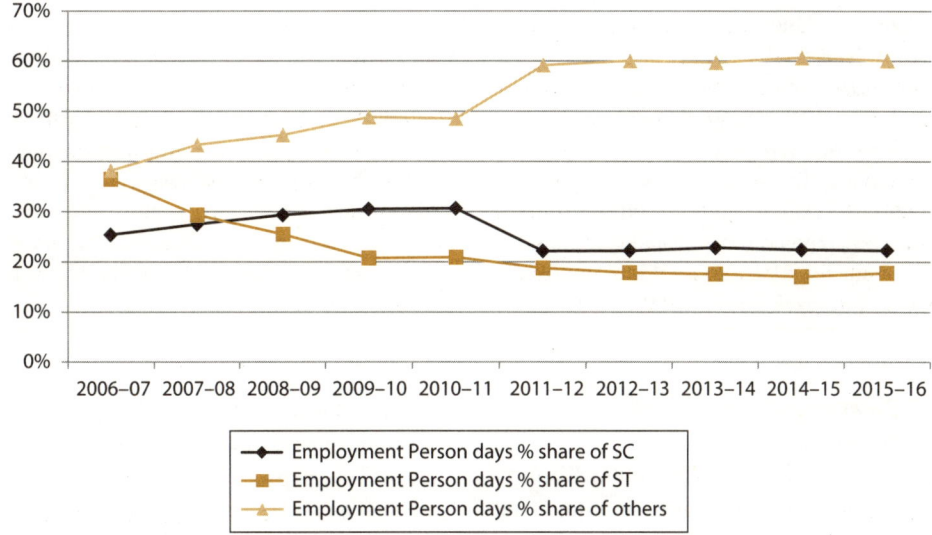

Figure 4.4: Employment of SC, ST, and Others

Source: MIS Data from the website of Ministry of Rural Development.

since it is free from the largely caste-based relations of subordination, discrimination, and exploitation that mark both agricultural daily wage work and nonfarm employment. Those normally employed in agriculture often work alongside their employers, who hassle them to work harder and faster; the work is closely related to past relations of subordination and servitude, which all Dalits aspire to move away from. Being a government scheme means that MGNREGA is considered 'respectable' and 'decent' work, which adds considerably to its success in the minds of its participants.

Box 4.3: *Who Benefits—Findings from Field Studies*

IGIDR[14] survey data of 4,881 households in Maharashtra shows that out of the works on private lands, 75% were on lands that belonged to small (53%) and marginal farmers (22%). Within this category, small farmer beneficiaries outnumbered marginal farmers, suggesting that the better endowed were more likely to benefit from MGNREGA works. This was consistent with the notion that small farmers are more able and willing to devote a part of their land for development works such as farm, ponds, and wells, while marginal farmers opt for land development works such as levelling, bunds, and so on. It could also reflect that small farmers are perhaps more aware of the possibilities of leveraging government programs to make investments on their private land.

Thus, fears of elite capture of MGNREGS works, or large farmers and absentee landlords benefiting disproportionately from having MGNREGS works on their lands, appeared to be misplaced. Of those who had carried out works on private lands, 92% said that farming was their main household occupation suggesting that in terms of creation of works, the scheme has been profarmer. That being said, 25% of the works were on lands owned by medium and large farmers, which raises questions on whether the selection criteria for works had been faithfully applied. Larger farmers were perhaps more likely to seek horticultural investments, both relative to marginal and small farmers and relative to other land improvement works. A disquieting

---

and GOI, *MGNREGA Sameeksha An Anthology of Research Studies on the MGNREGA, 2005 2006–2012*. Edited and compiled by Mihir Shah, Neelakshi Mann, and Varad Pande. New Delhi: Orient Blackswan, 2012.

[14] Krushna Ranaware, Upasak Das, Ashwini Kulkarni, Sudha Narayanan, "MGNREGA Works and Their Impacts A Study of Maharashtra" *Economic & Political Weekly* 1, no. 13 (March 28, 2015).

pattern was the relatively low representation of SC and ST beneficiaries in works on private land, at 7% and 6%, respectively. Even including Other Backward Classes (OBC), the beneficiaries were only 37%. It also appeared that many BPL households were urged to use the MGNREGA by village functionaries, rather than people proactively demanding such works.

A study by IDS, Sussex[15] in Tamil Nadu in two villages finds that the majority of MGNREGA workers are women (88%) and Dalits (76%). Divorced, separated, or widowed women were 25%, compared to around 10% for the whole village population. MGNREGA workers are drawn particularly from those households who depend on agricultural labor as their main source of income, rather than from households drawing their primary income from better paid, nonagricultural activities.

4.3.3 Participation of Labor Households

Dhanya,[16] analyzing NSSO (68th Round) data pertaining to the time period July 2011 to June 2012, concludes that

- Majority of MGNREGS households (82%) belong to casual labor households and agricultural households. Fifty-seven percent of casual labour in agriculture and 51% in nonagriculture households have MGNREGS job card. While their share is higher than the other categories, almost half of the casual labor households have still not even applied for a job card.
- Analyzing the percentage share of MGNREGS households in total casual and agricultural households that were provided job cards, it was found that Northeastern states, Chhattisgarh, Uttaranchal, Rajasthan, Jammu and Kashmir, and Himachal Pradesh, were more effective in providing MGNREGS job card. Haryana, Punjab, and Maharashtra are the worst performers among the major states.

The nonenrolment of 43% of agricultural casual labor and 49% of nonagricultural casual labor under NREGS is a matter requiring further analysis and action. Instead of reasoning that it is a demand driven scheme

and that these households could have easily enrolled, means of taking affirmative action should be explored. A campaign—such as the one carried out for opening bank accounts under Pradhan Mantri Jan-Dhan Yojana (PMJDY)—can be launched to enroll all casual labor households under the scheme. Once registered, the households can decide whether and when to avail of the employment on offer.

As Deep Joshi[17] points out

There continues to be widespread ignorance about the Act, many eligible people do not have job cards (though every adult living in rural areas is eligible), reports about delayed payment of wages are common, the process of implementation indicated under the Rules is not followed in spirit and there is no capacity in most places to truly follow the process (to make detailed plans for village development to generate opportunities for wage employment locally). Many people still do not know that, unlike government programmes, the NREGAct is judiciable, i.e. one can take the government to court for not being able to provide employment when demanded.

4.3.4 Differently Abled

Though there is no reservation for persons with disabilities under MGNREGS, but in the spirit of provisions of persons with disabilities (Equal Opportunities, Protection of

---

[15] IDS, "Employment Guarantee as Social Protection: Lessons from Tamil Nadu, India"

[16] V. Dhanya, "Implications of MGNREGS on Labour Market"

[17] Deep Joshi, a Magsaysay award-winning development expert was part of the National Advisory Council in early days of NREGS conceptualization and implementation. He graciously responded to a set of questions from the authors from which excerpts are reproduced.

Rights and Full Participation) Act, 1995, the MORD specifically monitors the coverage the persons with disabilities under MGNREGS. Based on the Tamil Nadu Model, wherein special rural schedule of rates (SoRs) have been fixed for differently abled population with special categories of work, an amendment had been carried out in Schedule-I of MGNREGA incorporating separate SoRs for the people with disabilities.

Box 4.4: *Special Initiative for Differently Abled by Government of Tamil Nadu*

In order to implement the provisions of the persons with disabilities (Equal Opportunities, Protection of Rights and Full Participation) Act, 1995 in MGNREGS, the Government of Tamil Nadu initiated time and motion studies through professional institutions and designed special activities and special provisions for undertaking earthwork-related tasks for the differently abled workers.

- The Special provisions include, waterman/waterwoman at the worksite, caretaker to look after children, assistance to the worksite supervisor in premarking, clearing uprooted jungle from the site (only scrubs, light jungle), watering the area to be desilted, compacting the earth deposited on the bund and benching, leveling, sectioning, and sloping of the bund.

- The differently abled, who are able to carry out physical work, are utilized for earthwork-related activities such as jungle clearance, desilting work, planting and refilling, watering, and so on. In terms of earthwork, the differently abled workers are required to make 50% outturn only or work continuously for four hours only for getting full wages.

During the past three years (from 2012–13 to 2014–15), 102.12 lakh person days have been generated for which ₹151.64 crore has been paid as wages in Tamil Nadu.

Source: GOTN, 2015, Policy Note 2015–16, Rural Development and Panchayati Raj Department, http://tnrd.gov.in/policynotes/ENGLISH%20POLICY%20NOTE%202015-16.pdf, accessed on October 19, 2016.

4.3.5 Women's Participation

As a rights-based legislation, MGNREGA has ensured gender equity in its design features. MGNREGA has incorporated gender equity in various provisions under the Act and its guidelines, to ensure that women have equitable and easy access to work, decent working conditions, equal payment of wages, and representation in decision-making bodies. Two key features of the MGNREGA set it apart from previous labor market interventions from the perspective of the opportunities it holds for women.[18] First, the Act prescribes that at least a third of all workers be women. Second, since the entitlement to 100 days of work is at the household level, the allocation of the work is left to the household members allowing space for the participation of women. MGNREGA's stipulation of work within 5 kilometers of the village where the job applicant resides makes participation in the scheme logistically feasible for women given their household roles and responsibilities. Even in the allocation of work, the guidelines recommend that women be given preference on worksites closest to their dwelling.

In 2012–13, to improve participation of women, the ministry issued further guidance and measure. These included (a) individual bank/post office accounts must compulsorily be opened in the name of all women MGNREGS workers and their wages directly credited to their own account for the number of days worked by them, (b) to identify widowed women, deserted women, and destitute women who qualify as a household under the Act and to ensure that they are provided 100 days of work, (c) to give less strenuous works nearer their dwelling to the pregnant women and lactating mothers (at least up to

---

[18] Sudha Narayanan and Upasak Das, "Women Participation and Rationing in the Employment Guarantee Scheme," *Economic and Political Weekly* 49, no. 46 (November 15, 2014).

8 months before delivery and 10 months after delivery), (d) to conduct time and motion studies to formulate gender, age, level of disability, terrain, and climate-sensitive SoRs and to ensure accurate capturing of work done by women at worksites, (e) to ensure that at least 50% of the worksite supervisors (mates) at all worksites are women, (f) participation of women groups, including SHGs in awareness generation, capturing of demand, planning, implementation, monitoring, and maintenance of works.

MGNREGA is gender sensitive in its formulation. How far the program has been gender sensitive in implementation is analyzed further;

Women work participation across states: At the national level, the participation of women in the scheme has surpassed the statutory minimum requirement of 33%; in FY 2015–16, women person days of employment was 55% whereas the proportion of women in total rural workforce is 34.9% according to the Census 2011. However, at a disaggregated level the interstate variation in women participation is an issue. The percentage of women participation from FY 2006–07 up to FY 2015–16 for all the states is provided in Annexure 4.2.

The extent of women's participation has been somewhat stable over the years in almost all the states. Kerala (97%) and Tamil Nadu (85%) have consistently had high women participation. Assam and Jammu and Kashmir have never achieved the minimum 33% participation of women. In Jharkhand (33%) and Odisha (38%), participation rates have been hovering closer to the minimum requirement. In places where the market wages are higher than MGNREGA, men undertake jobs in the market and women seek employment under the scheme;[19] while this is one of the reasons for high women participation in some states the important aspect is enabling state policy and implementation modalities. Another reason adduced for higher level of women participation is that the work is in mostly public spaces and less exploitative than wage labor in privately owned farms and enterprises.

While cultural aspects can be the reason for poor women participation in Jammu and Kashmir, in the other poorer states low participation of women could be due to a lack of awareness, and/or due to a high demand and limited supply of work opportunities wherein women are forced to compete with men for employment, and the latter are usually favored for manual labor. In many places, social norms against women working outside the household continue to prevent them from participating in the MGNREGA. Nonavailability of worksite facilities like crèches is also a huge disincentive for women.[20] In some states, productivity norms are too exacting, because the SoRs is yet to be revised in line with the norms of the scheme. In states where women's participation is weak, policies have to focus on enabling women to access work especially sensitizing the staff implementing the scheme.

There have been a few studies on factors of implementation that determine women's participation. Analyzing the NSSO 68th round data relating to MGNREGS, Sudha Narayanan and Upasak Das[21] find that for India as a whole, among households those headed by women face a lower rationing rate. Widows too face a lower rationing rate. The administrative rationing rate is higher for all other categories. While these are encouraging indicators, the difficulties faced by women-headed households are apparent in both participation rates

---

[19] Pellissery, Sony and Sumit Kumar Jalan, "Towards Transformative Social Protection: A Gendered Analysis of the Employment Guarantee act of India (MGNREGA)," *Gender and Development*, 19, no. 2 (2011).

[20] R. Bhattacharya, and P. Vaquoline, "A Mirage or a Rural Life Line? Analysing the impact of Mahatma Gandhi Rural Employment Guarantee Act on Women Beneficiaries of Assam" *Space and Culture, India*, 1, no. 1 (2013).

[21] Sudha Narayanan and Upasak Das, "Women Participation and Rationing in the Employment Guarantee Scheme."

and work seeking. For example, only 19% of all female-headed households with no adult males report having "sought" work. Those who worked in the MGNREGA sites in 2011–12 are even lower at 16%. These women are likely to value MGNREGA work a great deal and it is possible that they face substantial social barriers in accessing the program. Women in households with young children appear to face constraints in accessing the MGNREGA—they are less likely than all other types to possess a job card, less likely to have sought work, and least likely to have worked in the MGNREGA. This pattern reflects well-recognized difficulties faced by young mothers in terms of childcare that might prevent them from participating in MGNREGA.

Other studies[22] have found that single women are often routinely excluded, citing that the nature of work demands pairs. It has been reported that widows and single women sometimes were required to accompany men in order to get work. Even in states like Tamil Nadu, data from worksites suggest that of the complaints of harassment at the workplace, more than half of these are related to the issue of childcare.

Equal wages: MGNREGA offers equal wages to men and women. The NSSO 66th Round indicates that MGNREGS has reduced the traditional wage discrimination in public works. As per the NSSO 68th round data,[23] average wage for labor in MGNREGS was ₹112.46 per day for men, and for women it was ₹101.97 per day. The difference was larger for labor in other public works; ₹127.39 per day for men and ₹110 per day for women.

NCAER research study[24] finds that for nearly half the women participants, the program provides the first opportunity to earn cash income since many of the female MGNREGA participants were either not employed in 2004–05 or employed only on a family farm or in a family business. The mandatory transfer of wage payment through bank accounts has ensured that a greater number of women are brought into institutional finance from which they had previously been excluded.

However, lack of women's participation in the planning process is a significant issue in many states. Substantive participation of women in gram sabhas will ensure their contribution to decision making. This relates not just to the relevance and ownership of completing works and the selection of works but also to accurately capture demand and the utilization of the scheme by women who need it the most. Very few research studies have been done on the role of women in the planning of works either through the gram sabha or in panchayats.

Box 4.5: *High Women Participation in Kerala*[25]

Kerala is unique in the country for the extent of women participation in the MGNREGS. Not only is there the highest rate of participation of women in the program in the country, the rate is much higher than that of the four other states which have crossed 50% in women participation—Tamil Nadu (85%), Rajasthan (69%), Himachal Pradesh (63%), and Andhra Pradesh (58%).

Kerala faces shortage of manual labor, which is closely linked with casual labor migration to Gulf region. Furthermore, the inflow of

---

[22] R. Holmes, S. Rath, and N. Sadana, "An Opportunity for Change? Gender Analysis of the Mahatma Gandhi National Rural Employment Guarantee Act" (Project Brief No. 53, Overseas Development Institute, 2011).

[23] GOI, Key Indicators of Employment and Unemployment in India, 2011–12 (2013), Report no. NSS/KI 68/10, Page number 23. Table 6 daily wages received by casual laborers and regular wage employees of age 15–59 years.

[24] Sonalde Desai, Prem Vashishtha, and Omkar Joshi, MGNREGA A Catalyst for Rural Transformation.

[25] Largely adapted from (a) UNDP, *MGNREGS and Kerala, The Untold Story*, ftp://ftp.solutionexchange-un.net.in/public/gen/cr/res22031301.pdf, accessed on October 4, 2016; (b) UNDP, 2015, *MGNREGA Sameeksha II An Anthology of Research Studies (2012–2014)*, nrega.nic.in/Circular_Archive/archive/MGNREGA_SAMEEKSHA.pdf, accessed on October 4, 2016.

foreign remittances resulted in construction boom, which increased the demand of casual labor. The demand supply mismatch is evident from the high wages prevalent in Kerala when compared to other states. The higher wages attracted laborers from other states.

In normal circumstance, MGNREGS is redundant in such an economy as demand for labor already exists and thus invalidates the need for a government program providing employment. At the same time, Kerala is one state in which the scheme is effectively implemented. Only 6% of individuals did not get a job after seeking it making the state a high performer in implementing the program.[26]

With the wage rate on offer in MGNREGS being unattractive to male labor and the workforce participation of women being abysmally low, initially it was feared that the scheme would not take off in Kerala. MGNREGS had a very sluggish start in Kerala. The GPs in Kerala are powerful institutions, with both personnel and financial resources at their command and the power and authority for decision-making including administrative sanctions. It was the synergy that was built between the panchayats and Kudumbashree, the community organizations of women that turned the program around in the state.

Kudumbashree is the State Poverty Eradication Mission of the Government of Kerala, which has been federating neighborhood groups (NHGs) of poor women into ward level Area Development Society (ADS) and panchayat level Community Development Society (CDS). Unlike federated structures of SHGs in the other states, in Kerala the Kudumbashree CDS is embedded in the GP—the panchayat president is the patron of the CDS, five women members of the Panchayat are ex officio members of the CDS and the ward member, the patron of the ADS. Dissemination of information on schemes and mobilization of poor women to access entitlements is also an important function of the CDS.

Since 2008, CDS and ADS have spearheaded the MGNREGS implementation in the state through house to house visits, awareness building, job cards registration, arranging visits to work sites for the women, and so on. It is estimated that 90% of the workers are members of the Kudumbashree network. While the engagement of the network in dissemination and mobilization evidently helped in bringing women into MGNREGS, a small but significant decision of the state government to have all 'mates' (work supervisors) for the program from among the ADS of Kudumbashree helped in generating demand for work. Kerala became the only state in the country with 100% women 'mates' in the program. The 1.2 lakh women mates (selected from the general body of the ADS) who were jointly trained by Rural Development Department and Kudumbashree Mission, then proceeded to identify work opportunities, mobilize groups for work, prepare estimates in consultation with the overseer or engineer, supervise work and provide amenities and work implements at the worksite, prepare and submit muster rolls, and handle emergencies at work.

It was the responsibility of the CDS to coordinate the work of the mates. Nearly every panchayat in the state tapped into the resource pool of mates offered by the community-based organization (CBO), and used it to develop projects, coordinate workers, and make necessary arrangements at the worksite. The pressure of the SHGs ensured that these mates followed up on field checks and measurements, sanctions and release of wages. The work they did was regularly reviewed by the CDS.

There are 11.6 lakh women workers in MGNREGS in Kerala. A good proportion of the women who sought work under MGNREGS were not agricultural labor or casual laborers but housewives who were not in the labor market to begin with. In many cases their presence in MGNREGS was only grudgingly permitted by their families. What prompted these women to come out and undertake work—that they did not know and which involved a level of physical exertion that they were not accustomed to—was that this was work 'for the government', which gave it an aura of respectability that private manual work did not carry. Second was the power of the collective. The involvement of the network in nearly every activity of MGNREGS, the pressure from the panchayat, the presence of a mate who was identified as 'one of us', the opportunity to move into collective farming have all contributed positively.

[26] V. Dhanya, "Implications of MGNREGS on Labour Market."

The mates were particularly proud of their ability to size projects up, gauge the number of person days required, and prepare estimates for the work. All these were new skills, and in the time that they improved and honed these skills, they found themselves being sought-after by landowners to work on their properties and being offered wages to the tune of ₹250 to ₹350 for private work. This interest in the skilled woman laborer has led to the creation of the women's labor collective. The estimation and accounting skills of the mate have also come in handy in the labor collective. Across the state in various panchayats the workers of MGNREGS have been coming together to form labor groups that take on agricultural work and work on homesteads and plantations. Over a thousand of these collectives have begun working. Even while taking on outside work at rates roughly double of what MGNREGS offers, the women have not stopped seeking work through the program.

4.3.6 Demand Driven but Reality is Rationing …

According to MORD data, MGNREGS implementation is almost perfect—all who applied for a job card received one and most of the households that demanded work were allotted work. However, large sample surveys such as National Sample Surveys and IHDS-II (2011–12) showed a different picture. IHDS-II data shows that 48% of rural households applied for job cards, but only 44% received them, and NSSO data shows that only about 81% of the households that demanded work were allotted work.

NCAER study reports that despite MGNREGA's universal nature, not all interested households can get work. Work rationing occurs at different stages of the process, including getting a job card, getting any work at all, and getting the full entitlement. While a quarter of rural households participate in the program, nearly 60% of them would like to work for more days but are unable to find work. Of the households that did not participate, 19% would have liked to participate but could not find work. This widespread direct rationing affects all sections of society—about 29% of all rural households—but is particularly pervasive in some regions. The rationing rate for days of work is high for all households but particularly high for the poorest. In the lowest income quintile (2011–12 income), 92% of households experience rationing of days of work, whereas only 88% of the highest income quintile do so. Among interested households (those that applied for a job card and do not express lack of interest in MGNREGA work), households in the lowest income quintile worked only 23 days a year when they worked in MGNREGA, while those in the highest income quintile worked for 29 days. But much of this difference is due to the poor performance of states such as Bihar and Odisha, where many poor people live.

Local political economy also affects program implementation, creating tremendous variation between villages within the same state.

1. Lack of Capacity in Gram Panchayats to Plan and Implement—A multitier institutional structure has been set up for implementing MGNREGS with GPs playing a critical role in implementation. The implementation structure at the district level and below is crucial for successful implementation. GPs which are responsible for implementing 50% of the works under MGNREGS lack the capacity to plan and execute MGNREGS works. Line departments only typically have adequate sectoral capacity. Several studies have pointed out that lack of human and technical capacity at GPs is a limiting factor for addressing the demand.

2. Not Capturing and Reporting Unmet Demand—The rights-based framework of MGNREGA demands time-bound provision of work. As per the provisions of the Act, a rural household is entitled to unemployment allowance if the state fails to

Box 4.6: *Role of Gram Panchayats in Successful States—Two Different Approaches*

In the Sikkim state, 100% of the works (as against the suggested 50% by the Government of India) under MGNREGA are taken up by GPs. This ensured appropriate planning, execution, and monitoring of converged activities. The presence of infrastructure and staff at GP level made it possible to devolve implementation of the program activities to the GPs. However, it should be remembered Sikkim is a small state and has had continuing stable governance.

Tamil Nadu, which is leading in MGNREGS implementation in 2015–16, has not relied as much on GPs but more on the bureaucratic and administrative structures to ensure implementation. A policy study by IDS Sussex concludes that

the scheme has been successful because it has not been left to the whims of elected village leaders, but has remained in the hands of a bureaucracy that is at least to some extent independent from local village

elites.[27] There is high-level political will and commitment to implementing the policy which wants and ensures that adequate money is allocated to the MGNREGA budget, that money is spent, and a large number of person-days of MGNREGA employment is generated. The state imposes 'targets' for district and block level officials, such as numbers of people to be employed on MGNREGA per day and such targets, imposed top-down are key to implementation of the scheme.

Source: GOI, 2014, Enhancing Sustainable Livelihoods of the poor through convergence of MGNREGA with various schemes, Ministry of Rural Development, and IDS, 2013, Employment guarantee as social protection: lessons from Tamil Nadu, India, Global Insights, Policy Brief No.6, July 2013, IDS Sussex, United Kingdom.

provide it unskilled work within the stipulated 15 days and the liability of payment of unemployment allowance is on the states. So, state and local governments have an incentive not to report unmet demand given that this implies they should pay unemployment allowances.

Moreover, much depends on the GPs' willingness to implement. When there is high demand for work on the ground, the GPs must prepare project proposals and implement them. Panchayat members—many of whom are farmers—may pay less attention to the preparation of projects or may prioritize farmers' needs over laborers' needs. The role of local Panchayati Raj institutions as mediators between demand for work and supply of work often lends itself to making choices out of competing priorities. Even in states, like Rajasthan, with well-functioning MGNREGA programs there is evidence that GPs can easily block creation of employment opportunities through passivity.

Deepta Chopra using field research and secondary data, attempted to 'unpack' the reasons for a decline in Rajasthan's

performance, which was one of the best performers on MGNREGA till 2010[28]

There has been a three-sided negative cycle that has been initiated by supply-side factors. First, local power holders do not want to implement MGNREGA, instead masking their reluctance to engage in the MGNREGA by claiming that the state government does not provide work or wages in time. Secondly, workers have lost trust in obtaining MGNREGA work, and hence do not put pressure on local functionaries to register demand. Lastly, state functionaries have either inadvertently or consciously sent the message that demand needs to be captured in a controlled manner, because they do not have the capacity to deliver work or wages in time, and do not want to be caught out paying unemployment allowance from their state coffers. Instead they use the argument that there is no demand…

[27] IDS, "Employment Guarantee as Social Protection: Lessons from Tamil Nadu, India".

[28] Deepta Chopra, "'They Don't Want to Work' Versus 'They Don't Want to Provide Work': Seeking Explanations for the Decline of MGNREGA in Rajasthan" (Working Paper, Effective States and Inclusive Development Research Centre [ESID], Manchester, 2014).

What has been found as field reality in Rajasthan may be holding good for several other states.

3. Right or Favor—One of the factors for demand not getting registered is lack of awareness about the guaranteed employment. The demand is still seen in the social context as a 'request' or a 'favor'. Some households are deterred from formally obtaining job cards, demanding work from the officials, or do not even know that they have the right to make such demands. Moreover, there is low awareness among potential beneficiaries about certain provisions of the MGNREGA. This limits their ability to fully benefit under the Act. Infrequent meetings and low participation at the gram sabhas convened for planning MGNREGS works further limit the implementation of the scheme at the village level in many places.

4. Issues Related to Wages—The Act provides for prompt wage payment and as per the guidelines, MGNREGA workers are entitled to receive delay compensation at a rate of 0.05% of the unpaid wages per day for the duration of the delay beyond 16th day of the closure of the muster roll.[29] MGNREGA is largely implemented when there is slack season when workers need jobs and wages most, to meet their basic needs. A huge disincentive, which discourages potential workers to get involved in MGNREGA, has been the inordinate delays in wage payment.

Available information shows that in spite of being operational for 10 years, the system of timely wage payment to workers is not streamlined. In 2015–16, 56% of the wage transactions were delayed beyond 15 days; 65% of the amount paid as wages was delayed beyond 15 days, and as much as 10% of the payment was delayed beyond 90 days.[30] Reports from the field also suggest that wage payments are often less than the notified wage, primarily due to inaccurate SoRs. Being a government intervention, the financial transactions involve certain mandatory processes and paperwork; there is a considerable time lag between work completion and payment of wages.

The delays occur due to inadequate staff, delays in paperwork clearance and sanction, and also delays in release and flow of funds from the center to the banks. Coupled with the delays are the allegations of corruptions and siphoning of funds which make the rural households lose faith in the scheme to offer them an employment opportunity and dissuade them from demanding jobs. The government has been pushing for streamlining the funds flow to states down to panchayats for timely payment, the delays have to be addressed on war footing if workers' needs are to be fulfilled.

Right from inception, by endeavoring to make the payments of wages through banks or post office account, the government has tried to address the issue of leakages apart from promoting usage of banks among the financially excluded. However, ghost accounts and duplicate accounts have been issues. For addressing this, the government has been insisting on Aadhaar seeded bank accounts, uploading these details on MIS (NREGAsoft) and ensuring Aadhaar-based payment system. Aadhaar seeding in NREGAsoft is to help in de-duplication of the database and elimination of any fake beneficiary records. The states have been given a deadline of August 2016 to complete all tasks and switch to Aadhaar-based payment system. The Aadhaar-enabled processes in three states with the highest wage-related transaction are not very encouraging except in Andhra Pradesh. As

---

[29] MORD, *MGNREGA Newsletter*, 2, no. 3 (Dec–Feb 2015), MGNREGA Division, Ministry of Rural Development, on behalf of the Ministry of Rural Development, Govt of India, Krishi Bhavan, New Delhi

[30] MORD, http://164.100.129.6/netnrega/delayed_payment.aspx?fin_year=2015–2016&source=national&Digest=i67VyMD7xCwP1LGxHgYF1Q, accessed on October 4, 2016.

of June 2016, Tamil Nadu could seed 75% of the bank accounts with Aadhaar numbers and Aadhaar-based wage payments has been done in 41% of accounts, Andhra Pradesh could seed 94% of accounts and effect 74% of payments through Aadhaar-enabled payment, and for West Bengal the figures are 61% and 17%, respectively.[31] Thus, the progress in states with higher numbers of person days shows that this is still work in progress.

Economic Survey 2015[32] sums up the challenges the states face in streamlining payment

> MGNREGS is one of the government's largest schemes, and forms 41 per cent of Direct Benefit Transfer expenditure…. It is acknowledged that MGNREGA, despite its benefits as a well-targeted social insurance mechanism suffers from significant leakage. To reduce leakages and payment delays, Andhra Pradesh introduced direct benefit transfers, so that salaries would be paid directly to workers, with biometric Smartcards to reduce the scope of siphoning of funds via registering ghost workers. The Smartcards program was a tremendous success, reducing payment delays by 19 per cent, increasing MGNREGA wages by 24 per cent and reducing leakages by 35 per cent. The return on investing in Smartcards infrastructure was thus seven times the cost of implementation. Ninety per cent of beneficiaries also preferred the Smartcards. And yet, the perception was created that the program was mostly negative. In the case of administrative schemes, vested interests often create a market of their own, planning their actions to benefit from it: put differently, this is a case of supply creating its own demand.

MORD initiatives: In order to address the challenge of generating and accurately capturing demand in several states and for improving the implementation of MGNREGA, some initiatives have been taken up which include the Kaam Mango Abhiyan in six districts and IPPE for preparation of the labor budget for 2015–16.

Identifying the key gap of exclusion, especially of women in the planning process, MORD initiated IPPE in July 2014 for the preparation of the labor budget for FY 2015–16. IPPE interventions were carried out in 2,500 backwards blocks in around 100,000 GPs. The hypothesis appears to be that social inclusion in the microplanning process would lead to inclusive outcomes as well as better implementation.

The IPPE process is facilitated by block level teams and included participatory tools: social mapping for the priority of MGNREGS implementation, seasonality mapping for peak and low demand for work in each habitation of the GP, and type of works could be done in different seasons and resource mapping, for identification of the type of works most suitable and relevant for the villagers themselves using the natural resource management approach. In addition, an individual household survey was also conducted to capture demand and seasonality. The preliminary analysis of the data entered in the web-based MIS suggests that the IPPE has led to higher estimation of demand for work in 2015–16 as compared to the estimates for the labor budget 2014–15. From information received in a sample of 18 blocks from 10 different states MORD found an average 14% increase in estimated demand for work.[33] However, the budget allocations for the program for FY 2016–17 do not reflect such robust demand.

Union Budget 2016–17 has allocated ₹38,500 crores for the program as against ₹34,699 crore in 2015–16. However the current year's allocation is lower than the allocation in 2010–11 which was ₹40,100 crores. Taking in to account inflation, the real terms budget outlay is much less as

---

[31] http://nrega.nic.in/netnrega/writereaddata/Circulars/1692WestBengal.pdf, http://nrega.nic.in/netnrega/writereaddata/Circulars/1710AndhraPradesh.pdf, and http://nrega.nic.in/netnrega/writereaddata/Circulars/1597Tamilnadu_April2016.pdf, accessed on August 14, 2016.

[32] GOI, Economic Survey Volume 2 (2016), http://indiabudget.nic.in/es2014–15/echapter-vol2.pdf, accessed on October 4, 2016.

[33] MORD, *MGNREGA Newsletter*, 2, no. 3.

compared to that of 2010–11.[34] Again to quote Deep Joshi

> Budgetary allocations, however, make little sense in case of an Act where expenditure depends on demand. What does happen in practice is that 'indicative' budgets are provided to States and they 'manage' demand accordingly. No one actually breaks the law but the allocations are never exhausted.

Box 4.7: *How Far is the MIS Reliable*

Although Planning Commission applauded the MIS of the MGNREGA with more than 80 million muster rolls and over 120 million job cards online, some studies[35] which have tried to use the secondary data from the MIS, have found that many of the figures may not be reliable. Narayanan and Lokhande mention

> [O]ur analysis raises the question of the reliability of many of these figures, which partly reflects the institutional constraints of the MGNREGA implementation process. The general problems that we encountered with the MIS during data analysis were data entry errors, data exaggeration, data gaps, mismatch of data between derived entries, incomplete entries, and missing financial and audit reports. The data entry operator decides on some critical aspects of data entry … whether a work entered is a spillover or not, whereas it should have been a derived parameter.

IDS Sussex in the study of Tamil Nadu mentions

> Official data from the MGNREGA website was examined alongside independently collected survey and ethnographic data. This suggested that in certain ways the official MGNREGA data is robust: in particular absolute numbers were good for one of the villages, although they were not accurate for the other. However, in other very important ways, the data was highly problematic. The online data keeps a careful track of how many days each household has worked, but the data at the level of the individual is not reliable. Furthermore, the individual characteristics of MGNREGA workers (in particular age and caste) as inputted on the online database of Job Cards were shown to be unreliable. This is a note of caution to other researchers intending to use the official data, and in particular the individual characteristics part of the online dataset.

Source: N.C. Narayanan, Nitin Lokhande, 2013, Designed to Falter MGNREGA Implementation in Maharashtra, *Economic & Political Weekly*, vol. xlviii, nos 26 & 27; IDS, Employment guarantee as social protection: Lessons from Tamil Nadu, India, Global Insights, Policy Brief No. 6, July 2013, IDS Sussex, United Kingdom.

4.4 Asset Creation

The second core objective of MGNREGA is to create durable assets and strengthen the livelihood resource base of the rural areas. A 60:40 wage and material ratio has to be maintained while carrying out the expenditures. Contractors and use of labor-displacing machinery is prohibited.

The choice of works suggested in the Act address causes of chronic poverty such as drought, deforestation, soil erosion, so that the process of employment generation is on a sustainable basis.

The Act has been amended from time to time to enlarge the scope of the works and also in providing flexibility to the states to undertake location-specific works. While in the initial year largely community works were undertaken, a significant amendment was made in 2007, to include works on land owned by households belonging to SC and ST, BPL families, beneficiaries of land reforms, the beneficiaries under IAY for provision of irrigation facility, horticulture

---

[34] Connecting the dots, An analysis of the Union Budget 2016–17. Published by CBGA.

[35] N.C. Narayanan and Nitin Lokhande, 2013, "Designed to Falter MGNREGA Implementation in Maharashtra," *Economic & Political Weekly* 48, no. 26 & 27 (June 29) and IDS, "Employment Guarantee as Social Protection: Lessons from Tamil Nadu, India".

Table 4.4:   Asset Completion Rate

Year	No. of Works Started	Works Completed	Works Not Completed	Completion Rate
Till 2013–14	24,263,281	21,294,822	2,968,459	88
2014–15	4,380,027	2,915,602	1,464,425	40
2015–16	6,183,884	1,742,590	4,441,294	23
Total	34,827,192	25,953,014	88,74,178	75

Source: Website of Ministry of Rural Development.[36]

plantation, and land development facilities. Based on the experience gained, in 2013–14 substantial revision to the Schedules I and II of the Act was carried out and the list of works further expanded and classified into four categories—public assets, assets of poor and vulnerable households, works in relation to livelihood plans for SHG members, and rural infrastructure. In 2014–15 directions have been issued that 60% of the works are to be directly related to agriculture.

4.4.1 Works Undertaken and Assets Created

About 348 lakh works have been taken up since the beginning of the program of which about 75% are reported to be completed (Table 4.4).

Till 2012, water-related assets and works dominated NREGS, accounting in all for 52% of all assets crated;[37] individual works were at a minimum, accounting for 14%.

Since 2012, the individual works especially sanitation, irrigation works on individual farms has gained momentum. The top 3 categories in terms of numbers of works completed since 2012–13 have been (Table 4.5).

Selection of Durable Assets: Though MGNREGS is supposed to be demand driven and assets to be created are identified through participatory processes, other factors determine the type and nature of works and assets created. These factors can and do override demand considerations.

The first and foremost is the state-specific policy direction. The expenditure on the scheme includes both labor costs and materials. The pattern of expenditure on wages and materials clearly shows that some states such as Kerala, West Bengal, and Tamil Nadu have spent nearly all the budgets on labor till 2011 after which material component has been increasing. Kerala continues to spend almost 96% of the expenditure on labor.

In Tamil Nadu, there has been a ban on use of materials and contractors to reduce opportunities for corruption. As a policy decision, the schemes implemented under MGNREGA in Tamil Nadu ensure 100% unskilled manual works. The state has used the labor budget in improving natural resources and renovation of water resources. Up to 2010–11, the major works taken up were large water bodies and community

Table 4.5:   Types of Assets Created in XII Plan Period

2012–13	2013–14	2014–15	2015–16
Rural Connectivity 20%	Rural Sanitation 31%	Rural Sanitation 41%	Rural Sanitation 25%
Water Harvesting 17%	Irrigation Facilities to SC/ST/IAY 10%	Irrigation Facilities to SC/ST/IAY 13%	Irrigation Facilities to SC/ST/IAY 23%
Land Development 13%	Rural Connectivity 16%	Rural Connectivity 12%	Rural Connectivity 12%

Source: Calculated from the data provided on the website of Ministry of Rural Development.

[36] Data on yearly completion works rate, http://164.100.129.6/netnrega/takenup_compwrk.aspx?lflag=eng&fin_year=2015–2016&source=national&labels=labels&Digest=+WYLWwx19OhhVOg6q39p/g, accessed on August 16, 2016.

[37] GOI, *MGNREGA Sameeksha An Anthology of Research Studies on the MGNREGA, 2005. 2006–2012.*

Percentage Share Types of Assets Created till 2012

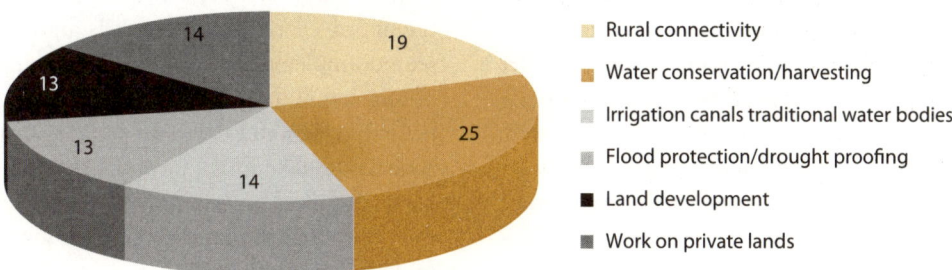

Figure 4.5: Types of Assets Created

Source: MIS Data from the website of Ministry of Rural Development.

assets. The impact of these works was realized by the entire community. However, focused attention to individual needs was not addressed till 2011. Irrigation facilities for individual farmers, that is, farm ponds and sanitation facilities for households are the major individual works undertaken since then, which has increased the material component. The expenditure on materials has gradually increased to 20% of expenditure in 2015–16 from near 0% earlier.

The second influencing factor is technical capacity at the block and GP levels. Several studies[38] show that vacant positions, lack of technical capacity, over dependency on block staff, and implementation coming to depend on line departments who have other competing programs and works are limiting choice of works as well as implementation process. Narayanan and Lokhande mention on the basis of a micro study in Maharashtra which incidentally is one of the better performing states that

> At the block level, the engineers and TAs were so preoccupied with the measurement of completed works and the preparation of wage payment orders that they did not have time

to design, supervise, and provide technical guidance for ongoing work. The distance of worksites from the line department offices varied, resulting in delayed measurements and wage payments. In some cases, this was done entirely by the GRS. Similarly, computer data entry operators were not able to keep pace with the task of uploading muster rolls and other data into the MIS system. The GPs were dependent on block-level officials for the preparation of plans due to lack of technical training.

The third influencing factor is the adoption of the prescribed processes. The prescribed way is to understand the scope and constraints of the natural resource base (using tools such as transect walks, and resource and social mapping) and plan works under the GP to create durable assets. Such an assessment requires a thorough analysis of the natural resource base including groundwater, surface flows, topography, soil types, land use, and so on. Each GP has to prepare a 5-year perspective plan which will outline the development requirements of the GP. The perspective plan will (a) assess natural resources, (b) analyze current use patterns, (c) identify opportunities provided by markets, and (d) identify natural resource constraints such as limited groundwater, endangered bio diversity, upstream/downstream of water harvesting, and the capacity of soils to support specific production systems. In the absence of such an exercise, works identified by GP members are normally included in the GP plan with designs

---

[38] (a) Pooja Datta et al. *Right to Work? Assessing India's Employment Guarantee Scheme in Bihar* (Washington, D.C.: The World Bank, 2014); (b) N.C. Narayanan and Nitin Lokhande, 2013, "Designed to Falter MGNREGA Implementation in Maharashtra"; (c) Kunal Sen. *Success and Failure in MGNREGA Implementation in India* (Manchester: Effective States and Inclusive Development, 2014).

and estimates prepared by line department engineers. The sequence of activities to be carried out—initial surveys, designs, and uploading of photographs before and after completion of works—are not properly done in many places due to a paucity of staff. Previous design and estimation sheets are often used as references, making appropriate changes in dimensions and costs.

4.4.2 Work Completion Rates

The available data on year on year work taken up, completed, and pending works is at best confusing; only from the year 2013–14 there is clear data on these aspects. Though overall the work completion rate is reported to be 75% (Table 4.4 and 4.5), the year on year data shows an average completion rate of 50%.

MIS data for 2015–16 shows that at the beginning of the year, 5,642,370 works were pending since 2012–13 out of which 42% were completed during the year and 6,248,484 new works were taken up out of which 17% were completed.

The period taken for completion depends on type of work. Comprehensive watershed program will take three to four years, roads may take two years, whereas farm ponds and wells can be completed within a year, thus some assets are, by design, meant to be completed over a longer period. Clubbing of all different types of works and information on whether they are complete or incomplete within a year gives a misleading picture. The MIS needs to identify clearly those works that are to be executed for more than a year. Such works may be split into annual work plans, with each annual plan given a distinct identity to track work completion.

Though there is no hard data available, some studies and anecdotal evidence have found that some works are not completed. MGNREGS works that are left incomplete because available technical capacity at the block and GP levels is grossly inadequate to design, monitor, and evaluate the available works. Revision of wage and material rates raise the actual cost beyond the approved estimates which is another reason. Implementing agencywise tracking of ongoing and incomplete works need to be undertaken and for those agencies that have incomplete works for more than one fiscal year after the year in which the works were proposed, no sanction is to be given for beginning new works.

Quality of Assets: Some opinions in public domain raised doubts regarding the nature of works undertaken and completed under MGNREGA and the existence of the assets. There had been concern regarding utility and quality of works as material use is capped on works undertaken. However, some systematic studies undertaken by reputed institutions show that the assets created exist and are providing benefits.

In a survey, carried out by a group of scientists from Chhattisgarh State Renewable Energy Development Agency (CREDA) and ICAR,[39] covering 2,381 households in the six states of Andhra Pradesh, Chhattisgarh, Madhya Pradesh, Odisha, Rajasthan, and Uttar Pradesh, it was found that MGNREGA works on the lands of individual beneficiaries had a significant impact. These are as follows:

1. **Groundwater levels** in the study blocks have either increased or remained at the pre-MGNREGA level though the numbers of borewells had increased in most locations.
2. **Area irrigated using groundwater** has increased in 30 of the 40 villages studied potentially leading to increased and sustained crop yields.
3. **Soil organic carbon:** 72% of the 899 samples of the beneficiary plots subjected

[39] Tashina Esteves, K.V. Rao, Bhaskar Sinha, S.S. Roy, Bhaskar Rao, Shashidharkumar Jha, Ajay Bhan Singh, Patil Vishal, Sharma Nitasha, Shashanka Rao, Murthy I.K., Rajeev Sharma, Ilona Porsche, Basu K., N.H. Ravindranath, 2013, "Agricultural and Livelihood Vulnerability Reduction through the MGNREGA," *Economic & Political Weekly*, 48, no. 52 (December 28).

to MGNREGA works' implementation showed an increase in the SOC content.

4. **Crop yields**: 32 of the 40 study villages reported an increase in crop yields (46% to 100%), both irrigated and rainfed. The remaining eight villages reported no change. However, the authors noted that it was not possible to attribute increase in crop yields to any single work or only to MGNREGA works.

5. **Migration:** Due to increased employment availability in the villages as a result of MGNREGA work implementation, migration of landless or unskilled laborers fell in 29 of the 40 villages (in the range of 8% to 100%).

IGIDR carried out a study[40] in 20 districts of Maharashtra[41] to verify (a) if the works created under the MGNREGA in Maharashtra exist, and their condition and quality and (b) to record perceptions on the impacts of these works through a systematic survey of beneficiaries. Of the 4,266 completed works in the sample GPs assigned for verification, the survey teams found that close to 87% assets existed and were in use. Of the works verified to exist, an overwhelming proportion supported farming activities, directly or indirectly. Over a third was land development on private lands. The distribution of works across districts reflected the diversity of the districts, pointing to their varying priorities. The individual benefit schemes are more likely to be in nontribal areas since tribal regions have traditionally been participating in large numbers on employment guarantee scheme worksites, and common works are necessary to cater to the high demand for work. There did not seem to be any clear evidence to show whether the choice of works was primarily driven by villagers' aspirations, officials' initiatives, or agroclimatic conditions. It was apparently a combination of all these.

Water works on public lands impacted more land and households than works on private land, because the public works were of a larger scale. Roads had the widest impact. For horticultural works, the land devoted was typically fairly small, at about three quarters of an acre, but the estimated annual net earning was close to ₹58,000 at 2013–14 prices. Interestingly, even for works on private lands, there was a perception that for each acre of the beneficiary's land it benefited, another acre of someone else's land also benefited, underscoring the positive spillover effects of these works. This ratio was more than two in the case of water works on common lands.

The study concludes that the widespread perception that the MGNREGA does not create anything productive or that many of its works exist only on paper appears to be exaggerated, with a majority of respondents suggesting that the assets are somewhat or very useful. Another perception, that MGNREGA assets are nondurable, is not entirely true either. Many works, including those on public land, appear to be maintained regularly, if not by local governments, by users themselves. There is merit, however, in the argument that greater attention to design and maintenance can go a long way toward ensuring that works rated as good now get better. Efforts to foster local participation, more careful selection of works, and a better design would ensure that the MGNREGA is effective in supporting livelihoods.

---

[40] Krushna Ranaware, Upasak Das, Ashwini Kulkarni, Sudha Narayanan, "MGNREGA Works and Their Impacts A Study of Maharashtra".

[41] The 20 districts accounted for 60% of the MGNREGA expenditure and 66% of the works generated in Maharashtra from 2010 to 2013. In each of the 20 districts, one block was sampled purposively to represent the best performing block in terms of expenditure and in each of these 20 blocks, five GPs were selected for the survey, and these five GPs were the best performers in terms of the cumulative number of works created and completed under the MGNREGA from 2010 to 2013. In the sample GPs, the survey considered all works completed between January 1, 2010 and December 31, 2013. Also, 4,265 households were interviewed.

In a rigorous study[42] in 2015 of utility of wells created under MGNREGS in Jharkhand, the authors observe that about 70% of the sanctioned wells get completed with 60% with parapet and the rest 10% without one. Not having a parapet is a serious risk and shows that functionaries and beneficiaries alike are unaware of the risks associated with it and the possible reduction in the life of wells since mud would slide into the well, slowly filling it up. Thirty percent of wells not getting completed are also an issue since the expenditure on them is wasted. NREGA wells are able to give about 5.3% of average rate of return on the total cost of construction of the wells. However, rate of return are largely underestimates of the actual returns since returns of only owners are calculated where a well is used by on an average by five households.

These positive experiences based on studies demonstrate the potential of MGNREGA works to provide sustained benefits, beyond employment. However, the observations that 20% to 30% of the works are not found or are incomplete does not augur well since it amounts to waste of public funds. With the recent government initiative of registering the expected outcomes of each work at the time of approval, follow up on completion, and measuring outcomes on completion will yield better results. More detailed cost–benefit analysis of MGNREGA works[43] will also enable better work selection.

4.4.3 Convergence with Other Programs

MGNREGS is labor-intensive scheme and convergence with other relevant schemes and programs can enable durable asset creation apart from ensuring more complete interventions that addresses livelihood resources of rural households. One of the major policy interventions is forging convergence between MGNREGS and other government programs. In 2008–09, based on convergence task force report, joint guidelines were issued on convergence of NREGS with ICAR, schemes of Ministry of Environment, Forest and Climate Change, schemes of the Ministry of Water Resources, River Development & Ganga Rejuvenation and within the same MORD—PMGSY, SGSY, and watershed development programs. In 2009–10, 115 pilot districts were identified in 22 states to carry forward the convergence initiatives. Since 2011, convergence gained momentum with several states showcasing good models.

However, some studies find that at field level except a few, many of the departments may not want their programs to converge with MGNREGS, as they apprehend that pressure would build on them to operationalize MGNREGS norms and processes in the implementation of their projects and schemes.[44] In spite of such reservations some of the states have built best practises and models in convergence. Institutionalization of convergence in the states' system, as in the case of Andhra Pradesh, Madhya Pradesh, and Tamil Nadu, and innovations by district administrations in few other states are well documented. Convergence of MGNREGS with other programs of other departments has been able to leverage additional resources for the rural households and leads to better outcomes especially of the livelihoods of the households. Some such examples are as follows:

1. **Rural Sanitation**: Individual household toilet units have been a priority for work under MGNREGA under 'individual assets'. Whereas, the construction of Individual

[42] Bhaskar, Anjor and Pankaj Yadav, 2015, All is Well that ends in a Well: An Economic Evaluation of MGNREGA Wells in Jharkhand, Report Submitted to National Institute for Rural Development Hyderabad by the Institute for Human Development, Eastern Centre, Ranchi, Jharkhand.

[43] Reetika Khera, "Digging holes, filling them up" http://indianexpress.com/article/opinion/columns/mgnrega-digging-holes-filling-them-up, accessed on October 4, 2016.

[44] Bhagirathi Panda, "National Rural Employment Guarantee Scheme Development Practice at the Crossroads," *Economic & Political Weekly* 1, no. 23 (June 6, 2015).

Household Latrines (IHHLs) was under convergence with Nirmal Bharat Abhiyan (NBA) earlier, currently this can also be done fully under MGNREGA. There are interstate variations with some states such as Karnataka, Andhra Pradesh, Madhya Pradesh, and Tamil Nadu making concerted efforts to construct IHHLs under MGNREGA, while several states still lag behind. However, out of the total assets generated rural sanitation works account for 31%, 41%, and 25%, respectively during the years 2013–14 to 2015–16.

2. **Kapil Dhara in Madhya Pradesh:** Madhya Pradesh was one of the first states in the country to conceptualize and implement an integrated area development approach for convergence of MGNREGA with other government schemes for rural infrastructure, Integrated Natural Resource Management, rural sanitation, and drinking water. The strategy involved identification of each subscheme according to specific livelihood of the region. The Kapildhara Yojana is one such successful subscheme that has shown a clear impact and has contributed to an increase in area irrigated. For Kapil Dhara, land development and dug wells are provided under MGNREGA. While several other state governments have provided farm ponds in farms of small and marginal farmers, the crucial factor of formulating convergence strategy to allow for water lifting pumps for irrigation has not been as frequently implemented. In Kapil Dhara, water-lifting devices (which run on diesel) for each farm were provided from different schemes. As of December 2015, over 3.6 lakh dug wells have been sanctioned and 1.44 lakhs have been completed and the estimated increase in the irrigable area is around four lakh hectares. Large parts of these areas have moved from single crop to double crop. An evaluation[45] looking at the impact of water-related works across the four states of Madhya Pradesh, Karnataka, Rajasthan, and Andhra Pradesh found that the increase in water availability was the highest in Madhya Pradesh. This was mainly attributed to the Kapildhara Yojana. The evaluation also mentioned that in the villages which were the subject of study, the percolation tanks, stop dams, ponds, and plantation works have contributed to groundwater recharge.

3. **Springs of Sikkim:** Springs are the main lifeline of the people of Sikkim and around 65,000 households, that is, about 80% of the state's rural households depend on springs for drinking water and irrigation throughout the year. Over the years, several of these traditional water bodies have become either dry or discharge water only seasonally, due to declining natural recharge and groundwater table leading to droughts. In order to address this water insecurity, the Government of Sikkim conceptualized and implemented a Dhara Vikas (spring-shed development) initiative with an objective to revive springs, streams, and lakes in the state. Following a convergence approach, MGNREGA provided necessary financial support to the initiative whereas activity-specific technical convergence was ensured through various line departments such as forest, mines, and science and technology and leading NGOs. Activities such as laying of trenches and galvanized iron (GI) pipes were taken up under the national flagship MGNREGA program. Using scientific and people-centric approaches, groundwater recharge activities were undertaken. In the last four years, this project has improved groundwater table and ensured irrigation for cash crops. Overall, 704 springs and four lakes have been resurrected covering an area of more than 8,000 hectares of irrigation apart from drinking water to the households.[46] While the latest data on impact is not available, a study of 50 revived

---

[45] GOI, 2014, Enhancing Sustainable Livelihoods of the poor Through Convergence of MGNREGA with various schemes, Ministry of Rural Development.

[46] Data taken on August 15, 2016, from the Government of SIKKIM portal, http://www.sikkim-springs.org/

springs shows that with an investment of ₹2.5 crore led to 900 million liters of annual groundwater recharge, reforestation of seven hilltop forests.[47]

4. **Solid Waste Management in Tamil Nadu:** The state has used the labor budgets under MGNREGA creatively along with Solid Waste Management program of the Government. This program is being implemented in 2,000 periurban GPs which is being extended to all the panchayats in 2016–17, where MGNREGA labor is used to collect segregated garbage from homes in a tricycle cart, brought to a yard where biodegradable waste is composted. Nondegradable waste is sorted and sold.

4.5 Impact on Agricultural Labor and Wage Rates

One significant policy decision taken in 2010–11 was to link wages under MGNREGS to CPI for agricultural labor. MGNREGA rates were revised on the basis of minimum of ₹100 or price indexed rate whichever is higher which led to enhancement in wages in different states in a range of 17% to 30%. At the national level, the average nominal wage paid under the scheme increased from ₹65 in FY 2006–07 to ₹115 in FY 2011–12. The present rates vary from ₹167 in northern and eastern states to ₹259 in Haryana.

A criticism of MGNREGA is that the scheme has created labor scarcity that causes escalating wages in agricultural work, thereby creating hardship for farmers. The other criticism is that the wage rate on the MGNREGS is being set too high, relative to actual casual labor market wages and so will bid up the market wage rate.

Some studies[48] that have examined the impact of MGNREGS on rural labor market

at a macro level find that only 10% of rural women and 13% of rural men aged 15–59 work in MGNREGA and consequently, although MGNREGA work plays an important role in labor allocation of participants, its overall role in the economy is limited. Since other work opportunities for women are more limited, MGNREGA contributes a very large proportion of overall work for women; the number of days worked in MGNREGA constitutes about 38% of work for female MGNREGA participants, compared with only 22% for male participants. The average increase in household income of ₹4,000 from MGNREGA work for one in four rural households can hardly create substantial changes in the wage structure of the rural economy, nor is it substantial enough to put individuals above a threshold where leisure is more valuable than work. Moreover, the implementation of MGNREGA varies widely from state to state, within districts in a well-performing state and even village to village within a district.

Ashok Gulati, Surbhi Jain, and Nidhi Satija[49] who carried out econometric analysis of real farm wages from 1990–91 to 2011–12 covering 16 major states that account for 93% of farm labor find that though real farm wages rose by almost 6.8% per annum from 2006–07 onwards, the impact of growth variables such as overall GDP, agriculture GDP, and construction GDP was almost 4–6 times higher than that of MGNREGA. Impact of MGNREGA is significant but is 4–6 times less effective than other growth variables. In other words, contrary to popular perception, MGNREGA was not the major reason for spurt in rural wages.

Some micro studies[50] in Kerala and Tamil Nadu, two of the well-performing states, have found that:

---

[47] UNDP., http://www.sikkimsprings.org/dv/research/dhara%20vikas-undp-2015.pdf, accessed on October 4, 2016.

[48] V. Dhanya, "Implications of MGNREGS on Labour Market"; and Sonalde Desai, Prem Vashishtha, and Omkar Joshi, "MGNREGA A Catalyst for Rural Transformation."

[49] Ashok Gulati, Surbhi Jain, and Nidhi Satija, "Rising Farm Wages in India The 'Pull' and 'Push' Factors," (Discussion Paper 5, Commission for Agricultural Costs and Prices, Department of Agriculture & Cooperation, Ministry of Agriculture, Government of India, New Delhi: April 2013).

[50] IDS, "Employment Guarantee as Social Protection: Lessons from Tamil Nadu, India." V. Dhanya, "Implications of MGNREGS on Labour Market".

1. MGNREGA helps to set benchmarks for local agricultural wages and enhance the bargaining power of rural laborers since they have an alternative source of income. Even when there is very little agricultural work available in the village, daily wage laborers are now better placed to negotiate a wage that is at least at the MGNREGA level.

2. For women it is not just that their bargaining power has improved, but also that they now have the choice between agricultural work and MGNREGA work, and that they can plan what work to do according to their own needs rather than being subject to the demands of landowners.

3. While nonagricultural jobs are already available to some rural workers, MGNREGA has now added a new employment opportunity. This is particularly significant for women and the elderly whose restricted access to alternative jobs has kept them in agriculture and their wages low. As women's agricultural wages are closer to the state-set MGNREGA wages, it is women's wages that are pushed up by rising MGNREGA wage levels.

4. Such wage hikes benefit all the rural poor who are dependent on agricultural work for their livelihood, not just those who participate in MGNREGA.

5. MGNREGS has resulted in shortage of women labor force involved in pre and postharvesting operations in agrarian districts (both the states have very high women participation rates) and as a result, wages for women labor force involved in this work has increased, which was earlier only marginally higher than the MGNREGS wages. However, labor shortage and wage hike was limited to only certain types of work and cannot be generalized across works and regions.

To conclude, nearly half of MGNREGS workers are new entrants to the labor force and are confined to the MGNREGS works only resulting in limited impact on the labor market and wages. However, restructuring the program to ensure that farmers can use MGNREGA workers through a cost-sharing arrangement will provide relief for landowning farmers. (NITI Aayog in a communication to MORD has suggested that during the peak period of the agriculture season, farmers experience acute shortage of labor and hence farmers may be allowed to hire the MGNREGA workers with them paying the bulk of wage [say 75%] and MGNREGA covering the remainder[51]).

4.6 Other Impacts of the Program

The research studies on implementation and impact of MGNREGS are well documented. MORD has commissioned two compilations of the studies—*MGNREGA Sameeksha* is an anthology of the studies conducted between 2006 and 2012 and *Sameeksha II* is the compilation of studies between 2012 and 14. Many of these are micro studies covering a few villages in a single state with few being multistate studies. Some of the larger studies have been referenced in the other sections of the chapter as well.

Major findings of research studies compiled in both *MGNREGA Sameeksha*[52] are;

1. MGNREGA is important as a supplementary source of income. MGNREGA income is being used by some of the rural households for starting their own ventures.

2. MGNREGA has caused a significant increase in monthly per capita consumption expenditure of rural households and improved household welfare. A positive impact of this wage transfer on household income, monthly per capita expenditure, food security, and health of the beneficiaries was observed.

---

[51] GOI, 2016, Suggestion of Niti Aayog Under MGNREGS, Unstarred Question NO. 800 Answered On 28.04.2016, Lok Sabha.

[52] GOI, *MGNREGA Sameeksha An Anthology of Research Studies on the MGNREGA, 2005 2006–2012.* UNDP, 2015, *MGNREGA Sameeksha II An Anthology of Research Studies (2012–2014).*

3. MGNREGA is succeeding as a self-targeting program with high participation from marginalized groups including the SCs and STs. In the case of both SCs and STs, the participation rate exceeds their share in the total population.

4. MGNREGA is an important work opportunity for women who would have otherwise remained unemployed or underemployed. MGNREGA has reduced the traditional gender wage discrimination, particularly, in the public works sector and has had a positive impact on the socioeconomic status of the women. Studies on widows and women-headed households show that MGNREGA is a substantial income earning opportunity for these women and a majority mention that MGNREGA had helped them avoid hunger. Findings from different studies also observe that post- MGNREGA, women have greater control over their wages and have been spending them on repaying small debts, paying for their children's schooling, bearing medical expenses, and so on.

   However, lack of women's participation in the planning process is a significant deficiency. This relates not just to the relevance and ownership of completing works and the selection of works but also to accurate capture of demand and the utilization of the scheme by women who need it the most. The type of works taken up may not be amenable to what women can do. Women also need decent work facilities including facilities for children.

5. Assets: The sustainability of an asset depends to a large extent on the soundness of its technical design. Inadequate staff was a major reason for poor quality and effectiveness of assets. Where planned and implemented well, MGNREGA works have led to a rise in groundwater, improvement in soil quality, and reduction in vulnerability of production system. However, some studies have pointed out that the extent and kind of impact of MGNREGA works on the environment depend on the scale of the activities undertaken, the technical design, the quality of assets created, and ownership and use of physical structures constructed. Research indicates that wherever village communities have taken enthusiastically to the idea of MGNREGA and their enthusiasm supported by an able, well-staffed administration, and capable local governance institutions and leadership, results have been positive. In other instances, lags in process and procedure have reduced the efficiency of assets.

   There are only a few studies that have conducted rigorous scientific analysis on the actual productive performance of these assets. Furthermore, the quality and durability of the assets vary vastly with district/region and cannot easily be generalized at the national level.

   Studies found that while creation of new assets was beneficial, investments in expanding, deepening, improving, and renovating existing assets provided the highest returns; existing assets renovation had a return of 136%, much higher than the return on new assets created which was 65%.

   Water-related assets created under MGNREGA have increased the number of days in a year water is available and also the quantity of water available for irrigation. The increased availability of water has also led to changes in crop patterns and increased area under cultivation according to some studies.

6. The impact of MGNREGA on agricultural productivity is neither uniform nor conclusive. There is also the problem of attributing changes in crop yield, increased water availability for irrigation, increase in crop area, productivity of agricultural land, and so on, to MGNREGA. The values of all these variables can be influenced by several other external factors, such as, rainfall and floods, and economic shocks like inflation.

7. Migration: MGNREGA has had a more direct and positive impact on reducing distress migration as compared to migration taken up for economic growth and other reasons.

8. Environmental Impact: While there are several studies that suggest that MGNREGA has had a positive impact on the environment, there are only a few studies that have actually attempted to quantify this impact.

9. Labor: The agriculture labor shortage is not caused entirely by MGNREGA; trends of reduced labor force in agriculture precede MGNREGA. Wages of MGNREGA provide an alternative source of income for rural laborers, raising the minimum wage threshold (the fallback position if a bargain is not struck) and implicitly offering laborers bargaining powers in an otherwise inequitable rural labor market. The scheme has also provided laborers (particularly those who are in debt bondage or contract labor) with a dignified choice of work. Thus, the diversion of labor in places may reflect an active choice made by the workers.

An impact assessment report carried by NCAER uses the data of IHDS conducted in 2004–05, just before MGNREGA was started, and the second survey conducted in 2011–12,[53] after MGNREGA had been extended to all rural districts. The key findings of the study released in 2015 are as follows:

- Although only 25% of the households in the sample participate in MGNREGA and half of these earn less than ₹4,000 a year, the program provides an important source of income for the participants, lifting many of them out of poverty.

- MGNREGA, by providing work on demand, creates employment opportunities during periods when other work is not available. And through bank payments it also generates financial inclusion for nonbanked households. Examination of household debt finds that MGNREGA participation decreases reliance of rural households on moneylenders who charge usurious interest rates and improves these households' ability to obtain formal credit.

- MGNREGA also seems to be associated with lower child labor and better education outcomes for children.

- Women's employment in MGNREGA is high, and for nearly half the women participants the program provides the first opportunity to earn cash income. The study also finds a substantial increase in women's control over resources and improvement in women's ability to make independent decisions about their health.

- Although the poor are far more likely than the rich to work in MGNREGA, nearly 70% of the poor remain outside its purview and unless the program expands its reach, its benefits will remain limited.

NREGS has been impactful in certain areas, but has not measured up to its potential in terms of comprehensive impact in local areas.

Deep Joshi sumps up the expectations and the shortfalls thus

> For every village where 100 households are willing to take up unskilled manual work, ₹30 lakh can be mobilized under MGNREGA year after year (₹180*100 days*100 people/0.6 as wage to material ratio can be 60:40)! In five years, such a village should be able to transform itself and no one would want to migrate in search of unskilled work for survival, no one would need to defecate in the open, the village would have paved roads with drainage, and so on! No State has looked at the Act this way even as they keep asking for Special Packages! There is no Central programme that gives this kind of money for land and water resource development, improving roads

---

[53] 42,152 households and 204,577 individuals in 2011–12—including 83% of the original households and 2,134 new households were covered making it one of a large sample study.

inside the village, building toilets, and so on as a matter of right and on demand. Of course, if States had taken such a stance—it would require working in a mission mode—one would have seen many court cases challenging the current practice of 'allocating' funds by the Centre as the law brooks no budgetary constraint!

To conclude, NREGS, at the end of the 10 years, has proved to be a clearly positive instrument that intervenes in the rural labor market, by creating new demand for casual labor at reasonable wage levels and thus influencing positive changes all around. While the initial design had a few flaws and incrementally these are being reset, the fundamental concept is seen to be sound from the impact it has had on women, and marginalized sections of population. The scheme has to come off its oft-repeated claim that it is demand driven and hence it cannot force people to enroll or take up a job. Since the employment guarantee is

an affirmative concept, there is no reason why the implementation processes cannot become affirmative and persuade vulnerable households to enroll under the scheme. The challenge is to find creative ways of providing employment in future that can lead to positive impacts through better asset creation and enabling conditions for other economic activities to thrive in local areas.

There is a lot to be proud of in MGNREGS, which is a unique scheme globally. In celebrating its uniqueness, we need to make it future ready. NREGS, with its statutory backing and demand-based funding can become a rural reconstruction program in a real sense in the hands of good state governments. At the village level, the program can do what is enjoined on several departments—water, soil, agriculture, roads, schools, sanitation, housing, and disaster proofing. What is needed is good planning, effective convergence, and quality governance.

ANNEXURE 4.1
NREGS Progress March 2016

Total No. of Districts					661
Total No. of Blocks					6,858
Total No. of GPs					2,62,256
I Job Card					
Total No. of Job Cards [in Cr]					13.34
Total No. of Workers [in Cr]					27.85
(i) SC worker % as of Total Workers					19.54
(ii) ST worker % as of Total Workers					14.97
Total No. of Active Job Cards [in Cr]					6.73
Total No. of Active Workers [in Cr]					10.7
(i) SC worker % as of Total Workers					20.69
(ii) ST worker % as of Total Workers					16.39
II Progress	FY 2016–2017	FY 2015–2016	FY 2014–2015	FY 2013–2014	FY 2012–2013
Approved Labor Budget [in Cr]	217	239.112	220.67	258.57	278.71
Person days Generated so far [in Cr]	35.0529	235.5695	166.21	220.37	230.46
% of Total LB	16.15	98.52	75.32	85.23	82.69
% as per Proportionate LB	49.67	0	0	0	0
SC person days % as of total person days	20.46	22.26	22.4	22.81	22.22
ST person days % as of total person days	18.5	17.69	16.97	17.52	17.79

Women Person days out of Total (%)	56.4	55.21	54.88	52.82	51.3
Average days of employment provided per Household	18.82	48.87	40.17	45.97	46.2
(i) Average Person days for SC Households	17.8	47.94	39.68	45.28	44.92
(ii) Average Person days for ST Households	19.76	51.68	40.11	48.93	49.97
Average Wage rate per day per person (₹)	154.88	154.14	143.92	132.7	121.41
Total No of HHs Completed 100 Days of Wage Employment	20,157	4,854,455	2,492,654	4,659,347	5,173,487
% Payments generated within 15 days	67.3	34.77	26.85	50.09	50.09
Total Households Worked [in Cr]	1.8623	4.8205	4.14	4.79	4.99
Total Individuals Worked [in Cr]	2.627	7.2337	6.22	7.39	7.97
% of Men Worked	44.25	49.7	49.77	52.03	52.93
% of Women Worked	55.75	50.3	50.23	47.97	47.07
% of SC Worked	21.05	22.3	22.26	22.93	22.79
% of ST Worked	18.57	18.21	18.39	17.88	17.92
% of Disabled Persons Worked	0.73	0.63	0.67	0.66	0.57
III Works					
Number of GPs with NIL exp	63,080	39,586	39,531	27,154	25,152
Total No. of Works Takenup (New + Spill Over) [in Lakhs]	96.04	117.36	97.65	93.52	104.62
Number of Ongoing Works [in Lakhs]	91.71	88.52	68.21	66.1	79.09
Number of Completed Works [in Lakhs]	4.34	28.84	29.44	27.42	25.53
% of Expenditure on Agriculture & Agriculture Allied Works	64.1	60.44	52.81	48.7	56.1
IV Financial Progress					
Wages [in Cr]	11,666.48	30,843.33	24,187.26	26,491.21	27,153.52
Material and Skilled Wages [in Cr]	2,517.19	10,719.42	9,421.11	9,693.72	10,429.97
Total Adm Expenditure [in Cr]	319.98	2,274.48	2,416.67	2,367.68	2,194.78
Total Exp [in Cr]	14,503.64	43,837.22	36,025.04	38,552.62	39,778.27
Total Release (center + state + received this year release last year) (in Cr)	21,783.22	39,844.18	35,046.91	36,597.1004	33,728.2764
Total Center Release (in Cr)	20,346.6	35,998.39	32,139.1	32,746.2675	29,908.681
Total Availability (in Cr)	21,815.71	43,327.55	37,588.03	42,103.8825	46,463.7895
Percentage Utilization	66.48	101.18	95.84	91.56	85.61
Average Cost Per Day Per Person (in ₹)	197.59	211.43	206.13	183.47	170.34

Source: MIS report from website of Ministry of Rural Development. http://mnregaweb4.nic.in/netnrega/all_lvl_details_dashboard_new.asp

ANNEXURE 4.2
Women Participation Rates in MGNREGS

No.	State	2006–07	2007–08	2008–09	2009–10	2010–11	2011–12	2012–13	2013–14	2014–15	2015–16
1	Andhra Pradesh	55	58	58	58	57	58	58	59	59	58
3	Assam	32	31	27	28	27	25	26	25	28	34
4	Bihar	17	28	30	30	28	29	31	35	37	41
5	Chhattisgarh	39	42	47	49	49	45	47	49	50	49
7	Gujarat	50	47	43	48	44	45	43	44	43	46
8	Haryana	31	34	31	35	36	36	40	42	42	45

(Continued)

(Continued)

No.	State	2006–07	2007–08	2008–09	2009–10	2010–11	2011–12	2012–13	2013–14	2014–15	2015–16
9	Himachal Pradesh	12	30	39	46	48	60	61	63	61	63
10	Jammu and Kashmir	4	1	6	7	7	18	20	23	25	25
11	Jharkhand	39	27	29	34	33	31	33	32	32	33
12	Karnataka	51	50	50	37	46	46	46	47	47	47
13	Kerala	66	71	85	88	90	93	93	93	92	91
14	Madhya Pradesh	43	42	43	44	44	43	42	43	43	43
15	Maharashtra	37	40	46	40	46	46	45	44	43	45
20	Odisha	36	36	38	36	39	39	36	34	34	38
21	Punjab	38	16	25	26	34	43	46	53	57	58
22	Rajasthan	67	67	69	67	67	69	69	68	68	69
23	Sikkim							44	45	48	48
24	Tamil Nadu	81	82	80	83	83	74	74	84	85	85
25	Telangana									61	61
26	Tripura							41	47	49	50
27	Uttar Pradesh	17	15	18	22	21	17	20	22	25	30
28	Uttarakhand	30	43	37	40	40	45	47	45	51	52
29	West Bengal	18	17	27	33	34	32	34	36	41	46
	Total	40	**43**	**48**	**48**	**48**	**47**	**51**	**53**	**55**	55

Source: MIS data from the website of Ministry of Rural Development. http://164.100.129.6/Netnrega/nrega-reportdashboard/index.html#/

Climate Change Adaptations: Farming in a Hotspot

5.1 Climate Change and Likely Effects in India

Rural India has faced for long the brunt of erratic weather systems, whether of scarcity or abundance of rains and droughts. While relief and rehabilitation from weather-induced problems has been ongoing for a number of years in some part of the country or the other, the recent years have seen extreme weather conditions inflicting heavier losses—of lives, assets, and incomes. Climate change impairing livelihoods is not a future scenario, but a compelling current problem. The cumulative build-up of greenhouse gases (GHGs), historically since industrial revolution, has significantly led to the current problem of global warming. Risk factors in addition to temperature increase include changes in the monsoon pattern and increased intensity of weather events including unprecedented rainfall, tropical cyclones, and extremes of heat. The resultant flooding, prolonged periods of drought, unseasonal frost, and hailstorms impact lives and livelihoods. Any adverse impact on water availability due to recession of glaciers, decrease in rainfall, and increased flooding would threaten food security and livelihoods, especially in rural areas.

Few countries in the world are as vulnerable[1] to the effects of climate change as India is with its large population dependent upon climate-sensitive sectors like agriculture, forestry, and livestock for its livelihoods. Climate Change Vulnerability Index released by global risks advisory firm, Maplecroft, has ranked India the second most vulnerable country to climate change next to Bangladesh due to the acute population pressure and a consequent strain on natural resources.[2]

The Indian government's National Communications report of 2004[3] identifies the following as the impacts of climate change most likely to affect India between 2004 and 2100:

- Decreased snow cover will affect snow-fed and glacial systems such as the Ganges and Brahmaputra. Most of the summer flow (70%) of the Ganges comes from melt water.
- Erratic monsoons will affect India's rainfed agriculture, peninsular rivers, and water and power supply.

---

of climate change, including climate variability and extremes. Vulnerability includes three components: exposure, sensitivity, and adaptive capacity. (IPCC 2007).

[2] Watershed Organisation Trust (WOTR), *Community Driven Vulnerability Evaluation* (Pune: CoDrive Programme Designer, 2013).

[3] Ministry of Environment and Forests, *India's Initial National Communication to the United Nations Framework Convention on Climate Change* (New Delhi: GOI, 2004), http://unfccc.int/resource/docs/natc/indnc1.pdf, accessed on July 16, 2016.

---

[1] Vulnerability is the degree to which a system is susceptible to, and unable to cope with, adverse effects

- Wheat production will drop by 4–5 million tonnes, even with a rise in temperature of only 1°C.
- Rising sea levels will cause displacement along one of the most densely populated coastlines in the world, also threatening freshwater sources and mangrove ecosystems.
- Floods will increase in frequency and intensity. This will heighten the vulnerability of people in the country's coastal, arid, and semi-arid zones.
- Over 50% of India's forests are likely to experience shift in forest types, adversely impacting associated biodiversity, regional climate dynamics, and livelihoods based on forest products.

India has always been prone to droughts, cyclones, and other disasters. India's disaster management programs rank among the most comprehensive in the world and have achieved considerable success in countering the severe effects of extreme events (Box 5.1).

When floods or droughts occur, governments implement cash and food distribution, arrange for emergency health care, and offer employment schemes. The extensive relief systems that governments have put

> The flood-affected land mass has more than doubled in size from about 5% (19 million hectares) to about 12% (40 million hectares) of India's geographic area in the past five decades. This has occurred despite the rising government spending on a multitude of flood protection programs.

in place have come at a substantial price. India's annual average flood damage during the period 1996–2005 was ₹47.45 billion (USD 753.2 million).[6] Several state governments spend significantly more on relief and damages than on core rural development programs. In the state of Maharashtra, a single drought (2003) and flood (2005) absorbed more of the budget (₹175 billion) than the entire planned expenditure (₹152 billion) on irrigation, agriculture, and rural development from 2002–07.[7]

While attribution of specific weather events to climate change is highly challenging, the occurrence of flash floods, prolonged droughts, extreme weather events, etc. has increased in frequency and become more unpredictable. With climate change, events such as floods, droughts, heat waves, and typhoons are expected to become more frequent and intense, the effectiveness of many development programs are being compromised.

5.2 Climate Change and Agriculture

Agriculture contributes about 18% to India's GDP and is the main source of livelihood for about 60% of the country's total population.

> **Box 5.1:** *Vast Areas are Drought/Flood Prone*[4]
>
> Covering an area of about 74.6 million hectare, 971 blocks of 183 districts have been identified as drought-prone areas of the country. Most of the drought-prone areas lie in the 'arid, semi-arid, and sub-humid' regions. Drought is a major contributing factor to low productivity in rainfed areas—estimated at 0.2, 0.6, and 1.0 tonnes/hectare against a potential of 1.0, 1.9, and 3.0 tonnes/hectare in arid, semi-arid, and sub-humid regions.[5]

---

[4] GOI, *National Disaster mitigation plan (Drought and Cold Wave/Frost)*, http://agricoop.nic.in/imagedefault1/draftdisplan7813.pdf, accessed on July 17, 2016.

[5] K.P.R. Vittal et al. *Guidelines on Drought Coping Plans for Rainfed Production Systems* (Hyderabad: Central Research Institute for Dryland Agriculture, 2003).

[6] GOI, *India's Intended Nationally Determined Contribution: Working Towards Climate Justice* (2015), http://www4.unfccc.int/submissions/INDC/Published%20Documents/India/1/INDIA%20INDC%20TO%20UNFCCC.pdf, accessed on July 16, 2016.

[7] Climate Change Impacts in Drought and Flood Affected Areas: Case Studies in India. June, 2008. Report No. 43946-IN. The World Bank. http://siteresources.worldbank.org/INTINDIA/Resources/295482–1243337137917/ExecutiveSummary.pdf, accessed on July 16, 2016.

The impacts of climate change on agriculture will therefore be severely felt in India. Agriculture plays the roles of both the victim and aggressor in climate change: On the one hand, it is severely affected by climate change; on the other hand, it is a significant contributor to greenhouse gas emissions.

India has seen a 0.4°C increase in mean surface air temperature over the past century (1901–2000),[8] and climate change projections up to the year 2100 indicate a possible overall 2°C–4°C rise in temperature.[9] A 2°C –3.5°C increase in temperature and associated increase in precipitation are estimated to lower the agricultural gross domestic product (GDP) by 9%–28%.[10] Increase in temperature and crop yields are influenced by the interplay of three key climate parameters: (a) the level of carbon dioxide (termed carbon fertilization); (b) the temperature change; and (c) the level and distribution of precipitation. For most crops, the elevated levels of carbon dioxide and higher precipitation rates (except where rainfall is excessive) promote crop growth. Since current temperatures throughout India are high, these beneficial effects are offset by further warming.

The overall impact of climate change on crop yields depends on the baseline conditions of the above three parameters and the balance of these conflicting forces. In arid locations, where crops already suffer heat stress, a small increase in average temperatures can lead to a dramatic decline in yields. The same temperature change in a cooler climate zone could produce an increase in yields. The clear implication is that broad generalizations of crop responses to climate change will be misleading if they do not take account of location-specific baseline climate and soil conditions. Due to India's vast geographic diversity, the impacts are likely to be varied and heterogeneous.[11]

Studies have been conducted on climate change and impact on farm yields.

(a) A major study[12] conducted by the Indian Network of Climate Change Assessment (INCCA) to assess the impact of climate change on four key sectors of Indian economy, namely, agriculture, water, natural ecosystems and biodiversity in four climate-sensitive regions of India, the Himalayan region, the Western Ghats, the Coastal Area and the Northeast Region, projects an overall warming, increase in precipitation with variable water yield, change in the composition of the forests, spread of Malaria in new areas, which are likely to cause an adverse impact on the lives. Crop yield models show that overall there is decline in the yields in the major crops grown in the regions (only in few areas the yields increase); the magnitude of change in yield, however, differs from location to location within the regions studied. The expected changes in yield of rice in irrigated and rainfed conditions in the four zones are given in Table 5.1.

(b) The Second National Communication to the UNFCC highlights the nature and magnitude of the expected impacts of climate change on agriculture.[13]

---

[8] Planning Commission, *Twelfth Five Year Plan (2012–2017). Faster, More Inclusive and Sustainable Growth, Volume I.* (New Delhi: GOI, 2013).

[9] B. Venkateswarlu et al., *Demonstration of Climate Resilient Technologies on Farmers' Fields Action Plan for 100 Vulnerable Districts* (Hyderabad: Central Research Institute for Dryland Agriculture, 2012).

[10] Planning Commission, *Twelfth Five Year Plan (2012–2017): Faster, More Inclusive and Sustainable Growth, Volume I.*

[11] World Bank. *Climate Change Impacts in Drought and Flood Affected Areas: Case Studies in India.* (June 2008), Report No. 43946-IN,. http://documents. worldbank.org/curated/en/263441468034787069/ Climate-change-impacts-in-drought-and-flood-affected-areas-case-studies-in-India

[12] Ministry of Environment & Forests, *Climate Change and India: A 4X4 Assessment—A Sectoral and Regional Analysis for 2030s* (New Delhi: GOI, 2010).

[13] Ministry of Environment and Forests, *India— Second National Communication to the United Nations Framework Convention on Climate Change* (New Delhi: GOI, 2012).

Table 5.1:   Likely Changes in Yield of Rice

Western Ghats	Irrigated	Change +5% to –11% depending on location; overall 4% decrease
	Rainfed	Range of –35% to +35% with a large part of the region likely to lose rice yields up to 10%
Coastal areas	Irrigated	10% decrease in majority of coastal districts
	Rainfed	20% decrease in west coast,15% increase in east coast
Northeast	Irrigated	Change range will be –10% to 5%,
	Rainfed	Range of –35% to 5%

Source: GOI, 2010, Climate Change and India: A 4X4 Assessment—A Sectoral and Regional Analysis for 2030s, Ministry of Environment & Forests, Government of India.

Simulation exercises showed that a 1°C increase in temperature alone could lead to decrease in wheat production of 6 million tonnes in the absence of adaptation and carbon dioxide fertilization benefits. An increase of temperature from 1°C to 4°C reduced the grain yield of paddy (0% to 49%), potato (5% to 40%), green gram (13% to 30%), and soybean (11% to 36%). The linear decrease per °C temperature increase was 14%, 9.5%, 8.8%, 7.3%, and 7.2% in paddy, potato, soybean, wheat, and green gram respectively. Chickpea, however, registered a 7%–25% increase in seed yield with an increase in temperature up to 3°C, but was reduced by 13% at 4°C increase in temperature. Rice showed no significant change in yield up to an increase of 1°C temperature.

Onion and tomato, two important commercial vegetable crops grown across the country, whose productivity levels are very low compared to major producing countries will face decreasing productivity under climate change scenario. Another fruit, the productivity of which is heavily linked with climatic variations, is apple; the temperature change will benefit apple cultivation in high altitudinal regions of Himachal Pradesh, but lower regions will be affected by the increase in temperatures. At present, due to climatic stress 1.8 million tonnes of milk production is being lost and global warming is expected to increase the loss by another 1.6 million tonnes by 2020.

High producing crossbred cows and buffaloes will be more adversely affected than indigenous cattle, which are better adapted to higher temperatures.

(c) The ICAR has conducted climate change impact analysis on crop yields for the whole country including the Himalayan region using different crop simulation models.[14] For irrigated maize, wheat, irrigated paddy, and rainfed paddy, the reduction in crop yields has been projected to the extent of 18%, 6%, 4%, and 6%, respectively, by 2020.[15] Further, the council has made vulnerability assessment on major food crops in different production zones to climatic variability under the 'National Initiative on Climate Resilient Agriculture' (NICRA). The study revealed that around 81.3 million hectare area in arid, semi-arid, and dry sub-humid regions of the country may suffer from extreme weather events. Out of 81.3 million ha, 46.0 million hectare are agriculture lands, spread over 122 districts in 11 States.[16]

(d) The World Bank commissioned a study on climate change impacts in two drought-prone regions in AP and Maharashtra and one flood-prone region in Odisha. It found that in AP, dryland farmers may see their incomes plunge by 20%, in Maharashtra, sugarcane yields may fall by 25%–30% and in Odisha, flooding may result in a drop in rice yields by as much as 12% in some districts.[17]

---

[14] INFO-CROP and HAD CM3 are the models used.

[15] GOI, 2015, Unstarred question no. 2501 answered on August 04, 2015.

[16] GOI, 2014, Starred question 137, answered on December 2, 2014. Adverse impact of global warming climate change on agriculture.

[17] World Bank, *Climate Change Impacts in Drought and Flood Affected Areas: Case Studies in India.* http://documents.worldbank.org/curated/en/263441468034787069/Climate-change-impacts-in-drought-and-flood-affected-areas-case-studies-in-India, accessed on October 20, 2016.

Water is the most critical resource for agriculture in India where large tracts of agricultural land are drought-prone. Groundwater is the major source of irrigation, accounting for about 65%. Rapidly declining groundwater because of overexploitation is a major cause of concern.[18] While public investment is available for large dams and surface irrigation commands, there is little for groundwater sources, although they contribute to half of agricultural production. Farmers often have to make repeated investments in drilling borewells and tubewells due to fall in water tables and failure of wells which causes financial stress. Current trends estimate that 60% of India's groundwater sources will be in a critical state of degradation within the next 20 years with the rate of exploitation exceeding recharge.[19] According to the IPCC, in the changing climate scenario, the demand for irrigation in arid and semi-arid regions of India is estimated to increase by at least 10% for an increase in temperature by 1°C. In contrast to surface water irrigation, groundwater irrigation in India is almost wholly self-financed and hence the climate change effect on dryland farmers will be direct and drastic.

There are certain segments in agriculture that climate change can impact with intensity. Within agriculture in India, rainfed agriculture, which constitutes nearly 58% of the net cultivated area in the country, is expected to be significantly impacted by climate change for two reasons: it is practiced on fragile, degraded lands which are prone to erosion; the people dependent on it are less endowed in terms of financial, physical, human, and social capital, thus limiting their capacity to adapt to changing climate.[20] Delayed onset of monsoon rains and mid–season and terminal droughts in rainfed areas are causing huge losses to agriculture and livestock production affecting livelihoods.

The agricultural sector in India is already stressed by the limited availability of water resources, land degradation, biodiversity loss, and air pollution; climate change is making already sensitive systems even more vulnerable. Modern intensive agriculture has also been a major contributor for the stress. Many small and marginal farmers have been shifting from low-input food crops to market-driven high external-input cash crops. With unanticipated climatic variations, farmers are prone to increasing risk of crop losses. Moreover, the trend of monocropping, with the increasing applications of fertilizers and pesticides, has been cited as the major cause of deteriorating soil quality, poor water retention capacity, decline in productivity, and ever increasing costs.[21] Thus, these agricultural practices are reducing the resilience of small farmers to face climate changes.

5.2.1 Agriculture's Contribution to Global Warming

Global warming is caused by the increase in the concentration of GHGs in the atmosphere. Three GHGs, that is, carbon

---

[18] The stage of groundwater development in the country is 61%. Highly intensive development of groundwater in certain areas in the country has resulted in overexploitation leading to decline in the level of groundwater and seawater intrusion in coastal areas. Out of 5,842 numbers of assessment administrative units (blocks/taluks/mandals/watershed), 802 units are 'over-exploited', 169 units are 'critical', 523 units are 'semi-critical', 4277 units are 'safe' and 71 units are 'saline'. (GOI, 2014, "Status of Ground water development," Ministry of Watersources, GOI, http://wrmin.nic.in/forms/list.aspx?lid=301&Id=4, accessed on July 17, 2016).

[19] World Bank, *Deep Wells and Prudence: Towards Pragmatic Action for Addressing Groundwater Overexploitation in India* (2010), http://documents.worldbank.org/curated/en/272661468267911138/pdf/516760ESW0P0951round0Water129101110.pdf, accessed on October 20, 2016.

[20] B. Venkateswarlu et al., *Demonstration of Climate Resilient Technologies on Farmers' Fields Action Plan for 100 Vulnerable Districts.*

[21] WOTR, *Towards Resilient Agriculture in a Changing Climate Scenario.*

dioxide, methane, and nitrous oxide trap the outgoing infrared radiation from the earth's surface and thus raise the temperature. Agriculture and livestock are sources of emission of GHGs. carbon dioxide emission arises from decay of organic matter, forest fires, burning of fields and crop residue, deforestation, and land-use changes. Agriculture is not considered as a major source of emission of carbon dioxide. The main agricultural sources of methane are organic decay, biomass burning, paddy cultivation, and livestock.

In ruminant animals, methane is produced as a by-product of the digestion of feed in the rumen under anaerobic condition. Methane emission is contingent on the composition of animal diet and the proportion of different feeds. Mitigation of methane emitted from livestock is approached most effectively by strategies that reduce feed input per unit of product output. Nutritional, genetic, and management strategies to improve feed efficiency increase the rate of product (milk and meat) output per animal.

As a greenhouse gas, nitrous oxide is 310 times more effective than carbon dioxide. Forests, grasslands, soils, nitrogenous fertilizers, and burning of biomass and fossil fuels are the major sources of nitrous oxide. Soil contributes to the largest amount of nitrous oxide emission. The major sources are soil cultivation, fertilizer and manure application, and burning of organic material and fossil fuels. From the agricultural perspective, nitrous oxide emission from soil represents a loss of soil nitrogen, reducing the nitrogen-use efficiency. Appropriate crop-management practices, which lead to increased nitrogen-use efficiency, hold the key to reduce nitrous oxide emission. Indian agriculture should learn to adopt soil management systems that are climate change compatible, where soil organic carbon is maintained or enhanced and GHGs emission is reduced. It would require increased mitigation and adaptation research, capacity building, and changes in land-use management. Increasing soil organic carbon content can be a good starting point in mitigation strategies for the agricultural sector.

5.3 Government Policies and Programs

India faces the double challenge of ensuring reasonable advance in human development: economic progress of its vast population with climate-sensitive carbon emission policies and at the same time investing in adaptive measures that will secure the livelihoods of the poor and vulnerable from adverse climate change impact. While the developed countries could grow somewhat irresponsibly without check on carbon emissions, developing countries like India do not have this luxury.

India follows a twin strategy of mitigation and adaptation to combat climate change. India's intended nationally determined contribution statement to UNFCC does not bind it to any sector-specific mitigation obligation or action, including in agriculture. India's goal is to reduce overall emission intensity and improve energy efficiency of its economy over time and at the same time protecting the vulnerable sectors of economy and segments of our society.

The mitigation strategy and plan of action focuses largely on clean energy, energy efficiency in various sectors of industries, steps to achieve lower emission intensity in the automobile and transport sector, a major thrust to nonfossil- based electricity generation (solar, wind, and bio mass), and energy conservation in building sector. The adaptation strategies are largely focused on rural areas and rural livelihoods, especially agriculture. India's expenditure on programs with critical adaptation components has increased from 1.45% of GDP in 2000–01 to 2.82% during 2009–10.[22] Expenditure on human capabilities and

---

[22] GOI, *India's Intended Nationally Determined Contribution: Working Towards Climate Justice.*

livelihoods, namely, poverty alleviation, health improvement and disease control, and risk management, constitutes more than 80% of the total expenditure on adaptation in India.

5.3.1 National Action Plan on Climate Change (NAPCC)

The government launched NAPCC in 2008 for tackling climate change with missions in the eight specific areas of energy efficiency, solar energy, sustainable habitat, water, the Himalayan ecosystem, forestry, agriculture, and strengthening the scientific knowledge on climate change. All the missions are anchored in the respective nodal ministries/departments and are under various stages of implementation. The implementation of the NAPCC is an integral part of the Twelfth Five Year Plan (2012–17), which contains an assessment of vulnerability of various sectors to climate change, and identifies specific adaptation measures to be implemented over the longer term. In addition to the NAPCC, 32 States and UTs have prepared their State Action Plan on Climate Change (SAPCC) in line with the objectives of NAPCC and also state-specific needs that include both mitigation and adaptation plans.[23] The total resource requirement is estimated at ₹11,336.92 billion for implementation of SAPCCs.[24] The SAPCCs provide a compilation of existing state government programs that contribute to climate resilience; however they lack the operating and institutional mechanisms required for implementation.[25]

5.3.2 Missions on Climate Change

Of the eight national missions on climate change, a separate mission, National Mission for Sustainable Agriculture (NMSA), focuses on agriculture and allied sector. However, the missions had been allocated small budgets till 2015 and expenditure till March 2015 was even lower at only 7%.[26]

5.3.3 NMSA

The government has made NMSA operational from 2014–15 and several ongoing schemes are subsumed under NMSA.[27] The NMSA as a programmatic intervention aims at making agriculture more productive, sustainable, remunerative, and climate-resilient by promoting location-specific integrated/composite farming system; soil and moisture conservation measures; comprehensive soil health management; effective water management practices; and mainstreaming rainfed crop technologies.

States prepare Mission Implementation Plan under NMSA indicating action plan and strategies for sustainable agriculture development with a horizon of 5–7 years which will emanate from District Agriculture Plans and State Agriculture Plan prioritizing the interventions from climate change point of view. NMSA converges, and consolidates all ongoing as well as newly proposed activities/programs related to sustainable agriculture with special emphasis on soil and water conservation, water

---

[23] GOI, 2016, Unstarred question number 335 answered on July 19, 2016, http://164.100.47.190/loksabhaquestions/annex/9/AU335.pdf, accessed on August 14, 2016.

[24] GOI, 2016, *Economic Survey 2015–16, Volume 2.* http://indiabudget.nic.in/es2014–15/echapter-vol2.pdf, accessed on June 15, 2016.

[25] World bank, 2014, Sustainable Livelihoods and Adaptation to Climate Change (SLACC) - P132623, http://documents.worldbank.org/curated/en/158021468253217344/Project-Information-Document-Appraisal-Stage-Sustainable-Livelihoods-and-Adaptation-to-Climate-Change-P132623

---

[26] GOI, 2015, Starred question number 102 answered on March 3, 2015 and annexure on budget allocations to unstarred question 4595 answered on April 21, 2015.

[27] As per the ministry, climate-resilient interventions have been embedded and mainstreamed into missions/programs/schemes of Department of Agriculture and Cooperation through a process of restructuring and consolidation. The Rainfed Area Development Programme (RADP), National Mission on Micro Irrigation (NMMI), National Project on Organic Farming (NPOF), National Project on Management of Soil Health & Fertility (NPMSH&F), and the central sector scheme of Soil and Land Use Survey of India (SLUSI) were subsumed to form the revised programmatic interventions under the NMSA in 2014.

Components of NMSA	Details
Soil and moisture conservation measures	Adopts watershed plus framework focusing on a cluster based approach of 100 hectare or more.
	Support to each farm family under this component will be restricted to a farm size of 2 hectare and financial assistance will be limited to ₹0.1 million.
	Introduce appropriate farming systems by integrating multiple components of agriculture such as crops, horticulture, livestock, fishery, forestry with agro-based income generating activities and value addition.
	Farming systems recommended by ICAR's contingency plans and findings of successful NICRA projects to be considered in development of integrated project plan.
On farm water management	Harvesting and management of rainwater, drip and sprinkler technologies, secondary storage and drainage development.
	Farm ponds to be dug using MGNREGA funds and earth moving machinery (to the extent manual digging under MGNREGA is not feasible)
	Support to each farm family under on farm water management (OFWM) component will be restricted to a farm size of 5 Ha.
Soil health management[28]	Location as well as crop-specific sustainable soil health management, organic farming practices, linking soil fertility maps with macro–micro nutrient management, appropriate land use based on land capability, judicious application of fertilizers, and minimizing the soil erosion/degradation.
Climate change and sustainable agriculture: monitoring, modeling, and networking	Bidirectional (land/farmers to research/scientific establishments and vice versa) dissemination of climate change related information and knowledge by piloting climate change adaptation (CCA)/mitigation research projects in climate-smart sustainable management practices and integrated farming system.
	Consortium approach to be evolved with various stake holders—State Agricultural Universities (SAUs), Krishi Vigyan Kendras (KVKs), Indian Council of Agricultural Research (ICAR) Institutes, etc. by the state government to provide a single window service/knowledge provider system.

use efficiency, soil health management and rainfed area development.

The mission requested budgetary support of ₹1,080 billion up to the end of Twelfth Five Year Plan period (2011–17) and as of December 2014, proposals for ₹130.34 billion have been approved.[29] There is little information on implementation aspects of the mission. As per IFMR-LEAD, which did an evaluation of the mission in 2015, the progress of the NMSA is being accounted predominantly through the achievements of the other ongoing programs of the DAC.[30] NMSA is being redesigned as per Government of India (GoI) guidelines.

5.3.4 NICRA

The second major government initiative is ICAR launching of NICRA in 2011. This initiative, being coordinated by Central Research Institute for Dryland Agriculture (CRIDA), Hyderabad, is a collaborative project by a number of institutes addressing the specific subsectors within rainfed agriculture. The key activities under NICRA include: (a) vulnerability assessment for climate change, (b) district-wise contingency

---

[28] To be implemented by state governments, National Centre of Organic Farming, Central Fertilizer Quality Control and Training Institute, and Soil and Land Use Survey of India.

[29] Ministry of Environment, Forests and Climate Change, *India's Progress in Combating Climate Change: Briefing Paper for UNFCCC COP 20 Lima, PERU* (GOI, 2015), envfor.nic.in/sites/default/files/press-releases/Indian_Country_Paper_Low_Res.pdf, accessed on October 20, 2016.

[30] IFMR-LEAD, Mission Brief Prepared as part of the Study: Implementation of the National Action Plan on Climate Change (NAPCC)—Progress & Evaluation (2015), http://www.ifmrlead.org/wp, accessed on July 17, 2016. content/uploads/2015/10/NAPCC/7_NMSA%20Brief_CDF_IFMRLEAD.pdf, accessed on July 17, 2016.

plans for 576 districts[31] to provide a broad advisory to farmers at the district level, (c) technology demonstration to combat climate change through 121 KVKs and 7 ICAR in one village each in 130 most vulnerable districts. The initiatives under NICRA are included in later sections of the chapter.

Both the NMSA as well as the NICRA are implementing innovative pilots and technology packages on farmers' fields. The total budget sanctioned under NICRA for the four years (2012–16) is ₹3,089 millions.[32]

5.3.5 The National Adaptation Fund for Climate Change (NAFCC)

NAFCC was established in 2015–16 with a budget provision of ₹3.5 billion for 2015–16 and 2016–17 to help in scaling-up CCA interventions in accordance with the NAPCC and SAPCCs. The overall aim of the fund is to support concrete adaptation activities identified under NAPCC and SAPCCs which are not covered under ongoing activities through the schemes of national and state governments. The adaptation projects contribute toward reducing the risk and vulnerability at community and sector level. The Implementation Guidelines for NAFCC have been prepared which outlines that the funding could be provided for adaptation projects in a variety of sectors including agriculture[33] to address climate change related issues. A total of ₹1 billion has been allocated for NAFCC for the Financial Year 2016–17 and further enhancement will depend on budget allocation. More details on the projects funded are given under the section on climate change funding.

5.3.6 MGNREGS

MGNREGS, with a budgetary annual allocation of about ₹347 billion (USD 5.5 billion) in 2015–16, aims at enhancing livelihood resource base in the rural areas apart from employment generation. A vast majority of works under this program aims at strengthening natural resource base of the rural economy and is linked to land, soil, and water. The Integrated Watershed Development Program (IWDP) also delivers better resilience. Although these programs integrate activities that improve coping capacity of local communities to potential impacts of climate variability and change (examples include afforestation, plantations, coastal vegetation belts, fodder development, drainage structures, water harvesting, soil moisture conservation works), they do not have a systematic approach to assessing and addressing climate change risks.

5.4 Climate-smart Agriculture

Climate-smart agriculture sustainably increases productivity, resilience (adaptation), reduces/removes GHGs (mitigation).[34] Indian farmers have evolved many coping and adaptation mechanisms over time, but these mechanisms are unable to cope with extreme weather events being witnessed in recent times.

Conservation techniques involving sustainable land and water management, organic farming, and diversified cropping can buffer against climate change: interventions such as watershed development, re-vegetation, physical structures for managing water flows, changes in cropping systems, and promotion of conservation tillage do enhance resilience to climate variability. However, new and

---

[31] These plans are placed in the websites of the Ministry of Agriculture & Cooperation, GOI (www.agricoop.nic.in) and CRIDA (www.crida.in).

[32] GOI, 2015, Unstarred question no. 2501 answered on August 4, 2015.

[33] Horticulture, agroforestry, environment and allied activities, water, forestry, urban, coastal and low-lying system, disaster management, human health, marine system, tourism, habitat sector, and other rural livelihood sectors.

[34] Food and Agriculture Organisation (FAO), *Climate-Smart agriculture: policies, practices and financing for food security, adaptation and mitigation* (Rome: Food and Agricultural Organization, 2010).

innovative measures to adapt to climate change need to be built along with the conservation techniques that include:

(i) Changes in agricultural practices to improve the fertility of soil and enhance carbon sequestration;

(ii) Changes in the management of agricultural water for more efficient use;

(iii) Crop diversification to enhance resilience;

(iv) Agricultural advisory services and information systems; and

(v) Improving risk management and crop insurance.

As per WOTR,[35] climate-resilient agriculture does not necessarily mean inventing/adopting new methodologies but it is more about applying appropriate strategies/approaches that address climate change.[36]

There are about 23 documented projects[37] on climate-smart agriculture in dry land areas which are largely funded by international NGOs, bilateral agencies, Global Environment Facility (GEF), NABARD, etc., While about four of them are found to

be scaling up, the others are in pilot stage or one-off projects. Additionally, NABARD has sanctioned 18 projects in 2015 which cover the vulnerable agroclimatic zones including Himalayas, northeast and coastal belt. The common elements that are tried and tested in some these projects that enable farmers to cope with climate change are described in this chapter.

5.4.1 Vulnerability Assessments

Most climate-impact and vulnerability assessment studies follow a top-down approach. These studies make use of simulation models to project future impacts. The findings of some of these studies have been covered in section 5.2. However, for planning and implementing interventions at a local level, local level assessments are needed. Bottom-up approaches to vulnerability assessments provide an analysis of what causes people to be vulnerable to a given natural hazard such as climate change. There are a number of tools that are now tested and available for vulnerability assessment. A few of the tested and used tools are;

CRiSTAL: Community-based risk screening tool	Project-planning tool that helps users design activities that support climate adaptation in the context of livelihood projects. Not widely used in India except by Bharatia Agro-Industries Foundation (BAIF). The key outputs are: List of livelihood resources that are most affected by climate hazards. Proposed adjustments to existing projects and new activities to support climate adaptation. List of desired adaptation outcomes and important influencing factors to be monitored.
CoDriVE: Community-driven vulnerability evaluation	WOTR has tested and fine-tuned this tool in four states over two years. Builds on CRiSTAL. While primarily developed for watershed development, can be useful for any livelihood based project. Generates 5 digit vulnerability code based on all five capitals—human, social, natural, physical, and financial that grades all highly sensitive and essential resources on a scale of 1–5. Web-based software enables processing and analysis of key data to generate vulnerability profile as well as situation-specific adaption action.
Framework for community-based climate vulnerability and capacity assessment in mountain areas	Developed by International Centre for Integrated Mountain Development (ICIMOD) presents an analytical framework and a participatory methodology for assessing climate change vulnerability in mountain communities.

[35] WTO is a pioneer in watershed development which is now working several CCA projects in agriculture.

[36] WOTR, 2015, *Climate Change and Agriculture; Moving Towards Resilience for Small Holder Producers*, Policy Brief No. 3, project on promotion of CCA in semi-arid and rainfed regions of Maharashtra, MP, and AP.

[37] Arivudai Nambi Appadurai et al. *Scaling Success: Lessons from Adaptation Pilots in the Rainfed Regions of India* (Washington: World Resources Institute, 2015).

| NICRA | Vulnerability index based on exposure (25 indicators), sensitivity (40 indicators), and adaptive capacity (35 indicators). |
| CEDRA—climate change and environmental degradation risk and Adaptation assessment | Explicitly combines assessments of risks from both climate change and environmental degradation. |

Assessment of vulnerability to climate change includes the following steps:[38]

1. Assess profile of the location (watershed, hydrological unit, cluster of villages, etc.,)
   a. State of natural resources
   b. Socio-economic dynamics
   c. Environmental issues
   d. Developmental issues
2. Assess the observed climate (exposure)
   a. Significant trend of minimum, maximum, and average monthly temperature
   b. Significant trend of minimum, maximum, and average monthly precipitation
   c. Standard deviation of average summer monsoon precipitation—degree of inter-annual variability of climate variable
   d. Frequency, intensity, timing, and duration of extreme events
   e. Observed key climatic hazards in the area
   f. Identification of hotspots, that is, where largest changes have occurred in climate variables from past and present conditions
   g. Evaluate trust worthiness of the data/observation/responses
3. Assess the effects of climate change (sensitivity)
   a. Impact of climatic variability and extreme events
   b. Impact of climate variables on non-climate stresses
4. Assess adaptation to climate change
   a. Social adaptation though formation of social networks
   b. Human adaptation through development of skills, education

c. Institutional adaptation through provision of infrastructure (electricity, connectivity, water) institutional building and services related to health, social support, and communication
   d. Natural adaptation through endowment of bio-physical resources such as forest, soil, air, water, genetic resources, environmental services, etc.
   e. Economic adaptation through availability of financial resources, livelihood, and employment opportunities
5. Assess overall current vulnerability
   a. Impact of climate variability and hazards on key environmental, natural resources and developmental issues
   b. Identification of most vulnerable sections of the community, groups, regions
   c. Identification of non-climatic factors that determine the severity of climatic impacts
   d. Identification of resources that have resulted in successful adaptation to climate variability and extreme events
   e. Identification of level of existing adaptation capacity
   f. Distribution of adaptive capacity across community classes (ethnicity, gender, cast, marginalized and poor population, etc.)

Other than the above tools for vulnerability assessment, there are at least six other tools that are specific to agriculture sector.[39] Tools

---

[38] NABARD, *Guidelines for Preparation of Detailed Project Reports by Project Facilitating Agencies for Climate Proofing.* (Mumbai: NABARD, 2016).

[39] Gesellschaft für Internationale Zusammenarbeit (GIZ), *A Framework for Climate Change Vulnerability Assessments* (2014), https://www.weadapt.org/sites/weadapt.org/files/legacy-new/knowledge-base/files/5476022698f9agiz2014–1733en-framework-climate-change.pdf, accessed on Chapter 4 has good descriptions on the tools.

for vulnerability assessment in general and agriculture sector in particular are plentiful. Vulnerabilities in India differ among states, among regions, and among different groups of people within the same region due to substantial variations in topography, climatic conditions, ecosystems as well as diversity in its social structures, economic conditions, and needs of different communities. Hence, it is all the more necessary that the results of the assessment need to inform the design of adaptation projects so that they reduce vulnerability over time.

At present, the aspects for vulnerability assessments are dovetailed to the projects being implemented by some agencies. For example, Indian Agricultural Research Institute (IARI) carries out climate analysis along with analysis of parameters like soil profile, water availability, and vegetative cover that have enabled an appropriate choice of seed varieties for a given location. Others like Watershed Support Services and Activities Network (WASSAN) and WOTR carry out more comprehensive assessments as a preparatory exercise at the early stage of projects in selected locales. BAIF, which implements climate adaptive agriculture projects, has conducted assessments in seven climatic zones of the country using CRiSTAL tool and the summary of the findings inform the project design.[40] NICRA on the basis of its vulnerability index has chosen 130 vulnerable districts in different climatic zones for carrying out technology demonstration.

However, many projects that carry out such assessments do not thoughtfully include them in project interventions. World Resources Institute (WRI), which studied 23 adaptation pilots[41] in India,

---

Box 5.2: *Community Perceptions on Climate Change*[42]

MRDS as part of community-based planning assessed the perceptions on climate change and coping mechanisms by the community. Community to community interphase within the project areas (across 7 districts covering 709 villages) showed that the community are aware of the changes in the climate and are in their own ways coping with it. Some of the key observations are as follows:

(a) Some of the community members were digging a pond in the middle of their paddy field, not for availing of the grant given by the Government of Meghalaya under the Aquaculture Mission as perceived by most but because they have observed the changes in rainfall pattern. Though the quantity of rain is the same in the past and present, the duration of rain is now shorter and hence there are flash floods and most importantly the quantity of water in the short span of time could not moisten the soil adequately for them to grow the same quantity of paddy like in the past. Hence, digging of the pond in the middle of the field is to ensure adequate water for paddy and for off-seasons vegetables as well as they could get a supplementary income from the fishes reared in these ponds.

(b) An interesting observation was made regarding the erratic occurrences of hailstone. Though the occurrence of hailstones can result in crop damage but the farmers pointed out that it is the timing of the occurrence that is important which can be a boon or curse to the farmers. If the hailstones occur when fruit trees are just flowering, the weaker flowers will fall resulting in fewer and bigger fruits rather than many smaller-sized fruits. Bigger fruits also fetch a better price for the farmers. However, the size of the hailstones is increasing which are having other effects. Earlier in paddy fields there were fewer pests and insects because the small freshwater fishes and aquatic animals residing in these paddy fields would devour off these pests. These large-sized hailstones are pounding the medicinal plants and herbs available in the slopes adjoining these paddy fields and these are leaching into these paddy fields killing many aquatic animals there leading to increased pests in paddy fields.

---

[40] A summary of findings from the seven climatic zones is provided in Annexure 1.

[41] Appadurai et al. *Scaling Success: Lessons from Adaptation Pilots in the Rainfed Regions of India*.

[42] Contribution from Augustus S. Suting, Project Director, Meghalaya Rural Development Society (MRDS).

found that 10 projects undertook vulnerability assessments, but only 5 of these made use of assessment findings significantly in the project action plan.

Apart from vulnerability assessments, institutions also carry out other need-based studies to understand farmers' preferences. BAIF in partnership with Climate Change, Agriculture and Food Security conducted a study on assessment of farmers' preferences and willingness to pay for climate-smart technologies in diverse rainfall zones in India, which included a quick vulnerability assessment along with other tools for measuring farmer preferences.

5.4.2 Key Interventions for Climate Change Adaptations

Based on vulnerability assessment and after assessing farmer preferences, the key interventions are drawn up; the list of interventions usually includes both conventional as well as new ones to adapt to climate change. While many of the interventions are conventional, there are new interventions such as agromet/hydromet services, water budgeting, climate-resilient crop varieties, etc., A brief description of interventions is given below:

(i) Soil and Water Conservation
- Redesigning of existing soil and water conservation measures and works[43] taking into account climate change information and availability of water and construction of new works.
- Vegetation cover on existing treated and reclaimed land such as grasses and trees, development of pastures, adoption of silvi-pasture models, afforestation, development of fuel wood and energy plantations, shelter belts and wind breaks, etc.

---

[43] Continuous contour trenches, stone bunds, water absorption trenches, gully plugs, farm bunds, earthen gully plugs, stone outlets, percolation pits/tanks, well recharge pits, sunken ponds, other water storage structures, and drainage line treatment such as loose boulder structures, nala bunds, gabion, check weir, and check dams.

- Irrigation management: participatory water budgeting and introduction of group irrigation systems with common facilities and equipment (drip, pumps, water pipes, etc.).
- Land reclamation measures such as land levelling, field contour terracing, de-siltation of village ponds, bunding, etc.

(ii) Soil Health Improvement and Productivity Enhancement Measures
- Soil testing and introduction of soil health cards;
- Deep ploughing and summer ploughing;
- Application of organic fertilizers, farm yard manure, green leaf, tank silt, vermin-compost;
- Replacement of chemical fertilizers and introduction of integrated nutrient management systems;
- Treatment of alkaline soils;
- De-acidification;
- Decontamination and de-toxification – use of organic pesticides.

(iii) Flood Management
- Early warning systems and flood forecasting;
- Reservoirs for storing excess water and subsequent safe release;
- Diversion of flows through safer areas;
- Embankment strengthening of river courses and water bodies;
- Channel improvement through desilting, dredging, and lining;
- Improving drainage capacity—by mapping inadequacies in drainage and improving natural as well artificial channels to carry the flood water;
- Community mobilization and training to manage the water bodies and drainage courses;
- Introduction of crop varieties that are resilient to inundation in flood-prone lowlands.

(iv) Promotion of CCA Farming Practices
- Crop diversification;
- Inter cropping;

- Multiple cropping with agrobiodiversity, crop rotation;
- Crop intensification, for example, Systematic Crop Intensification (SRI);
- Seed replacement;
- Introduction of new climate-resilient crops;
- agroforestry;
- Introduction of diversified sources of food such as kitchen gardens with back yard poultry and fish farms as integrated farming systems (animal husbandry, fisheries, vegetable, etc.);
- Preparation of household food and nutritional budgets;
- Establishment of fodder bank that is run commercially;
- Creation of postharvest storage facilities to reduce wastages and add value;
- Convergence with other research institutions, other central, and state-sponsored programs and institutions.

(v) **Measures to Mitigate Climate Change Risk**
- Introduction of resource centers/agri-clinics, seed farms, common equipment and agro-input centers, village knowledge centers, fodder banks;
- Improved connectivity with farmer call centers;
- Linkages with India Meteorological Department (IMD) weather stations and advisory services;
- Market information collection and dissemination;
- Crop Insurance.

(vi) **Capacity Building, Institution Building, and Knowledge Management**
- Training and capacity building of farmer households (HHs) on CCA measures, risk mitigation measures, integrated farming systems, etc., sustainable farming practices including organic farming, soil health management, water budgeting, and management;
- Knowledge dissemination through publication material, exposure visits, workshops for knowledge sharing, documentation of best practices/success stories.

At present, many of the above interventions are being implemented as stand-alone activities; however, resilience develops only if they are taken to the ground level as an integrated package of practices, which the vulnerability assessments should lead to. Some recent initiatives that hold promise are described below.

5.5 Recent Initiatives in Climate Adaptive Agriculture

5.5.1 Contingency Planning for Crops and Livestock

Climate variability in terms of frequency and quantum of rainfall and temperature necessitates a contingency plan for crops, fodder, and livestock rearing. Such plans have been found beneficial for farmers for dealing with weather aberrations.

CRIDA and ICAR under NICRA have developed detailed district-wise contingency plans for 576 districts[44] to provide a broad advisory to farmers at district level, prescribing alternate strategies in the event of climate variability, by factoring in crops, livestock, aquaculture practices, soil characteristics, infrastructural facilities, etc. These plans are developed based on certain simulated models for different weather conditions like delay in monsoon, occurrence of drought, flood, cyclones, frost/cold wave, etc. However, the cropping patterns and practices even within a block differ and hence such plans at district level are far too general; it is necessary that such plans are prepared and disseminated at least at the block level to make them closely relevant to local farms.

WOTR has facilitated contingent crop planning in a few blocks where they are

---

[44] These plans placed in the websites of the Ministry of Agriculture & Cooperation, GOI (www.agricoop.nic.in) and CRIDA (www.crida.in).

working in collaboration with CRIDA. Additionally, WOTR in collaboration with CRIDA has facilitated preparation of crop calendar and crop management plans in partnership with the State Agricultural Universities and India Meteorological Department for three main crops of Akole Block of Ahmednagar district. The plan spells out week-wise crop related activity to be carried out by the farmer under normal rain conditions as well as with delayed rains.

5.5.2 Agromet Advisory Services (AAS)

IMD has been issuing district-level weather data for seven weather parameters with weather forecast up to five days since 2008. Ministry of Earth Sciences has set up 130 Agrometeorological Field Units (AMFUs) in different agroclimatic zones of the country: each covering five to six districts operated by agricultural universities, ICAR, etc. AMFUs use these weather data along with district crop data to provide AAS. Twice a week through mass media agricultural bulletins are issued with specific advice covering crops, livestock, and horticulture crops. Increasingly this information is disseminated to farmers via mobile and Internet who subscribe for such services. However, the forecast being made at district/block level is far removed from the farmers' villages.

Some projects are being piloted for providing weather-based agricultural advisory services based on local weather data. WOTR's experience has been that to better equip farmers to respond appropriately to climate variations and minimize risks, local automated weather stations at appropriate distances to generate locale-specific crop-weather advisories is necessary. Contingent crop plans specific to the sub-agri-climatic zone, coupled with weather advisory will increase the response capacity of farmers and will minimize losses.

Box 5.3: *Weather-based Agro-advisory Services by WOTR*

The Agrometeorology service consists of four components that are interlinked:

- Acquisition of local weather data through automated weather stations, short range village-level weather forecasts from the IMD, and awareness creation of the impacts of weather variability on crops and livestock. Three-day village-level weather forecasts are received daily from IMD. Unusual/extreme weather event forecasts are immediately disseminated to villages.
- Crafting of agro-advisories based on weather forecasts and crop calendars prepared in collaboration with the State Agricultural Universities, and their dissemination (twice a week) followed by feedback gathering. Weather forecasts from IMD are fed into AGRIMATE (an automated crop weather calendar software). Indigenous knowledge and traditional agricultural practices of area are referenced. Geographic Information System (GIS) data base containing details of farmer-wise land, soil, water, farm resources, and crops grown together with socioeconomic data are prepared. In-house experts prepare weather-based crop growth stage and locale-specific agro-advisories.
- An automated content management system generates agro-advisories and disseminates them using a user profiling system. User profiling system matches the advisory with the farmer and disseminates the same through mobile SMSs in local language at least twice, weekly or whenever required. Multiple channels are used, SMSs, weekly wall-papers in local language and public announcement system, for advisory distribution. SMS service has been launched with six crops, sorghum, gram, onion, rice, wheat, and groundnut, and feedback loops have been set up. A weekly 'Krushi Salla' wall newspaper is also displayed in villages.
- On-site capacity building through farmer field schools, on-site knowledge, and technology transfer. Farmers' feedback sessions and feedback from field investigations are looped into the AGRIMATE to help generate

effective advisories, knowledge acquisition, and system development.

This system helps farmers to respond appropriately to local climatic variations. Crop calendars have been prepared for different crop varieties and crop growth stages for various meteorological conditions and soil types. The crop calendar helps prepare real-time crop-specific agriculture advisories based on local weather conditions and in accordance with crop growth stage. Crop mapping helps in monitoring yearly seasonal changes in the cropping pattern at plot level.

Source: WOTR[45] and NABARD.[46]

Cost benefit analysis for this service has not been assessed and WOTR at present does not charge fees for such services. They have measured only the overall impact of the range of services provided under the climate adaptive agriculture. There have been some studies on the impact of the weather-based agro-advisory services. While the studies generally mention that farmers gained by 10% by using weather services, more detailed studies are needed on crop-specific, location-specific as well as weather parameter-wise analysis.

NICRA has attempted such an exercise. A major objective of NICRA project is the customization of micro-level agromet advisories and their effective dissemination to help the farmers in enhancing the economic benefit by suggesting management practices suiting the anticipated weather conditions. Economic impact assessment of AAS issued to farmers of NICRA villages was carried out at six centers.[47] There were mixed results, farmers gained and in few cases there were losses as well. The losses were due to inaccurate prediction of weather and resultant advice.

Weather-based agro-advisory services can help farmers make climate-smart decisions but operation and maintenance of the weather stations need a lot of attention.

5.5.3 Climate-resilient Cropping Systems

Traditionally, technology transfer in agriculture has aimed at enhancing farm productivity. However, in the context of climate variability, farmers need to adapt quickly to enhance their resilience. Over the years researchers have developed many improved practices and technologies toward stabilizing agricultural production amidst seasonal variations. Adoption of such resilient practices and technologies by farmers appears to be a necessity than an option. Therefore, a reorientation in technology transfer approach is necessary.

Participatory on-farm demonstration of site-specific technologies is being carried out under NICRA in 100 villages spread over the different agroclimatic zones facing different effects of climate change. Some government programs are also propagating climate-smart practices. The climate-smart practices being carried out in scale include the following:

(a) **Community Nursery:** A staggered community nursery under assured irrigation is established at the village level as a local adaptation strategy in 11 states under NICRA. Three different nurseries at an interval of two weeks are raised to combat the problem experienced by farmers during deficit rainfall seasons. The two weeks gap in nursery rising makes available planting material for

[45] WOTR, "E-Technologies and Agro-Met Advisories: Helping Farmers Stay Ahead in the Weather Game" (presentation made in the National Workshop on Scaling Up Good Practices on Climate Change Adaptation, New Delhi, October 19, 2014).

[46] NABARD, *Weather Based, Farmer-Centric Agrometeorology* (Mumbai: NABARD, 2015).

[47] NICRA, "All India Co-ordinated Research Project on Agrometeorology: Annual report, 2014–15" (2015), http://www.nicra-icar.in/nicrarevised/images/publications/NICRA_APR_2014–15.pdf, accessed on August 31, 2016.

crops that need transplanting and enables farmers to face delay in monsoons. In Bihar, state department of agriculture is promoting farmer-managed community nurseries under assured irrigation to make available paddy seedlings for transplanting to meet contingent situations. Under the scheme, a community nursery in 5 acres per panchayat and 150 acres in each district is taken up. The subsidy for each nursery given to the farmer is ₹6500 per acre to cover the cost of production and ₹1,000 per acre to farmers for purchasing of seedlings for transplanting in 10 acres from 1 acre of nursery. The total amount supported by the department for 1 acre of community nursery is ₹16,500. Promoting community nursery with short duration varieties is found to be an effective strategy in the event of deficit rainfall situation in July as being experienced in several districts in Bihar in recent years.

(b) **Direct Seeding of Paddy:** In direct-seeded rice cultivation, raising of nursery for transplantation is done away with. In case of delay in monsoon or shortage of water, direct seeding gives the farmer flexibility to take up direct sowing with a suitable duration variety to fit into the shorter growing season. This allows timely sowing of the succeeding Rabi wheat. Direct sown paddy consumes relatively less water compared to transplanted flooded paddy. Energy demand for pumping of irrigation water is also less and saving can be much higher during deficit rainfall situations compared to transplanted rice. Direct sowing is being adopted for cultivating both coarse rice and basmati rice.

(c) **Drought Tolerant Paddy Cultivars:** Deficit rainfall in July affects the timely transplanting of paddy in several rainfed districts. Long duration (140–150 days) cultivars are preferred by farmers who take up sowing of nursery in June and transplanting in July. However, due to deficit rainfall situation in July, farmers wait for transplanting till August. This results in low productivity and can affect the timely sowing of succeeding Rabi crop. Stress tolerant paddy varieties of shorter duration that are amenable both for transplanting and direct sowing are being promoted. Yields with short duration varieties are slightly lower due to early maturation. However, short duration varieties serve as best bet options for drought proofing in rainfed rice cultivation as they provide a significant yield advantage in drought years over the traditional long duration varieties. Short duration finger millet varieties, pulses, and oil seeds for delayed monsoon/deficit rainfall districts are also being promoted.

(d) **Inter Cropping in Scanty Rainfall Area:** In scarce rainfall zones of India, practice of sole cropping (cotton, soybean, pigeon pea, and millets) is predominant but is risky and often results in low yields or sometimes even in crop failure due to erratic monsoon rainfall and skewed distribution. In such areas intercropping with a legume crop to minimize risk in crop production, ensures reasonable returns at least from the intercrop and also improve soil fertility with a legume intercrop is being advocated.

(e) **Farmer field schools** have been the medium of working with farmers on transfer of technology. Farmer water schools and farmer climate schools are also functional under a few projects. However, post-project availability of the technology will be critical for wider adoption. For example, regular supply of climate-resilient seeds needs to be ensured in the seed supply chain

5.5.4 System of Crop Intensification (SCI) for Climate Change Adaptation:

Green revolution advocated increased production by adopting improved varieties of seeds which needed more water and more inputs of agro chemicals thus raising costs of production and also risks. The SCI aims to get higher output with less use of and less expenditure on land, labor, capital, and water by making agro-ecological modifications[48] in crop management. SCI which was originally carried out for rice are now being widely adopted for rainfed finger millets, wheat, sugarcane, mustard, and maize in hill districts, pigeon pea, chickpea, moong, vegetables, turmeric, and lac in India. The detailed costs and return data show that average increase in profits have been 250% for rice, 86% for wheat, 67% for pulses, 93% for oilseeds, and 47% for vegetables.[49]

WOTR promotes the system of crop intensification as part of climate adaptive agriculture.[50] This low-input crop production methodology enhances productivity and uses inputs more efficiently while maintaining the resource base and appears to withstand some shocks due to climate variability, especially in poor soils. Field trials were conducted across WOTR project locations for various crops, namely, maize, groundnut, sunflower, turmeric, wheat, and a variety of vegetables. Almost all field trials have shown significant impacts in increased agricultural productivity ranging from 30%–80%, while reducing the cost of production by 40%–50%. Through crop demonstrations with regular on-site technical hand-holding, farmers were encouraged to have small demonstration plots beside their regular fields. In this manner, the difference in the crops between the two methods was immediately visible.

5.5.5 Watershed Management Plus

Watershed management results in increased soil moisture, groundwater recharge, and water percolation, enhanced water storage in tanks and increased soil fertility. Moreover, degraded lands are reclaimed and carbon sequestration is improved. Additionally, it has resulted in increased intensity of agriculture, increased private investments on irrigation infrastructure (mainly borewells), and increased area under irrigated agriculture.

However, the watershed programs have had certain shortcomings as has been the experience of WOTR, WASSAN, BAIF, etc.:

- Indiscriminate Exploitation of Water Resources: With the augmented groundwater resources, private investments also increased considerably. The competitive exploitation of augmented groundwater by individual farmers is pushing the villages toward irretrievable positions. Absence of institutional arrangements for groundwater management and equitable water use by the watershed HHs is a critical issue.
- Commercial and Water-intensive Crops: The watershed development program encouraged farmers to choose low water-consuming crops. However, these efforts may not be sustainable in the long run, as market forces for immediate gains influence farmers to choose commercial and water-intensive crops.
- Weak Institutional Base: Only few of the watershed-based user groups and committees work well after the project period. As a result there is no social mechanism in place to restrain farmers' crop choices or water usage. These institutions need a revised action plan and goal beyond water shed development on how to sustain and manage investments and common resources.

---

[48] These modifications include (a) planting young seedlings singly with optimally wide spacing for better exposure to sun and air, (b) providing only sufficient water to support growth of roots and soil organisms, (c) adding as much organic matter to soil system to support soil health and functioning, and (d) breaking up soil surface in the process of controlling weeds actively aerating the soil.

[49] NABARD, *The System of Crop Intensification* (Mumbai: Department of Economic Analysis and Research, NABARD Head Office, 2016).

[50] WOTR, *SCI: System of Crop Intensification—A step Towards Climate Resilience* (2015), http://www.wotr.org/sites/default/files/SCI-System-of-Crop-Intensification-Booklet.pdf, accessed on July 16, 2016.

The experience of WOTR, WASSAN, BAIF, and others working on watershed development indicates that climate variability is already affecting crop production, causing economic losses for the farmer despite the tangible benefits of participatory watershed development. Additional initiatives are needed to build on the watershed development programs which include (a) water budgeting and crop budgeting/choices based on water availability, (b) modifications for community ponds for storing more water in good monsoon years, (c) individual farm ponds for storing excess runoff during monsoons and to ensure water availability for irrigation in critical crop growth periods, etc.

(a) Water and Crop Budgeting: Groundwater is considered to be less vulnerable than surface sources to climate fluctuations and can therefore help to stabilize agricultural populations and reduce the need for farmers to migrate when drought threatens agricultural livelihoods.[51] Groundwater is a sensitive resource in that people who own its sources need to use it judiciously, while ensuring that the needs of the community are met. This is particularly important in semi-arid regions. Since groundwater is an open-access, common pool resource, protection of the resource is not possible unless the users agree to cooperate and manage the resource themselves in a sustainable manner. This requires local data of the water available to plan its use to meet the community's various needs—domestic, livestock, agriculture, and other livelihoods. There is better acceptance of water budgeting when it is participatory, with data displayed, accompanied by appropriate crop planning and microirrigation (MI) with agricultural guidance. Adaptive capacities are built to face summer months and years of drought. These interventions have to be embedded in institutions that have regular working beyond the typical project phase.

Community-based Groundwater Management has been scaled up in AP under three different projects—Andhra Pradesh Farmers Managed Groundwater System(APFAMGS),[52] Social Regulations in Water Management (SRWM) by the Centre for World Solidarity (CWS) and its partner NGOs, and Andhra Pradesh Drought Adaptation Initiatives (APDAI) program being implemented by the WASSAN with its partner NGOs. All the three models focus on influencing communities through generation of information on groundwater though the degree of using scientific methods varies.

Community Groundwater Management Models

Community-based Groundwater Management Models	Description
APFAMGS (APWELL)	Dug new borewells for a group of HHs not having access to water, with clear sharing, groundwater monitoring, and water use efficiency measures. Limited to 'new unexploited' areas. APWELL has been transformed into the largest groundwater awareness program in the state premised on: (i) communities monitoring the groundwater status regularly with knowledge and scientific principles. (ii) sharing knowledge of alternative crop systems and evolving norms for groundwater management (with facilitation).
SRWM (CWS and partners programme)	This program was initiated on a limited scale and based on regulations: (i) the community adopts a norm of 'no new borewells'. (ii) increasing system efficiency through the provision of collective sprinkler irrigation sets. (iii) borewell owners share their water with neighboring farmers, leading to a substantial reduction of the number of families in the village without water.
APDAI (facilitated by WASSAN)	This initiative followed an 'area approach' for groundwater management where the borewell owners pool their individual borewells to provide supplemental critical irrigation to a larger rainfed area (entire block) for survival of rainfed crops. The community has to abide by the following rules: (i) no new borewells for at least 10 more years. (ii) all the land within the specified area (including those without water) will have a right to supplemental irrigation for Kharif rainfed crops. (iii) pipeline network is provided by the project so that water can be taken to any part in the block/area.

---

[51] P. S. Vijay Shankar, Himanshu Kulkarni and Sunderrajan Krishnan, "India's Groundwater Challenge and the Way Forward," *Economic and Political Weekly* xlvi, no 2. 37 (2011).

[52] Food and Agriculture Organisation (FAO), *Andhra Pradesh Farmer Managed Groundwater Systems Project: Terminal Report* (GCP/IND/175/NET) (2010), Rome: Food and Agriculture Organization of the United Nations.

The major differences between the models include: (i) two of the models are on a small scale while APFAMGS is on a bigger scale; (ii) two of the models use social regulation as a means to achieve sustainable groundwater use, while the APFAMGS depends on awareness building; and (iii) contribution of farmers varies between 75% APDAI to zero APFAMGS.

Features of the three institutional models[53] are compared below:

Features	APFAMGS	SRWM	APDAI
Awareness on groundwater situation	High	High	High
Participation in management	Limited to well owners	Well owners as well as well sharing farmers (high)	All the farmers in the well network area (high)
Rules and regulations	Yes (informal and voluntary)	Yes (formal)	Yes (formal and binding)
Extent of well-sharing	Limited	High	High
Cost sharing	No	Yes	Yes
Practicing recommendations	Moderate	High	Low
Additional infrastructure support	Nil	Yes (MI)	Yes (pipelines and MI)
Key to success	Professional approach	Leadership and incentives (subsidy for MI)	Incentives (subsidy for pipelines and MI)
Impacts on access to water	Moderate	High	Moderate
Impacts on cropping pattern	Limited	High	High
Nature of key impact	Reduction in overexploitation of groundwater	Conservation of water and sharing of water	Conservation and sharing of water
Impact on equity	No	Yes	Yes
Scalability	Good	Poor	Moderate
Sustainability	?	?	?

Sustainability of these initiatives is a major concern in all the approaches. None of the approaches have a well-defined exit protocol, while the APDAI appears to be well placed in this regard as its process involves a number of departments and formal institutions. At the same time, it requires strong leadership at the village level to implement and take the initiative forward, especially in the context of people's contribution. In the case of SRWM, its present success is mainly due to the commitment of NGO partners in the absence of any contribution from the farmers. Besides, in the absence of contribution the financial sustainability of the initiatives would be a big concern, especially once the external funding stops. The weak sustainability of APFAMGS initiative was evident during the no-fund phase.[54] Hence, fund flows appear to be critical for the success of the initiatives. The initiatives may continue in some of the villages due to strong leadership and commitment of the local NGOs even beyond the present funding, as they are at a smaller scale. Thus, scaling up these initiatives requires much more planning and designing.

(b) Community Ponds: Large number of tanks, with substantial water storage capacity constructed long ago, have become defunct due to neglect, non-maintenance and silting up, especially in peninsular India. Due to neglect of community tanks, surplus rainfall (runoff) is not stored properly and used. During prolonged dry spells at critical stages, on account of no or low storage of water for protective irrigation, crop failures and production shortfalls are experienced in some years.

Identification of these structures to carry out desiltation with farmers' participation has been an activity which has been carried out successfully by many projects and programs. The rich silt deposited in these structures is used by farmers for spreading in the fields, to improve the water holding capacity of soils. This intervention has helped in increasing the surface water resource availability and increased the groundwater recharge observed through water table measurements in wells located nearer to the tanks.

---

[53] V.R. Reddy, M.S. Reddy and S.K. Rout, "Groundwater governance: A tale of three participatory models in Andhra Pradesh, India," *Water Alternatives* 7 no. 2 (2014): 275–297.

[54] Shilp Verma et al. *Andhra Pradesh Farmer Managed Groundwater Systems (APFAMGS): A Reality Check* (2012), www.iwmi.org/iwmi-tata/apm2012, accessed on July 18, 2016.

(c) Individual Farm Ponds: Small scale water harvesting structures at individual farm level enable reuse of harvested water during critical periods of growth stage and for providing pre-sowing irrigation to next crop. Various models of small scale water harvesting systems have been promoted by governmental and non-governmental organizations involving different farm pond sizes, lining material, and reuse of harvested water for different crops at critical crop growth stages. Farmers earlier were reluctant to dig farm ponds in their lands since they lost cultivable land and income from the pond area. However, with repeated failure of monsoons and erratic rainfall, there is more interest in farm ponds from farmers. If constructed well, the farm ponds have the following benefits; (a) increased area under irrigation, (b) two crops per year, (c) many farmers undertake higher value vegetable farming earning additional income, and (d) increase in groundwater recharge.[55]

5.5.6 Custom Hiring Centers (CHCs):

About 80% of the land holdings in the country are operated by small and marginal farmers owning < 1 and 1–2 ha holdings, respectively. Labor shortage at peak times of demand is a serious problem faced by these farmers. With fewer rainy days and also delayed monsoons, in rainfed areas, the window for taking up of timely land preparation, and sowing operations is narrow. Adoption of climate-resilient practices such as soil incorporation of legume catch crops and crop residues to improve soil health and resource conservation technologies are linked to timely access to appropriate farm machinery at reasonable cost. Small and marginal farmers cannot invest in costly farm machinery and depend on hiring of implements to carryout agricultural operations in their fields. Mechanization brings

in timeliness and precision to agricultural operations, greater field coverage over a short period, cost-effectiveness, efficiency in use of resources and applied inputs, conservation of available soil moisture and provision of adequate drainage of excess rain and floodwaters.[56] It also reduces drudgery.

CHCs for farm implements are being set up to ensure that equipments are made available at village level by different governments, under NICRA as well as some externally aided projects. Usually a village organization (VO) of farmers is set up and committee of farmers manages the CHC. The rates for hiring the machines/implements are decided by the committee. The revenue generated from hiring charges is used for repair and maintenance of the implements and remaining amount goes into the revolving fund. Different types of farm machinery are stocked in these CHCs; the most popular are reported to be rotavator, zero till drill, drum seeder, multi-crop planter, power weeder, and chaff cutter. Usually the village-level CHCs are set up with a capital of ₹0.7 million to ₹1 million; some are fully supported by grants while in some others the village-level organization of farmers contribute a part of the cost to ensure ownership and good governance.

Many government programs are providing grants for setting up CHCs; however, they need to identify and work with well-governed grassroot institutions so that these equipments are available for all the farmers in the village and not just a few elite farmers.

5.5.7 Microirrigation

Microirrigation, with drip and micro-sprinklers, owing to its ability of applying water to only a small portion of soil volume resulting in minimal surface evaporation, and deep percolation, is a far more efficient method having an overall irrigation

[55] NICRA, *Smart Technologies and Practices for Climate Smart Agriculture* (2014). http://www.nicra-icar.in/nicrarevised/images/publications/Smart%20practices%20&%20technologies.pdf, accessed on July 18, 2016.

[56] NICRA, *Smart Technologies and Practices for Climate Smart Agriculture* (2014). http://www.nicrai-car.in/nicrarevised/images/publications/Smart%20practices%20&%20technologies.pdf, accessed on July 18, 2016.

Box 5.4: *CHCs by Community Managed Resource Centers (CMRC), Maharashtra Arthik Vikas Mahamandal (MAVIM)*

MAVIM has promoted three-tiered grassroot institutions of women SHGs, VOs, and federation of SHGs. In Thane district, the Zilla Parishad developed a scheme to set up village-level equipment and tool banks since monsoon was erratic, sowing window was limited, labor shortage was acute, and there was a rush for hiring such equipments. Usually the poorer farmers suffered the most. The CMRCs developed convergence plans for this scheme. VOs consulted the SHGs on the equipments in demand and in short supply and thus carried out a need assessment. CMRCs informed the Zilla parishad that they will collect VO contribution at 10% of the cost of the equipment bank in order to ensure good governance. In

Thane district, 33 VOs are operating these equipment banks with total outlay of ₹0.0226 billion.

VO has hired a small shed to park the equipments and tools. Norms for hiring have been made in consultation with members. Some of the women members have been trained in operations of the machines. Funds collected from the service charges are paid for maintenance as well as for wages for operators. Women mention that the equipments have enabled timely agri operations apart from reducing their drudgery.

Source: Contributed by Mahila Arthik Vikas Mahamandal (MAVIM), Maharashtra.

---

efficiency of almost 90%. Apart from saving irrigation water, the MI system enhances the economic returns from crop by increasing the yield, reduces energy requirements due to pumping of lesser amount of water while also enabling the uniform application of precise amount of nutrients and pesticides along with irrigation water. Thus, its potential to combat the vagaries of climate change, especially in water scarce areas is very high.

Launched in 2006 as centrally sponsored scheme, the MI scheme was revised and up scaled to NMMI in June 2010. It was subsumed under NMSA as OFWM since 2014 and the MI component of OFWM has been subsumed under Pradhan Mantri Krishi Sinchai Yojana (PMKSY) since 1 April 2015. PMKSY with ₹500 billion allocation for next 5 years has major thrust on farm ponds and MI. The government's key policy instrument for MI promotion continues to be subsidizing farmers' capital costs of drip and sprinkler systems.

Since its inception, most of the states have taken efforts to popularize the scheme by increasing the state's share of the subsidy. Five states (Andhra Pradesh, Gujarat, Karnataka, Maharashtra, and Rajasthan), belonging to the water scarce areas, recorded relatively higher area coverage under both the drip and

sprinkler irrigation systems. Farmers' acceptance of the technology was high in areas (a) experiencing chronic water deficit and over-exploitation of groundwater and (b) water scarce areas with undulating topography and sandy soils, where the topography and soil characteristics restrict the use of conventional irrigation systems.

AP and Gujarat (Box 5.5) had created special purpose vehicles for the implementation of the scheme that had led to an improved performance in these two states. Both these models emphasize safeguarding farmers' interests and have in place various oversight measures to this end.

An evaluation by the Planning Commission[57] of MI is one of its kind since there have been very few assessments on the impact of MI.

(a) Overall, an overwhelming majority of the beneficiaries reported their net returns from crops irrigated with MI systems as better in comparison to that earned before adopting the MI systems.

---

[57] Planning Commission, Evaluation Study of Integrated Scheme of Micro Irrigation, PEO Report no 222 (2014), http://www.indiaenvironmentportal.org.in/files/file/micro%20irrigation.pdf, accessed on November 8, 2016.

Box 5.5: *Gujarat Green Revolution Company Model*

- Single window approach, farmer does not need to go to different places for sanction of application.
- Farmer has the choice of MIS supplier and type of MI system.
- Free access to farmers of same quality product linked with market with a competitive edge.
- System design as per cropping pattern and as per farmer's/field requirement.
- Maintenance, warranty and guarantee of MI components for five years.
- Inbuilt agronomic as well as system maintenance advisory services through SMS services.

- Inbuilt insurance of the MIS system as well as farmer's life.
- Effective complaint redressel system and toll free helpline number.
- Promotion of high nutrient use efficiency: water soluble fertilizers.
- Third party inspection at the factory site and also on every farmers MI System installed on his field.
- Per hectare additional income after installation of MI is reported to be ₹17,000.[58]

As of March 2016, Gujarat has covered 8,13,499 farmers and 13,08,143 hectares under MI, that is, about 15% of farmers and 10% of agricultural land.

(b) The area under irrigation increased by 10%.

(c) One of the implicit objectives of the MI scheme is to bring about a change in the water-intensive cropping patterns with that of other high-value cash crops requiring less irrigation water through the MI systems. The survey finds that the cropping pattern shifted toward that of other high value crops, as the areas under soybean, cotton, paddy, wheat, maize, cumin, bajra, etc., registered a decline, while, that under the crops like, groundnut, mustard, banana, kinnow, orange, chillies, sugarcane, gram, guar, etc., increased.

(d) The adoption of MI systems significantly reduced the farm labor requirements by over a quarter, particularly during the application of irrigation and weeding. Nearly 100% of the beneficiaries reported a significant reduction in the occurrence of weeds on their farms irrigated with the MI systems.

(e) Only about one-fourth of the sample beneficiaries were applying fertigation/chemigation to their crops through their MI systems. The proportion of such beneficiaries was the highest (74%) in Maharashtra, followed by

AP (52%), and Gujarat (26%), while no beneficiary farmer was applying fertigation/chemigation in the states of Chhattisgarh, Odisha, and Karnataka. Among the beneficiaries who were applying fertigation/chemigation through MI systems the consumption rate of fertilizer declined significantly by an overall average of 24% after the adoption of MI systems. Among those beneficiaries who were applying insecticides/pesticides with their MI systems the average consumption of insecticides/pesticides recorded a decline of 18%.

(f) A substantial reduction in electricity consumption due to MI was observed among the sample farmers. The average annual savings in energy was higher (370 kWh/ha) for the sample farmers practicing drip irrigation, as compared to the sprinkler irrigation where a reduction of about 198 kWh/ha was observed.

---

[58] GGRC, *Micro Irrigation in Gujarat: A Case Study of State Effectiveness* (2015), https://macrofinance.nipfp.org.in/PDF/10_Sugoor_Micro_Irrigation_in_Gujarat.pdf, accessed on July 16, 2016.

(g) The economic analysis of MI has revealed that drip and sprinkler methods have generated additional income among the sample farmers.[59]

With 50% subsidy being available from governments, the rest of the cost has to be borne by the farmers. However, the loan off-take for MI is very limited. The evaluation study by planning commission[60] shows that only a miniscule proportion (4%) of beneficiaries availed loan from the bank, almost all of the remaining farmers did not apply for the loan. In most of the cases, farmers were not aware about the availability and processes involved. A significant proportion has availed loan facility only in the states of Gujarat (14%) and Rajasthan (10%). The minimum payback period was found to be less than one year for cash crops and the maximum duration spread over a period of two to three years in both drip and sprinkler methods. With thrust on crop loans and interest subsidy being available only for short-term loans of less than a year, longer term loans for MI did not seem popular.

Some issues in adoption of MI include the following:

- Rarely, a farmer has all his lands in a continuous stretch at a single place. Installing separate MI units for each fragment of land results in cost escalation.
- Resource-poor farmers having marginal landholdings are not able to bear the high initial investments for adopting the MI technologies. On account of such a sizeable chunk of farmers being left out of the ambit of the scheme due to their being unable to afford even their own share of the costs after the subsidies, the adoption of MI systems remains largely/limited to those few who have the resources to afford them.
- Poor quality of after sales services even in states like Gujarat and AP (despite support by special purpose vehicles) highlights the need for better quality of service by private sector.
- As the MI scheme focuses on the horticultural crops and other high-value cash crops, the lack of agronomical support services demotivates farmers from adopting the MI systems. However, only a few of the states, Gujarat and Punjab, have provisions for the agronomic support services to the farmers.

The potential for adoption of MI in the country is estimated to be 69.5 million hectares. The potential realized is only 18%. With per hectare average cost of ₹50,000, the total funds required are ₹3125 trillion. With yearly budgets of ₹30 billion by the central and state governments, for MI to realize its potential will take several decades. MI potential can be realized only if farmers and financial institutions come forward to make the necessary investments instead of depending on government subsidies.

5.5.8 Solar Pump Sets

Solar installations are considered as climate mitigation and adaptation strategy. India has approximately 18 million grid connected pump sets and 7 million diesel pump sets. India uses more than 4 billion liters of diesel and around 85 million tons of coal per annum to support water pumping for irrigation.[61] The farms are partly irrigated due to erratic grid supply, increasing unreliability of monsoon rains, nighttime supply

[59] The drip method has proved to be the most efficient mode of irrigation in the water scarce areas, providing additional annual income that was more than one lakh per hectare in case of chilly cultivated by sample farmers. Similarly, sprinkler methods provided an additional income of nearly 60,000 per hectare for the farmers growing garlic.

[60] Planning Commission, Evaluation Study of Integrated Scheme of Micro Irrigation.

[61] Shakti Foundation, Feasibility Analysis for Solar agricultural Water Pumps in India (2014), http://shaktifoundation.in/wp-content/uploads/2014/02/feasibility-analysis-for-solar-High-Res-1.pdf, accessed on July 18, 2016.

for agricultural operations during peak demand seasons and high cost of diesel. The main advantage is that solar radiation is intense when the need for irrigation is high. Further, solar power is available at the point of use, making the farmer independent of fuel supplies or electrical transmission lines.

Union budget 2014–15 had allocated ₹4 billion for installation of 0.1 million solar agricultural pump sets. Ministry of New and Renewable Energy (MNRE) launched the "Solar Pumping Programme for Irrigation and Drinking Water" for promoting solar agricultural pump installations. The program targets to implement 0.1 million solar pumps every year and it is expected that by the year 2020–21, at least 0.1 million solar pumps will be deployed out of which 60% are expected to be for irrigation purposes. As per the scheme, the ministry provides 30% of the cost, beneficiary 10%, and the rest from state subsidies/loans, etc., capital subsidy level varies between 40% and 80%.[62]

Studies are needed on actual benefits to the farmers. Current economics indicate an internal rate of return (IRR) of 10% for replacement of diesel pumps with solar pumps without factoring in crop yield improvement benefits due to water availability on demand. Considering even 10% yield benefit, the IRR would be 19%. However, the upfront cost of a solar pump (2.2 KW) is about 10 times of a conventional pump (₹0.35 million versus ₹30,000) and hence capital subsidy and financing support are needed. Subsidy is essential for development of solar-based pump set market but heavy dependence on subsidy is unsustainable in the long term. However, with improvements in scale of economies, local manufacturing, adoption rates by

farmers, and marketability and also bankability of such investments, the subsidy rates can come down and affordability can go up. Adoption rates by farmers will improve with trust worthiness of the product and after sales services. The costs and economics of solar pumping system have to be more closely studied as to whether the avoided costs of fossil fuels is sufficient to recover the high initial investment costs of solar pumps. Only then it will be clear as to whether solar pumping systems can offer a mainstream solution for irrigation problems.

For the governments the benefits can be high. Replacement of 1 million diesel pumps with solar pumps would result in diesel use mitigation of 9.4 billion liters over the life cycle of solar pumps which translates into diesel subsidy saving of ₹84 billion and carbon dioxide emission abatement of 25.3 million tonnes. Forex savings of USD 300 million per annum on diesel imports for replacement of 1 million diesel pumps translating into Forex savings of USD 4.5 billion over pump life.

Solar pumps work better in areas with better water tables, surface irrigation mechanisms, and in terms of affordability medium and large farmers will be able to afford as of now. Solar pumps are considered ideal for ground and surface water abundant areas such as North Bihar, coastal Odisha, North Bengal, Assam, and eastern UP. However, in western and southern regions, replacing electric and diesel pumps by solar pumps can result in accelerated withdrawal and depletion of groundwater. In western and southern India, a better option may be to connect solar pumps with grid, treat farmers as independent power producers and offer them guarantee to buy surplus power at an attractive price.[63] As irrigation

[62] Rajasthan has been a pioneer in promoting solar water pumps and offers an additional subsidy of 40% over and above the MNRE subsidy, which means that the solar water pump owner gets 70% subsidy in total. In Tamil Nadu, a total of 80% subsidy is provided, whereas in Punjab, the total subsidy comes to about 70%.

[63] Tushaar Shah and Avinash Kishore, *Solar-powered Pump Irrigation and India's Groundwater Economy: A Preliminary Discussion of Opportunities and Threats* (2012), http://www.iwmi.cgiar.org/iwmi-tata/PDFs/2012_Highlight-26.pdf, accessed on July 18, 2016.

needs are intermittent, between 200 and 250 days in a year, a solar pump can feed surplus power back in the grid in collaboration with electricity authorities and local utilities. Innovations like that of Solar Pump Irrigators' Cooperative Enterprise (SPICE) selling power to the grid needs to be the way forward—see Box 5.6 below.

Box 5.6: *A Climate-smart Sustainable Agriculture*[64]

SPICE has been set up in Dhundi, Anand district, Gujarat. Members of this cooperative are using solar power not only to run irrigation pumps but also pool their surplus energy to sell to the Madhya Gujarat Vij Company Ltd (MGVCL) at ₹4.63/unit under a 25-year power purchase agreement (PPA). International Water Management Institute (IWMI) has installed the pump sets for this pilot. Gujarat Energy Research and Management Institute is training and providing technical support to the farmers. The cooperative society members being small farmers, IWMI has supported them financially for purchase and installation of pumps and solar panels. The institute has so far funded about ₹0. 04 million in the project which includes project management costs as well.

The Dhundi SPICE's six solar pumps, can generate nearly 85,000 units (kilowatt-hours) of energy annually, assuming 5 units per kW on an average daily over 300 sunny days. Of this, the six farmer-members would use 40,000 units for watering seven acres land and inject the balance 45,000 units into the grid, grossing over ₹0.2 million revenues per annum from power sales to the distribution company or Discom.

Benefit to farmers: Under the PPA contract, the six farmers have surrendered their right to apply for grid power connections for 25 years. Solar power is much cheaper than diesel—roughly 3,600 liters are required to produce 40,000 units—and is also more reliable than subsidized grid power that is available for only 7–8 hours daily, with voltage fluctuations and during nighttime in half of the days every month. Solar power, by contrast, is uninterrupted, predictable, available during daytime, and free of cost. Income from solar power sales is also free of risk from drought, floods, pests, and diseases. All that is required is land for erecting panels.

The Dhundi farmers initially were worried about the land footprint of the solar panels. But they are already experimenting with a range of high-value crops like spinach, carrots, garlic, beet, and a few medicinal plants that grow well under panels.

The Dhundi-pattern SPICEs, will liberate the Discoms and state governments from debilitating farm power subsidies. Had the Dhundi farmers obtained grid power connections for 56.4 kW instead of solar pumps, MGVCL would have to provide them over 162,000 units of electricity—taking 8 hours supply for 360 days—at ₹0.7/unit, as against its cost of ₹4.5/unit to deliver. Even if only two-thirds of the power supplied was used, the annual subsidy burden on MGVCL would have worked out to well over ₹0.4 million. Besides, MGVCL would have had to invest ₹1.2 million on poles and cables to connect the tubewells to the grid, at ₹0.2 million for every new connection. The annual interest and depreciation cost on this investment, even at a conservative 10%, would be ₹0.12 million.

The Dhundi SPICE will also enable MGVCL earn money from the sale of renewable energy certificates. As per the PPA, the sale of Renewable Energy Certificates (RECs) against the entire 85,000 units generated by the SPICE would accrue to the Discom. Taking the current value of ₹3,500/megawatt-hours for RECs being traded on electricity exchanges, it comes to an income of almost ₹0.3 million.

Taken together, the subsidy on grid power saved, not having to bear the amortized cost of connecting tubewells, and sale of RECs would leave MGVCL better off by about ₹0.82 million annually for 25 years. That, over 45,000 units, translates into a gain of ₹18.2 per unit. State governments have until now been promoting solar irrigation pumps by offering around ₹90,000/kW subsidy on capital costs to farmers

---

[64] Tushaar Shah et al., "Sustainable agriculture: A new Anand cooperative model—this time, in solar farming", http://indianexpress.com/article/india/india-news-india/sustainable-agriculture-a-new-anand-cooperative-model-this-time-in-solar-farming-2807828/, accessed on July 18, 2016.

opting out of grid power connections. A better way, however, would be through PPAs that guarantee attractive feed-in tariffs. The capital cost subsidy on solar pumps can actually be scaled down to ₹50,000/kW and farmers instead be offered feed-in tariffs of ₹8–9/unit.

India's currently grid-connected irrigation tubewells account for some ₹700 billion of power subsidies. Dhundi-pattern SPICEs can, however, painlessly eliminate farm power subsidies once and for all. They can also be the answer for groundwater overexploitation. The existing regime of electricity subsidies mutes farmers' incentive to conserve both power and water. By weaning them off grid power, farmers are being helped to make money from conserving energy and water. Moreover, metering energy will make it possible for measuring water withdrawals to manage a scarce natural resource better.

A 7.5 kW solar pump with an assured power buy-back contract at ₹8/unit can enable a one hectare of farm to meet irrigation needs and generate extra income of ₹60,000, equivalent to what three buffaloes give.

Besides, there is the promise of making irrigation climate-smart. Using electricity and diesel in groundwater irrigation produces about 26 million tonnes of carbon emissions—about 5% of India's total. Solarizing the groundwater economy could eliminate this huge carbon-footprint, reducing the carbon intensity of the country's economic growth. Though Dhundi SPICE is a small experiment, it can go a long way in reconfiguring groundwater economy and agrarian livelihoods.

Some of the states like Rajasthan and Gujarat are combining drip irrigation, rain water harvesting, and solar pumping to bring additional area under irrigation, especially horticulture and cash crops and increase farmers' income. Such an approach can ensure adaptation gains and immediate benefits to farmers along with possible reduction in GHG emissions and global warming potential of agriculture.

5.6 Livestock-related Interventions

There are several environmental factors that contribute to heat stress to livestock which includes high temperature, radiant solar energy, high relative humidity (RH), wind velocity, etc. therefore, methods to mitigate the heat stress are useful to dairy farmers. During heat stress, feed intake of livestock generally reduces and therefore impacts livestock production. Several research findings envisaged that diets high in grain and low in fiber cause less heat stress in animals. Increasing potassium to 1.3%–1.5%, sodium to 0.5%–0.6% and magnesium to 0.3%–0.4% may reduce heat stress to animal. There are a number of measures available and NICRA has also undertaken a project under multi-institutional mode for climate-resilient livestock farming system. These research findings require to be adopted in field condition.

Selective breeding of indigenous breeds which are adapted to local climate, having high milk yield and other economic traits of competitive advantages need to be undertaken/strengthened in their native breed tract. These breeds required to be identified in consultation with line departments/ICAR institutes/veterinary universities, etc. and area-specific approach needs to be undertaken for proliferation, conservation, and genetic upgradation of indigenous breeds of cattle, buffaloes, sheep, goats, draught animals, etc. At present, banks are reluctant to finance indigenous breed.

Slaughter of cow is banned in most of the states in India. Extra males/unproductive females are very difficult to be disposed off which has increased the uneconomic stray cattle population (Cattle have been orphaned as they have lost their economic productivity). This is also another cause of concern as they tend to compete with common pool of available feed resources apart from generating emissions leading to global warming. Sex selection toward females will help in producing larger number of females and also will help in strengthening food production.

The other measures being undertaken are environmental modification by providing appropriate sheds, shelters for reducing solar radiation, suitable spaces for comfort, orientation of shed, creating provision for ventilation, providing cooling infrastructure depending upon various agroclimatic zone, etc. could be useful for heat stress mitigation.

5.7 Himalayas and Northeastern States: Struggle Between Adaptation and Mitigation

The Himalayan states and northeastern states are ecologically more fragile and more vulnerable to climate change impact. Increase in temperature affects the fruit crops and forces the horticultural farmers to move plantations to higher elevations. High intensity, shorter duration rains make cropping difficult. Floods from snow melt, heavier than usual rains, longer intervals between rains, and emergence of certain types of insects are issues that require adaptation measures. Rising temperatures also provide opportunities for newer crops and higher productivity of traditional crops, but can impact biodiversity and local ecology. Water conservation, flood management, and improved crop management practices using a combination of traditional knowledge and modern advancements in CCA are needed. There are a number of localized actions and projects that have been tried successfully in the NER—such as aquifer management, spring development, improved jhum cultivation that is environmentally sustainable, integrated farming systems, and afforestation.

The Himalayan states and Northeast states have been identified to act as the carbon sink for the rest of the country with their low density population, forest friendly ecosystems and people. Many such afforestation programs are being implemented through forest department leading to local tensions around livelihood issues since lands and local natural resources are becoming inaccessible. More and more community-managed models from which community distinctly benefits are needed in this region.

5.8 Community-led Climate Change Adaptation: World Bank Funded Sustainable Livelihoods and Adaptation to Climate Change (SLACC)

This USD 8.0 million project financed with grant funds from the Special Climate Change Fund intends to incorporate climate resilience in the GoI's NRLM. The proposed SLACC project seeks to establish a large scale proof-of-concept on integrating community-based CCA planning and implementation into livelihood support activities of the National Rural Livelihood Mission (NRLM)/National Rural Livelihoods Programme (NRLP), Mahila Kisan Sashaktikaran Pariyojana (MKSP), and Mahatma Gandhi National Rural Employment Guarantee Scheme (MGNREGS). The SLACC project will be implemented in the states of Bihar and Madhya Pradesh; the NRLM/NRLP will cover about 10,000 farmers' HHs, 200 villages corresponding to approximately 8–10 blocks over a 3.5-year period. At the end of the project it is expected that a) at least 50% of the targeted HHs adopt livelihoods with enhanced climate resilience, b) at least 50% of the targeted HHs demonstrate strengthened awareness and ownership of adaptation and climate risk reduction processes/measures.

The project will cover drought- and flood-prone areas and the agriculture sector will be at the core of the SLACC project. It will address all aspects of farm-based livelihoods that may be affected by climate change by helping the community choose interventions for the: production system such as participatory selection of climate-resilient varieties/breeds; ecological system such as tree-based farming or soil moisture conservation; knowledge system such as local weather-based agro-advisories, and financial system such as weather index insurance. Though the project became effective in February 2015, it is slow to take off with no disbursements made so far. Both Bihar and Madhya Pradesh are engaged in the transfer of funds to the VOs, roll-out of CCA interventions and recruitment of technical resource and partner agencies.

5.9 Climate Change Financing

All actions and solutions to address the adverse impact of climate change ultimately involve costs. Maximum share of India's current climate finance comes from budgetary sources as most of the resources for adaptation and mitigation are built into the ongoing sectoral programs. The availability of funds for such purposes is largely guided by the overall resources and requirement of different sectors. Government is also experimenting with market mechanisms together with fiscal instruments and regulatory interventions to mobilize finance for climate change. These include:

- Setting up of ₹3,500 million (USD 55.6 million) National Adaptation Fund.
- Reduction in subsidies on fossil fuels including diesel, kerosene, and domestic LPG.
- Coal cess quadrupled from ₹50 to ₹200 per tonne to help finance clean energy projects and Ganga rejuvenation.
- Introduction of tax-free infrastructure bonds for funding of renewable energy projects.

Funds are being collected for compensatory afforestation from agencies and projects that divert forests for other use. The funds so far collected remain unutilized to the extent of ₹370 billion. The funds are available for use specifically for forestry projects—rejuvenation and afforestation by the states. The slow pace of utilization of funds and slow progress in compensatory afforestation has necessitated fresh legislation

(the Compensatory Afforestation Fund Bill, 2015), which has been passed by the parliament.[65]

5.9.1 NABARD's Funding of Climate Change Initiatives

At the country level, NABARD is operating three funds for supporting projects in the climate change space. The Adaptation Fund Board (UNFCC) has appointed NABARD as the National Implementing Entity. Six projects involving a total outlay of USD 9.8 million have been sanctioned (Table 5.2). It is learnt that no fresh funding has been

Table 5.2: Projects Under Adaptation Fund Board Funding (UNFCCC)

Name of project	State/Implementing agency	Amount USD milllion
Conservation and Management of Coastal Resources as a Potential Adaptation Strategy for Sea Level Rise; Regeneration of mangroves and the surrounding ecosystem for livelihoods and sea water surge	Andhra Pradesh/MS Swaminathan Research Foundation (MSSRF)	0.69
Enhancing Adaptive Capacity and increasing Resilience of Small and Marginal Farmers in Purulia and Bankura Districts of West Bengal	West Bengal/Development Research Communication and Services Centre (DRCSC)	2.51
Building Adaptive Capacities of Small Inland Fishermen Community for Climate Resilience and Livelihood Security	Madhya Pradesh/Towards Action And Learning (TAAL)	1.79
Climate Proofing of Watershed Development Projects in the States of Rajasthan and Tamil Nadu; strategic water management	Tamil Nadu and Rajasthan/Multiple agencies	1.34
Climate-smart actions and strategies in north western Himalayan region for sustainable livelihoods of agriculture-dependent hill communities	Uttarakhand/BAIF	0.97
Building Adaptive Capacities in Communities, Livelihoods and Ecological Security in the Kanha–Pench Corridor (PCN approved)	Madhya Pradesh/ Royal Bank of Scotland Foundation, Madhya Pradesh Forest Department	2.50
Total		9.80

Source: NABARD Annual Report 2015–16, https://www.nabard.org/Publication/Annual-Report-2016.pdf

---

[65] Parliamentary Standing Committee on Science and Technology, Environment and Forests, Two Hundred Seventy Seventh Report: The Compensatory Afforestation Fund Bill, 2015. Published by Rajya Sabha Secretariat in 2016. http://www.prsindia.org/uploads/media/Compensatory%20Afforestation/SCR%20Compensatory%20Afforestation%20Fund%20Bill%202015.pdf, accessed on October 20, 2016.

received under this facility after the initial allocation. Projects sanctioned have NGOs and technical agencies as implementing partners.

The NAFCC was constituted in August 2015, with an initial budget allocation of ₹3.5 billion by the GoI for the years 2015–17. GOI will replenish and augment the allocation depending on usage. So far 12 projects for a value of ₹2.35 billion have been sanctioned under this fund (Table 5.3). The projects under this fund facility are typically implemented by state government

departments and technical agencies set up by the states.

The Green Climate Fund (GCF) is a dedicated fund facility set up under the UNFCCC. NABARD has been designated as the national implementing agency. The fund can be approached for large projects in mitigation and adaptation. NABARD has been accredited for submission of large projects in excess of USD 250 million. So far no sanctions have been received. It is understood that a few project proposals are under preparation for submission to this fund.

Table 5.3: Projects Sanctioned Under NAFCC

Name of Project	State/Implementing agency	Outlay ₹ million
Toward Climate-resilient livestock production system in Punjab; with focus on tropical, indigenous breeds	Punjab/State Council for Science and Technology	174.0
Conserve water through the management of run-off in the river basin to reduce vulnerability and enhance resilience for traditional livelihood in Nuapada	Odisha/Department of Water Resources	200.0
Sustainable livelihoods of agriculture: dependent rural communities in drought-prone district of Himachal Pradesh through climate smart solutions	Himachal Pradesh/ Department of Environment, Science and Technology	200.0
Model carbon positive eco-village in Phayeng Of Manipur	Manipur/Directorate of Environment	100.0
Management and rehabilitation of coastal habitats and biodiversity for climate change adaptation and sustainable livelihood in Gulf of Mannar, Tamil Nadu, India; regeneration of coral colonies and the ecosystem	Tamil Nadu/Department of Environment	247.4
Promotion of integrated farming system of Kaipad and Pokkali in coastal wetlands of Kerala	Kerala/Agency for Development of Aquaculture	250.0
Sustainable agriculture development through expansion, enhancement and modelling; homestead farming with multiple, interdependent activities	Mizoram/Department of Agriculture	103.8
Climate adaptation strategies in wetlands along Mahanadi river catchment areas in Chhattisgarh	Chhattisgarh/State Center for Climate Change	214.7
Climate-resilient sustainable agriculture in rainfed farming (Kandi) areas of Jammu and Kashmir	Jammu and Kashmir/ Agriculture Production Department	225.2
Spring-shed development works for rejuvenation of springs for climate resilient development in the water stressed areas of Meghalaya	Meghalaya/Directorate of Soil and Water conservation	229.2
Resilient agricultural households through adaptation to climate change in Mahbubnagar District, Telangana	Telangana/Environment Protection Training and Research Institute (EPTRI)	240.0
Integrated surface water management through rejuvenation of 20 tanks and 32 village ponds for climate change adaptation in Puducherry	Puducherry/Department of Science and Technology	167.6
Total		2,351.9

Source: NABARD Annual Report 2015–16, https://www.nabard.org/Publication/Annual-Report-2016.pdf

Apart from these specific funds, NABARD also finances climate change initiatives under its other funds, namely Rural Infrastructure Development Fund (RIDF), Tribal Development Fund (TDF), Integrated Watershed Development Programme, Umbrella Programme on Natural Resource Management (UPNRM), and NABARD Infrastructure Development Assistance (NIDA). Initiatives in emission reduction including forestry, biogas digesters, rural energy management (pump replacement, HVDS, etc.), renewable energy, and improving energy efficiency have been supported under these funds.

NABARD has adequate technical expertise that enables it to visualize how to translate concepts into actions in the field. On account of its technical and financial expertise, the GCF has entrusted NABARD with roles in facilitating identification of project ideas/concepts from SAPCC, project formulation, appraisal, sanction, disbursement of fund, monitoring and evaluation, and above all capacity building of stakeholders including state governments.

A review of the sanctioned projects indicates that the focus is on geographies experiencing climate change impact. The projects involve traditional natural resource management practices as well as some innovative measures. All the projects explore the link between climate change and impact on livelihoods and seek to stabilize livelihoods and mitigate adverse impact. However, in a few projects, it is difficult to escape the feeling that conventional responses to droughts and floods are passed off as CCA measures. While the identification of geographies and communities is done with rigour using vulnerability assessment tools, measures designed are not always fully addressing the adverse impact. With more experience in the hands of NABARD, this is bound to change.

Another issue is that the funds, as in the case GCF, are not always grants, but in the nature of loans. Given the unpredictability of nature, climate change coping measures are better delivered as a public good, particularly when affected communities are at the bottom of the pyramid. A further issue is that most projects concentrate on adaptation rather than mitigation. Emission reduction, renewable energy, carbon sequestration and such measures will provide long-term ability to manage climate change and should be prioritized under the different funds.

5.10 Cost Benefit of Climate Adaptation Projects

Some of the long-standing programs for water shed development, soil and water conservation, improving irrigation at farm level, and research and field trials in drought-resistant farming have helped to build resilience to climate shocks, though the impacts and benefits of the programs on combating climate change are not well-researched and documented.

An Independent Evaluation Group (IEG) study[66] of 22 bank projects, initiated between 1998 and 2011 on adaptation to climate variability and change, found that projects in the areas of 'watershed management' and 'sustainable land and water management' had positive payoffs and increased crop yields affecting positively the livelihoods of HHs in the project areas. Where reported, the economic returns to these projects were high, with a median economic rate of return of 20% and yield increases of 20%–70%.[67] Initiatives on improving hydromet services were also reported to offer potentially high economic returns. Further, a recent study conducted by the Economics of Climate Adaptation Working Group based on test

---

[66] Independent Evaluation Group, *Adapting to Climate Change: Assessing the World Bank Group Experience* (Advance Edition), Phase III of the World Bank Group and Climate Change, http://ieg.worldbankgroup.org/content/ieg/en/home/reports/climate_change3.html, accessed on April 26, 2013.

[67] Independent Evaluation Group, *Adapting to Climate Change: Assessing the World Bank Group Experience* (Advance Edition), Phase III of the World Bank Group and Climate Change, http://ieg.worldbankgroup.org/content/ieg/en/home/reports/climate_change3.html, accessed on April 26, 2013.

case studies in several countries showed that climate adaptation activities tend to have very favorable cost-benefit ratios.[68]

5.11 Conclusions

Climate change is probably the most complex and challenging environmental problem the world is facing and is increasingly recognized as a threat to livelihoods, in general, and to agriculture and food security, in particular.

Building greater climate resilience requires a combination of measures packaged with the right incentives and implemented at multiple levels of government (local, state, and national). Reactive or singular approaches to droughts, such as relief and emergency assistance or debt relief alone for that matter, are essential to appease suffering, but these should be complemented with a combination of other initiatives that promote longer term climate resilience.

The government has to be prime mover in facilitating farmers to adapt to climate change, the district plans for agriculture and irrigation have to follow a bottom-up approach, and there is a need to have climate-related analysis, programs, and budgets. Specific projects focusing on climate change vulnerabilities are necessary but not adequate as a complete response to the problems. Actions of a regulatory nature with robust implementation mechanisms, fiscal incentives and disincentives, and community mobilization for social monitoring and enforcement of desirable practices in the millions of farms are an integral part of the comprehensive set of responses. The real challenge lies in the creation of an enabling institutional and administrative framework that will facilitate the technical solutions to

be accepted and implemented. Local-level actions can be changed to encourage adaptive practices by creating new incentives such as subsidies or sanctions.

There is a significant scope for scaling up CCA into a wider array of state rural development programs by incorporating a dedicated climate change component into each rural livelihoods program. In general, the integration of Low External Input Sustainable Agriculture (LEISA) models will lead to better adaptation and partly answer mitigation needs. LEISA models require policy reversals in both government and research institutions. For long the focus has been increasing productivity through intensive application of inputs that exacerbate the adverse impact of climate change and reduce farm incomes in the long run. LEISA, with its lower demand on inputs, might not serve the commercial interests of those engaged in marketing of inputs but can improve sustainability of small farms and build better resilience to climate change.

The other aspect for focus is on conservation and frugal use of water, soil, and forest resources. Agriculture, irrigation, and forestry projects should focus on soil conservation and improvement of quality, economic use of water, and sustainable exploitation of forests for livelihoods. There is political reluctance to control water-hungry crops in low rainfall regions such as sugarcane in Maharashtra and paddy in Punjab. One would need stricter implementation of environmentally sound cropping patterns and regulation of use of groundwater. Incentives should be given to farmers to move away from crops that tempt them to "steal" water from their neighbors.

Since more than 80% of farmers are small holders the need for climate-smart approach to agriculture is critical. Climate change impacts on small farms are disproportionately adverse. The small holders are unable to make on-farm investments and contribute to common adaptation mechanisms. Projects dealing with CCA

---

[68] Economics of Climate Adaptation Working Group, Shaping Climate Resilient Development: A Framework for Decision-making (2009), http://www.mckinsey.com/App_Media/Images/Page_Images/Offices/SocialSector/PDF/ECA_Shaping_Climate%20Resilent_Development.pdf, accessed on July 18, 2016.

should facilitate inclusion of small holders in a facile manner so as to secure their livelihoods.

India's immense geographic diversity adds to the complexity of developing an adaptation strategy. Climate variations in India will be varied and heterogeneous, with some regions experiencing more intense precipitation and increased flood risks, while others encounter sparser rainfall and prolonged droughts. The impacts will vary across sectors, locations, and populations. The implication for a country so diverse is that broad generalizations on ways to promote adaptation to climate change will be misleading. Consequently, there can be no one-size-fits-all approach to developing a climate risk management strategy; approaches will need to be tailored to fit local vulnerabilities and conditions.

ANNEXURE 5.1
Vulnerability, Impact, and Adaptation Analysis (CRiSTAL Tool, 4.0)

Climatic Hazards	Impact	Coping Mechanism
Amreli, Gujarat		
Drought	Scarcity of water, fodder, loss of crop, and loss of income; increased soil salinity.	Ground nut cultivation is stopped; cultivation of improved varieties of bajra, cotton, and sesame has been started, free grazing of animals; fodder purchase by selling assets; migration; secondary income from gem polishing work.
Cyclonic Activities	Damage to crops, land, infrastructures, seepage of seawater to adjacent land, increase in salinity, water logging, and incidence of more diseases.	——
Unseasonal Rains	Late flowering and fruiting, damage in standing crops, and finally yield and net returns.	Cultivation of fodder rather than food crops to get minimum yield/produce; changing cropping pattern.
The Dangs, Gujarat		
Drought	Dry spell during May–July affect negatively the sowing for many crops; inadequate irrigation and drinking water; crop loss; adverse effect of shortage of water on livestock, small ruminants and poultry.	Adoption of late sown crops; work in "work and payment for food" system; migration; loan lending from local and big landowners (*Sahukars);* collection and sale of wild fruits, seeds from the forests; secondary occupations-carpentry, masonry; collection of natural medicines from surrounding forest; in dry spells, feeding of animals with dry fodder while small ruminants are given leaves, collected from the forest. In extreme conditions—selling their assets; change in cropping pattern and mixed cropping.
Unseasonal Rains	Unseasonal, heavy showers of rains have adverse impact on standing crop—more incidence of disease and pests or lodging of crops, poor quality of produce, reduced net returns. In livestock, small ruminants and poultry—more incidence of various diseases.	Plant protection by using some plant extracts (*Van Aushadhi* – bio medicine from plant extracts); processing of food grains to improve quality of produce, to get good price in market; use of traditional medicines to cure diseased animals.
Hailstones	Less frequency but damage associated is quite large.	Produce is for only home consumption; work as farm laborers; use of hot water/heat treatment, to protect animals; the damaged crop in field is used to feed the animals; low cost shed for animals to protect them in extreme conditions.

(Continued)

(Continued)

Climatic Hazards	Impact	Coping Mechanism
Barmer, Rajasthan		
Drought	Increasing desertification and erosion, higher sand dunes—adverse effect on agriculture; adverse effect on health; less productive animals.	Use of *Pukka Tanka* (cemented tank) to store rain water; mixed cropping, to minimize losses from a single crop failure; use of preserved seeds for sowing; secondary occupations—wood carving, rope making and mat making with camel and goat hairs are some common nonfarm activities to withstand the situation; migration (in extreme conditions).
Flood	Flood has direct negative impact on natural, physical, and human resources of livelihoods. Occurrence of waterborne diseases, bacterial infection, and mass mortality also happened due to flood.	*Pukka Tanka* got filled during flood.
Unseasonal Rains	Adverse effect on economic returns; unwanted rains at the time of flowering of Khejri (*Prosopis cineraria*) and other vegetations indirectly affect production of milk and wool from small ruminants due to dependency on vegetation.	Marginal/landless families compel to make premature distress sale of kids of goat due to crisis of cash income.
Nandurbar, Maharashtra		
Drought	Short supply of water at the time of sowing of major crops; loan lending (in case of repeated sowing or crop loss); adverse effect on animal's well-being and production; dry spell clubbed with high temperature leads to death of animals.	Cultivation of only one crop (depending upon the onset of rains), low water requiring crop are preferred, and animals are fed with dry fodder or left for open grazing, migration to nearby areas for work; preparation of low cost sheds for animals to protect them from heat stroke.
Unseasonal Rains	Badly affects the standing crops and results in higher incidences of diseases and pests; lodging of crops; adverse effect on the quality and productivity of grains which results in low net returns; more diseases of animals leading to poor health and death.	Processing of food grains to improve the quality; Pesticides are sprayed for plant protection; the diseased animals are given treatment with traditional medicines.
Champawat, Uttarakhand		
Reduced Snow Fall	Adverse effect on production of temperate fruits, especially apple; impaired quality of wheat; more pest incidence.	Instead of apple, fruits like malta, peach, etc. that require low chilling hours are grown now. Since horticulture has been mainly affected, people have now started growing vegetables.
Drought	Scarcity of water, crop loss, and animal deaths.	Changes in cropping pattern; started digging wells.
Unseasonal Rains	If it rains by last week of June, then only the rains are beneficial for the crops otherwise they are not. Reduction in rainy days; delayed onset and early conclusion.	Changed cropping pattern. Nowadays, Kharif crops are cultivated on a large scale as compared to Rabi crops.
Haveri, Karnataka		
Drought	Scarcity of water—loss of food security, nutritive value of food and income; fodder scarcity; declined milk production; due to fodder scarcity, animals are sold with fewer rates; drinking water scarcity; major effect on crossbred animals—decline in milk production; bound to take loans against their assets.	Crops diversification/integrated farming system. Drought resistant and short duration varieties of crop; tree-based farming system (Wadi). Adoption of MI, water conservation—farm ponds, borewell/open well recharging. Fields left as fallow and temporary migration for brick making, construction labor. Agronomic practices

Climatic Hazards	Impact	Coping Mechanism
		like ridge and furrow system, compartment bunding, frequent intercultural operations, soil much, etc. Distress sale of bullocks and goats. Keeping local Pandharpuri buffalo, Khilar/Hallikar cows seasonal migration with animals in case of sheep and goat. Soil/water conservation measures. Land leveling and terracing. Organic material/biomass recycling.
Unseasonal Rains	More incidences of insect–pests; more soil erosion.	Drain out excess water and weeding; proper drying of produce and fumigation of stored grains for avoiding fungus/pests; crops diversification/integrated farming system, tree-based farming system (Wadi); Cattle sheds for shelter; maintain hygienic condition in animal shed soil conservation measures.
Anantapur, Andhra Pradesh		
Drought	Adverse effect on crop growth and yield; less availability of fodder for farm animals (usually sourced from nearby villages) has also reduced; decreasing water table.	Started growing groundnut (short duration variety TMV-2) and pigeon pea; reduced paddy cultivation; sale of large ruminants; migration of farmers with small ruminants.

Source: Contributed by BAIF, Pune, based on their study using CRiSTAL tool.

Handloom: Need for Result-oriented Policy Support

I feel convinced that the revival of hand-spinning and hand weaving will make the largest contribution to the economic and the moral regeneration of India. The millions must have a simple industry to supplement agriculture.

Mahatma Gandhi

6.1 Introduction

Handloom weaving is the largest employment generation activity after agriculture, providing direct and indirect employment to an estimated 4.204 million workers in about 1.873 million handloom units.[1] The strength of the sector lies in its heritage, uniqueness of designs, flexibility of production, low level of capital investments, openness to innovations, adaptability to the buyer's requirement, and the wealth of its tradition.

With 2.377 million handlooms, this sector supplies nearly 11% of the cloth production in the country and also contributes to the export earning of the country. Of the world's hand woven fabric, 95% comes from India.[2] The cloth production details and share of handlooms for past seven years (Table 6.1) show that after a three-year stagnation, the handloom production level is gradually rising in the last two years.

Production in the handloom sector recorded a high of 7,203 million sq. meters in the year 2014–15. The share of handloom sector which had touched a low of 11% in 2012–13 has climbed back to 15% since 2014–15. Though competition from power loom and mill sector, availability of cheaper imported fabrics, and changing consumer preferences are threats to the sector, due to policy initiatives and marketing efforts the handloom sector has shown positive growth.

The sector engages largely economically and socially backward communities.

---

[1] Ministry of Statistics and Programme Implementation, All India Report of Sixth Economic census 2014 (March 2016).

[2] GOI, Annual Report of 2013–14 (2014), Ministry of Textiles, Government of India.

Table 6.1: Cloth Production by Handloom Sector

Year	Cloth Production by Handloom Sector	Share of Handloom to the Total Cloth Production	Ratio of Handloom to Power Loom (in terms of cloth)	Total Cloth Production*	Export
2008–09	6,677	15.9	1:5.04	42,121	
2009–10	6,806	14.6	1:5.59	47,083	
2010–11	6,949	14.6	1:5.59	47,083	
2011–12	6,900	14.8	1:5.42	46,600	
2012–13	6,952	11.22	1:5.47	61,949	
2013–14	7,104	15.30	1:5.18	46,425	
2014–15	7,203	15.18	1:5.24	47,438	
2015–16 (up to November)	4,904	15.51	1:5.13	31,624	

Source: GOI, Annual Report 2015–16 (2016), Ministry of Textiles, Government of India.
Note: *The total cloth production includes handloom, power loom, and mill sector excluding hosiery, khadi, wool, and silk.

Marginalized population of SCs and STs and other backward communities are engaged in the sector. Of people employed (including proprietor weavers) in the sector, 12.4% are from SCs, 6% belong to STs, 45.3% belong to other backward classes, and 36.3% are from other castes. The statewise number of handloom weavers and allied workers and number of handlooms are provided in Annexure 6.1. The top five states, in terms of number of handicraft/handloom establishments are West Bengal (17.6%), Uttar Pradesh (16.5%), Odisha (7.8%), Andhra Pradesh (7.5%), and Tamil Nadu (6.8%). In terms of persons employed, Uttar Pradesh topped the list (Table 6.2). Assam which had the highest weaver population in the 2009–10 census does not figure in the top five states either in handloom enterprises or people employed. Andhra Pradesh which was in the top five in terms of people employed is now sixth in the list.

It is noteworthy that the Northeastern states which were significant in the sector in the last census have lost their position with the number of enterprises and people employed drastically lower.

The handloom census 2009–10 was carried out by NCAER and the sixth Economic Census was carried out by the Central Statistical Office (CSO), Ministry of Statistics and Programme Implementation

MOSPI, GOI. After the 2009–10 Census some state authorities were concerned that since three different agencies carried out the census with different definition of working weaver and loom, the data may not be uniform and thus not accurate. In some states, looms currently in use were only considered; since some weavers migrate for part of the year, these looms were considered idle and were not counted. In other states looms that worked at least one day in a year were considered. Thus, with a common definition and understanding the numbers can change. The sixth economic census shows that the people employed in handloom sector remains more or less the same as in 2009–10, but the distribution of these people across states has changed. While the numbers of weavers has remained stagnant over the last five-year period, the increasing production of handloom cloth suggests that the sector is growing, perhaps on account of better efficiency and productivity.

6.2 Classification of Weavers

Income Earning Potential: Depending on their specialization and skill sets the weavers can be classified into seven categories in the order of their earning potential. These are as follows:

1. Contractual cotton weaver—either under societies or master weavers.
2. Contractual silk weaver—either under societies or master weavers
3. Entrepreneurial weaver—independent.
4. Tie and dye design entrepreneurs—they make the yarn design and sell in the market.
5. Traditional master weavers—many are usually national awardees making traditional designs aimed at niche market both national and international. Each product will take three to six months. They have few weavers (10 to 20) work under them and usually have huge margins and profits. Some of the renowned designers are working with master weavers.

Table 6.2: Top 5 States in Handloom Sector

State	No. of People Employed (Millions)	State	No. of Handloom Weavers & Allied Workers (Millions)
2014 VI Economic Census[3]		2009–10 Census	
Uttar Pradesh	0.769	Assam	1.643
West Bengal	0.746	West Bengal	0.779
Tamil Nadu	0.31	Andhra Pradesh	0.355
Odisha	0.305	Tamil Nadu	0.352
Rajasthan	0.263	Uttar Pradesh	0.257

Source: Handloom Census 2009–10 by NCAER.

[3] Ministry of Statistics and Programme Implementation, "All India Report of Sixth Economic census 2014".

6. Commercial master weavers—they have many weavers[4] attached to them. Common designs for local markets are their target.
7. Traders from weaver community.

Full-Time and Part-Time Weavers: There is increasing trend of weavers undertaking other livelihood activities on part-time basis to enhance their income. While weaving is their main occupation, they undertake farming, work as farm laborers during agriculture season. Sarba Shanti Ayog (Sasha),[5] a private sector marketing initiative, finds that during peak Kharif season there are very few weavers available in West Bengal and nearby states to execute orders. Similarly, in the state of Odisha it is common for weavers from marginalized community to migrate for four to five months to nearby states to work in brick kilns and as agricultural labor. The sixth economic census has categorized the handloom units into three—perennial, seasonal, and casual. Of the handloom enterprises, 88.7% of the handloom enterprises are perennial and 9% operate seasonally. The remaining 2.3% units are operated casually.

During field interactions, weavers including those making silk saris mentioned that they work as casual unskilled wage laborers under MGNREGS. Though women typically undertake such work, most of these women are also weavers and not mere workers. The MGNREGS work is undertaken for about 40 to 50 days in a year and is considered as light and easy with four hours of work near to their homes.

Skill sets of Weavers: Though there are no clear census data on the classification of weavers as per their skill sets, both government functionaries and organizations working with the weavers estimate

that about 25% of the weavers are highly skilled, weaving intricate designs and weaves such as Jamdani, Kanchi silks, Benarasi silk, Paithani, patola, and so on. About 60% of the weavers undertake medium skill jobs such as simpler saris, bedsheets, daily men's wear, and so on. About 15% are not very skilled and weave low-value items with mass market like towels. While the top 15% are able to earn a decent income the other two segments are vulnerable to income fluctuations. Weavers who make low value products such as towels, lungis and so on are not able to compete with power loom sector since these products are cheaper by 50% when made in power looms. Some of the state governments are the major procurer of the lower value handloom products such as saris, dhotis, materials for uniforms for government staff and so on thus enabling the medium and low skilled weavers to have a livelihood.

Semiorganized and Unorganized: State authorities mention that 50% to 60% of the weavers and working looms are organized as weavers' cooperative societies (WCSs). Most of the rest are attached to master weavers while a few work independently with their own marketing arrangements. Tamil Nadu leads in cooperative networking of weavers followed by Odisha.

Master weavers usually provide employment apart from taking care of the family requirements of the weavers. While the wages paid are lower than that of societies, regularity of work, financial support for emergent needs, and so on, make the weavers loyal to the master weavers. It is not unusual for weavers to be working with a society and a master weaver in an attempt to spread sources of income and risks.

The weavers' societies operate like employers with weavers being job workers. The societies provide the yarn, dyes, and patterns and the weavers return the finished goods and get payment. The benefits of the government schemes such as yarn supply, loom provisions, skills training and so

---

[4] As high as 1,000 weavers in some pockets.

[5] Sarba Shanthi Ayog, Sasha, works with 120 group enterprises of weavers and other handicrafts all over the country for improving the designs for better marketing linkages. Since 1980s the organization has been facilitating market linkages especially for export markets.

on, are largely routed through the WCSs. However, getting enrolled as a member is not easy with entry barriers being set up by the Board of Directors. These barriers are because of marketability of products and inclusion of members who will execute orders in time. However, whenever there is a window opened for including new members other factors such as gender and political affiliations also come into play; supporters of the party in power only are admitted. Women appear to face difficulties in getting membership or even changing membership from the husband to their own names.

There is no reliable statistics on how many weavers' cooperatives are functioning and also how many of them are financially sound. In West Bengal, Odisha, and Andhra Pradesh discussions with Directorate of Handlooms reveal that 40% to 60% of the weavers' societies are inactive. On an average only 20% to 30% of the societies are consistently supplying to the apex marketing agencies and these can be considered active. Since cooperatives are not functioning in all states and districts, many weavers are outside their purview. However, weavers attached to cooperatives are able to get better remuneration. Others are at the tail end of a longer value chain of weaver-trader-agent-master weaver-apex marketing society/private shop-customer and suffer in income terms as a result.

> One trend seen is more and more women are operating looms and are undertaking actual weaving than merely doing pre loom activities. Under master weavers about 70 to 80% are women. Weaving is found suitable by women since they are able to combine house work with the production and use their time flexibly; master weavers are also lending looms at their homes, set time targets and piece rates.
>
> Managing Director, Utkalika.

Women's Role: As per the last handloom census (2009–10), out of the 3.847 million adult weavers and allied workers in the country, 77% are women and 23% men. Though women traditionally carry out the preloom activities, in recent times more women are under taking weaving and some of them are organized into SHGs as well. Weaving clusters closer to semiurban centers see this trend of males taking up jobs and women carrying out livelihoods as weavers.

6.3 Government Initiatives

A total amount of ₹7.1 billion has been allocated for handloom-related programs in the current year's budget. For a sector that is the second largest informal sector employer, the allocation is meager. However, this is a significant step-up from the previous years as seen in Tables 6.3 and 6.4.

Table 6.3: Central Government Budget Allocations for Handloom Sector

Programs for Handloom Weavers	Plan	Nonplan	Total
National Handloom Development Programme	150		150
Handloom Weavers Comprehensive Welfare Scheme	30		30
Yarn Supply Scheme	260		260
Trade Facilitation Centre and Craft Museum	107		107
Comprehensive Handloom Cluster Development Programme—Handloom Mega Cluster	65		65
Weavers Service Centre		47	47
Others Handloom Programmes		51	51
Total	612	98	710

Source: Authors based on Expenditure budget, Ministry of Textiles—Union Budget—www.indiabudget.nic.in

Table 6.4:   Union Budget Allocations for Handloom Sector (₹ millions)

Scheme	2012–13	2013–14	2014–15	2015–16	2016–17
National Handloom Development Programme			2,880.0	1,250.0	1,500.0
Comprehensive Handloom Development scheme		1,070.0	–	–	–
Integrated Handloom Development Scheme (central sector schemes [CSS])	1,700.0		–	–	–
RRR package (CSS)	22,050.0	1,570.0	–	–	–
Market and Export Promotion Scheme (CSS)	480.0	–	–	–	–
Diversified Handloom Development Scheme	200.0	–	–	–	–
Weaver Service Centre	325.0	350.0	330.0	380.0	470.0
Handloom Weavers Comprehensive Welfare Scheme	1,050.0	650.0	550.0	150.0	300.0
Mill Gate Price Scheme	3,500.0	965.0	1,250.0	1,400.0	2,600.0
Scheme for Grant of Special Rebate		0.10	0.10	–	–
Trade Facilitation Centre and Crafts Museum				800.0	1,070.0
Others	300.0	329.9	375.0	420.0	510.0
CHCDS—Handloom Mega Cluster		260.0	260.0	66.0	650.0
Lump sum provision for Northeast and Sikkim			570.0	400.0	**
Total	2,9605.0	5,195.0	6,215.1	4,866.0	7,100.0

Source: Authors based on Expenditure budget, Ministry of Textiles—Union Budget—www.indiabudget.nic.in
Note: ** Included in the budget provision under relevant heads.

The major programs of the Central Government for the handloom sector include the following:

1. National Handloom Development Programme with two components: Revival, Reform, and Restructuring (RRR) package for handloom sector and Comprehensive Handlooms Development Scheme.
2. Handloom Weavers Comprehensive Welfare Scheme—two components: Health Insurance Scheme for access to health care facilities and Mahatma Gandhi Bunkar Bima Yojana for life insurance.
3. Yarn Supply Scheme.
4. Comprehensive Handloom Cluster Development Scheme (CHCDS, Mega Cluster Scheme).

RRR package has been completed and hence no further allocations are being made for the same. Significant allocations are to National Handloom Development Programme, yarn supply, and trade facilitation centre (which is a common one for handlooms and handicrafts).

The cluster development programme is the flagship scheme of the Central Government at present. The cluster development programme aims at development of clusters in terms of increased market share and ensuring higher productivity with interventions such as skill upgradation, formation of SHGs, corpus fund for yarn depot, CFC/dye house, and so on for a period of 3–4 years. Three types of clusters are being supported: existing clusters, setting up new clusters, and support to smaller groups. Two mega clusters (with 15,000 looms each) are also being developed.

The focus of the Ministry appears to take up maximum number of clusters (Table 6.5). Clusters are developed by the private sector including civil society organizations and states have to certify implementation progress. The State Directorates find that while some states get more clusters others only few. Moreover, the period of three years for development of a cluster is insufficient to enable clusters to achieve

Table 6.5: Cluster Development Programme (till 31.3.2015)

Components	Targets (No. of Weavers)	Achievements (No. of Weavers)
1. Consolidation of Clusters	116,000	63,400
2. New Clusters	80,000	12,908
3. Group Approach	1,000	3,150
Total	197,000	79,458

Source: Development Commissioner Handlooms, GOI, Note on Handloom Sector—31-12-2015, http://handlooms.nic.in/writereaddata/2486.pdf, accessed on October 7, 2016.

self-sustainability. Instead of adopting a target-driven approach for adopting more and more new clusters, efforts should focus on select promising traditional/heritage clusters and work with them for a longer period of time, about seven years. These clusters need to be provided the required support across all important areas including marketing, social welfare, credit availability, and technological upgradation.[6]

Social protection insurance schemes are the other major expenditure that the Central Government incurs. Social protection is offered to weavers through two insurance schemes—one each covering life and health risks. Weavers highly appreciate the health insurance scheme given the high incidence of diseases and health-related expenditure being high.

Apart from the above, each state government also has their own schemes and funds. According to the states, the budget from the Central Government is often inadequate, irregular and of late budget provisions are also getting reduced.

Schemes of the Odisha state governments for weavers include (a) housing cum loom provision (₹70,000 per weaver), (b) solar lanterns to facilitate working at all times even during power cuts (40,000 households), (c) concretization of pit in the pit looms to manage the rainy season (8,000 covered), (d) skill training for basic weaving as well as new techniques—basic weaving—dobby and jhala, jacquard, tie

and dye making, natural dyeing and so on (six months training with stipend—15,000 weavers trained), (e) technology intervention for modern looms and weaving accessories with 90% support from the state government. The unique initiative of the government is to ensure that these schemes reach all weavers not just those attached to Primary Weavers Cooperative Society (PWCS).

Similarly, the Government of West Bengal has introduced Tantisathi scheme in 2015 with a total budget of ₹1.2 billion. Looms and accessories are to be supplied to 100,000 weavers, who do not have looms or whose looms are in dilapidated condition so that weavers can weave at home. While 20,000 looms have already been supplied the rest are to be distributed during the current year.

Government of Andhra Pradesh has a number of schemes for the weavers aimed at improved credit. To reduce the interest burden to the weaver cooperative societies on the credit limits, government makes available loans at 3% interest rate. The government offers an additional 10% yarn subsidy to PWCS.

> **Box 6.1:** *Old Age Pensions to Weavers of Andhra Pradesh*
>
> Financial assistance of pension is provided to the old-aged eligible weavers; 86,065 old age pensions are allocated exclusively for weavers in the state. The age of weaver pensioner is reduced from 65 to 50 years, as a special case because of crippling effect in weaving profession. Old age pensions to weavers are being disbursed at ₹1000 per month with effect from September 2014.

The states also have programs for improving weavers' skills and design inputs. Each state visited had trained between 15,000 and 35,000 weavers in skill upgradation with duration of 45 days to 6 months. West Bengal has planned training statewide through the Department of Technical Education and Training.

---

[6] GOI, Draft Consultation Paper on Handlooms (October 2014), Planning Commission Government of India.

Government initiatives on skilling are aimed at upgrading the skills of medium-skilled persons for making niche products. While responding to public demand for such products is one of the reasons, states also see that niche products face negligible competition from power loom sector. However, focusing on niche products is proving to be an uphill task due to (a) limited interest of weavers in the older age group, (b) Paucity of trainers and designers to upgrade skills for weaving such products, and (c) limited markets for niche products which makes weavers cautious.

1. Marketing support to Primary Weavers' Societies and Apex Marketing Societies

Marketing incentives are provided by the Central and state governments. The Central Government scheme provides for 10% to be shared equally between the state and the center. Apart from this, each state provides for additional rebates to be offered for marketing which varies from state to state. These incentives are available for both the apex marketing society and also to the primary weavers' cooperatives. Directorates, apex societies and primary weavers' societies found the rebates to be the game changer and if these rebates are withdrawn, cooperatives may not be able to market effectively and compete with private sector.

The state governments have extended financial support to the apex marketing societies and also primary weavers' societies for capital investments in terms of modernization of showrooms for apex marketing societies, funds for other special initiatives such as e-marketing, computerization, international, and national exhibitions. While salary costs and other overheads are being largely covered by the societies out of their margins, capital investments are funded by the states. Moreover, primary weavers' societies also get support for showrooms, dyeing units, and other common facilities shared by weavers in the area.

2. Revival Reform and Restructuring Scheme

The RRR package for handloom sector was implemented from 2011 and declared closed in 2014. The basic purpose of the package was revival of the handloom sector and unclogging the choked lines of bank credit to viable/potentially viable WCS and no individual weavers. Recapitalization assistance was to facilitate increasing the borrowing power of the primary WCS and enable them to enlarge their client base.

The package was to be implemented, as a centrally sponsored plan scheme, with a total outlay of ₹38,840 million; the share of the Government of India was to be ₹31,370 million and that of the state government to be ₹7,470 million. Both GOI and state governments contributed the funds required for loan waiver and recapitalization of handloom WCSs and individual weavers.

The package included the following:

i. Reformation of the legal and institutional framework of the handloom WCS.
ii. Detailed assessment of losses and subsequent one-time recapitalization of viable and potentially viable WCS at the primary and the apex level; funds are provided to repay 100% of the principal and 25% of the interest[7] (as on the date of loan becoming NPA) which was overdue as on March 31, 2010, for viable and potentially viable societies, groups, and individual weavers, provided the banks agreed to sanction fresh loans;[8] For individual weavers, there was an overall ceiling of ₹50,000.

[7] The balance 75% of overdue interest and the entire penal interest, if any, will have to be written off by the bank as a precondition to avail assistance under the package.
[8] On the lines of Agriculture Debt Waiver and Debt Relief (ADWDR) scheme of Government of India, wherein banks agreed to issue fresh loans once the overdue agricultural loans were written off, the recapitalization and repayment of outstanding loans of handloom cooperative societies to banks under the package would be subject to a commitment by the bank concerned to give fresh loans.

iii. The quantum of assistance for weavers' societies and individual weavers was based on audits and recommendation of state implementation, monitoring, and review committee.

iv. Provision of low-cost credit to handloom weavers by providing interest subsidy of 3% for an annual cycle of up to three years for each fresh loan.

v. Creating mechanism for credit guarantee.

vi. Computerization of accounts of all viable and potentially viable primary weavers' societies and putting in place a common accounting system for all weavers' societies across the country

vii. Launch of credit guarantee scheme for loans to weavers.

Keeping in view the limited coverage under RRR package, the government modified the package in 2013, by relaxing the eligibility norms. The condition of minimum net worth was relaxed and even cooperatives with negative net worth were to be considered provided its net worth becomes positive after adjustments of loans waiver. The revised scheme also facilitated cheaper credit at 6% interest rate to the handloom sector in line with budget announcement. The package is closed as of February 2014.

Twenty-seven states have signed tripartite memorandum of understanding MT metric tons (MoUs) for the centrally sponsored plan scheme with GOI and NABARD. Under RRR, 39 Apex Weavers' Cooperative Societies (AWCS), 9,642 PWCS, 6,310 SHGs, and 54,226 individual weavers have been assisted. To settle claims under the package, an amount of ₹7410 million was released by GOI in four tranches. Total utilization under the package stood at ₹7,090 million as on March 31, 2016.[9] Weavers' societies and weavers in Kerala, Andhra Pradesh, Tamil Nadu, and Odisha received nearly 75% of the amount. The expenditure incurred under the RRR package incidentally is nearly the same as that of current year's allocation for the handloom sector.

Cooperative banks' exposure to handloom weaving has been included for coverage under Credit Guarantee fund Trust for Micro and Small Enterprises (CGTMSE) administered by SIDBI.[10] Furthermore, an amount of ₹134.6 million was released to seven states as 50% mobilization amount for computerization of 4,170 PWCSs.[11] The flip side is that less than 50% of the PWCS assisted under RRR package are being covered for computerization.

Two clear outcomes expected from banking sector out of the package were (a) fresh financing to weavers' societies at subsidized rates and (b) financing of individual weavers up to ₹200,000 under weavers' credit card scheme and margin money scheme. There is widespread disappointment that these outcomes are not getting achieved and the scheme benefitted the banks most with their books becoming clean but very little fresh credit have been lent.

The sixth economic census investigated the sources of finance for weavers. The worst fears about the paucity of resources have come true in the findings of the survey. Almost 86% of the handloom enterprises were financed from own sources; only 1.19% of the units had financing from financial institutions. Government support was reported by 1.84% of units and 6.70% units reported other sources including donations and transfers. Money lenders were the largest financiers as they account for 3.81% of the units.

Though overall data on financing of weavers' societies by banks is not available, Directorates of Handloom as well as the apex marketing societies mention that credit is an issue only for some of PWCS.

---

[9] NABARD, Annual report, 2015–16 (2016).

[10] Govt. will make necessary provision for payment of guarantee fee @1% and annual service fee @0.5% to CGTMSE, for credit guarantee for a period of three years from the date of first disbursal of the fresh loan.

[11] Development Commissioner Handlooms, GOI, "Note on Handloom Sector—31-12-2015".

RRR package had six subcomponents and has been implemented in such a way[12] that the societies in some states have balance funds left with after the NPAs were settled. Many weavers' societies buy yarn on credit from wholesalers or apex marketing societies and hence working capital need is limited to payment of wages to weavers and holding on to stocks if sales realization takes long. Interactions with weavers' societies show that well-functioning ones are able to get working capital limits from the banks.

The weavers' societies are eligible for concessional finance at 6%. The usual procedure is that the Directorate will release the interest subsidy to the PWCS based on audit report.

Individual loans to weavers: The state directorates of handloom have been setting targets for financing weavers by banks in state level bankers' committee. The response from the banks has not been encouraging as shown in Table 6.6.

NABARD is the implementing agency to channel interest subsidy to banks of up to 7% for providing concessional credit to handloom sector at 6%. The assistance is limited to the difference between the prevailing rate of interest charged by the banks and concessional rate of interest. The margin money assistance to enable weavers, SHGs, and joint liability groups (JLGs) through banks was enhanced from ₹4,200 at the start of the scheme to 20% of loan amount subject to a maximum of ₹10,000 per weaver, since 2013. Under the scheme, banks are allowed to claim interest subsidy upfront. A sum of ₹0.2285 billion was released to 77,863 beneficiaries under the package during the year 2015–16.

How far the weavers' credit card scheme reflects ground reality needs introspection. Most of the weavers are either attached to cooperatives or to master weavers. Hence

Table 6.6: Loans to Weavers Under Weavers Credit Card

	Target for Cards Issuance	Cards Issued	Loan Sanctioned (₹ in millions)	Loan Disbursed (₹ in millions)
2012–13	160,000	53,629	1,714	
2013–14	200,000	71,643	1,942	
2014–15	200,000	79,210	2,335	1,006
2015–16	200,000	33,444	968	677

Source: Annual report, 2015–16 of Ministry of Handlooms, Government of India.

their production-related needs—yarn, dyes, (even looms are supplied by some of master weavers)—are provided for. In such a situation the weavers do not require much for production credit. In the societies visited in Odisha and West Bengal most of the weavers have been provided a Weavers' Credit Card (WCC) though the usage and repayment performance was a concern. Societies do not play a role in WCC. The experience of the bankers has been poor with mounting NPAs reported under the WCCs[13]. As per bankers, most weavers are job workers and the bank loan has been misutilized and there is hardly any possibility for recovering the money back. Hence, there is natural reluctance from banks to issue cards or sanction credit limits under the scheme.

This scheme requires reexamination. In the meanwhile, MUDRA loan scheme for weavers has been launched with targeted coverage of 0.5 million weavers during the current year. If targeted clearly at entrepreneurial weavers, this scheme has the potential to spur growth of the sector.

6.4 Yarn and Dyes Availability

Access to raw material such as yarn, dyes, and dye stuffs has been an issue. The Government of India has promulgated the hank yarn packing notification (HYPN) to ensure sufficient availability of hank yarn for the handloom sector under the provision of Essential Commodity Act, 1955. The Office of Textile Commissioner has been entrusted with the responsibility of monitoring the compliance

---

[12] Many primary weavers' societies maintained kutcha sales registers and recorded sales to many individual traders who have not paid and thus are losses. Government has accepted these records in the audit.

[13] Personal interactions with NABARD and SLBC convenors, bankers in four states.

of HYPN. Presently, every producer of yarn is to pack at least 40% of yarn in hank form and not less than 80% of the hank yarn packed should be below 80 counts.

Government of India launched mill gate price scheme in 1992–93 to make available all types of yarn at mill gate price to facilitate regular supply of Yarn to the handloom sector. National Handloom Development Corporation (NHDC), a Government of India undertaking, is the only agency authorized to implement the scheme. Furthermore, to provide the subsidized yarn only to handloom weavers in order to compete with power loom and mill sector, a component of 10% price subsidy on hank yarn is applicable on cotton, domestic silk, and woolen yarn with some quantity limitation. The scheme is extended to weavers' societies, SHGs, JLGs, weaver entrepreneurs, and individual weavers.

While NHDC is exceeding the target set in terms of quantity of yarn supplied year on year (about 150 million Kilograms of yarn is supplied by NHDC), still they are reported to be catering to only 10% of the demand. The other major issue is the time lag between the placement of order and actual supply which is as high as three months as per some of the weavers' societies. Moreover, the price difference between the order placement and supply has to be borne by the societies. Lack of adequate depots also leads to delays and increase in transportation costs. Moreover, weavers have to pay in cash to NHDC whereas other private players provide yarn on credit. With private agencies the other advantage is that weavers are able to demand and are assured of quality.

Assam has large numbers of weavers and as per the Directorate of Handlooms the yarn market is controlled by private trade. Since there is no spinning mill in the state and the yarn has to come from Coimbatore, the price is high pushing up cost of production. Under the mill gate price scheme, there is a minimum waiting period of one and half months and the weavers also need to buy a minimum threshold quantity which is

With increasing cotton and cotton yarn exports, yarn prices are steadily increasing. The availability of hank yarn—the basic material from which handloom weaving is done—is an issue because it is controlled by modern spinning mills, which see more profit in large volume cone yarn. Second, since hank yarn is tax-free and has subsidies, enormous amounts are diverted to the power loom and mill sectors. As a result, there is a shortage of yarn for the weavers. Colors (for dyeing) are expensive, and presently there is no system or mechanism to increase their availability.

Source: A sector expert.

far higher than what they need. Thus, they need to depend more on private trade for costly yarn which is making the products less competitive.

Some of the apex marketing societies and PWCS act as implementing agency of NHDC and supply yarn to the weavers' societies. Boyanika, the apex cooperative handloom marketing society in Odisha, emphasizes that the societies attached to them use only the yarn supplied by them. Societies are not allowed to purchase yarn from elsewhere; as per senior management "We source yarn from different parts of the country. What we supply is good quality as per demand. They may be interested to procure low quality but we don't allow."

Andhra Pradesh State Handloom Weavers' Cooperative Society, APCO, procures and supplies cotton yarn from NHDC to the weavers' societies; 30% to 40% of cotton yarn requirement is fulfilled by APCO. The apex is not supplying silk yarns, since the yarn is costly and due to quality issues if weavers' societies refuse to lift the supply, it results in losses. For government orders, polyester yarn is supplied by APCO to the societies. Similarly, Tantuja, the West Bengal state handloom marketing society, calculates the yarn requirement for the government purchase orders and supplies to the weavers.

Serifed, Odisha Cooperative Tassar and Silk Federation Limited, which works with both cocoon rearers as well as weavers mentions that only 50% of the demand could be met by Serifed. NHDC procures Korean Tussar and supplies through the implementing agencies. With funding support for additional plantations and cocoon production, more tussar, eri, and mulberry can be produced in the state.

The other raw material is color dyes. The usage of Azo dyes is hazardous to the environment and is banned. But because of low prices and easy availability, these dyes continue to be being used. NHDC is also supplying quality dyes and chemicals to the handloom weavers in small packets at competitive rates; however, supply to individual weavers is needed in much smaller quantities as compared to existing NHDC supply.

Hence, certified and standards compliant Azo-free dyes in smaller quantities need to be freely accessible and available to the weavers. State directorates mention that training and awareness building on the usage of natural dyes, reactive dyes, and color-fastening techniques are a priority especially if export and niche markets are to be addressed. The Directorate of Handlooms West Bengal mentions that 100,000 kilogram of natural dyes are in short supply in the state and also only about 30 weavers are well trained in vegetable dyeing. The state is improving infrastructure for dyeing and planning to launch more training courses for production of natural dyes as well as dyeing process.

The next related issue is color fastness of the cloth produced with frequent complaints about color leaking. While this is partly due to lack of availability of good quality colors, it is also due to lack of awareness of different kinds of dyes and dyeing processes. Currently, most individual weavers use local dye houses or purchase small quantity of dyes from local traders. These dyes, which are available in paper sachets, are often adulterated with common salt making them less effective. Constant exposure to the atmosphere also reduces their potency leading to inconsistent quality. To improve the quality of dyeing, provision of dyeing training and upgradation of existing dye houses are being taken up under the cluster development schemes and also under other state schemes.

6.5 Productivity Enhancement

Modernization of looms and mechanization of preloom activities are two major initiatives to improve the productivity of the weavers. State governments have schemes for providing better looms and weaving accessories. Most of them offer grants with only a few governments like Tamil Nadu which has designed partial loan schemes especially under housing cum loom improvement. However, PWCS mention that the targets are too small to satisfy the large demand.

Preloom mechanization reduces the drudgery and also enables another person to carry out this work while the weaver is free to work on the loom nonstop. Moreover, the dobby system was found to be tedious and hence the system simplification enables weaver to have free movement so that work can be carried out for longer hours. In tie and dye, mechanization of preloom process is reducing drudgery to a large extent and also improves productivity. Weavers prepare tie and dye weft yarns manually, by grouping them in calculated quantities. With the introduction of the Auto Ikat Group Former (AIGF) machine, the time required for this process was greatly reduced, freeing the weaver for other tasks. Importantly, this machine also track-monitors jobs from start to finish, through an electronic control unit—including accurate control over motif and design formation—so that the weaver can leave off during the process, if need be.[14]

---

[14] GOI, Ministry of Textiles, Prayas, A Compilation of Success Stories of Handloom Clusters (2016). http://handlooms.nic.in/writereaddata/PRAYAS635785218515448945.pdf, accessed on October 7, 2016.

Similarly, the spinning in charkhas is also getting mechanized though these measures are yet to be widely adopted.

The recent initiative of some governments to offer specific schemes for cementing the pit looms in order for weavers to work in the rainy season will not lead to increased productivity according to the weavers. Some moisture is needed to weave and in cemented looms it becomes hot leading to breakage of the yarns.

The introduction of jacquard machines has led to additional expenditure since the roofs of the houses had to be raised to fit the machine above the frame of the loom. Weavers are still using their feet to operate leg pedals against a load of 15–20 kg especially in jacquard looms. This results in quick fatigue and thus declining productivity. Therefore, use of pneumatic lifting mechanism for jacquard shedding can lead to increased comfort level of the weavers and higher productivity. Simple mechanical (nonelectrical) innovations that have been done by weavers' service centers need to be promoted to reduce strain for weavers, thus improving productivity.

6.6 Product Diversification and Design Inputs

In various handloom hubs and clusters, the growth of computer-aided design capacity is very visible enabled by private sector. Master weavers and independent weavers have spurred this movement and now PWCs are also increasingly availing of the services to develop designs and get them approved by prospective buyers. Earlier the weavers used to develop the design on graph paper, then developed sample which was time consuming and costly as well. Use of computer-aided applications now makes designs in different color combinations and once the purchaser approves, the designs are converted in the looms. This is a boon to the weavers, especially individual weavers. A sector expert form West Bengal mentions

The design development and fitting it into a loom takes 10 to 15 days. The cost of the design can be recovered only if 50 saris are sold. Now with good designer and the computer aided applications, the approval of the design is possible and thus there is some certainty of customer approval and sales.

The apex marketing societies are also engaging designers to work with the weavers for value addition into garments. Utkalika, Orissa State Co-operative Handicrafts Corporation Limited, has engaged two designers to be attached to the weavers for value addition of cloth to ready-made garments but finds that only few weaver entrepreneurs are keen to experiment. APCO has engaged a designer since 2014 and out of 380 weavers' societies that are supplying cloth, only about 20 are keen to work with the new designs and move into value-added products like garments.

In West Bengal, the Directorate of Handlooms has developed a State Design Center in collaboration with Tantuja. Designers are selected from various districts and their design skills and computer skills are further honed and improved through master textile designers. In all about 160 designers are attached to 8 master designers and these designers work with weavers, societies, and so on. This initiative is expected to yield better results. Biswa Bangla, an initiative to showcase the rich heritage weaves of West Bengal, aims at high end of the market.

However, the apex marketing societies find that for high end of the market, design development work being done is inadequate. Engagement of international designers should be facilitated by the government to work with grassroots which can fetch more profits for societies and better wages for the weavers.

Designers having their own export business are now working with weaver clusters, developing designs, and entering into exclusive clauses for not selling these designs to anywhere else. Some of PWCS complain that sample development is time taking and is also proving to be costly with very few orders placed so far. Moreover, they do not pay equitably and weavers remain where they are whereas the profits are garnered by the design houses.

But not all design improvement is aimed at high end market. In Odisha, lower middle class buy Khandua silk while middle class and rich buy high cost Sambalpuri and Bomkai. Since same design became repetitive over time there was stagnation in sale of Khandua saris. Over the last five years, new designs have been developed with the support of government and as a result sales of these saris have improved. Design plays a vital role in effective access to markets.

While the current initiatives are aimed at external designers working with weavers, there is another school of thought that weavers are the best designers and all along it is their imagination and creativity that has given identity to the handloom products. So, weavers must be encouraged to come up with new designs and must be involved in the design workshops in periodical intervals where they can be informed about trends and where needed get help from the professional designers.

Ready-made garment is seen as the major market segment next to saris which has been recording the highest growth rates in

The government had in a great initiative taken a bunch of designers to Varanasi to market the weaves at international fashion shows. But the thing is we have to also ensure that we can generate enough woven material for designers to work with. Have we considered the fact that Banarasi weaves are not good for western cuts because they were imagined as drapes? If we have, how do we use textile technology to make the changes needed? Can the weaver create several hundred yards with the shortage of raw material? Most of the silk is being imported from China now. The promotion and marketing cannot be done in isolation..... it needs thorough economic intervention.

Source: Laila Tyabji, Founder, Dastkar.

last three years. Dastkar Andhra Pradesh, Sasha, a private marketing initiative in West Bengal, and e-commerce platforms dedicated to handlooms and handmade crafts are offering more ready-made garments to cater to the younger generation's demand.

6.7 Marketing of Handloom Products—Role of Apex Handloom Marketing Societies

Each state has its own apex handloom weavers' marketing societies. They are federated organizations with the primary weavers' societies being members. The primary weavers' societies sell to the apex marketing societies, private traders and some have even their own showrooms. Many of them participate in regional, state, and national exhibitions for sales. Though PWCS sell to different sources, they prefer to sell to the apex societies.

Apart from the apex handloom marketing societies, the state handicraft marketing societies also procure and sell handlooms from the primary weavers' societies. Since tie and dye is considered a handicraft, the textiles with this craft are sold through the apex handicraft societies such as Utkalika, Lepakshi, and so on. While they sell these crafts, the emporia also sell other types of handlooms to offer a choice to the customers. Moreover, within the product mix of handicrafts and handlooms, handlooms move faster and offer better margins and thus there is an incentive for these handicraft apexes to sell handlooms.

However, not all apex marketing societies are vibrant nor all sell only handlooms. While few, such as Boyanika, Tantuja, and Co-optex, are well integrated with the member PWCS and sell their products, there are others especially from North India which reportedly are selling more of power loom products for their survival. Even presently well-functioning apex marketing societies, such as Boyanika, Co-optex, Tantuja, and so on, were once in losses and had to be restructured and revived with considerable reduction of staff and closure of sick units.

6.7.1 Procurement

The apex societies largely procure the goods from their weavers' societies. However, it is not unusual for them to directly buy from some of the master weavers and large traders. The handicraft apexes bought more from the master weavers cum large traders than the primary weavers' societies; capacity in terms of quality control, timely delivery, and also ability to tide over delayed cash payments were found to be better in the case of private trade.

APCO has about 900 PWCS as members out of which products are procured from 358 societies. Tantuja, in West Bengal, has 468 primary WCSs as equity shareholders and procurement is made from 300 to 400 societies depending on the ability to sell. Boyanika, Odisha has 607 working societies as members and during procurement was done from 195. Serifed, Odisha is marketing silk cocoons and finished products. Through Amlan, a marketing initiative, sale of finished goods is undertaken. To Serifed, 163 societies are affiliated—62 primary tussar rearers' cooperative societies, 37 mulberry rearers' cooperative societies, and 64 WCSs, which are getting marketing facilities through Serifed[15].

Utkalika does not have shareholding from PWCS but procures goods from 60 societies regularly. It has three kinds of suppliers for handlooms: (a) weaving cooperatives, from five districts of Odisha, usually standard items up to ₹5000 value per piece are procured from cooperatives; (b) handloom SHGs undertaking value addition such as cushion making, home usage products; (c) individual weavers and entrepreneurial traders supply 60% of handloom procurement; only high value exclusive items (usually ₹10,000 and above per piece) are procured from them.

Similarly, Lepakshi, handicraft development agency in Andhra Pradesh, procures handloom products from 10 to 15 societies every year but buys mostly from master weavers.

In terms of numbers of members versus those who had patronage with the apex handloom marketing societies, it is seen that these numbers varied between 30% and 50% in any year. Stringent quality and delivery schedule controls set by some apexes resulted in fewer societies being able to sell their production to apex marketing societies.

6.7.2 Procurement Plan

Before the start of the financial year, the apexes draw up sales and procurement plan. These are shared on quarterly basis with the PWCs in Andhra Pradesh and Odisha. Usually, the targets are arrived at by increasing the sales targets by 20% year on year minus the actual stock in hand. While this system is confirmed to be working in Odisha, in states like West Bengal, the PWCS mention that the apex societies do the procurement for high value, niche products only before festival seasons to manage their stocks and working capital. PWCS, to provide regular employment to their members and also to stock, adequately invest more in working capital due to bunching of purchase near festival season.

6.7.3 Product Mix

Niche products, standard products and low-value daily use items, and so on are all sold by the apexes. Niche products and common design products are limited in the

---

Regarding product mix, the bulk of the materials sourced are saris. With the rich traditional weaves in West Bengal (Tangail, Jamdani, Balucheri, Phulia cotton weave, Shibori (tie and dye) etc., produced in many natural fibers (cotton, jute, linen, mulberry and tussar silk) and the local culture of wearing saris, Tantuja caters to lower middle class to rich households. Since last year exports of scarves and stoles are being attempted.

Source: Managing Director, Tantuja.

---

[15] Data on weavers' societies seen from the website of SERIFED, http://odisha.gov.in/textiles/, accessed on May 23, 2016.

product mix of some the apexes. Saris are the major product segment for the apex marketing societies.

Some of the state governments are the major procurer of the daily use handloom products such as saris, dhotis, materials for uniforms for government staff, and so on, thus enabling the medium and low-skilled weavers to have a livelihood. In West Bengal, the government utilizes Tantuja for placing orders for lower value items. During 2015–16, the total sales of Tantuja are ₹1240 million, out of which ₹520 million are from execution of government orders for saris (0.6 million saris) and dhotis as part of poverty reduction measures uniform material, disaster management-related relief material, and so on. Tantuja places orders with primary WCSs and the societies have the freedom to say no to low-value orders. However, even those societies with skilled weavers also rarely decline these orders since looking to the condition of semiskilled and low-skilled weavers outside the society, these orders are executed through these weavers though they are not members. Tantuja estimates that about 0.2 million such weavers execute the bulk orders from government.

The chief minister of Andhra Pradesh directed all the departments to purchase their liveries from the handloom sector. APCO, as a nodal agency, coordinates the orders between the departments and weavers' societies. In 2014–15, out of sales of ₹2420 million, ₹1674 million (69%) were that of the government departments and in 2015–16, the same was 66%. These orders are executed through weavers' societies. Similarly, in Tamil Nadu free supply of uniform to school children under noon meal scheme is implemented with procurement from handloom weavers' societies through Co-optex.

While government procurement orders provide livelihoods for low-skilled weavers, this also provides a ready market for the apex handloom societies. However, the pitfall is that this does not foster marketing capacities and producing for meeting consumer demand and facing competition.

6.7.4 Market Intelligence

The apex marketing societies have not undertaken any major studies on customer preference and what different age groups prefer in handloom products. The front office sales staff is often found to be the ears and eyes for understanding customer preferences. The senior management of the apex marketing societies relies more on them for market preferences.

Utkalika has point of sale and inventory management process; reportedly the only organization to have developed such a process. A 19-digit code helps track supplier-wise, designwise information on what sells. Color tracking could not be implemented and Utkalika proposes to include this in 2016–17 to watch market acceptance rates of different colors and fabrics. Customer satisfaction with pricing is also being monitored.

6.7.5 Staff Capacity

All the apexes had to shed some staff in the process of restructuring. While governments are encouraging outsourcing, the apexes find that service providers cannot be trusted with safeguarding products. Two apex marketing societies have commissioned studies through management institutes to assess the capability of staff especially sales counter staff and the findings and video recordings of the staff behavior are being used to improve their skills in customer relations and marketing.

6.7.6 Market Share

APCO's market share is estimated to be about 10% in silk varieties and 50% in cotton and other natural fibers segments. Tantuja mentions that 15% of what WCS produce is procured and marketed by them. Utkalika procures less than 10% of what the societies produce. All the marketing societies agree that private wholesale dealers are the major procurers of handlooms who provide spot payment and some advance as well.

6.7.7 Procurement Cost and Margins

All the apex societies have a technical advice division to assess costs which are determined by the cost of materials including yarn and thread count used, weaving days and the wages determined by the government where applicable, and margins to society. While the primary costing is done by the society, the technical division assesses the design and salability. Boyanika has more than 6,000 product codes and costs. Utkalika has about 4,000 codes. Stringent quality controls are now being adopted by some of the apexes.

The apex societies keep a gross margin of 50% to 80% but ultimately aim for a net margin of 8% to 10%. The offer of rebates throughout the year eats into the margins and reduces the net profits. APCO has a markup of 80% on the goods procured but offers 30% discount for 185 to 200 days in a year. Even on other days 20% discount is made available to the customers. Boyanika has a markup of 50% to 70% and offers rebate of 20% plus 10%. The 20% rebate is offered throughout the year to compete with private traders. The senior management mentions that this is a very old practise since inception of Boyanika; 10% is the rebate that comes from the Central Government scheme to be shared equally between state and the center. The state provides 20% additional rebate for 100 days; 10% extra rebate is offered from Boyanika's margins. The net margin Boyanika aims at is between 8% and 12%. Tantuja aims for 15% to 20% net margin. Utkalika, on the other hand, is able to give discount for only 100 days at 20% as set by the state government. In some

of the apexes, the profits from marketing of handloom products are low and in fact they earn more from managing the state government funds parked with them.

While Boyonika charges 6% commission from the marketing societies for effecting sales of their produce, the other apexes are not having such a practise. PWCS in Odisha have a fixed margin of 17.5% on cost of the saris and hence they are able to pass on 6% commission (please see the section on pricing). In Andhra Pradesh, the PWCS get a net margin of 6% to 6.5% profit whereas in West Bengal the PWCs have a net margin of 8%

However, the apexes are not able to support creativity of individual weavers. High value purchase is proving to be difficult when a weaver brings his product since the weaver inspector, store manager have to carry out costing which has to be approved by the managing director after which the code is given. The pricing also does not adequately compensate creativity. So these weavers prefer to deal with private players where decision-making is quick and handled efficiently.

6.7.8 Marketing Channels

Marketing is carried out largely through showrooms followed by exhibitions (both national and international) and e-marketing. All the apexes have showrooms within the states as well as in other states—metros and major cities. While a few apexes like in Odisha are well supported by the states in showroom-related expenditure, others are constrained by lack of budgets. All of them are exploring export markets for some of the niche products as well as commonly used products such as scarves, stoles, and so on. Overall, Tantuja and Boyonika mention that 80% of the sales happen within the state since the locals have the culture of wearing handloom products. The different states' apex marketing societies also cooperate to sell each other's products on reciprocal basis. However, such sales volumes are very minimal. Boyonika, Serifed, and Co-optex have online marketing and sales platform.

> Apex marketing societies add 50% as mark up, offer 20% discount, and another 10% of Central Government subsidy. Thus, a sari bought for ₹1,000, is priced at ₹1,500 but after discounts will be sold for ₹1,080 thus 8% is the actual margin for the apex marketing society. It is a social cause and not a business.
>
> *Source:* Sector expert, Odisha.

Tantuja has an agreement with Flipkart. Apexes see this as way forward for expanding sales especially overseas markets.

6.7.9 Payments to Societies

The marketing societies are able to pay to the weavers' societies normally in three months. Where the apexes supply yarn to the weavers' societies, as in the case of Boyanika, the payments are net of yarn prices. Tantuja mentions that weavers' societies deliver the goods in local procurement centers and usually the payments are made within two months of procurement. Serifed, Odisha reportedly makes payment within a month to the weavers' cooperatives since they procure smaller volumes and retaining weavers is critical to compete with Boyanika and Utkalika.

Utkalika has two procedures for making payments. For materials procured from cooperative societies, 2% to 5% extra payment is made since they are community-owned organizations. The low-value items produced by the cooperatives—*gamcha* (thin cotton towel), short dhoti, and so on—are accepted without any prior orders to extent of production. For exclusive and high-priced items (more than ₹5,000 per piece) specific orders with specifications are placed, an advance is paid, and acceptance of the products is subject to stringent quality check. In the tribal belts of Kalahandi, Balangir, and Koraput immediate payment is made since the weavers come from far off places and special provision for making cash payments where demanded has been made. Small volumes are accepted from the region. For the rest of suppliers, an initial advance is paid and a 3-months cycle is maintained for settlement. Since Utkalika does not supply yarn, they try to settle the payments within this time frame.

The payment from government (for supplies against its orders) is often delayed. The marketing apexes mention that they get paid after five to six months and hence the payment to weavers' societies can be delayed. APCO borrows about ₹1 billion a year to meet the payments to PWCS. The apexes borrow subsidized loans from National Cooperative Development Corporation or cash credit facility from the banks and utilize this to make payments to the societies. However, the weavers' societies are also investing their own funds or borrowing from the banks to meet the working capital needs since the government payments are delayed.

6.7.10 Unsold Stock

Apexes keep the stock for two years under normal pricing and stocks beyond that period are sold at discounts of 50% to 70%. Beyond third year, the good quality stock is converted to garments. Otherwise it is discarded. Since audit looks at such procedure in detail, due processes need to be followed. All the apexes mention that such weeding out is very less and not more than 0.01% to 1% of the value of sales in a year. These losses are not passed on to the societies but borne by the apexes.

6.7.11 Unique Selling Proposition of the Apexes

Apexes find that customers prefer to buy from them in spite of higher price due to authenticity, quality control, and guarantee for color which is not ensured by private sellers.

6.8 Working of Primary Weavers' Cooperative Societies;

To get field level perspectives, five weavers' societies in three states (Odisha, West Bengal, and Tamil Nadu) were visited. All of them were more than 40 years old with well-established processes.

Membership: While membership ranges between 120 and 1,254 weavers in these societies, the active members with working looms range between 94 and 350. In Tamil Nadu, the society had nearly 75% idle members—the reason being employment opportunities from nearby factories. However, with closure of a big factory in the vicinity, more weavers are reported to be resuming weaving. In Odisha more looms have been added at PWCS, from funds released from RRR package. Usually women who do not own looms weave in these looms. While normally work is provided only to members, it is not unusual for the PWCS to get work done from outside weavers in the village when a large order is to be executed.

Most of the societies are not interested to add new members looking at the production and marketing issues. In the field interaction it was also seen that though women are the actual weavers now, with men being seasonal weavers or absentees, there is reluctance to change the membership from husband to the wife.

As per the information provided by these societies, these villages traditionally have a few thousand weavers. However large numbers of weavers, ranging between 30% and 90%, are outside the cooperative fold primarily due to defunct societies, weavers selling off their shares and membership, and inability to get back into cooperative fold. Some of the members were working on both power looms and handlooms.

Services to Members: Apart from providing yarn and dyes for weaving and providing the weavers the conversion wages, the WCS also link up their members with the government schemes for weavers and BPL cardholders. Housing, looms, and accessories are the usual schemes accessed. Apart from these, weavers are provided information on weavers' credit card and MUDRA loans. Weavers have direct dealings with banks and the WCSs are not involved, except to give information. The societies also enroll the members for the government insurance and pension schemes.

Products and Markets: These societies specialize in specific natural fibers such as cotton, silk, tussar, and so on. While saris are the main output, they are diversifying into other products such as dress material, stoles, and shawls. The change to new products is not easy; many weavers very adept in sari weaving expressed dissatisfaction at being trained for shawls and stoles since they are shorter cloths. This training is not considered as skill enhancement.

Since these societies are well established, one would expect steady and assured markets. The weaving societies have three to four channels for sales. The apex marketing societies is a dependable channel though their sales volumes range from 30% in the case of Odisha WCS to less than 20% in West Bengal to about 5% in the case of Tamil Nadu. All of them sell a part of production to master weavers and also to wholesale traders. In Andhra Pradesh and West Bengal, the wholesale markets are the major source of sales. Export-oriented production has been volatile with steady decline in an assured market and exploration of

	Nuapatna WCS, Odisha	Maniabandha WCS, Odisha	Tussar and Silk WCS Gopalpur, Odisha	Shantipur WCS, West Bengal	Silk Weavers' Society, Kanchipuram, Tamil Nadu
Registered	1948	1948	1976	1977	1965
Members	439 members; 239 looms thus active members; 39 looms added out of RRR packages.	422 members, 368 with looms, 122 BPL. 2 looms added out of RRR.	120 members; 94 working looms	538 members and all are active	1,254 members— active members are 350 to 400
Village	2,100 looms—27 WCS and 17 are working.		14 WCS and all are tussar weavers	90% of weavers outside cooperatives. 46 societies—only 6 are active.	16 working WCS— additionally some are defunct

	Nuapatna WCS, Odisha	Maniabandha WCS, Odisha	Tussar and Silk WCS Gopalpur, Odisha	Shantipur WCS, West Bengal	Silk Weavers' Society, Kanchipuram, Tamil Nadu
Products	Largely silk—silk saris, cotton dress material, silk shawls of late.	Cotton saris— now diversifying to dress material.	Tussar	All types of clothing in all natural fibers— cotton, linen, tussar, silk, jute and combination thereof.	Silk saris, pavadai, dress material. Specialization in pure zari and pure silk.
Major markets	Boyanika 30%; Exhibitions 50%, master weavers and traders 20%.	Sambalpuri Bastralaya 40%, Boyanika 30%, exhibitions 15%; Local traders 15%.	Make on orders 40% Boyanika and Serifed 30% Local exhibitions and trades 30%.	Tantuja 30%; Exports through middlemen 20%; Wholesale market 50%.	Own showrooms 70%; Co-optex 30%

new export markets proving to be time and resource consuming. E-marketing is being explored in tie-ups with both Amazon and Flipkart in West Bengal with government support.

The silk weavers' societies in Odisha as well as Tamil Nadu have piled up stocks and have issues with sales. The cotton and tussar weaver societies expressed adequate and quick moving sales. In spite of having 12 modern showrooms in all major cities in Tamil Nadu, the stock piled up in PWCS in Tamil Nadu is high at 150% of yearly sales.

While the apex marketing societies regularly lift the goods in Odisha and Tamil Nadu, in West Bengal more goods are procured by Tantuja from September onwards for puja sales. This necessitates stocking of production at PWCS. While apex weavers' societies and also local master weavers pay regularly, the settlement with the wholesale traders is reported to be once in a year. However, these wholesale traders also supply yarn on credit which accounts for 50% of the cost and to that extent the working capital is avoided.

Payment to Weavers: All the societies report to settle wages at least within 15 days. Since yarn and in some cases the dyes are also supplied by the societies, the weavers are paid only conversion charges/wages. All of them have a working capital limit from cooperative bank/public sector bank and are able to get interest subsidy under the government scheme after the audited statements are filed with the Directorate.

Pricing of the Products: All the WCSs have costing norms as per design and maintain cost sheets. Except in West Bengal, the other two states are guided by the state government rules on how much should a weaver be paid. In Odisha whenever a new design or product is designed, the cost norms are decided by a committee consisting of representative of technical advisory department of Directorate of Handlooms, WCSs representative; the weaver is also consulted on the number of days spent. Separate costing register is maintained and used for future.

Similar procedure is followed by WCSs in Tamil Nadu where the state directorate has norms of payments to skilled workers and artisans and per piece rates are settled depending on the design involved. For example, for weaving a silk sari with pure zari a weaver is paid ₹5,000 which takes about 10 to 12 days. The costs are arrived at by individual WCSs. While fixing rates, they also check on the salability and market acceptance of the price. Though the societies aim to give wages of ₹250 to ₹300 per day, these are only for the weaver's time spent on the loom. Invariably some of the preloom activities are carried out by an additional person usually women in preparing the yarn and dyeing and these are not counted. Similarly, to set a design for the loom takes anywhere between 3 and 10 days depending on the design and this is also not calculated. As a result, weavers are not paid for the total labor that goes into the final product. The final payment to weavers works out to less than minimum wages for casual laborers!

Mark-up and Margins: WCSs in Odisha adopt a government-approved rate of 17.5% on the cost price for mark-up for sales. In Tamil Nadu, the rates are dependent on the price of the product; ₹4,000 and below—32%, ₹4,000 to 10,000—34%, and above 10,000—37%. In West Bengal, the mark-up is usually 8%. In spite of such mark-ups, the Tamil Nadu WCS after the RRR package has accumulated losses, which is getting reduced in the last two years with profits being posted.

6.8.1 Problems Highlighted by Weavers' Societies

All the societies are concerned about the conversion charges being paid to the member weavers. They feel that at least 50% increase in the current rates is needed. Minimum conversion charges for low-skilled workers should be ₹200 per day.

Power looms are copying the simple handloom designs giving unfair competition to the handlooms. Only high end and artistic products, such as silk, tie and dye works, Jamdani, and so on, are not copied by the power looms. According to the PWCS though enforcement department offices are situated close by and they try to carry out inspections, the political clout that the power loom owners enjoy ensures that no action is taken.

While yarn supply has improved, for good quality cotton yarn of more than 100 counts the WCS have to rely largely on spinning mills from South India. The farther the societies are from the production area, the higher the costs thus affecting their competitive ability. While state governments are reportedly considering setting up of spinning mills in the state but these are not translated into action.

Marketing, especially understanding new markets, is a major issue. Usually exporters engage middlemen with very few purchasers willing to directly deal with PWCS. Similarly though there are chains of stores set up by big industrial houses, they also prefer to deal through middlemen and not directly with PWCS which leads to uncertainty of contracts and execution. Reliability of apex marketing societies is being questioned by some of the societies due to increasing rejection rates citing quality parameters. PWCS feel that the apexes have more supplies than sales and hence manage the situation by higher rejection.

Though the PWCS visited did not have a problem of shortage of working capital, they point out that other societies in the village/area face serious working capital shortage. Banks have not been willing to provide fresh loans after the RRR package. The payments from apexes to PWCS take between 15 days and 3 months and the PWCS pay interest on the working capital; but neither the apexes nor the wholesale traders reimburse this interest cost.

6.9 Working of Master Weavers

Master weavers are an important link in the handloom value chain. They have better skills, contacts with bulk buyers, are able to arrange for some working capital, and get work done by other weavers. The master weavers have a reputation based on their skills and managerial capabilities to run a weaving enterprise. However, the capacities of master differ. Some of them are dependent on buying agents and can be subject to exploitation. In other cases, they keep the weavers they employ under control, limit their wages, and ration out work. On account of their better (and many times exclusive) access to yarn, dyes and dyehouse facilities, and market information, they tend to garner a large part of the value realizations. There are also master weavers known for their original work and award-winning creations. Some of them train a number of weavers providing them an opportunity to develop.

In a study of master weavers, Suresh Bhagavatula[16] concluded that master weavers are the risk-takers and entrepreneurs.

If one were to view the handloom industry from a firm level, establishing a venture in handloom industry is fraught with risk. Firstly, master weavers need to raise capital and more often than not, they have to rely on informal financial systems that charge interest rates higher than 36%. Secondly, they need to coordinate their production, which spreads across various locations, to ensure that the products are marketable. Third, they need to market their products to retail stores, which are again spread across various locations. Cash transactions are rare in handloom marketing. Store owners need to be provided with credit periods of 30 to 90 days depending on the season. An immediate difficulty with sales on credit is the recovery of it. Fourth, many weavers require their master weavers to upgrade to more expensive looms which means that capital, which cannot be used in the production cycle, has to be infused initially and the profits are likely to come only later. Finally, raw material needs to be purchased mostly on credit for about a period of a week to a fortnight which is much shorter than the sales cycles. Therefore, master weavers producing expensive fabric need to invest heavily in raw material upfront on the premise that the product will eventually be saleable and generate profits months later.

On account of the diverse risks, master weavers seek higher returns and a larger share of value realized. If the government makes functional use of master weavers and reduce their risks as well as costs of operation, they might be in a position to pass on a larger share of value realized to the other weavers.

---

[16] Suresh Bhagavatuls, 2010, The Working of Entrepreneurs in a Competitive Low Technology Industry: The Case of Master Weavers in the Handloom Industry, IIM Bangalore.

6.10 Do Weavers Get a Decent Livelihood?

According to the Directorates of Handlooms, apex marketing societies and PWCS highly skilled weavers such as Baluchari, Jamdani, double Ikat, and silk saris with zari works are expected to earn ₹300 to ₹400 per day. The medium skilled weavers weaving standard items earn ₹200 and low-value item weavers are expected to earn ₹150 per day. However, the apexes are also concerned about the salability of goods if increasing wages hike the prices with competing private traders quoting lower prices.

Director of Handlooms Odisha along with apex marketing society drive the pricing especially cloth conversion charges/wages for the weavers. Their staff attends the technical meetings at PWCS when the cost norms are arrived at. Weavers also mention that for a new item they are consulted on how much time is taken. For old items, wage revision is undertaken every six months.

> Odisha is the only state where income is much higher for weavers as compared to other states; the state has artistic weavers and so they deserve more income. In Western Odisha, with more artistic weaving of Sambhalpuris, 60% to 80% of the costs are conversion charges and the rest being raw material costs. In mass commercial production area of coastal areas the wages form 60%. Every year Government enhances the conversion charges (wages) by at least 10%. In the last 10 years, the cost of sari has increased 3 times.
>
> *Source:* Directorate of Handlooms, Odisha.

Not all states are able to ensure such close involvement of government officials in pricing and wage fixing nor do they find it desirable. For instance, Director of Handlooms West Bengal mentions that with 300 technical staff they cannot manage pricing in 700 PWCS. While government nominee is on the boards of PWCS, they hardly have time to attend these meetings.

The government seems to believe in creating an enabling environment than guiding or controlling PWCS. The government has fixed the minimum wages for weavers in West Bengal.

Supplying to export markets bring in better income for weavers but very marginally. Some of the private initiatives like that of Sasha, West Bengal, Fabindia, and so on are also able to provide 10% more than prevailing government rates even when the woven goods are exported. The PWCS in Shantipur has been able to pay 20% more wages for export orders. With export markets turning sluggish even Sasha and other private marketing agencies are looking to niche markets within India and have been able to sustain only the existing local wage rates.

The more skilled silk weavers in well-established societies/clusters are able to earn between ₹6000 and ₹10,000 per month whereas simple cotton saris weavers are able

---

Box 6.2:   *Caselets from the Field on Earnings of Weavers*

Tulasi has been weaving silk saris for the last 25 years. Her husband used to be a weaver but now is employed in a factory. Her husband, as the member of a PWCS, deals with the society including marketing. The society provides yarn and other materials. She gets designs made in computer for the jacquard weaving which costs ₹3,000 to ₹15,000 based on the design. Depending on the market acceptance, a design can run up to two years. A loom is set for weaving three saris and this may take three days since she has to depend on an external person to set the loom with jacquard design. Though the jacquard setting can be finished in one day, the external person delays it to maximize his income. In about 45 days, 3 saris are woven. She gets ₹5,000 as wages per sari and after deductions of 10% toward PF and other savings she gets ₹4,500. Thus, her net earnings are ₹12,500 for two months.

Velu is 22 years old, resides in the same area as Tulasi, and works for a master weaver. He gets ₹4,000 per silk sari as compared to ₹5,000 being paid by PWCS. He has fit in a small motor for the leg operations in the loom which makes him more productive and he is able to weave three saris in a month. His mother helps in preloom activities and thus saves some labor. Net earnings are ₹10,000 per month after payments for loom setting.

Shanthakumari, a widow and staying alone, carries out weaving of only silk borders. She earns ₹600 per week. She has not undertaken regular weaving since two persons are needed for weaving. She undertakes MGNREGS work when it is available in the village; on an average five days in a month.

Gajalakshmi and her husband are private silk sari weavers. They make their own designs, weave them, and then sell them to master weavers for ₹20,000 netting ₹10,000 per sari. However, they are aware that the saris change three other hands and ultimately sold for ₹35,000 to ₹40,000.

Sujoy Meher weaves lungis with an output of eight lungis per week with average earning of ₹1,500 per week and monthly earnings of ₹6,000 to ₹8,000 depending on his health. He has taken up lungi work since it is fast moving. The village is famous for silk and tie and die weaving, but there is a waiting period of four to six weeks for wages in silk weaving. His wife is involved in preloom activities.

Gopal Meher weaves cotton saris, both simple puja saris as well as Ikat (tie and dye) weaves. The last sari he had woven was an Ikat and the costing norms came to ₹3,170 and his wages were ₹1,100 for weaving for five days. His wife does the preloom activities of starching, prewinding, and so on, and is engaged at least for 4 to 5 hours for 20 days in a month. Her wages are neither accounted for nor reimbursed.

Amitava Basak's last piece was a simple cotton sari; the cost price was ₹1,020 out of which wages were ₹450 for 2.5 days of work. His wife carries out preloom activities for 4 hours each day for 18 days in a month. This is not accounted for. He is able to work for 25 days in a month with average earnings of ₹5,000.

Biren Basak is adept in weaving any type of natural fiber into sari. The last sari he had woven was linen saree and costing was for ₹3,200 out of which wages were ₹1,000 for three days.

to earn much less. However, if the time of other household workers are reckoned, the earnings per head per day comes down drastically by at least 60%, which is much lower than the prevailing wage rate for casual unskilled labor work prevailing in the states. Some small sample field studies find the monthly income even lesser at ₹1,500 to ₹2,000 per month. A study on position of traditional weavers in Varanasi in 2013 found that the income of weavers ranged between less than ₹1,500 and ₹5,000 with more than 81% of weavers earning less than ₹3,500 per month.[17] Similarly, a study in Kallidaikurichi in Tamil Nadu found that 90% of the small sample of 50 weavers earned less than ₹2000.[18] However, the recent publication on "Handloom Day" 2016 by the Ministry of Textiles showcases some success stories of cluster development and improvement in income of weavers because of several initiatives in the cluster. The weavers showcased therein have almost doubled their income in two to three years.[19] Thus, while there is possibility to raise the incomes, this requires concerted efforts and well-planned interventions. PWCS mention that weaving is family work and almost all family members are involved. Husband, wife, children, everyone plays a part and it is very difficult to measure level of per head income and level of employment or unemployment. When the entire family gets involved it is difficult to reckon the entire labor contribution and cost the same, let alone pay a reasonable wage.

All the weavers interacted with except Velu were middle aged and have severe joint pains. Few have problems with eyesight as well. Some of the weavers do not want their children to take up this profession due to the physical strain as well as low incomes. They are educating their children to find regular jobs.

Directorates of Handloom and marketing apexes opine that weavers' interests are protected though they agree that wages for such skilled artisans need to increase. However, the exodus of youth and the reluctance of weavers to involve their children in the profession tell a different story. Other than the income factor, the weaving process itself is considered very laborious. Weaving is painstaking and meticulous work and thus the younger generation is not keen to take this up. In a recent initiative, Co-optex began to showcase the efforts put in by the individual weaver in making the final product as part of its marketing strategy.

The tags showcase the specific weavers who had woven the material, in a bid to give them some positive recognition and some connect with the customer. The tag also indicates that the weaver had to move their hands and legs 19,000/20,000 times in 2 days to weave a sari. The wear and tear of the limbs is an aspect that was highlighted by the weavers as one of the reasons for less productivity and thus income beyond 45 years. Probably that is the reason for Government of Andhra Pradesh to offer pension from the age of 50; and for many weavers to say categorically that they will educate their children to have jobs than do the traditional family work. With the youth not being attracted to weaving, the question arises whether the industry is in its sunset days.

---

[17] Shaw Tanusree, "A Study of the Present Situation of the Traditional Handloom Weavers of Varanasi, Uttar Pradesh, India," *International Research Journal of Social Sciences,* 4, no. 3 (March 2015): 48–53. Available online at www.isca.in. ISSN 2319–3565.

[18] A. Venkateswaran, "A Socio Economic Conditions of Handloom Weaving In Kallidai Kurichi of Tirunelveli District," *International Journal of Social Science and Humanities Research* 2, no. 2 (April–June 2014): 38–49. Available online at www.researchpublish.com. ISSN 2348–3164.

[19] Ministry of Textiles, GOI, Prayas, a compilation of success stories of handloom clusters (2016), http://handlooms.nic.in/writereaddata/PRAYAS635785218515448945.pdf, accessed on October 10, 2016.

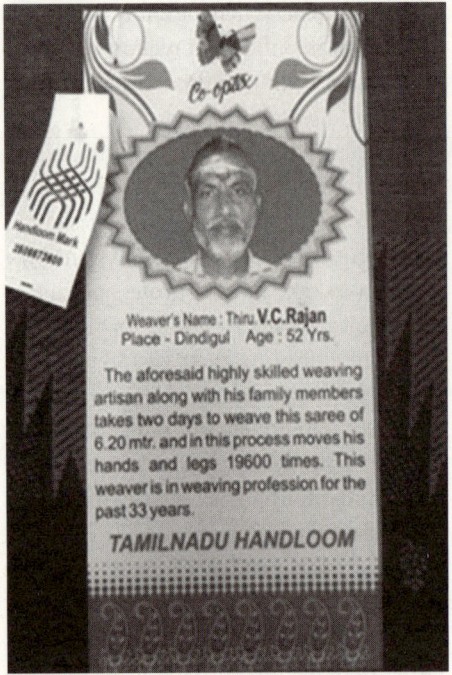

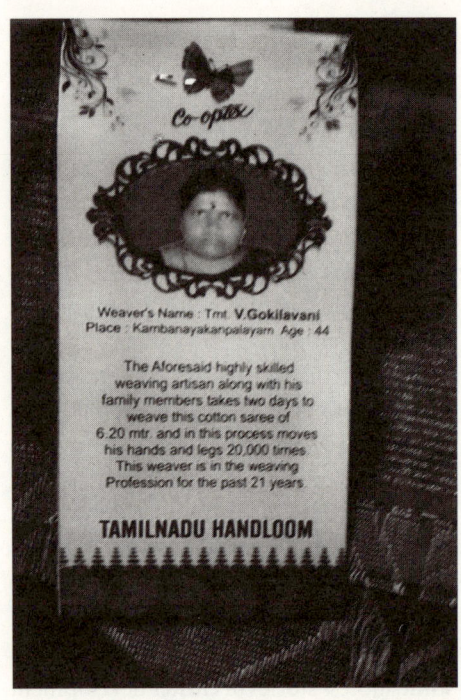

6.10 Sunset or a Rising Industry?

Global demand for quality handloom is high, with a demand for green, ethical handmade products that offer individual identity through a skilled hand. Boyanika mentions that in some seasons there is inadequate supply to meet demand since WCSs are fully engaged in executing different orders. In locations like Maheshwar in Madhya Pradesh there are reports that the numbers of weavers had increased from 200 in 1978 to over 2,000 now since the industry has been growing. Similarly in Odisha certain clusters are attracting more youth as per the sectoral experts. Nuapatna and Gopalpur clusters are picking up with more youth joining. Some clusters are also moving up the value chain in terms of quality, design, tie-up with designers, value addition, and so on.

Dastkar pointed to the growth in handloom demand over the last five years, covering a range that extended from exquisite products as well as functional ones—*gamchas* and *jharans*. These claims are also backed with sales statistics from some apexes, few master weavers, and design firms and retail entities such as Sasha and Fabindia. However, more or less the growth is seen in high value high skilled segment. In other standard segments and low value daily items there does not seem to be such vibrant growth.

One view is that since Indian population is young, unless the middle income youth purchase handlooms, the sector does not have much future. NHDC had commissioned a study across 13 cities including 7 metro cities to understand the awareness and perception of the younger generation of the handloom products and explore market opportunities and ways to popularize the increased usage of handloom within the target group. The study has thrown up suggestions on the attributes that may be improved to make handloom products more acceptable to the mass and specifically to the younger generation:[20]

---

[20] NHDC, Report on Market research for promotion of India Handloom brand (2016), http://handlooms. nic.in/writereaddata/2534.pdf, accessed on October 10, 2016.

1. Fusion designs (traditional and contemporary designs)
2. Varieties of clothes for men
3. Smoother finishing to make it easier to wear in any kind of climate
4. Easily available—through ecommerce.
5. Awareness to make it popular and trendy among the youth.
6. Variety in sizes as well as fittings.
7. Contemporary colors and more of color combinations.
8. Economical price (or have different pricing for regular wear and special occasion wear)

The weaving community can respond to changing demand and thus capture better value for themselves with new skill sets within the community and PWCS. Attaching young weavers to designers, new skills in management, e-commerce opportunities, and language capacities to deal with distant markets thus ensuring that adequate income will attract more youngsters into weaving.

6.11 Power Loom Sector and Handloom Sector—How to Coexist?

Power looms are rated as the topmost threat by both apex marketing and primary weavers' societies. Power looms dominate India's textile production, contributing to 60% of textile output. Handlooms follow with 15%, although handlooms employ more persons. In 1977, it was estimated that every Indian handloom offered employment to six persons.[21] Subsequent loom improvements (not requiring power) have brought the estimate to four. In contrast, a single power loom worker may supervise no less than four looms and possibly as many as eight. The power loom sector is estimated to employ less than 1.4 million people on a three-shift basis. Handloom production has grown steadily in real terms while maintaining a 15% share of the country's total cloth production. However, even GOI document on the status of the sector mentions that one of the challenges for the sector is "low productivity in comparison to power loom and mill sector."

There have been many instances by power loom operators, backed by an influential lobby, to redefine handloom technology and revise the Handloom Reservation Act, 1985 (HRA). Despite their larger numbers, dispersed handloom weavers are not able to match the power loom sector's political clout and lobbying capacity.

The HRA listed 22 items to be reserved for weavers in the face of rising competition from power looms intending to protect a range of handwoven products, including sarees, dhotis, and lungis identified for excellence in a particular craft. Within a decade, the power loom lobby's growing clout reduced items reserved under the HRA from 22 to 11. However, with power looms making inroads into almost all clusters of handlooms, the real threat to traditional weavers is that cheap fakes of the handloom designs are flooding the market making a mockery of the reservation. The government machinery has not been able to enforce the reservations—inspections are few and detection of violations and penalties are rarer. Even when the Directorate mounts raids reportedly political pressure is mounted on them to ease up and let go the violators.

During 2015 there were reports that ministry is considering revision of the definition of handloom with just one symbolic hand operation sufficient to qualify power loom fabric as "handmade." With strong protests from handloom sector, the ministry clarified no changes are being proposed.

The state departments are not only concerned about the survival of the sector but they also need to coexist. Unique products and artistic weaves cannot be replicated in power looms. Handlooms are yet to be

---

[21] Ashoke Chatterjee, "India's Handloom Challenge Anatomy of a Crisis," *Economic & Political Weekly* 1, no. 32 (August 8, 2015).

> **Box 6.3:** *Handloom Identity and Survival*
>
> I can understand the mixed responses to our insistence on reservations. But the field reality cannot be ignored. The existence of the HRA is a deterrent to the proliferation of powerloom imitations. It is the sole remaining instrument that defines handloom. It is ironic that we need to hold on to a definition of handloom to ensure its survival, just as a definition still protects an adivasi's rights to exist.
>
> Shyama Sundari, Dastakar Andhra.[22]

clearly linked to current Skill India and Make In India Programs and policies. There is global demand for sustainably produced goods, unique designs, and contemporary handcrafted items.

Reservations cannot remain the handloom's only insurance, however critical these may be for survival. Intense competition is faced in every market segment demanding an ability to negotiate with and respond to market forces with speed and quality. Lasting security requires a market in which handmade quality is demanded and paid for, and the ingenuity of artisans respected for delivering what mechanized mass production can never match. Technologies will continue to evolve, hopefully led by weaver service centers and their deep understanding of handloom technology and artisan need. In the long run, only connoisseurs and a well-informed consumer base can make handloom survive.

In conclusion, it is difficult to escape the feeling that weaving as a mainstream livelihood in rural areas might vanish over the next few years unless result-oriented actions are taken at different stakeholder levels. The lack of a discerning mass market, competition from power looms, symptomatic policy response that does not attend to root causes and paucity of political power in weavers' organizations all lead to a livelihood situation that can rapidly deteriorate. However there are bright spots within the sector that produce high end products for niche markets where higher order skills and innovations ensure that weavers get a decent income. The future of the sector would rest solely on such unique weaves, designs, and artistic skills of the weavers. The mass market will survive as long as government support in terms of procurement continues and reservation of certain items for handlooms is retained and enforced. The existing government spending in clusters has an impact, but needs to become more inclusive. Master weavers and buying agents seem to capture more of the value added leaving the weavers with just the labor component, and the weavers' skills go unremunerated. The cooperative societies suffer from both governance deficit as also lack of business management expertise. The RRR package should have gone the extra mile and worked with weavers' cooperatives, consolidated them into fewer numbers, and strengthened managerial capacity in financial and commercial aspects. This is something doable even now. The recently finalized weavers' skills courses should be popularized. The weavers' image should be glamorized, with due recognition for high quality work. A mass campaign to restore customer interest and confidence on handloom fabrics is needed as a priority action to sustain the sector and the heritage.

---

[22] Ashoke Chatterjee, "India's Handloom Challenge Anatomy of a Crisis".

ANNEXURE 6.1
Handloom Enterprises—Statewise[23]

State/UT	Number of establishments by type			% of Establishments Without Hired Workers	% Share of State/UT	% Share of Rural in Total No. of Establishments
	Without Hired Workers	With at least One Hired Worker	Total			
Jammu & Kashmir	47,821	6,616	54,437	87.8	2.9	76.7
Himachal Pradesh	11,424	748	12,172	93.9	0.6	93.3
Punjab	10,676	4,482	15,158	70.4	0.8	40.7
Chandigarh	174	82	256	68.0	0.0	10.2
Uttarakhand	7,914	1,484	9,398	84.2	0.5	66.5
Haryana	13,221	3,466	16,687	79.2	0.9	56.4
Delhi	3,911	5,349	9,260	42.2	0.5	1.0
Rajasthan	96,883	27,060	123,943	78.2	6.6	56.2
Uttar Pradesh	245,969	64,028	309,997	79.3	16.5	49.9
Bihar	24,448	7,352	31,800	76.9	1.7	71.7
Sikkim	611	159	770	79.4	0.0	77.3
Arunachal Pradesh	115	90	205	56.1	0.0	50.2
Nagaland	4,217	596	4,813	87.6	0.3	86.8
Manipur	52,517	4,487	57,004	92.1	3.0	67.0
Mizoram	1,370	996	2,366	57.9	0.1	26.8
Tripura	8,680	2,245	10,925	79.5	0.6	60.4
Meghalaya	3,081	725	3,806	81.0	0.2	82.7
Assam	65,085	26,038	91,123	71.4	4.9	77.0
West Bengal	259,964	70,149	330,113	78.8	17.6	63.7
Jharkhand	11,164	3,792	14,956	74.6	0.8	78.7
Odisha	128,063	18,075	146,138	87.6	7.8	88.7
Chhattisgarh	19,245	2,147	21,392	90.0	1.1	69.7
Madhya Pradesh	42,074	8,485	50,559	83.2	2.7	59.4
Gujarat	42,056	25,881	67,937	61.9	3.6	29.3
Daman & Diu	20	8	28	71.4	0.0	17.9
D & N Haveli	26	28	54	48.1	0.0	16.7
Maharashtra	56,746	27,930	84,676	67.0	4.5	41.6
Karnataka	47,753	15,116	62,869	76.0	3.4	51.6
Goa	776	131	907	85.6	0.0	48.1
Lakshadweep	8	11	19	42.1	0.0	21.1
Kerala	24,846	5,447	30,293	82.0	1.6	51.0
Tamil Nadu	89,432	37,933	127,365	70.2	6.8	41.7
Puducherry	232	121	353	65.7	0.0	25.8
A & N islands	95	63	158	60.1	0.0	69.6
Telangana	33,745	6,645	40,390	83.5	2.2	63.3
Andhra Pradesh	123,018	18,279	141,297	87.1	7.5	65.6
Total	**1,477,380**	**396,244**	**1,873,624**	**78.9**	**100.0**	**59.6**

---

[23] *Source:* Ministry of Statistics and Programme Implementation, All India report of Sixth Economic Census 2014 (March 2016).

ANNEXURE 6.2
Handloom Weavers and Workers as Per 2010 Census

	State	No. of Handloom Weavers & Allied Workers	No. of Handlooms	Weavers and Workers Per Loom
1	Andhra Pradesh	355,838	124,714	2.9
2	Arunachal Pradesh	33,041	27,286	1.2
3	Assam	1,643,453	1,111,577	1.5
4	Bihar	43,392	14,973	2.9
5	Chhattisgarh	8,191	2,471	3.3
6	Delhi	2,738	2,560	1.1
7	Goa	0	0	0.0
8	Gujarat	11,009	3,900	2.8
9	Haryana	7,967	4,876	1.6
10	Himachal Pradesh	13,458	5,578	2.4
11	Jammu & Kashmir	33,209	7,301	4.5
12	Jharkhand	21,160	2,128	9.9
13	Karnataka	89,256	40,488	2.2
14	Kerala	14,679	13,097	1.1
15	Madhya Pradesh	14,761	3,604	4.1
16	Maharashtra	3,418	4,511	0.8
17	Manipur	218,753	190,634	1.1
19	Meghalaya	13,612	8,967	1.5
18	Mizoram	43,528	24,136	1.8
20	Nagaland	66,490	47,688	1.4
21	Orissa	114,106	43,652	2.6
22	Pondicherry	2,803	1,771	1.6
23	Punjab	2,636	261	10.1
24	Rajasthan	31,958	5,403	5.9
25	Sikkim	568	345	1.6
26	Tamil Nadu	352,321	154,509	2.3
27	Tripura	137,177	139,011	1.0
28	Uttar Pradesh	257,783	80,295	3.2
29	Uttaranchal	15,468	3,766	4.1
30	West Bengal	779,103	307,829	2.5
	Total	4,331,876	2,377,331	1.8

Source: Handloom Census, 2010, carried out by NCAER, New Delhi. http://handlooms.nic.in/Writereaddata/Handloom%20report.pdf

ANNEXURE 6.3
Employment in Handloom Enterprises[24]

State/UT	Number of persons employed by Type of establishment and Sector									
	Without Hired Workers	With at least One Hired Worker	Total	Without Hired Workers	With at least One Hired Worker	Total	Without Hired Workers	With at least One Hired Worker	Total	% Share of State/ UT
Jammu & Kashmir	60,071	16,438	76,509	13,762	10,310	24,072	73,833	26,748	100,581	2.39
Himachal Pradesh	12,633	2,732	15,365	744	1,121	1,865	13,377	3,853	17,230	0.41
Punjab	6,426	8,756	15,182	9,127	15,612	24,739	15,553	24,368	39,921	0.95
Chandigarh	8	60	68	220	263	483	228	323	551	0.01
Uttarakhand	7,430	3,637	11,067	3,743	3,628	7,371	11,173	7,265	18,438	0.44
Haryana	10,816	11,377	22,193	6,554	13,075	19,629	17,370	24,452	41,822	0.99
Delhi	89	141	230	6,504	28,819	35,323	6,593	28,960	35,553	0.85
Rajasthan	93,656	43,735	137,391	56,049	69,861	125,910	149,705	113,596	263,301	6.26
Uttar Pradesh	255,506	98,833	354,339	240,119	175,149	415,268	495,625	273,982	769,607	18.30
Bihar	27,720	14,327	42,047	9,079	9,658	18,737	36,799	23,985	60,784	1.45
Sikkim	569	267	836	97	638	735	666	905	1,571	0.04
Arunachal Pradesh	69	225	294	91	262	353	160	487	647	0.02
Nagaland	4,881	7,447	12,328	608	653	1,261	5,489	8,100	13,589	0.32
Manipur	40,895	8,459	49,354	18,843	6,924	25,767	59,738	15,383	75,121	1.79
Mizoram	545	577	1,122	1,255	3,474	4,729	1,800	4,051	5,851	0.14
Tripura	7,399	2,807	10,206	3,666	4,328	7,994	11,065	7,135	18,200	0.43
Meghalaya	4,364	1,876	6,240	502	1,005	1,507	4,866	2,881	7,747	0.18
Assam	83,996	54,886	138,882	15,130	35,859	50,989	99,126	90,745	189,871	4.52
West Bengal	284,537	122,566	407,103	124,395	214,711	339,106	408,932	337,277	746,209	17.75
Jharkhand	15,691	7,626	23,317	2,216	5,231	7,447	17,907	12,857	30,764	0.73
Odisha	223,880	44,701	268,581	22,775	14,190	36,965	246,655	58,891	305,546	7.27
Chhattisgarh	22,736	3,982	26,718	9,914	5,442	15,356	32,650	9,424	42,074	1.00
Madhya Pradesh	43,302	11,242	54,544	28,249	16,057	44,306	71,551	27,299	98,850	2.35
Gujarat	24,490	16,183	40,673	39,063	166,057	205,120	63,553	182,240	245,793	5.85
Daman & Diu	5	4	9	26	14	40	31	18	49	0.00
D & N Haveli	4	35	39	29	61	90	33	96	129	0.00
Maharashtra	44,436	17,265	61,701	39,171	114,487	153,658	83,607	131,752	215,359	5.12
Karnataka	40,367	32,563	72,930	31,267	45,168	76,435	71,634	77,731	149,365	3.55
Goa	511	143	654	524	299	823	1,035	442	1,477	0.04
Lakshadweep	0	11	11	9	31	40	9	42	51	0.00
Kerala	17,345	12,384	29,729	13,893	23,327	37,220	31,238	35,711	66,949	1.59
Tamil Nadu	78,891	54,592	133,483	93,076	83,667	176,743	171,967	138,259	310,226	7.38
Puducherry	90	98	188	285	2,257	2,542	375	2,355	2,730	0.06
A & N islands	110	111	221	22	143	165	132	254	386	0.01
Telangana	29,735	14,167	43,902	15,135	15,452	30,587	44,870	29,619	74,489	1.77
Andhra Pradesh	129,598	27,742	157,340	64,295	32,340	96,635	193,893	60,082	253,975	6.04
Total	**1,572,801**	**641,995**	**2,214,796**	**870,437**	**1,119,573**	**1,990,010**	**2,443,238**	**1,761,568**	**4,204,806**	**100**

[24] Ministry of Statistics and Programme Implementation, All India report of Sixth Economic Census 2014.

ANNEXURE 6.4
Access to Finance for Handloom Units in Different States[25]

State/UT	Self-finance	Financial Assistance from Govt. Sources	Borrowing from Financial Institutions	Borrowing from Non-institutions/ Money Lenders	Loan from Self-Help Group	Donations/ Transfers from Other Agencies	Total
Jammu & Kashmir	43,784	704	436	5,566	95	3,852	54,437
Himachal Pradesh	11,279	176	131	4	33	549	12,172
Punjab	13,953	305	86	38	12	764	15,158
Chandigarh	249	1	3	0	0	3	256
Uttarakhand	8,651	198	123	7	21	398	9,398
Haryana	15,629	289	178	41	19	531	16,687
Delhi	8,377	136	68	137	11	531	9,260
Rajasthan	115,825	1,625	1,105	1,200	118	4,070	123,943
Uttar Pradesh	280,131	4,196	1,174	2,541	728	21,227	309,997
Bihar	26,796	808	395	761	76	2,964	31,800
Sikkim	618	137	2	1	0	12	770
Arunachal Pradesh	163	21	2	3	0	16	205
Nagaland	4,533	50	7	9	13	201	4,813
Manipur	54,715	156	188	227	77	1,641	57,004
Mizoram	2,191	101	26	2	7	39	2,366
Tripura	9,870	327	189	119	49	371	10,925
Meghalaya	3,475	130	6	8	5	182	3,806
Assam	84,001	1,521	1,510	1,332	965	1,794	91,123
West Bengal	244,918	5,098	4,875	44,404	1,630	29,188	330,113
Jharkhand	12,791	545	101	126	44	1,349	14,956
Odisha	128,215	2,790	2,529	4,322	963	7,319	146,138
Chhattisgarh	18,737	805	277	290	22	1,261	21,392
Madhya Pradesh	44,542	892	235	455	79	4,356	50,559
Gujarat	57,622	1,943	702	172	159	7,339	67,937
Daman & Diu	22	0	0	0	1	5	28
D & N Haveli	48	0	1	0	0	5	54
Maharashtra	75,466	1,560	1,793	365	314	5,178	84,676
Karnataka	52,384	2,880	1,785	887	1,200	3,733	62,869
Goa	828	27	32	0	3	17	907
Lakshadweep	15	4	0	0	0	0	19
Kerala	27,367	1,161	663	129	212	761	30,293
Tamil Nadu	107,283	2,428	1,072	4,300	468	11,814	127,365
Puducherry	274	29	5	15	3	27	353
A & N islands	133	7	17	0	0	1	158
Telangana	36,856	473	421	480	149	2,011	40,390
Andhra Pradesh	117,350	2,979	2,131	3,475	1,858	13,504	141,297
All India	**1,609,091**	**34,502**	**22,268**	**71,416**	**9,334**	**127,013**	**1,873,624**
% share	**(85.88%)**	**(1.84%)**	**(1.19%)**	**(3.81%)**	**(0.50%)**	**(6.78%)**	**(100%)**

[25] *Source:* Ministry of Statistics and Programme Implementation, All India report of Sixth Economic Census 2014.

Livelihoods in the Northeast[1]

Chapter 7

The Northeastern states comprise Arunachal Pradesh, Assam, Manipur, Meghalaya, Mizoram, Nagaland, Tripura, and Sikkim. Sikkim is the last state to enter the region which originally was called the region of seven sisters. The region has unique geophysical features with hills and the Bramhaputra River cutting its path through the region separating the north from the south. The NER is also located sensitively with China, Bhutan, Bangladesh, and Myanmar at the borders of the region in different states. Heavy rainfall, lush tropical rainforests, and diverse flora and fauna add a lot of charm and mystique to the region. Traditionally, these states were famous for their unique spices, fruits, handloom, and handicrafts. Silk, tea, honey, and aromatics from the northeast have unique characteristics. Access to northeast from within India is constrained through a narrow passage from West Bengal called the Chicken's Neck.[2] Connectivity through road, rail and air have improved over the years and most states enjoy reasonable connectivity through rail. Air connectivity can improve further considerably in some of the states.

The northeast accounts for 7.9% of the geographical area of the country but has about 25% of the country's forest cover. In many ways, northeast is ahead of the rest of India in environmental terms. As per the 2011 census, the population in the NER constituted 3.07% of the all India population. While most of the NER is sparsely populated, Assam had a density of 397 persons per km^2, which was higher than the all India average of 374 per km^2. Arunachal Pradesh with 16.5 persons per km^2 had the lowest population density in the entire country. In fact, it also had a large area counting for 2.54% of India's land area. Barring Assam and Arunachal Pradesh, other states had a higher literacy rate than the all India average. Livelihoods of people in the bottom of the pyramid in the northeast have always been vulnerable in the sense that income opportunities were much lower than those available in the rest of the country. The local governance in these states is left to traditional tribal governance mechanisms and district autonomous councils as per the Sixth Schedule of the Constitution (Box 7.1). The implications are that the laws of the state do not fully apply where the same are different from the local traditions and rules adopted by the tribal governance structures.

---

[1] This chapter draws substantially from the contributions of 32 participants who came from all over northeast to the exclusive consultation meet held at Indian Institute of Bank Management (IIBM) on July 30, 2016. A list of participants is given in Annexure 7.3.

[2] Chicken's Neck refers to the Siliguri Corridor which is a narrow stretch of land in West Bengal, and which connects India's northeastern states to the rest of India. Nepal to the west and Bangladesh to the east are on either side of the corridor.

Table 7.1: Geography and Demography of Northeast

State	Area km²	Population	Population Growth Rate	Density Persons per km²	Sex Ratio Women per 1,000 Males	Literacy %
Arunachal Pradesh	83,743	1,383,727	26.03	17	938	65.38
Assam	78,438	31,205,576	17.07	398	958	72.19
Manipur	22,327	2,570,390	12.05	115	992	79.21
Meghalaya	22,429	2,966,889	27.95	132	989	74.43
Mizoram	21,081	1,097,206	23.48	52	976	91.33
Nagaland	16,579	1,978,502	−0.58	119	931	79.55
Sikkim	7,096	610,577	12.89	86	890	81.42
Tripura	10,486	3,673,917	14.84	350	960	87.22
All India	**3,287,240**	**1,210,193,422**	**17.64**	**382**	**940**	**74.04**

Source: Census of India 2011.

Box 7.1: *Constitutional Protection to Traditional Rights of Tribal Areas to Govern Themselves*

The Sixth Schedule provides for administration of certain tribal areas as autonomous entities. The administration of an autonomous district is to be vested in a district council and of an autonomous region, in a regional council. These councils are endowed with legislative, judicial, executive, and financial powers. Most council consists of up to 30 members including few nominated members. (The newest Bodoland Territorial Council is an exception; it can have up to 46 members). These constitutionally mandated councils oversee the traditional bodies of the local tribes such as the Syiemships and Dorbars of the Khasi hills of Meghalaya. There is a significant degree of variation in the functions devolved to various autonomous councils. For instance, the Bodoland Territorial Council has more power compared to the North Cachar (NC) Hills Autonomous District Council, though the latter has been in existence for decades before the former. This resulted in other areas also demanding further powers and greater autonomy. The Sixth Schedule applies to parts of Assam, parts of Tripura, Meghalaya, and Mizoram.

Source: Based on Ministry of Law and Justice write up "Provisions as to the Administration of Tribal Areas in the States of Assam, Meghalaya, Tripura and Mizoram" sourced from http://lawmin.nic.in/olwing/coi/coienglish/Const.Pock%202Pg.Rom8Fsss(34).pdf, accessed on September 13, 2016.

Table 7.2: Food Grains—Area and Production

States	Area (ha)		Production (tons)		Yield (kg/ha)	
	2012–13	2013–14	2012–13	2013–14	2012–13	2013–14
Arunachal Pradesh	203.8	214.4	364.0	384.6	1,786	1,794
Assam	2,691.5	2,660.0	5,280.6	5,096.8	1,962	1,916
Manipur	174.8	281.1	336.7	490.6	1,926	1,745
Meghalaya	132.7	134.1	265.0	320.0	1,997	2,387
Mizoram	23.8	48.4	41.8	72.8	1,756	1,506
Nagaland	285.7	309.5	579.1	624.6	2,027	2,018
Sikkim	68.9	64.9	106.0	102.4	1,538	1,577
Tripura	267.5	271.1	725.2	726.7	2,711	2,680
All India	**120,778.7**	**125,042.0**	**257,124.7**	**265,043.2**	**2,129**	**2,120**
Share of Northeast (%)	3.2	3.2	3.0	2.9		

Source: Ministry of Agriculture, GOI, 2015.

Table 7.3: Horticultural Crops—Area and Production (2014–15)

	Share of India	
Crop	Area Cultivated (%)	Production (%)
Fruits	8.5	5.9
Vegetables	5.4	4.6
Flowers	2.0	12.4
Aromatics	2.0	13.3
Spices	6.4	11.1
Plantation Crops	4.4	2.0
Food Grains	3.2	2.9

Source: Ministry of Agriculture, GOI, 2015.

Agriculture

The NER had a diverse range of crops on account of conducive soil and climatic conditions. In case of food grains, northeast had significant disadvantages and hence, the shares of northeast in area cultivated and production were 3.2% and 2.9% of the all India cultivation area and production volumes.

In case of horticultural crops, northeastern states had a large variety and significant production levels (Table 7.3). In the year 2014–15, northeast accounted for 12.4% of flowers, 13.3% of aromatics, and 11.1% of spices produced all over India. Northeast also produced 5.9% of fruits and 4.6% of vegetables.

Agriculture in most parts of northeast is carried out without fertilizers and pesticides. The produce is naturally organic. However, certification of these produce as organic has been difficult on account of the verification processes involved. Even if the produce is certified organic, premium pricing will not be possible for producers as the market linkages are weak. While the statistics related to production show a healthy share for northeast compared to its share of population in the country, there are factors that affected agricultural livelihoods in these states. The first of these is the small landholdings except in a couple of states in northeast. The quality of soil was not high and in a few states, acidic soils with low organic content affected productivity. Soil health testing had not

been a priority on account of lack of testing facilities and very limited government extension efforts. Irrigation facilities in northeast were much lower than the all India averages. While, across the country, 47.6% of the total cropped area was irrigated, no state in the northeast had more than 37% of the irrigated area. Assam with the largest area under cultivation had only 3.8% of the cultivated area under irrigation. This low level of irrigation was not a constraining factor in some of the states and locations on account of heavy rainfall and resultant soil moisture as well as existence of streams. However, the recent experience has been one of springs dying a slow natural death on account of both negligence and active degradation of the catchment areas. The reduced number of crops on account of reduced water availability through natural sources has shifted some of the households from agricultural to nonagricultural activities. Lack of mechanization in the northeast is on account of the type and topography of landheld, low purchasing power as also absence of tools and equipment customized for small plots of land in undulating terrain. The access of farmers to better-yielding varieties and crop practices is very limited. At times, high-yielding and hybrid seeds suitable for different agroclimatic conditions have been brought in with poor results, further impairing the farmers' confidence to take up new varieties. Seed replacement was not much in practice and the usage of the same tired seed material over a number of years has resulted in low productivity. Lack of capital and also a reluctance to borrow from formal financial institutions limited the capital investments direly required in agriculture for improving productivity and profitability. The farming systems have been under a subsistence mind-set rather than a market-oriented income earning mind-set. In the recent past, there have been indications of change in farming systems and farmer attitudes. There has been greater interest in taking up cultivation of commercial crops and changing to production systems oriented toward markets. The abundance of production also leads to glut and losses. For pineapple and jackfruit, producers have reported low prices that make even harvesting uneconomical. Jack Fruit is in fact fed to pigs for want of viable markets. Initial investments in some locations in processing facilities have sparked off interest in improving production for supplying these processing units. However, this will have to be watched over a long term to come to conclusion on whether agriculture in northeast is taking a distinct turn toward market-oriented environment. While institutions such as North Eastern Regional Agricultural Marketing Corporation Limited (NERAMAC) are active in processing and finding markets for the produce of northeast, a large part of the production, especially fruits, does not find its way to markets. Annexure 7.1 at the end of the chapter provides an indication of the marketable surplus for different horticultural produce in the northeast.

Sericulture

Sericulture in the northeast has a much wider variety than in silk heartland in the southern states of India. Eri, Muga, Tussar, and Mulberry silks are all produced in the northeastern states. Eri and Muga are traditional silk varieties produced almost exclusively in the northeast. Assam and Meghalaya specialize in Ericulture. Muga is traditional in Assam and has been introduced in Arunachal Pradesh in the recent past. The data on silk production in the northeastern states is provided in Table 7.4. In the year 2014–15, northeast accounted for 98.8% of Eri silk and 99.5% of Muga silk. The northeast thus has an exclusive monopoly over supply of Eri and Muga silk

yarn and fabric. Of the total silk of different types produced in the country, the share of northeast is almost 18%.

However, promotion of silk fabrics across India as well as elsewhere has not been taken up in earnest by the concerned state governments. There have been sporadic programs of silk development which have created localized impact for temporary periods. Increasing the number of skilled weavers, bringing in better designs, and finishing processes and improved marketing of high quality fabrics for higher price realization are all aspects that need to be attended to. Marketing of handloom products in the northeast generally has been left to groups of women who traditionally are the weavers. Indian Institute of Entrepreneurship (IIE),[3] for example, had supported 20 clusters of 3,000 artisans in Eri silk production. The project included introduction of natural dyes and new designs for stoles and shawls oriented toward market demand. The project ended in 18 months when the weavers actually required more funding and support after absorbing the technical inputs.

The marketing avenues available are subject to exploitation by traders from neighboring states. Financing of silk production as also making of silk fabrics is virtually unheard of. Silk yarn spinning and weaving are seen more as part time activities of a kind that does not require serious finance. Silk carries good potential for supporting quality livelihoods in the northeast as most of the processes involved can be carried out by women during their spare time. Specialized skills can also be imparted onsite for weavers in their locations. On account of the non-perishable nature and light weight transport of the produce, marketing in distant markets will not pose major problems and cost disadvantages. A few organizations in the field have introduced design colour and form in innovations while linking the

Table 7.4:   Sericulture in Northeast (Production of Silk Metric Tons 2014–15)

	Mulberry Silk	Nonmulberry			
		Tussar	Eri	Muga	Total
Northeast	298.00	4.29	4,671.46	157.27	5,130.60
India	21,390	2,434	4,726	158	28,708
Share of Northeast (%)	**1.4**	**0.2**	**98.8**	**99.5**	**17.9**

Source: Central Silk Board, Ministry of Textiles, GOI, 2016.

[3] Baruah, "Role played by IIE in North East" (Paper presented at the IIE in the consultation meet at IIBM, Guwahati on July 30, 2016).

Table 7.5: Number of Households Engaged in Sericulture (2015)

States	Mulberry	Tussar	Eri	Muga	Total
Arunachal Pradesh	770	110	3,410	3,930	8,220
Assam	31,731	–	182,991	37,434	252,156
Manipur	2,500	2,229	23,500	500	28,729
Meghalaya	1,368	–	26,472	160	28,000
Mizoram	2,500	650	7,200	1,650	12,000
Nagaland	1,825	330	10,998	515	13,668
Sikkim	189	–	160	44	393
Tripura	5,000	–	–	–	5,000
Northeast	45,883	3,319	254,731	44,233	348,166
India	**489,591**	**160,111**	**262,455**	**45,791**	**957,948**
Share of Northeast (%)	9.40	2.10	97.10	96.60	36.30

Source: Reply to Lok Sabha's question No. 533 dated February 26, 2015.

weavers to other markets. The potential for Eri and Muga varieties of silk to be geographically identified and made niche products is high.

Livestock

Northeastern states have more than a proportionate share of livestock; with about 3% of India's population, these states have 5.2% of India's livestock and 6% of India's poultry. There is high demand for meat, chicken, and other products in the northeastern states. Livestock-based livelihoods are popular in the region. While dairying

Table 7.6: Livestock in Northeast

States	Livestock	Poultry
Arunachal Pradesh	1,412,666	2,244,231
Assam	19,082,171	27,216,169
Manipur	695,772	2,499,516
Meghalaya	1,957,627	3,400,032
Mizoram	311,856	1,271,353
Nagaland	911,162	2,178,470
Sikkim	291,626	451,966
Tripura	1,936,179	4,272,733
NER	**26,599,059**	**43,534,470**
All India	**512,057,301**	**729,209,320**
Share of NER (%)	**5.20**	**6.00**

Source: 19th National Livestock Census 2012, June 2014, http://dahd.nic.in/sites/default/files/19%20th%20Livestock%20%202012.pdf, accessed on September 13, 2016.

is carried out in pockets, piggery is popular throughout the region. Poultry farming is also gaining acceptance, especially broilers. Backyard poultry of local variety is reared in many areas.

Piggery seems to be the largest source of protein in the northeastern food. Of the total pig population of 10.29 million in 2012, 3.95 million was in northeastern states. Assam accounted for 16% of India's pig population. Compared to 24% of pigs being crossbred across the country, the northeastern states had 45% of pig population as crossbreed animals. Between 2007 and 2012, the pig population dwindled by 11% in NER with Nagaland and Assam recording significant reductions. As for consumption, Nagaland and Mizoram had the highest per capita consumption in the country followed by Meghalaya. On account of high consumption, the northeast continues to import pork from the other states.

Between 70–90% of tribal households in the different northeastern states rear pigs. Typically, they rear one to three animals and mostly the pigs are fattened and sold. The pig rearing practices have by and large been traditional with modern practices being adopted only in the recent past. Artificial insemination is not practiced in most of the states. Natural breeding is the most predominant approach preferred but a more expensive one. Crossbreeding occurs indiscriminately in the field. The lack of attention to indiscriminate crossbreeding taking place in the field reduces the quality of animal and erodes the pure breed indigenous varieties of pigs which need to be preserved. As far as feeding is concerned, kitchen waste is fed to the animals besides jungle forage. Wheat bran and rice polish are additional feed bought out for being fed. There is no practice of cultivation of feed crops to improve the nutrition quality of food provided to the pigs. Given the high cost of feed brought in from other regions, the immediate priority is look for alternatives locally available for feeding.

One of the major problems in pig rearing relates to health care. Different types of diseases have from time to time impacted the pig population. It ranges from skin diseases, respiratory infections, foot and mouth disease, and also parasitic infections. The two diseases that can assume epidemic proportions are Classic Swine Fever (CSF) and Porcine Reproductive and Respiratory Syndrome (PRRS). Access to veterinary services is very poor on account of very thin presence of veterinary doctors in the field as also the difficulty of transport. A survey by International Livestock Research Institute in 2011 indicated that 68% farmers treat their animals by themselves. Vaccines against diseases that are epidemic are not readily available. These vaccines have to be bought only through the government agency and are also not available in sufficient quantities. The NER is estimated to require 4 million doses of vaccines for pigs. The availability has been less than 25% of this requirement. Last year, Mizoram reported the death of 3,000 animals in a PRRS epidemic, which could have been prevented had vaccines been available. However, a recent development is that of synthesis of a vaccine using local strains in Meghalaya by ICAR.

Deworming is not in practice in most pig rearing households. The pigs are also not maintained under hygienic and sanitary conditions. The diseased animals are not separated from the rest of the animals and often, animals carrying diseases are sold in the market without notice, posing health risk to human beings. Market access for pig farmers has not been a problem except in very remote and hilly terrain. The local markets in villages seem to have unlimited demand with almost all northeastern states importing pigs or pork to meet their consumption requirements. Almost 80% of the price realized is estimated to reach the producer, which is a very high percentage in terms of market efficiency. However, transportation of pigs can be an

---

Box 7.2: *Odourless Pig Sty, Healthy Pigs, and Compost as a By-product*

Bokashi Piggery is a Japanese and Korean pig conservation and rearing system propagated by practitioners of natural farming which uses "microorganisms" techniques. It has been introduced for the first time in India, in Meghalaya. The Bethany Society, a local NGO, had been advocating the Bokashi model in the state. This technique keeps the pig pens odourless, ensuring hygienic practices, better health, and faster growth of pigs. This has had a positive impact on the traditional pig rearing system of rural poor farmers of Khasi hills. Rice bran is used as part of the flooring in the pigsty as it is recommended as an important ingredient of the Bokashi compost. Indigenous microorganism (IMO) also plays a major role in conserving and propagating this technique, as its application on the floor of the pig shed deodorizes it. Moreover, it also provides organic compost as a by-product which is being used by farmers. Advantages of the Bokashi method are:

1. Minimal use of water
2. Pigs are protected against diseases
3. Pigs are fed at sunset and only once a day
4. The farmer has time to take up other income generating activities
5. Even local breed of pigs can weigh 100 kgs in 7–8 months
6. High Grade Organic Manure becomes available

Source: Brochure of Bethany Society, NGO, Shillong, Meghalaya, http://www.bethanysociety.org/, accessed on September 14, 2016.

expensive proposition and hence selling pigs in a distant market does not usually take place. In order to improve the systems of pig rearing and stabilize the small holders' livelihoods around pig rearing, strategies have to be designed. Improving health care and training local lead farmers and other interested persons in preventive health care as also reporting of diseases to qualified veterinary personal. Exploring substitute for feed and fodder that improve nutrition levels as also animals' health, improving sanitary conditions and hygiene in and around areas where pigs are housed, better control over breeding through artificial insemination, and prevention of crossbreeding in the field. Access to finance and introduction of effective insurance arrangement would increase investment and also reduce risk for the pig farmers. Insurance companies are not interested in offering insurance for piggery on account of difficulties in identification, remote locations, proving death claims with veterinary doctors' support as also moral hazard issues. But the epidemics of CSF and PRRS wipe out large herds at a time inflicting losses on farmers and making pig rearing a very risky enterprise. There is a need to design group-based insurance products covering a number of animals in a location backed up by quality health care support system that can also maintain health records of the animals.

Climate Change and Forestry

Northeast has an important role to play in the climate change mitigation processes on which India has given commitments under the Paris Agreement. The extensive forest resources in NER act as a cushion against the damage caused to forests and environment elsewhere in India. A cause for concern is the reduction in forest cover reported in a recent assessment. The forest cover in NER as a percentage of geographical area has been falling from 2007 onwards (Table 7.7). During the same period 2007–2015, the forest cover in the country

Table 7.7: Forest Cover as % of Geographical Area

	2005	2007	2011	2013	2015
Northeastern States	66.11	66.28	66.07	65.83	65.6
India	20.6	21.02	21.05	21.23	21.35

Source: Forest Survey of India, GOI, *India's State of Forest Report 2005, 2007, 2011, 2013, and 2015.*

as a whole has been increasing. The forest cover of NER as a proportion of Indian forest cover has also been declining from 25.6% in 2005 to 24.5% in 2015 (state-wise details are given in Annexure 7.2 at the end of this chapter).

The northeast has for long been considered the carbon sink of the country, accounting for a fourth of all forests. The high rainfall, low density of population, the natural conservation attitude among the tribal communities, and the cultural practices that are in harmony with forests have all combined to ensure that the forest cover in NER is intact. However, the development projects in mining, infrastructure, and commercial crops have been intruding in to the environment. The introduction of exotic species such as rubber, cashew, and eucalyptus in some of these diverse ecologies carries damage potential. Oil palm has also been advocated under a national mission for this region. Exotic commercial crops that are not native to the local ecology can destroy the forest cover and lead to irreversible damage.

Jhum cultivation, also known as Shifting cultivation, has been in practice for a long time in this region. There have been several calls to prohibit slash and burn methodology for Jhum on account of perceived damage to forests and environment. In Nagaland, an evaluation of Jhum was carried out by Nagaland Environment Protection and Economic Development (NEPED).[4] NEPED concluded that shifting cultivation is more beneficial for farmers, environment, and

---

[4] Nakeu, "Sustainable Development Foundation of Nagaland," (paper presented at the IIE in the consultation meet at IIBM, Guwahati on July 30, 2016).

climate change mitigation. With a mix of 15–60 crops, the farmer is able to diversify risks and absorb failure of some crops. The vegetative cover increases as a result of Jhum cultivation. A study of 21 villages showed that on an average, 870 trees per ha have been raised. With better planning, it is possible to raise this to 1,500 trees, leading to higher levels of carbon sequestration. The main problem is that of soil erosion of about 30 metric tonnes per ha in the first and second year of Jhum. With soil conservation measures, the erosion can be brought down to 13 metric tonne per annum. Jhum with soil conservation can protect the environment better than monocropping that is practiced in plantation crops such as in Tea and Cardamom.

Climate change effects have been felt in different forms in the NER. In Ukrul, Manipur, for example, the village ponds which used to freeze in winter do not freeze anymore. In Sikkim, orange crop has moved up on account of higher temperatures in the lower slopes. In Meghalaya, reports of new types of pests and plant diseases have been reported. Communities have tried to adapt to these changes. In some cases, the coping behavior has degraded the environment such as drying up of springs, receding tree line in forests and so on. In the different states, several measures are being taken to deal with climate change issues. Each state has drafted its own action plan on climate change. Catchment area treatment is a prime need. Sikkim has been taking measures to rejuvenate and protect springs that have reduced or dried up and other states are following the lead of Sikkim. Tripura has put together an ambitious Climate Change Adaptation (CCA) plan with a budget of ₹350 billion. One of the problems is that the NER has been awarded the role of being the carbon sink for the entire country. There are questions on whether this is fair to the local people who will also like to benefit from alternative uses of forests and land. The second issue is that lands are owned by tribes, clans, and communities. How does the state plan to afforest land that is owned by these? Such afforestation measures lead to conflicts over ownership and control over forests. The third issue is that of equating climate change adaptation with forestry. The result is that of budget allocations going to the forest department when water and soil issues also require attention as part of CCA.

The access to forests for NTFP is an area that needs to be understood better. Honey, lac, agar, bay leaf, broom grass, fuelwood, wild pepper, bamboo and so on, are such fruits of the northeastern forests. The need for protection of forests should not threaten the livelihoods of those dependent on forest resources. Awareness building and skill development among such communities on conservation and safe extraction of NTFP will reduce the overall long-term costs and improve the quality of forests. Participatory mechanisms involving the user communities will succeed better than the control and enforcement regimes that deny traditional rights of tribals over their forest-based livelihood. After an in-depth survey of 10 villages in Arunachal Pradesh, Saha and Sundriyal[5] identified as many as 343 plant species used by five different tribes for food, medicine, beverages, dyes, oil, fodder, and firewood uses. The user communities recognized that customary laws for management of plant resources were important. They perceived threats for the species that were collected for commercial uses on account of high volume and unscientific collection, excessive lopping of branches of tree species, maximum collection per unit labor to gain maximum profits, and least consideration for sustainable use of species. They desired awareness, knowledge sharing, and capacity building on allowable harvest levels using the means of productive forestry. The communities will be able to use their forests in a sustainable manner while eking out their livelihoods with capacity building.

[5] Saha and Sundriyal, "Perspectives of Tribal Communities on NTFP Resource Use in a Global Hotspot: Implications for Adaptive Management," *Journal of Natural Sciences Research* 3(2013).

Box 7.3: *NTFPs Sustainable Use for Livelihoods*[6]

It must be clearly understood that a low level of subsistence need must not pose threat to the biodiversity and isolation of local communities needs for mere conservation needs may lead to conflicts. A participatory mechanism is needed to be established for NTFPs management by bringing together all the stakeholders. Since all households use a wide diversity of NTFPs, they are sensitive for their regular and sustained supply. There is a need of cohesive approach in adopting traditional harvesting technique and scientifically established method of harvesting regime. Therefore, strong community participation is expected in NTFPs management programs. There is a strong need to incorporate NTFPs in forest working plans for long-term management of forest areas. Moreover, the residents can easily identify options, threats, and possible adaptive management strategies for local species in demand, which can help to develop an effective in-field management plan.

Their perception for extraction and enrichment practices can directly boost a sustained NTFPs management work plan. Community demands, rights, and tenures from forests are needs that needs to be given due considerations. Furthermore, improvement of organizational capacity of communities for decision-making and running forest-based enterprise, and equitable benefit sharing will help to sustainably manage NTFPs resources. A combined effort of communities with line departments (such as forest department) can lead to produce best feasible approach for NTFPs management and livelihood upgradation along with biodiversity conservation across the complex and diverse but integrated mountain landscapes of global significance. Since there are cases that have proved NTFPs are more profitable and sustainable than timbers, perhaps, similar approach can also work in northeast India to upgrade rural livelihood and forest management.

Employment and Skill Development

The annual employment–unemployment survey for 2012–13 conducted by Labour Bureau brought out that some states in the northeast have high rates of unemployment compared to the rest of the country (Figure 7.1). The unemployment rate per thousand persons of age 15 years and above was 40 across the country. The same was 84 in Tripura, 62 in Nagaland, 43 in Assam, 102 in Arunachal Pradesh, and 122 in Sikkim. Only 3 states in the northeast, that is, Manipur, Meghalaya, and Mizoram had

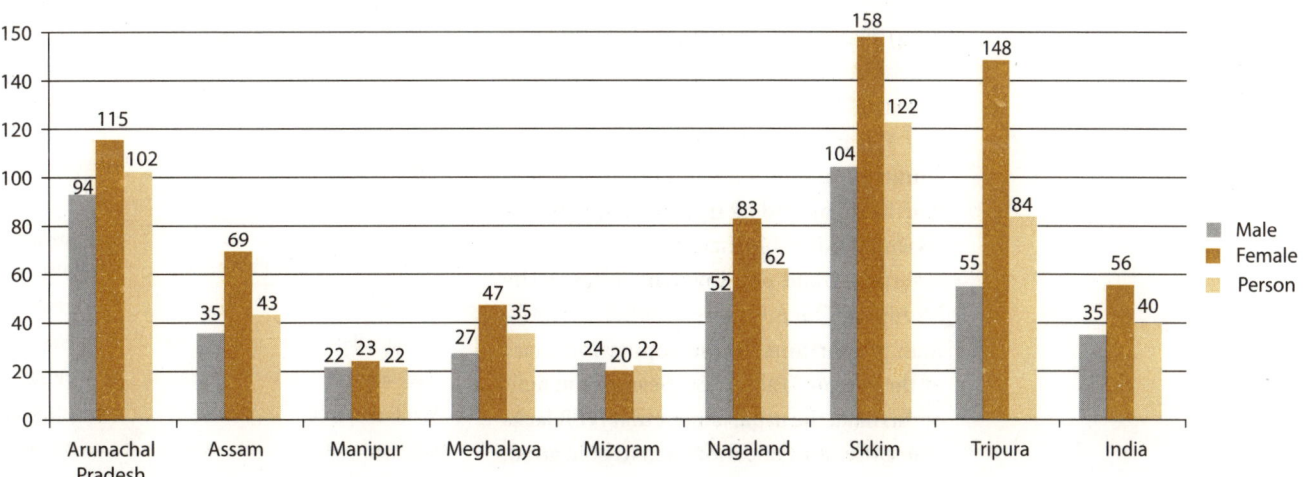

Figure 7.1: Unemployment Rate per 1,000 Population of Those Aged 15 years and Above

Source: Labour Bureau, Chandigarh, GOI, *Annual Employment Unemployment Survey* 2012–13.

---

[6] Saha and Sundriyal, "Perspectives of Tribal Communities on NTFP Resource Use in a Global Hotspot: Implications for Adaptive Management," *Journal of Natural Sciences Research* 3(2013).

an unemployment rate lower than the rest of the country. The unemployment rates among women was much higher both in rural and urban areas.

According to the study carried out by ICSI,[7] the NER will have only 2.6 million jobs between 2011 and 2021. During the same period, the supply of young persons to the labor force would be of the order of 17 million which is roughly 5 times the available jobs. The need to cater to such a large number of people in search of livelihoods is a cause for greater concern in a region that is sensitively placed on account of socio-economic reasons. Studies suggest that skill building can be a partial answer. The ICSI study had concluded that five segments of services can accommodate a number of persons from the northeast both in the region and outside the region. These segments are (a) aviation, tourism, and hospitality, (b) media and entertainment, (c) health and wellness, (d) information technology and telecom industry, and (e) retail logistics, handloom and handicrafts. Several youth from these states have migrated to take up careers in hotels, restaurants, shopping malls and the like in many cities and metros across the country.

The VI Economic Census counted the enterprises (except those engaged in cropping) that are set up all over the country and the number of people employed therein. The census results show that NER had a share of 4.8% of enterprises in the country, but only 4.2% of the employment had been provided in such enterprises. Assam, predictably, had the lion's share of enterprises and employment followed by Manipur. The numbers in NER are more than proportional to the population share of the region (Table 7.8). Seen in the light of this data, the usual lament that NER lacks enterprise spirit does not seem to hold good.

---

[7] International Chamber for Service Industry, "Potential of the service sector catering to domestic and international demand" (paper presentation in Advantage northeast conference, February 2016).

Table 7.8: VI Economic Census

State	No. of Enterprises	No. Employed
Sikkim	37,219	91280
Arunachal Pradesh	36,415	108936
Nagaland	60,937	161,818
Manipur	229,838	409,617
Meghalaya	105,556	289,431
Mizoram	57,486	122,226
Assam	2,030,042	3,953,563
Tripura	236,773	404,024
NER	2,794,266	5,540,895
India	58,495,359	131,293,868
Share of Northeast (%)	**4.8**	**4.2**

Source: MOSPI, GOI, *VI Economic Census*, 2012–13, 2016.

A number of arts and crafts provide livelihoods through wage employment and enterprise ownership in the northeast (Table 7.9). The region is famous for its unique products and curios. Shawls, stoles, articles made of bamboo, wood, horn, silk, forest products, baskets, mats, metal casting and the like have caught the imagination of buyers for many years. The skills of making such products have been passed on from generation to generation. Bamboo products, pottery, wood carving, textiles, and musical instruments and weapons are the top five categories of products in demand. In case of handlooms, only women weave in the region

Table 7.9: Workers Engaged in Handicrafts/Handlooms

Handloom/Handicraft Workers		Share of All India (%)
Sikkim	1,571	0.04
Arunachal Pradesh	647	0.02
Nagaland	13,859	0.32
Manipur	75,121	1.79
Mizoram	5,851	0.14
Tripura	18,200	0.43
Meghalaya	7,741	0.18
Assam	189,171	4.52
NER	312,161	7.44

Source: MOSPI, GOI, *VI Economic Census*, 2012–13.

unlike in other states of India, where men weave. Apart from design interventions, custom-designed better hand tools can make a difference to productivity. Skill development courses that integrate recent advances in consumer tastes, preferences, better production processes using specialization on specific processes in making a product, and emphasis on quality will help improve product quality and customer satisfaction. Bamboo-based craft initiatives have provided additional livelihoods in the region and connected the producers to markets in different parts of India. The problem faced by traditional crafts is that the younger generation is unwilling to learn these crafts and looking forward to white collar jobs in cities.

The consultation meet participants expressed concerns over the plight of handloom weavers and workers depending on handlooms. The wage rates are very low and lower than the minimum wages fixed by the government. The skilled weavers were better off taking up manual wage labor under NREGS as the wages were more than double what they earn by applying their weaving skills. The looms are owned by entrepreneurs who offer skilled weavers work on a piece rate basis. Finance for looms and technology upgradation to improve productivity are direly needed.

In the consultation meet at Guwahati, the participants brought in a variety of perspectives on skill building in the northeast. The skill development programs offered in the NER mimicked the ones across the country and were not suited locally. The courses assumed that people want to migrate to some other part of the country which is only partially true. The courses did not take in to account resources available locally. The delays in assessments, issue of certificates, and release of stipends to students created problems in implementation of PMKVY. Classroom training of 150 days is not relevant and not appropriate for most of the skills. The training should be more in the farm or enterprise where it is possible to learn by doing. The states should develop their own vision on skill building rather than bring models from Delhi or other states. While a large number of skill trainings have been planned, training institutions for doing such large numbers do not seem to exist. While skills are being built so that unemployed can find good jobs, skilled handloom workers are shifting to manual labor under NREGS program as the wages there are better than in weaving. A thorough gap analysis on skills in demand locally will help to make better plans. However, the quality of trainers and training institutions will determine the outcomes.

Tourism

Northeast with its attractive natural locations and scenic beauty has the potential to attract tourists which can form the basis for a number of livelihoods. The tourist arrivals in northeast have been a very small proportion of the total numbers in India (Table 7.10). Less than 0.6% of tourists in India visited northeast in 2013. The foreign tourists were a small proportion than the domestic tourists. The difficulty of access even by air, the absence of a marketing

---

Box 7.4: *Bamboo and NTFP-based Livelihoods*

TRIBAC is working on bamboo and cane-based livelihoods. It works with the community to increase their awareness, study, and exploit the scope for community enterprise clusters, development of need-based tools, upgrading the value chains and exploring PPPs in the space. It has introduced *agarbatti*-making with bamboo and treatment of bamboo for longevity for use in construction and furniture and NTFP-based livelihoods. TRIBAC is concerned that young persons do not want to practice bamboo crafts and the present craftsmen are all of 60+ years of age. It also finds that some of the rules and forestry regulations on bamboo and NTFP are too restrictive and affect the practice of livelihoods.

Source: Reza, *TRIBAC in the NER consultation meet*, July 30, 2016.

Table 7.10: Tourist Arrivals

States	2012			2013		
	Domestic	Foreign	Total	Domestic	Foreign	Total
Arunachal Pradesh	132,243	5,135	137,378	125,461	10,846	136,307
Assam	4,511,407	17,543	4,528,950	4,684,527	17,638	4,702,165
Manipur	134,541	749	135,290	140,673	1,908	142,581
Meghalaya	680,254	5,313	685,567	691,269	6,773	698,042
Mizoram	64,249	744	64,993	63,377	800	64,177
Nagaland	35,915	2,489	38,404	35,638	3,304	38,942
Tripura	558,538	26,489	585,027	576,749	31,698	608,447
Sikkim	361,786	7,840	369,626	359,586	11,853	371,439
Northeastern India	6,478,933	66,302	6,545,235	6,677,280	84,820	6,762,100
All India	**1,045,047,536**	**18,263,074**	**1,063,310,610**	**1,145,280,443**	**19,951,026**	**1,165,231,469**
Share of Northeast (%)	**0.62**	**0.36**	**0.62**	**0.58**	**0.43**	**0.58**

Source: Ministry of Tourism, Government of India, 2015.

effort, lack of facilities for the tourists, and a negative perception on account of frequent disturbances both natural and manmade in the region have reduced appetite for people to visit this region. A concerted effort at marketing specific locations in the region which carry some of the rarest flora and fauna and natural features has to be carried out. Investment in tourist infrastructure comprising of transport, logistics, accommodation, catering, entertainment facilities as also showcasing local art and culture will go a long way in improving tourist arrivals. Tourism has the potential to add significantly to the employment in the northeast. A range of activities that are possible in providing jobs to the youth can be exploited. Sikkim attracts tourists on account of comparatively better local environment and a combination of places of religious and natural interests. The state has a good network of transport, stay, and catering establishments. However, the livelihoods dependent on tourism will be seasonal and will have to find alternative livelihoods in the lean season for tourism.

KPMG and FICCI in their joint report[8] have proposed a strategy for developing

[8] KPMG and FICCI, "Northeast India—Economically and Socially Inclusive Development" (November 2015).

tourism in the region comprising of marketing, promotion, advertising, development of tourism circuits, and also popularizing wellness tourism in a welcoming environment as the key ingredients. Development of ecoresorts, creation of convention facilities, developing 2–3 star category hotels, notification of restricted ecotourism zones, and setting up an overarching northeast tourism development authority are some of the key actions that have been suggested. Tourism would also help in marketing some of the unique products of the northeast and provide access to distant markets in the form of tourist who return with pleasant experiences and memories. Youth withdrawing from traditional skill-based jobs, are interested in new economy jobs in sectors such as tourism. Hence, a focus on tourism as a livelihood supporting sector is necessary and should be taken up in right earnest.

NER in the Union Governments Reckoning

The union Budget allocated ₹330 billion for northeast, a step-up of about 11% over the previous year (Table 7.11). Most schemes implemented by the NER states will enjoy a high level of GOI funding. Given the low productivity of the region, the allocation for

Table 7.11:   Union Government Budgetary Support for Northeast

Sector	2015–16 RE	2016–17	Increase (%)
Agriculture, Cooperation, and Farmers Welfare	1,369.37	1,274.42	–6.9
Environment, Forests, and Climate Change	146.29	172.5	17.9
Labor and Employment	64.17	155	141.5
New and Renewable Energy	24.65	496	1912.2
Rural Development	3,780.5	4,164.5	10.2
Skill and Enterprise Development	100	0	–100.0
Tribal Affairs	429.22	449	4.6
Water Resources	213.6	261.36	22.4
Total Budget for NER	**29,669.22**	**33,097.02**	**11.6**

Source: Ministry of Finance, *Union Budget*, 2016–17, Indiabudget.nic.in, accessed on September 14, 2016.

agriculture appears to be low. Similarly, allocation for environment and forests is also low considering the declining forest cover over the years. Labor and employment as also renewable energy have got significant resources in recognition of the problems in both fronts. The zero allocations for skill development is surprising as the problems on the employment front are severe, with job seekers outnumbering jobs by many multiples.

In the recent restructuring of funds allocation to states under the revised devolution, the Center has not significantly changed the funding pattern of northeastern states.

Access to Finance for Livelihoods in NER

Access to finance is not easy in NER on account of low presence of bank branches and the low population density. The branch network of banks which is a critical requirement for physical access is geographically thin with less branches per km^2 compared to other Indian states (Table 7.12). The population per bank branch is higher than all India average (except in Mizoram) and very high in some of the states such as Manipur. NER has 3.72% of India's population but only 1.8% of savings deposits and just 0.8% of credit.

Table 7.12:   Branch Network and Savings in NER

NER	No. of Offices 2012	Population per Branch	State Share of Population (%)	Bank, Post Office, Cooperative Society Outlets/ Sq. km	Savings 2013 (₹ Billion)	State Share of Savings 2013 (%)	Average Savings per A/C 2012 (₹)
Arunachal Pradesh	91	14,108	0.11	5	72.15	0.10	116,998
Assam	1,574	18,925	2.58	159	777.29	1.10	135,343
Manipur	87	27,773	0.22	44	53.55	0.10	114,770
Meghalaya	231	12,350	0.24	36	139.72	0.20	139,380
Mizoram	104	9,405	0.09	28	42.29	0.10	154,414
Nagaland	99	18,339	0.16	126	64.58	0.10	113,599
Tripura	257	13,205	0.30	106	119.13	0.20	178,515
India	**96,059**	**11,821**		**83**	**70,513.32**		**270,860**

Sources: RBI, 'Database for All Banking Statistics', 2016, https://dbie.rbi.org.in/DBIE/dbie.rbi?site=home, accessed on September 14, 2016; NAFSCOB Database, 'Cooperative Societies – NAFSCOB data base (www.nafscob.org, accessed on September 15, 2016) Post Office Data—India Post Annual Report 2014–15; https://www.indiapost.gov.in/VAS/DOP_PDFFiles/AnnualReport2014-2015English.pdf, accessed on September 14, 2016.

Table 7.13: Snapshot of Bank Credit Situation in NER

NER	Credit Outstanding 2013 (₹ billion)	State Share of Credit 2013 (%)	State Share of No. of Small Loan A/Cs (%)	Average Amount per Small Loan A/C ₹	CD ratio
Arunachal Pradesh	15.31	0.03	0.19	66,606	28.4
Assam	285.76	0.52	2.54	53,973	40.3
Manipur	14.69	0.03	0.19	63,509	33.2
Meghalaya	32.74	0.06	0.38	52,132	28.2
Mizoram	14.90	0.03	0.14	64,196	41.9
Nagaland	18.02	0.03	0.36	55,869	47.6
Tripura	38.69	0.07	0.33	44,215	31.7
India	**55,064.96**			**56,019**	**79.0**

Source: RBID database, 'DBIE,' www.rbi.org.in, accessed on September 13, 2016.

Table 7.14: KCCs Issued in NER 2013

State	No. of KCC Issued (000)	Average Limit Sanctioned ₹
Assam	251	31,076
Arunachal Pradesh	7	24,286
Meghalaya	25	28,000
Mizoram	6	45,000
Manipur	3	20,000
Nagaland	11	36,364
Tripura	**92**	**15,217**
India	**11,760**	**77,959**

Source: Srinivasan, 'State of Rural Finance in India,' 2016.

Table 7.15: Access to Finance for Establishments by Source of Finance

	Self-finance (%)	(%) of Formal Loans	(%) of Informal Loans
Sikkim	79.5	14.6	0.2
Arunachal Pradesh	67.6	16.9	0.6
Nagaland	82.4	7.9	0.5
Manipur	89.5	3.2	0.5
Mizoram	72.4	15.4	0.1
Tripura	81.4	11.3	0.6
Meghalaya	75.8	15.1	0.5
Assam	84.3	8.4	0.9
NER	83.6	8.8	0.8
All India	**80.1**	**7.8**	**0.8**

Source: VI Economic Census, MOSPI, GOI, 2016.

In terms of credit, banks tend to restrict loans in northeast. Credit Deposit (CD) ratios have remained very low in almost all NER states (Table 7.13). Banks have high risk perception and tend to avoid extending loans to the extent possible. The fact that livelihoods in NER are similar to other states has been lost on banks. Despite high power committees headed by deputy governor of RBI, credit for livelihoods has not been forthcoming to the extent needed.

Agricultural credit through KCCs was popular in NER among banks. However, the issuance of KCC and the size of loans reflected low enthusiasm among banks. Less than 4% of all KCCs had been issued in NER. The average loan size in NER states was lower than the national average by a large margin. It is difficult to discern the reason for the low average loans sanctioned and how the loans can actually finance crop-based livelihoods as the costs of cultivation are not much lower in NER compared to other states (Table 7.14).

The establishments (other than those engaged in cropping) also did not fare better in access to finance. The VI Economic Census found that most establishments in NER had been self-financing their requirements. Formal loans were availed by 7.8% of the establishments. Informal credit access was not that prevalent (Table 7.15).

The remoteness of parts of the region, sparse population density, small ticket size of transactions and services, impaired credit culture on account of "subsidy expectation", inappropriate short duration staffing by banks in the region and law and order problems in most of these states in past two decades are major reasons for underperformance of the financial sector in NER compared to the rest of the country. Unwillingness to borrow from banks in some parts of the region was also a factor for low credit penetration for livelihoods. Banks have been reluctant to use full-fledged business correspondents (BCs) to extend banking services to remoter areas. Even where BCs are appointed, credit transactions are not put through these agents.

The solutions in some of the remoter parts of these states may lie in encouraging local financial institutions and linking them with formal mainstream financial institutions rather than setting up bank branches. Meghalaya is implementing a project from IFAD that intends to set up localized cooperatives in a bid to ensure timely and affordable financial services in the larger villages and village clusters.

Microfinance institutions have commenced financing in all the states in the northeast. They have financed more than 1 million customers with a loan outstanding of more than ₹15 billion. Compared to Self Help Groups (SHGs) funded by banking system, the MFI loans in northeast are much higher reflecting their robust business model. RGVN Microfinance (northeast) operates in six states of the northeast (except Mizoram and Manipur) with 131 branches. It provides small loans to its customers formed in to JLGs. By the end of March 2016, it had a portfolio of ₹4.88 billion in loans to 0.304 million customers in northeast. Its average loan size is of about ₹16,000, which emphasizes the small nature of its customers. RGVN has been issued a licence to set up a SFB and it is in the process of transforming itself in to a bank. It will be the first bank dedicated to northeast.

Northeastern region has also benefited from the SHG movement. At the end of

Table 7.16: MFIs in Northeast

State	Number of Clients (millions)	Amount of Loan Outstanding (₹ billions)
Assam	7.00	1,013
Tripura	1.00	70
Manipur	0.88	134
Mizoram	0.65	170
Sikkim	0.28	34
Meghalaya	0.19	29
Arunachal Pradesh	0.17	49
Nagaland	0.04	4

Source: Sa-Dhan, *Bharat Microfinance Report 2016.*

March 2016, there were 0.15 million SHGs which had borrowed ₹8.8472 billion from the banking system. The banking system had been conservative in lending to the groups as evidenced from the disproportionately lower share of loan disbursements and outstanding.

The number of groups is too small in Arunachal Pradesh, Meghalaya, and Sikkim to make an impact. Assam and Tripura seem to be doing well in formation and credit linkage of SHGs with banks. While NABARD had special programs for the northeast in microfinance, the progress did not reach expected levels mainly on account of paucity of NGO promoters. Willingness

Table 7.17: SHG Bank Linkage

| State | Loan Disbursed (2015–16) | | Loan Outstanding March 31, 2016 | |
	No. of SHGs	Amount (₹ millions)	No. of SHGs	Amount (₹ millions)
Assam	22,625	15,865.56	107,137	6,6031.12
Arunachal Pradesh	57	66.79	408	365.44
Manipur	382	360.59	2,063	934.84
Meghalaya	204	180.25	1,573	1167
Mizoram	327	473.05	2,156	2,963.48
Nagaland	1,255	1,360.09	3,348	2,963.25
Sikkim	134	90.28	632	618.55
Tripura	1,053	3,527.09	33,543	13,429.05
NER	26,037	21,968.7	150,860	88,472.73
India	**1,832,323**	**3,728,690.09**	**4,672,621**	**5,711,923.47**
Share of NER (%)	**1.4**	**0.6**	**3.2**	**1.5**

Source: NABARD, *Status of Microfinance in India 2015–16, 2016.*

of banks to provide credit to SHGs is also an issue.

Conclusion

The northeast is a net importer of food. Pulses, pork, fish, meat, chicken, eggs, milk and the like are brought in from other states. In all these, northeast has the capacity to produce a significant part of its requirements. However, the cost disadvantages will make it unprofitable for these states to produce these products and sell the same in other states. The livelihood strategy in such a situation should look to organize production to meet the demand within the region for produce of mass consumption. In case of unique products such as spices, quality fruits, handicrafts, and speciality handlooms, the strategy should be to focus on productivity, cost efficiency, and organized marketing. Aggregation of producers for pooling of resources, cost savings and improved negotiating capacity should be a necessary part of the livelihood strategy.

The livelihoods in northeast are mingled with the lifestyles of the local communities, whether it is farming, livestock, or handloom and handicrafts. The challenges in improving livelihoods are that of raising productivity and profitability. The risk averse nature of several communities makes the task of convincing them to make investments in productivity improvements harder. The recent past has seen greater acceptance of market-oriented production and a willingness to look at land-based livelihoods as businesses and not subsistence activities. More commercial crops and increased market arrivals are seen all over northeast. But, the physical difficulties posed by infrastructure limitations have to be overcome. Another key development is that of changing lifestyles and the consequent higher aspirations of youth. The youth in northeast no longer are content to remain in farm-based livelihoods, but seek white collar employment. They are willing to migrate.

Already in several cities across the country, the youth from northeast are employed in several vocations in new economy jobs. While skill development initiatives will help aspiring youth to migrate on their own terms, there should be a continuing focus on preparing people to render services especially in agriculture, horticulture, and livestock that are relevant in the region.

While introducing innovations for improved sustainability of livelihoods, one has to be conscious of not disturbing the local ecosystems. The agricultural produce markets are not well organized. The market access and market conduct issues also deserve a close look. The opaque and unfair market systems erode value from producers who are typically small. The traders finance inputs at the beginning of the season and hence are able to dictate produce prices. The difficulty of transporting goods to distant markets in an uncertain and often opaque price discovery process compels farmers to sell the produce to traders who appear in their villages. Collective action by farmers to pool produce and market the same is gaining momentum over the last few years. There are examples of pooled marketing of bay leaf, turmeric, ginger, pineapple, and oranges in some states.

Access to finance has been a continuing problem on account of demand and supply side issues. The actions from the supply side should go beyond tokenism; try to understand the real issues in livelihoods and design processes and products that are aligned to the socioeconomic conditions of communities. Insurance penetration in the region is abysmally low and requires serious attention. While several programs operate in the northeast, some of them seem to be working cross-purposes as was indicated earlier. Developing livelihoods in northeast without damaging its ecosystem and socio-cultural mores requires sensitive designs and implementation processes. The objectives of promoting livelihoods and developing the northeast economy should be rooted in the local area—not in the national objective of finding carbon sinks for the rest of the country or finding natural resources that would profit businesses elsewhere. The northeast also deserves to be freed of the shackles of dependency and subsistence.

Livelihoods should be oriented to a market environment and built to the best of efficiencies. The uniqueness of products that only northeast can offer should be preserved, geographically identified where possible, and marketed as niche products.

ANNEXURE 7.1
Marketable Surplus of Horticultural Produce in Northeast

Metric Tons

Pineapple	Production	Consumption	Surplus
Assam	216,059	64,818	151,241
Nagaland	8,290	16,608	66,300
Meghalaya	81,723	24,517	57,206
Tripura	42,270	11,413	30,857
Citrus Fruits			
Assam	64,367	19,311	45,056
Nagaland	33,026	6,605	26,421
Meghalaya	32,311	12,925	19,386
Mizoram	25,050	5,010	20,040
Banana			
Assam	590,095	177,029	413,066
Nagaland	55,060	16,578	38,482
Ginger			
Assam	112,935	33,881	79,054
Meghalaya	44,900	2,245	42,655
Mizoram	31,136	3,114	28,022
Arunachal Pradesh	27,681	8,304	19,377
Nagaland	13,411	2,682	10,729
Turmeric			
Meghalaya	8,565	857	7,708
Assam	8,032	2,410	5,622
Nagaland	3,544	44	3,500
Mizoram	2,785	279	2,506
Black Pepper			
Assam	3,470	1,041	2,429
Meghalaya	440	22	418
Cardamom			
Sikkim	3,500	500	3,000
Nagaland	2,535	35	2,500

Source: –NERAMAC, *Agricultural Map of Northeast*, http://www.neramac.com/

ANNEXURE 7.2
Forest Cover in Northeast (km²)

States	2005 Total Forest Cover	2005 % of (Gross Acreage) GA	2007 Total Forest Cover	2007 % of GA	2011 Total Forest Cover	2011 % of GA	2013 Total Forest Cover	2013 % of GA	2015 Total Forest Cover	2015 % of GA
Arunachal Pradesh	67,777	80.93	67,353	80.43	67,410	80.5	67,321	80.39	67,248	80.3
Assam	27,645	35.24	27,692	35.3	27,673	35.28	27,671	35.28	27,623	35.22
Manipur	17,086	76.53	17,280	77.4	17,090	76.54	16,990	76.1	16,994	76.11
Meghalaya	16,988	75.74	17,321	77.23	17,275	77.02	17,288	77.08	17,217	76.76
Mizoram	18,684	88.63	19,240	91.27	19,117	90.68	19,054	90.38	18,748	88.93
Nagaland	13,719	82.75	13,464	81.21	13,318	80.33	13,044	78.68	12,966	78.21
Sikkim	3,262	45.97	3,357	47.31	3,359	47.34	3,358	47.32	3,357	47.31
Tripura	8,155	77.77	8,073	76.99	7,977	76.07	7,866	75.01	7,811	74.49
Northeast	173,316	66.11	173,780	66.28	173,219	66.07	172,592	65.83	171,964	65.6
Share of Northeast (%)	**25.60**		**25.15**		**25.03**		**24.73**		**24.51**	
All India	**677,088**	**20.6**	**690,899**	**21.02**	**692,027**	**21.05**	**697,898**	**21.23**	**701,673**	**21.35**

ANNEXURE 7.3
List of Participants in the Northeast Consultative Meet on July 30, 2016

Name	Organization and Address
Shri Nayan Kakati	North East Rural Livelihoods Project (NERLP), MDoNER, GOI, Dispur, Guwahati
Shri Abhijit Mohapatro	NERLP, MDoNER, GOI, Dispur, Guwahati
Dr N.S.R. Prasad	National Institute of Rural Development and Panchayati Raj (NIRDPR), Khanapara
Shri G. Sarkar	Handloom and Textiles
Shri Vikramaditya Das	Grameen Sahara
Shri M.P. Bezbaruah	Guwahati University
Shri Partho Patwari	Centre for Microfinance and Livelihoods (CML), TATA Trust
Shri Kalyan Das	Omeo Kumar Das Institute of Social Change and Development (OKDISCD), Guwahati-36
Shri Mrinal Gohain	Action Aid Association
Shri Anupam Dutta	State Institute of Ruralo Development (SIRD)
Dr Debabrata Das	Tezpur University, Tezpur
Dr Sriparna B. Baruah	IIE, Guwahati
Shri Parag Boruah	Seven Sisters Development Assistance (SeSTA) Development Services
Shri A.M. Sharma	Grameen Sahara
Shri Dhrubajit Sarma	NULM
Shri K.N. Hazarika	North Eastern Development Financial Institution (NEDFI)
Dr Abhijit Sharma	Indian Institute of Bank Management (IIBM)
Shri Sabyasachi Dutta	Asian Confluence
Ms Sabhari Chaudhuri	Asian Confluence

Name	Organization and Address
Shri Augustus Suting	Meghalaya Basin Development Agency (MBDA)
Ms Dimple S. Das	North Eastern Region Community Resource Management Project (NERCORMP), 1st floor, Sympli Building, Shillong
Shri Indraneel Bhiwmik	Tripura University
Dr Selim Rezq	TRIBAC, Agartala
Shri Pawan Kr. Kaushik	CFLE, Agartala
Shri Daniel Lalawmpuia	NULM
Ms Guddy Singh	NULM
Capt. Ashok Y. Tipnis	Mission Fraternal, C/O VVD, Ukhrul
Dr K.I. Meetei	Institute of Cooperative Management (ICM)
Shri Swapan Singha	Action Aid
Shri Joshi Tuisum	Action Aid
Shri Vengota Nakeu	Sustainable Development Forum Nagaland (SDFN)
Shri R.P. Gurung	Ecotourism and Conservation Society of Sikkim (ECOSS), Gangtok

Financing Livelihoods: Search for Alignment

Livelihoods at individual, household, and tiny enterprise levels operate throughout the country. Livelihoods are also created and sustained by large entities that provide wage employment to people. The problems of those operating at individual and micro-levels in accessing financial services are severe, and continue to limit the viability and sustainability of such livelihoods. The VI Economic Census studied the enterprises that operate in the country to get a sense of how many enterprises exist and how many people are employed in these enterprises. As indicated in an earlier chapter, almost 58.5 million establishments (excluding those engaged in cropping) were operating across the country in 2013–14 when the census was carried out (Table 8.1). Out of these, 80% were self-financed and did not access funding from anywhere. Bank funding was accessed by just 2% of these units. In case of agricultural enterprises, only 1.1% were able to access funds from financial institutions.

NSSO Survey 70th round[1] found that out of the 90.2 million agricultural households in the country, above 48% did not access finance from any source and were dependent on their own funds (Table 8.2). Access to financial institutions was much better in case of agricultural households than the situation evidenced in the case of other establishments

not engaged in cropping. However, it should be noted that the establishments or agricultural households do not voluntarily refrain from taking institutional loans; while many find access to bank loans difficult, there are others who find it impossible. Access to finance from formal institutions continues

Table 8.1: Sources of Finance for Enterprises—VI Economic Census

Source of Funds	Agricultural Enterprises		All Enterprises	
	No. of Units	% of Units	No. of Units	% of Units
Self-finance	11,376,635	86.6	46,856,468	80.1
Financial Assistance from Government Sources	277,318	2.1	3,386,684	5.8
Financial Institutions	141,256	1.1	1,180,007	2.0
Money Lenders/Informal Sources	65,544	0.5	492,975	0.8
Loan from SHGs	85,444	0.7	312,172	0.5
Donations/Transfers from Other Agencies	1,185,376	9	6,267,053	10.7
Total Units	**13,131,573**		**58,495,359**	

Source: GOI, *VI Economic Census 2013–14*, Central Statistical Office, MOSPI, 2016.

Table 8.2: Sources of Loans for Agricultural Households

Sources of Funding	No. of Farm Households	% to Total 2012–13
Government	983,810	1.1
Cooperative Societies	6,933,519	7.7
Banks	20,097,835	22.3
Informal Sources	13,820,190	15.3
Relatives and Others	5,012,747	5.6
Self-finance	43,353,000	48.1
Total Farm Households	**90,201,100**	**100**

Source: MOSPI, GOI, 2015, *Key Indicators of Situation of Agricultural Households in India NSSO Survey 70th Round 2012–13.*

---

[1] MOSPI, GOI, "Key Indicators of Situation of Agricultural Households in India NSSO Survey 70th Round" (2012–13).

to be a matter of concern despite all the progress made in financial inclusion space.

Agricultural households continue to depend on informal sources to a significant extent. While banks and financial institutions provided funding to 22.3% of households, informal sources (including relatives) funded 20.9% of households. Compared to 2002–03, the proportion of indebted farmers had increased marginally from 48.5% to 51.9% in 2012–13. The proportion of farmers that remained without access to external funding (voluntarily or otherwise) continued to be high over the 10-year period.

Institutional Finance

In the last three years, the retail credit environment for agricultural, tiny, and household enterprises has significantly improved. The increasing flow of loans from banks, MFIs, cooperative societies, and SHGs (Table 8.3) has made access to credit easier.

The total number of loan accounts reported by formal financial institutions for livelihoods is about 235 million. The total loan amount outstanding in these accounts is of the order of ₹19,803 billion. A large proportion of these 100 million loans (given by SHGs to their members and MFIs to their customers) are very small. These loans at best support individual livelihood activities and at worst supplement livelihood activities of the household. The loans given by banks, cooperative societies for agriculture, and MSMEs are more likely to be for full-fledged livelihoods.

Scheduled commercial banks credit portfolio was dominated by agricultural sector in a number of accounts, but by a much smaller proportion of credit outstanding (Table 8.4). Industry and trade accounted for the bulk of credit outstanding. Most bank credit went for enterprise or income generating activities.

Agriculture is the largest livelihood driver in the country and the credit allocations from banking sector have been cognizant of this. The last five years have seen an average increase of about 18% in agricultural credit flow. The notable feature of institutional credit is the increasing share of regional rural banks in the total credit flow (Table 8.5). The commercial banks' share in credit flow to agriculture has stagnated in 2015–16 compared to 2014–15.

An analysis of the 20-year data on agricultural credit flows show a vigorous spurt from 2003 to 04 onwards (Figure 8.1). The interest subvention scheme for crop loans was introduced in 2005–06 and the GOI started setting targets for agricultural credit from that time onwards. It does not seem a coincidence that the agricultural credit

Table 8.3: Loans from Formal Institutions

Type of Institution/Purpose	No. of Accounts (million)	Loans Outstanding (₹ billion)
Commercial Banks		
Agriculture (March 2016)	63.3	8,625
Small Enterprises (March 2016)	20.5	9,957
Cooperative Societies (March 2015)—Mostly Agriculture	49.8	14.72
SHGs (March 2016)	Groups 4.7	571.19
Different Activities	Members 60.7	
MFIs (March 2016) Different Activities	39.9	638.53

Sources: RBI banking statistics, https://dbie.rbi.org.in/DBIE/dbie.rbi?site=home; NAFSCOB cooperative Statistics, www.NAFSCOB.org; Status of Microfinance 2015–16, NABARD website, www.nabard.org; Bharat Microfinance report, 2016, Publication by Sa-Dhan, New Delhi.

Table 8.4: Share of Sectors in Outstanding Credit (March 2016)

Types of Sector	Number of Accounts (%)	Outstanding Credit Amount
Agricultural	46	12
Industry	3	40
Trade	6	9
Personal	36	18

Source: DBIE, *RBI Quarterly Data on Depsoits and Credit*, https://dbie.rbi.org.in/DBIE/dbie.rbi?site=home, accessed on September 17, 2016.

Table 8.5: Ground Level Credit Flow for Agriculture

(₹ billion)

Agency	2011–12	2012–13	2013–14	2014–15	2015–16
Commercial Banks	3,68,616	4,32,491	5,27,506	6,04,376	6,04,668
Regional Rural Banks	54,450	63,681	82,653	1,02,483	1,19,261
Cooperative Banks	87,963	1,11,203	1,19,964	1,38,469	1,53,295
Total	**5,11,029**	**6,07,375**	**7,30,123**	**8,45,328**	**8,77,224**

Source: NABARD, *Annual Report 2015–16*, 2016.

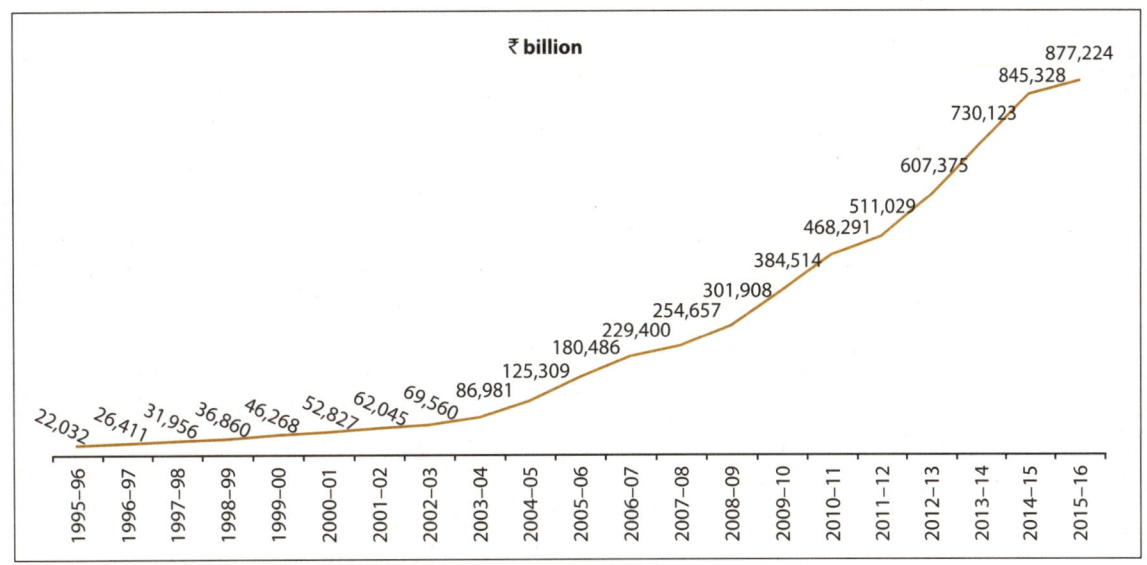

Figure 8.1: Ground Level Credit Flow to Agriculture

Source: Annual Reports of NABARD various issues, figure by the authors.

spurt also commenced around the same time. The increasing loan disbursements for agriculture still do not seem to reach all the needy farmers.

The increasing targets have resulted in a skew in credit disbursement towards short-term loans. The proportion of long-term loans required for investments in agriculture that can improve productivity and sustainability has been declining (Figure 8.2) from 35.4% in 2006–07 to 16.6% in 2015–16. This shift is caused on account of both demand side and supply side reasons. From the supply side, the banks, concerned about default risks, keep the period of exposure short and tend to recover loans quickly. From the demand side, farmers tend to demand short-term loans as they are available at a subsidized rate of 7% (or lower, subject to conditions), and try to divert the same for other purposes. But, short-term loans cannot be applied for long-term investments without adverse consequences to the farm level cash flow. The distortions arising from

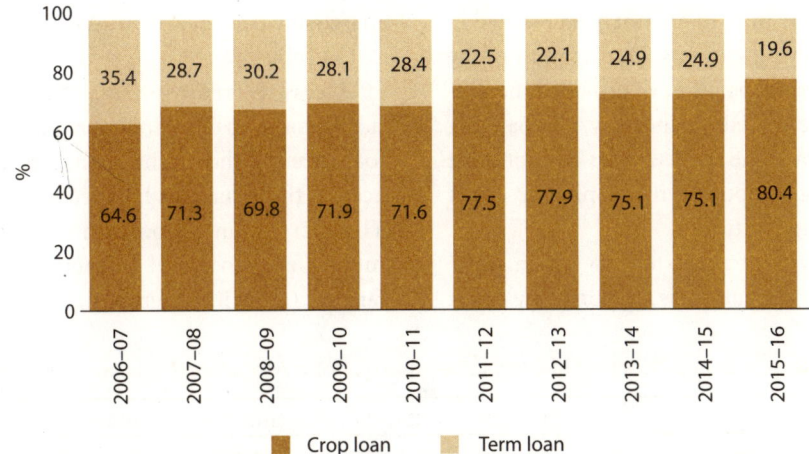

Figure 8.2: Skew Towards Short-term Credit in Agriculture

Source: NABARD, *Annual Report 2015–16.*

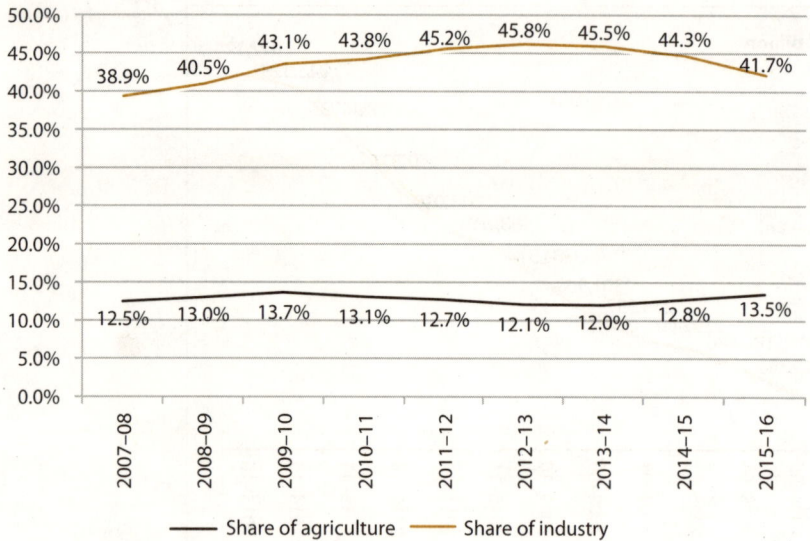

Figure 8.3: Share of Agriculture and Industry in Outstanding Bank Credit

Source: RBI Database DBIE, *Handbook of Statisticson the Indian Economy*, https://www.rbi.org.in/scripts/annualPublications.aspx?head=Handbook%20of%20Statistics%20on%20Indian%20Economy, accessed on September 17, 2016.

skewed credit flow is an aspect that needs immediate attention.

While credit flow to agriculture seems to be increasing rapidly year after year, a macro view shows that the claims of increased focus of banks on agricultural sector are illusory. The share of agricultural credit outstanding has not significantly changed; if anything, the share of outstanding credit to agriculture to total nonfood credit was lower in March 2016 compared to March 2008 (Figure 8.3). The level of 13.7% share of credit to agriculture in 2010 has not been reached in the following six years. During most of the same period, banks have provided increasing share of credit to industry. The banking system over the last few years has not done anything exceptional in stepping up credit flow to agriculture.

Analysis of the extent to which value added in agriculture is supported by credit shows that in the last two years credit support has improved significantly (Table 8.6). However, the improvement seems to be more on account of low growth rates in agricultural GDP in the last two years.

In the midst of claims of increased access to credit, there have been continuing problems. One of the assumptions made at the policy level is that if access to finance for inputs is ensured, all problems of farmers will stand solved. Cost and quantum of credit are thought of as critical issues and over the last several years, governments have subsidized crop loans and pushed for higher farm credit disbursements. Banks have been meeting higher targets for farm credit each year, but still many farm households report that they do not access bank credit. During the 10-year period from 2002–03 to 2012–13, despite the massive increase in flow of agricultural credit, the proportion of households accessing credit from formal sources remained almost the same. There was a marginal increase from 55.2% to 57.7% in the proportion of households availing formal credit even when the credit flow to agriculture increased from ₹695.6 billion to ₹6073.75 billion. Agricultural credit flow increased by 730% in the 10-year period, but the access to formal credit for farms in terms of households increased by 10%. In terms of loan amounts, the proportion of institutional loans increased marginally from 57.7% in 2002 to 59.8% in 2013 (Table 8.7).

Access to credit for small farmers has not become easier. However, in terms of loan size for those who managed to gain access, the situation has become better. The increase in proportion of disbursement going to small farmers/marginal farmers (SF/MF) is significant (Table 8.8).

Table 8.6: Credit as a Proportion of Gross Value Added (GVA) in Agriculture (₹ billions)

	2011–12	2012–13	2013–14	2014–15	2015–16
GVA in Agriculture	15,018.16	16,807.97	19,024.52	19,952.51	20,930.8
Outstanding Credit to Agriculture	5,466.26	5,899.14	6,659.79	7,658.8	8,829.42
Credit as % of GVA	36.4	35.1	35.0	38.4	42.2

Source: Handbook of Statistics on the Indian Economy, RBI Database DBIE, www.rbi.org.in.

Table 8.7: Trends in Access to Credit for Farmers

Source of credit (amount of loans)	2002 (% of loan)	2013 (% of loan)
Institutional	**57.7**	**59.8**
Of which from coop societies	19.6	14.8
From commercial banks	35.6	42.9
Non-institutional	42.3	40.2
Of which from money lenders	25.7	25.8

Source: MOSPI, GOI, *Key Indicators of Situation of Agricultural Households in India NSSO Survey 59th Round 2002–03 and 70th Round 2012–13.*

Table 8.8: Bank Credit to SF/MF

	2007–08	2014–15
SF/MF Loan Accounts	257.5	486
Share of SF/MF Loan Accounts (%)	58.6	56.9
Loan Disbursed (₹ billion)	898.59	3466.66
Share of SF/MF Loans to Total (%)	35.3	41
Average Loan per SF/MF (in ₹)	34,897	71,326

Source: NABARD, *Annual Report 2015–16.*

The average loan per SF/MF has more than doubled in the 7-year period. The decline in the proportion of SF/MF loan accounts (though there is a substantial increase in absolute terms) is a reflection of the continuing problems in access to formal credit.

The tendency of farm households borrowing from informal sources does not seem to be on account of lack of access or familiarity of banks. Even farmers, who are able to access bank loans, find it necessary to borrow from informal sources. While such borrowing from informal sources, if taken for emergent reasons, is understandable, it will be difficult to explain if the same is taken for cropping and so on for income generating purposes. But, this is precisely what seems to happen in the field; famers who have access to banks for crop loans, also have to borrow from informal sources during the cropping season. IFMR LEAD[2] had

[2] Nair, July 1, 2016, "Why Small farmers in Tamil Nadu borrow money at 60% interest," http://www.indiaspend.com/cover-story/why-small-farmers-in-tamil-nadu-borrow-money-at-60-interest-58892.

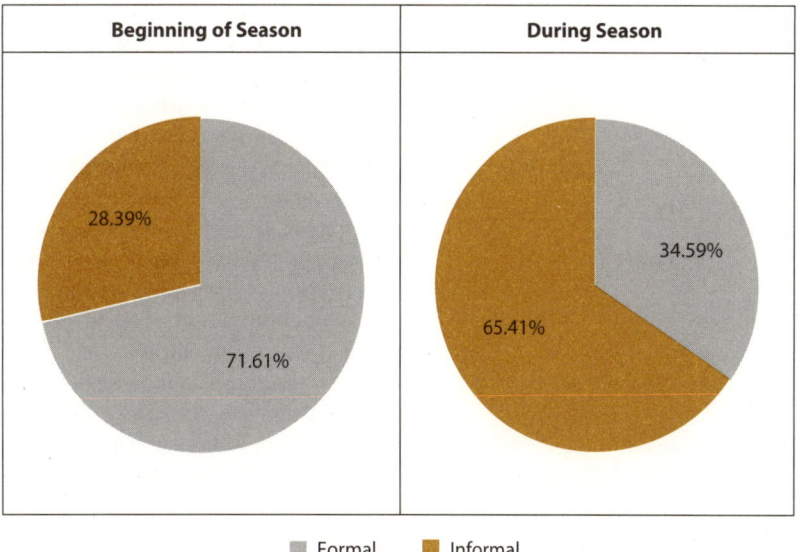

Figure 8.4: Total Borrowing By Source Across a Single Farming Season (2014–15)

Source: Reproduced from the article by Suraj Nair, IFMR LEAD, http://www.indiaspend.com/cover-story/why-small-farmers-in-tamil-nadu-borrow-money-at-60-interest-58892, accessed on September 17, 2016.

carried out a study to gain a nuanced understanding of farmers' credit requirements and borrowing behavior by surveying about 350 farmers in Tamil Nadu during the paddy crop season of 2014–15. The report brings to the fore the issues in responsiveness and timeliness of formal credit institutions. The report finds that formal loans are available at the beginning of crop season, but as the season progresses, formal credit is not easily available (Figure 8.4). Farmers are unable to access formal institutions on account of delays and difficulties in the processes.

The average loan taken by a marginal farmer in the study sample from an informal source is ₹8,643 with annual interest rates of nearly 60%. Marginal farmers seemed to prefer borrowing smaller amounts from informal sources, despite high interest rates.

The study rightly points out

Farmers often require credit at very short notice during a farming season. For instance, given the uncertainty in the arrival of rains in the 2014–15 cropping season in the delta districts of Tamil Nadu, even a slight delay in rainfall would have been enough to prompt farmers to rent a pump-set for irrigation. In such a situation where unforeseen expenses are necessary, it would be most convenient for farmers, especially small and marginal holders, to borrow from informal sources, given the speed and convenience in getting these funds and despite an average annualised interest rate of at least 60% (according to an on-going survey of the informal lending market in the same areas, by the same team of researchers). While larger loans are often taken by farmers pre-season, the potential losses of not being able to access credit during the season are the highest. This means that failure to get loans could adversely affect harvests, creating, for the farmer, a situation potentially more damaging than not having farmed at all. (Nair, IFMR LEAD)

The destination of low-cost credit is not fully documented. The low rate of interest provides a window of opportunity to those with access to banks. The crop loans are in demand, and the loans are used for a variety of purposes other than farming. A further problem with the subvented credit is that it causes losses to banks, especially cooperative banks which can ill afford the liquidity loss when the subsidy from the government is delayed. A study by the Bankers Institute of Rural Development[3] concluded that District Central Cooperative Banks and Primary Agricultural Credits suffer losses under the scheme. Instead of subsidizing the interest on loans and waiving loans once in a few years, can the resources be applied to build a sound safety net, by restructuring the crop insurance scheme? Marketing crop insurance as a commercial product and hoping cost recovery through premium is pretentious. The product design, delivery, and claim settlement have not found favor with farmers. NSS 70th round found during the crop season July 2012–December 2012 that out of 21 crops in 19, 90% or more households did not insure the crops. In the remaining two crops, 25% farmers in case of groundnut and 14% farmers in case of Soyabean had insured the crops. Even after

30 years of working on crop insurance, the coverage is less than 20% of cropped area! A thorough revamp of crop insurance scheme is warranted, with a clear understanding that the government funding for the entire deficit in settling claims will be made available. Setting up a separate corpus will give comfort to Agricultural Insurance Corporation of India (AICI) to operate the scheme with a focus on farmer benefit, rather than introducing restrictive features that limit claim payouts. The recently launched PMFBY is expected to provide much better support to farmers by offering coverage without a cap and having Gram Panchayat as the unit of crop loss or damage measurement. The scheme has been covered in Chapter 3 in greater detail.

Financing livelihoods is beset with many problems from demand and supply sides. Formal financial institutions have preset schemes full of what banks feel their customer should do. Where customer has new ideas for a livelihood, banks may not fund the same for want of a scheme in their hands. The multiple activities in different seasons of the year pursued by households do not fit in to schemes for financing by banks. NABARD experimented with financing the homestead instead of specific activities in Kerala about 20 years back. While some banks gave the product a try, it did not catch up. Financing the package of activities at the households provides the autonomy of action to the household and makes them use the money wisely in accordance with the income potential at any point of time in the year. A further problem is that banks are not very keen on small uncollateralized loans.

Value chain based financing in agriculture is talked about, but practiced very less in banks and financial institutions. A review of the credit products and arrangements available reveal that some parts of the production and marketing processes get funded, through loans that are fixed in terms of tenure, repayment terms, and use. Postharvest activities in value chain get much less support, especially in the hands

---

[3] BIRD, "Study Report on Impact of Interest Subvention Scheme (ISS) for Crop Loans on Cooperative Banks," (Lucknow, May 2015).

of farmers. Whatever credit is available in the postharvest stage is directed towards traders and procuring entities rather than to farmers and their collectives. Farmers badly need cash at the harvesting time. Loans to increase holding capacity of farmers, loans for aggregation of produce in farmer collectives, loans for primary processing (and secondary processing where possible), loans for warehousing of goods and so on are not common. Often the loan required is for the crop value, but for short periods of time. The time taken from procuring produce from members and selling to others can be as little as seven days and the farmer collective might require a 10-day facility—which can be against a bill drawn by farmers collective on the buyer. In case of input supplies too, the ability to pay an advance to suppliers can bring down the cost of inputs. Farmer collectives look for loans for short periods till the inputs are sold to members, which are not available from banks. Creation of captive collection, sorting, grading, and packing facilities requires investments. Financial structures such as equipment leasing, lending against future cash flows, suppliers credit for equipment suppliers, lending against escrow of future cash flows and so on which are used in other sectors are not available in financing agricultural value chains and farmer collectives. Despite the big schemes launched for FPOs, access to finance has been difficult for these entities. The conclusions from the National Seminar on financing agricultural value chains[4] were:

1. Lending institutions must ensure that agri-value chain financing products address the concerns of small holders. The requirements of sanitary and phytosanitary measures to be adopted by the farmers, cultivating vegetables and fruits, are required to be studied and popularized among SF/MF. Government departments have an important role to play in this regard.

2. Sound business and financial planning lies at the core of sustainable FPOs. For value chain financing, banks have to appraise the project reports keeping in view the five pillars of value chain: (a) factors of production, (b) financial constraints, (c) consumer's demand, (d) marketing constraints, and (e) government priorities,

3. NABARD should create awareness among the bankers on value chain financing. A set of regional workshops may be conducted for bankers, Agriucltural Produce Market Committees (APMCs), and other agencies who are involved in agriculture value chain.

In its annual report 2015–16, NABARD had dwelt on the producer companies, thus, GOI's decision to create a Producers' Organization Development and Upliftment Corpus (PRODUCE) Fund with a corpus of ₹2 billion in NABARD for the promotion of 2,000 FPOs by March 2016, was a major intervention aimed at facilitating aggregation of input supplies and output marketing, besides village level value addition. During the financial year 2015–16, 1,371 FPOs have been approved taking the total to 2,173 FPOs under PRODUCE Fund as on March 31, 2016, in various parts of the country. Out of ₹1.99 billion with NABARD in the PRODUCE Fund, ₹0.21 billion were utilized during the year 2015–16 for supporting FPOs, indicating that the progress is slow.

Credit Access in Nonagricultural Sectors

PMMY sought to fill the gap in credit requirements of small, micro, and tiny enterprises. It typically targeted enterprises requiring loan of ₹50,000 to one million to start or expand their enterprise activity. 34.88 million loans have been given till March 2016 involving a sum of ₹1,329.54 billion. In its very first year, the PMMY has captured the imagination of both banks and the people. The targets set for the first year were comfortably achieved. For the year 2016–17, a higher target of ₹1800 billion has

---

[4] Excerpted from Monograph by Ashok, Mani, and Panwar "Financing Value Chains—Challenges and Opportunities," (NABARD, November 2015).

been finalized. Women customers had been sanctioned more than three out of every four loans under MUDRA. This is on account of substantial involvement of MFIs in the scheme which exclusively focus on women on account of their superior repayment record. Three categories of loans based on loan size have been introduced (Box 8.1). A Mudra card has been introduced on the Rupay platform. It is a debit card which enables drawing of the loan amount in a hassle-free manner.

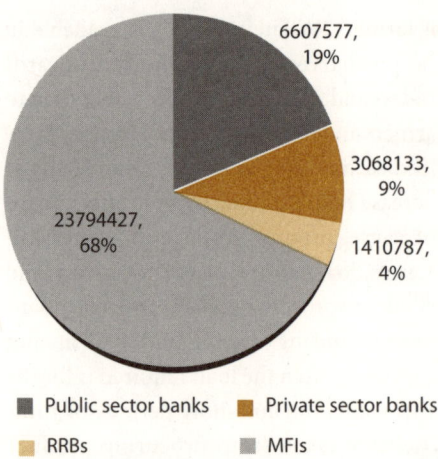

- Public sector banks
- Private sector banks
- RRBs
- MFIs

Figure 8.5: Institutional Shares in Loan Accounts

Source: Chart prepared by authors based on data from PMMY reports 2015–16 in www.mudra.in, accessed on September 17, 2016.

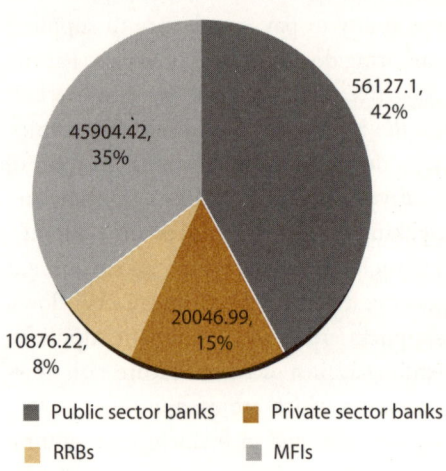

- Public sector banks
- Private sector banks
- RRBs
- MFIs

Figure 8.6: Institutional Shares in Loan Amount Disbursed

> **Box 8.1:** *The MUDRA Portfolio*
>
> MUDRA loans are extended by banks, NBFCs, MFIs, and other eligible financial intermediaries as notified by MUDRA Ltd. The scheme envisages providing MUDRA loan, up to ₹1 million, to income generating microenterprises engaged in manufacturing, trading, and services sectors. The overdraft amount of ₹5,000 sanctioned under Prime Ministers Jan Dhan Yojana (PMJDY) has been also classified as MUDRA loans. The MUDRA loans are extended under following three categories: (a) Loans upto ₹50,000 (Shishu), (b)Loans from ₹50,001 to ₹0.5 million (Kishore), and (c) Loans from ₹5,00,001 to ₹1 million (Tarun). More focus would be given to Shishu. All advances granted on or after April 8, 2015 falling under the above categories are classified as MUDRA loans under the PMMY.
>
> *Source:* Excerpted from MUDRA information kit.

While banking system participated in providing MUDRA loans, in terms of number of accounts, MFIs had the larger share of 68% of accounts (Figure 8.5 and 8.6). In terms of amount of loans sanctioned, the public sector banks had the highest share of 42%. The progress in its first year and the high new target for the current year are commendable. The concerns are about the purpose of these loans, verification of end use, and hand-holding of especially new entrepreneurs.

On account of the automatic classification of loans of size less than ₹1 million as

MUDRA loans, impressive numbers have been recorded even in the first year of the scheme. One of the concerns raised in case of PMMY is the extent to which these loans are incremental to the loans provided to similar categories of people by banks till the previous year. Data available shows that a significant proportion of loans are new loans to micro units and as such financially inclusive from a credit access point of view. Under MUDRA, 12.47 million new loan accounts had been added during the year, which was about 45% of all loans (Table 8.9), indicating that banks were not just relabeling renewal/enhancement of old

Table 8.9: Share of New Accounts and Women under MUDRA (2015–16)

	Loan Accounts	Amount Sanctioned (₹ billion)
Total	34,880,924	137,449.27
Of which new (%)	12,474,668 (35.8)	61,649.95 (44.9)
Women loanees (%)	27,628,265 (79.2)	82,183.55 (59.8)

Source: Review of the performance of Pradhan Mantri Mudra Yojana 2015–16.

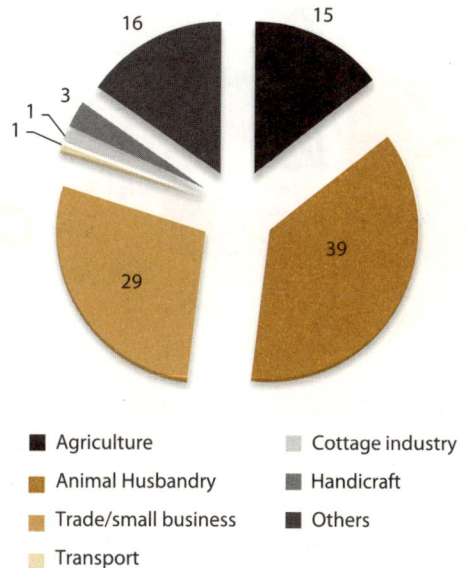

- ■ Agriculture
- ■ Animal Husbandry
- ■ Trade/small business
- ■ Transport
- ■ Cottage industry
- ■ Handicraft
- ■ Others

Figure 8.7: MFIs Loans for Income Generation

loans as MUDRA. However, in case of MFIs, the new customers would have anyhow been added. Inclusion of MFI customer numbers and loan amounts and reporting the same under MUDRA should have had a stronger basis. MUDRA sanctioned refinance of ₹10.62 billion to MFIs and disbursed ₹6.16 billion during the year. The disbursed refinance constituted 0.85% of loans disbursed by all MFIs during 2015–16. With a less than 1% share of resources employed, and without any significant policy intervention relating to either MFIs or their customers, it is a stretch to claim credit under MUDRA for sector achievements. But the fact that MUDRA is in its first year of operations should be noted. It has ambitious plans for supporting different institutions as also the MUDRA loanees on the ground. Their performance will be watched with interest in the coming years.

Microfinance

MFIs had increased lending significantly during the year 2015–16. With their basic orientation toward small and vulnerable people and the RBI's stipulation that 70% of MFIs portfolio should be for income generation activities, MFIs have been a leading financier of very tiny livelihoods on the ground. In 2015–16, 94% of the loans provided by MFIs were for income generation purposes, compared to 80% in the previous year. Animal Husbandry was the most financed segment on account of the regular cash flows of the farmers

helping them to repay periodic installments of loan (Figure 8.7). Agriculture and petty trade are the next best options in terms of livelihoods that came up for MFI funding. The high rates of interest and small size of loans have been held against the MFIs and SHGs. In case of MFIs, the interest rates ranged from about 19% to 26% with most loans being offered below 23.5%. In case of SHGs, the loans were priced between 7% and 24%, depending on whether interest subvention was available.

Loans to SHGs continue to be concentrated in the southern states. While the others are gradually increasing their share of number of accounts, southern region accounts for a substantial part of outstanding credit (Figures 8.8 and 8.9). A large number of these accounts are under NRLM, which also supports the groups with revolving fund and community investment funds. The low interest rates (effective rates range from 4% to 7%) are a key driver of these loans. However, the livelihood impact of the SHG loans is not adequately studied and documented.

The criticism against the microfinance by SHGs and MFIs is that they give very small loans for short durations that might not help livelihoods in any significant manner.

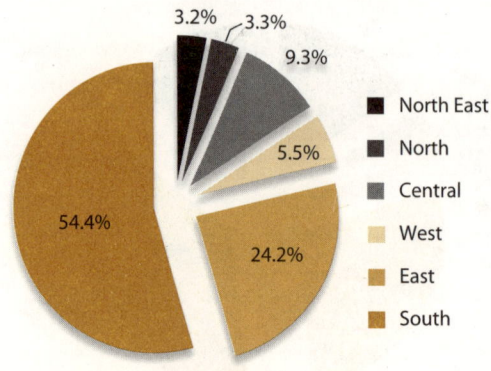

Figure 8.8: Bank Credit Across Regions to SHGs (accounts)

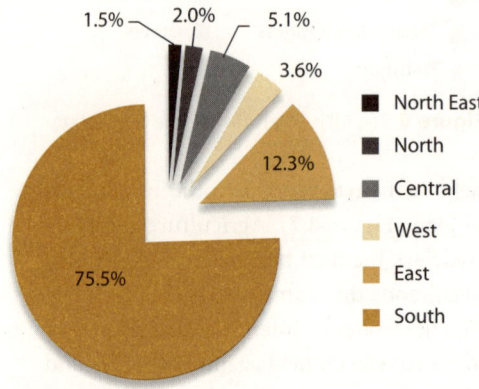

Figure 8.9: Bank Credit Across Regions to SHGs (amount)

Where the loans are available over a long time, the borrowers are able to utilize the same effectively in accordance with their priorities. Continuity of the credit access with normal growth year after year for a number of years is what builds livelihoods rather than one large loan. Data gathered on SHG members that were part of their groups for a long time clearly shows that (a) members are responsible and do not borrow excessive amounts, (b) they have clear priorities on why and how much they want to borrow, and (c) they do not need large loans every year and they have the patience to grow their livelihoods over time.

A sample of 25 SHG members[5] were obtained and analyzed as to how the loans

had progressed over the years. The analysis showed that though the loans started small, they could access very large loans. Some members could avail loans that were 200 times of the first loan. The purposes were varied—agriculture, dairy, goatery, poultry, small business, petty shops, house construction, health, and education. The sizeable loans taken in the last four years of the membership is a telling comment on building credit capacity first and providing credit according to absorption capacity. The loan size grows along with their businesses and there is increasing confidence from both the lender and borrower as to appropriate use of credit.

Other Issues

As for SMEs, collateral has been a big barrier. Banks tend to compensate for inadequate understanding of customers through excessive collateral. Some NBFCs have shown how to finance SMEs and tiny enterprises with limited financial records and limited collateral through creative means and strong customer relationships. New institutions at different levels continue to be introduced to fill the gaps in financing. MUDRA had been set up last year to cater to the missing middle, as explained earlier in the chapter. RBI has on its part issued letters of intent to 10 small finance banks. These banks are expected to focus on small loans, especially to the excluded persons and entities. Typically, these are small, microenterprises and own account establishments that have low or no records, limited collateral, but a lot of ideas and enthusiasm. The progress of these banks will certainly be watched with great interest especially because of the fact that eight of these licensees are MFIs. The start-up and stand-up India programs aim to improve the ground conditions for small and tiny units. The stand-up India programs in particular will be helpful to entrepreneurs from disadvantaged communities and women. The stand-up India

---

[5] The data was made available by Padmashri Al Fernandes, former Executive Director, MYRADA. See Annexure 8.2 for individual member-wise information.

aims to aid and back the Women and SC/ST entrepreneurs. The overall intent of the proposal is to leverage the institutional credit structure to reach out to underserved segments of the population by facilitating bank loans in the nonfarm sector for SC, ST, and women borrowers. The initiative intends to support 0.25 million borrowers over a 3-year period.

Key features of the stand-up India are:

1. Composite loan between ₹1 million and up to ₹10 million, inclusive of working capital component for setting up any new enterprise.
2. Refinance window through Small Industries Development Bank of India (SIDBI) with an initial amount of ₹100 billion.
3. Creation of a corpus of ₹50 billion for credit guarantee through NCGTC.

4. Hand-holding support for borrowers with comprehensive support for preloan training needs, facilitating loan, factoring, marketing and so on.
5. Web portal for online registration and support services.

On the financial inclusion front, impressive gains have been made (Table 8.10). The rural branch and agent network has expanded exponentially. PMJDY accounts amounted to 214 million. Credit expansion for agriculture and SMEs has increased significantly in the last five years.

RBI had set up a committee[12] on financial inclusion headed by Shri Deepak Mohanty, Executive Director. The committee examined issues relating to credit and insurance in great detail and covered issues of exclusion beyond the household level. It made recommendations on achieving comprehensive

Table 8.10: Financial Inclusion—Some Numbers

No. of Adults	840 million
No. of Households (2011)[6]	246.6 million
No. of Rural Households (2011)	167.8 million
No. of PMJDY Accounts (March 16)	214 million
No. of Basic Savings Bank Deposit Account (BSBD) Accounts with—Banks (March 16)[7]	469 million
Banking Outlets in Villages (March 16)[8]	586,307
Of which branches	51,830
No. of Loan Accounts Commercial Banks (March 15)[9]	144.2 million
Of which rural accounts	49.9 million
No. of Loan Accounts MFIs (March 16)[10]	39.9 million
No. of Saving SHG members (March 16)[11]	103 million
No. of Borrowing SHG members (March 16)	60.7 million

Source: Census of India estimates the population at 210 million people in 2011. The National Population Commission estimates that the adults of 15 years and more will be about 71% of total population in 2011. The adult population is taken at about 70% of population.

---

[6] As per the 2011 Census of India.

[7] Annual Report of RBI 2015–16, www.rbi.org.in, accessed on September 20, 2016.

[8] Annual Report of RBI 2015–16 www.rbi.org.in

[9] RBI, Basic Statistical Returns of Banks.

[10] Sadan, Bharat Microfinance Quick Report [2016].

[11] NABARD, Status of Microfinance [2015–16], www.nabard.org, accessed on September 17, 2016.

[12] RBI, Report of the Committee on Medium-term Path on Financial Inclusion, https://rbidocs.rbi.org. in/rdocs/PublicationReport/Pdfs/FFIRA27F4530706A41A0BC394D01CB4892CC.PDF, accessed on September 18, 2016.

Table 8.11:   Product Basket Offered in SMEcorner's Portal

Product	Maximum Loan Size (₹)	Maximum Loan Tenor	Typical Interest Rate Range (%)	Collateral Typically Required?
Unsecured Business Loan	0.05 billion	3 years	16.5–22 per annum	No
Secured Working Capital Loan	0.25 billion	7 years (for term loans)	10.5–16 per annum	Yes (e.g., stock property, book debts)
Machinery Loan	0.025 billion	5 years	10%–15 per annum	Yes (the machinery itself)
Loan against Property	0.25 billion	15 years	12–15 per annum	Yes (the property itself)
E-commerce Loan	7.5 million	Up to 8 months	1.5 per month	No
Home Loan	5 million	Up to 25 years	9.50	Yes
Salaried Personal Loan	2.5 million	5 years	12–18	

Source: www.smecorner.com, accessed on September 1, 2016.

inclusion across savings, credit, insurance, and geographical coverage. Some of its major recommendations are (a) step-up efforts in the NER, (b) open more accounts targeting women, (c) phase out existing interest subvention schemes and turn them into a crop insurance scheme for SF/MF, (d) restructure Agricultural Insurance Corporation in to Crop Insurance Corporation, (e) improve credit flow to MSMEs through institutional, informational, and collateral substitute options, (f) enhance range of credit guarantees to small and micro units, (g) introduce a Geographic Information System (GIS) mapping system for locating banking access points across the country, (h) increase use of mobile technology for last mile delivery of financial services, and (i) open more rural ATMs to serve the millions of new debit cards that have been issued. The recommendation to phase out subsidies in credit and introduction of collateral substitute options for MSME loans will improve the credit environment and increase bank appetite for lending. The suggestion for increasing rural ATMs is timely and will help millions of Rupay cardholders under PMJDY access services in a facile manner.

Loans from Cyberspace?

With the technological innovations available in the financial sector, web-based lending for SMEs has become mainstream. A number of web-based lenders have set up shop. Some of these are agents, partnering financial institutions; there are peer-to-peer lending facilitators and some are lending on own account. SMEcorner is one such online marketplace that enables MSMEs to find competitive offers for business loans from different NBFCs. The online marketplace we have created gives SMEs easier, faster, and more transparent access to financing that can help them grow, expand, or finance a project. The basket of loans available is significantly large and varied (Table 8.11).

The minimum loan size is ₹0.3 million. There are NBFC partners and at times banks that offer loans through the SMEcorner platform. The decision time promised is between 3–20 days depending on the type of loan. SMEcorner reports covering 18,500 customers so far in more than 2,300 cities in India. Such technology-based platforms are proliferating and several have been able to access private equity funding. The web-based lending platforms are set to expand and make access to mid-size finance especially for small businesses easier.

Some Nimble Footed Niche Institutions in Financial Sector

There are niche institutions providing differentiated products that are aligned to the customers' needs. These institutions represent the hope that eventually the formal financial sector with its technological prowess will be able to offer services that are customized to each customer's requirement. Some of these small, dynamic institutions are portrayed here.

The Kshetriya Gramin Financial Services (KGFS) Group of Institutions

The philosophy of the KGFS institutions is customer-centric financial services. According to KGFS, four critical ingredients that ensure high quality delivery of financial services are convenience, flexibility, reliability, and continuity. Convenience and flexibility are essential characteristics for ease of transactions. On the other hand, continuity and reliability bring in predictability for customers and are required for long-term financial decisions. The existing channels of financial services delivery in remote rural areas in India, though contributing to access in some ways, fall short on one or the other criterion. These shortcomings have come in the way of these providers transforming themselves into models that support complete financial inclusion on full scale. There is also shortage in number of financial service delivery points in the rural India. KGFS operates six NBFCs in this format from six locations of which four are in Tamil Nadu and one each in Uttarakhand and Odisha. It has 0.65 million customers in three states with a loan portfolio of around ₹5.5 billion.

The KGFS model is based on the **three basic operating principles**.

1. Geographic Focus

Each KGFS institution is designed to be a regional institution serving a specific territory with distinct geographic, economic, and linguistic characteristics. The geographic focus of the model makes sure that uniqueness of each service area is captured. This helps in getting better knowledge of the customer and the local economy which in turn helps in providing better products for the customers.

2. Wealth Management Approach

The second principle of the KGFS model is to provide tailored financial advice to every enrolled client. This is called a "wealth management" approach, a term common in private banking for affluent clients. The goal of this approach is to ensure that every client uses a tailored combination of financial services that best promotes the financial well-being of the client's household. The model believes that clients can make "informed" choices if they have a better understanding of financial products and services available.

3. Wide Range of Financial Products

Central to the KGFS vision of complete financial inclusion is the conviction that households need a diverse range of financial services. This is reflected in its wealth management approach that takes a holistic view of the financial needs of a household. KGFS units in turn offer a bouquet of products (Table 8.12) to its customers including credit, insurance, savings, and remittance products.

Vistaar Financial Services Private Limited

The company focuses on the missing middle segment, which is not served well by the formal financial institutions. Its objective is to make finance available at a reasonable cost and deliver it transparently. Vistaar aims to attract mainstream capital and skilled personnel to serve the chosen segment of SMEs. Vistaar's approach to credit decision (Figure 8.10) is rooted in studies to understand the customer's enterprise in depth and the peculiarities of that trade. Vistaar

Table 8.12: KGFS Product Bouquet

Loans	Insurance	Savings and Investment	Remittances
JLG Loan	Personal Accident Insurance	National Pension Scheme (NPS Lite)	International
Jewel Loan			Domestic
Salary Loan	Term Life Insurance	Savings Bank A/C	
Crop Loan	Livestock Insurance	FD & RD	
Education Loan	Shop and Content Insurance	Index Fund	
Microenterprise Loan		Gold Fund	
Emergency Loan	Weather Insurance	Liquid Fund	
Personal Loan	Health Insurance		
Livestock Loan	Crop Insurance		

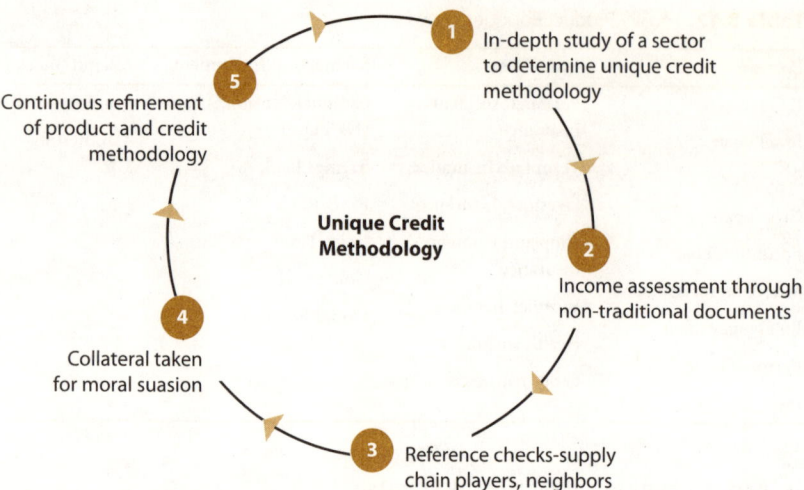

Figure 8.10: Vistaar's Credit Methodology

does not lend to sectors and trades before it achieves a good understanding of their business practices, challenges, and prospects. The income, ability, intention, business sustainability and credit behavior of the borrower are verified through traditional and nontraditional income documents, and reference checks and credit bureau checks. The database of references is maintained trade wise and updated regularly. The trades are continuously monitored and studied and the changes are incorporated in the credit assessment accordingly. The credit assessment gets additional strength from the collateral which is taken for all the facilities for moral suasion.

Vistaar makes loans for 90 days and up to 5 years. The loan basket includes small business hypothecation loan, small business mortgage loan, equipment finance, and bill discounting. The maximum loan size is ₹2.5 million which underlines the focus of the company on small enterprises. Over the last five years, Vistaar has shown impressive growth, increasing customer base six times from 12,600 in 2012 to 78,700 in 2016. It has a presence in 12 states through its 198 branches and 2,100 employees. On its ₹8.44 billion portfolio in March 2016, it carried non performing assets (NPAs) of 2.23% which is far lower than what the banks are able to manage in MSME finance.

Samunnati Financial Intermediation and Services Private Limited

Samunnati's objective is to work to enhance the value of all players across the agriculture value chain by providing financial intermediation, aggregation, market linkages, and advisory services. By identifying and interacting with existing community-based organizations, processors, and aggregators, Samunnati is able to develop or arrange customized financial interventions, while also encouraging aggregation, which is critical for lowering the risks faced by the small producers. Samunnati works through Points of High Impact (PHIs) and Channels of High Impact (CHIs). A physical office, also called the base PHI, is set up at a place and assisted by a set of mobile PHIs in chosen districts. This approach enables Samunnati to have a "rural+urban" reach in understanding and working with local value chains. In CHI, a service delivery partner route, partner entities like FPOs, cooperative societies, or processing units aggregating farm produce act as gateway agencies between Samunnati and producers or farmers. The unique features of Samunnati's processes are paperless enrolments and cashless operations. Samunnati has only two broad product categories—agri-business loan and agri-receivable finance—which are customized (Box 8.2) to suit the differences in working cycles of different value chain actors. Hence, product features such as the amount, disbursement as well as repayment schedules, and charges are all customized to suit the cash flow patterns of the specific value chain (Figure 8.11).

Do We Have the Right Models and Approaches

Financing vulnerable livelihoods by banks still continues to be under government schemes, rather than being a voluntary, well-thought-out banking business strategy. The

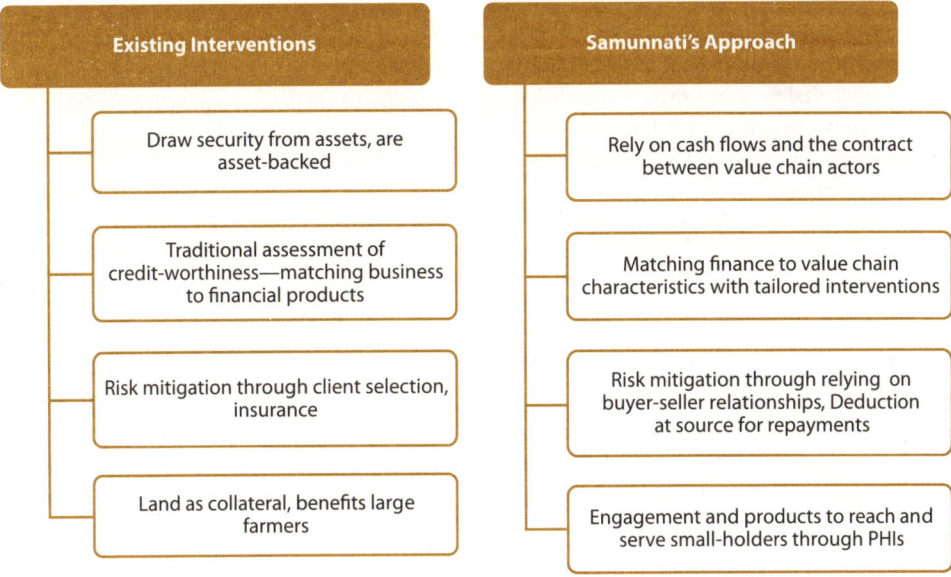

Figure 8.11: Differences in Samunnati's Approach

Source: Contributed by Samunnati Financial Intermediation and services Limited, Chennai.

Box 8.2: *Partnership Beyond Finance*

Sagar district-based Mahila Aajeevika, a producers' society, was started as a part of District Poverty Initiative Project (DPIP) of the Madhya Pradesh Government. In 2012, after visiting turmeric growing farmers in Sangli, Maharashtra, it started a turmeric cluster for which the society itself provided seeds, technical guidance, and support for sales to its members across nine villages. The society, which currently has 1,520 members in all, also began a dairy milk collection project to supply to the state's cooperative milk federation. The society soon acquired the necessary infrastructure for grinding the turmeric and expanding into pickle-making and bulk cooling plants for milk collected from members. Its Deori office manages the turmeric cluster with about 265 members and Kesli taluk has the two bulk milk cooling plants that service 1,255 members. The turmeric pickle is sold under Aajeevika brand and has raked in more revenues than turmeric powder.

However, raising turmeric production and, through that, the number of members, remained a challenge. The 9-month turmeric crop meant that no other crop could be grown and farmers were not keen to overly rely on one crop. The society's research led them to Prathibha, a variety of seed available in South India, which could help them to shorten their cropping cycle and persuade more farmers to enter the turmeric cluster. But how to get access to the seed variety from far of South India where the society had contacts? A Samunnati executive came across the turmeric pickle and through it, Mahila Aajeevika. Sensing the need for a market linkage, the Chennai-based Samunnati linked Mahila Aajeevika to one of the Turmeric Seed Traders in Erode, Tamil Nadu who could supply the Prathibha seeds at an affordable cost. This intervention is likely to help Mahila Aajeevika increase yields by more than 50% and shorten cultivation duration by 3 months. Samunnati also facilitated a customized loan to the society for improving marketing of chilli, turmeric, and coriander powder, besides the turmeric pickle. This was a critical intervention since retailers prefer sourcing multiple products from a smaller number of suppliers.

When crop loans to members were proving difficult because KCC imply land being mortgaged, Samunnati sat with the society's members to work around the problem. Smaller sized loans that do not require mortgage over land are now being facilitated with Mahila Aajeevika's guarantee. Samunnati has already disbursed loans to turmeric and dairy farmers for inputs. While the dairy loan has weekly repayments, the turmeric loan has a different repayment schedule reflecting the different working capital cycles of these value chains. The society itself does not have to collect repayments—it simply deducts the repayment portion from the sales revenue and transfers it to Samunnati's account directly. Samunnati participates in meetings with members at the Kesli headquarters, as Mahila Aajeevika, charts out plans for taking the producers' collective forward.

Source: Contributed by Samunnati Financial Intermediation and Services Limited.

low interest rates, existence of subventions and periodic waivers have fettered banks' enthusiasm to lend for small cultivators, enterprises, and service units. Even the priority sector obligations are being met through lending to MFIs and purchase of portfolios. However, the recent RBI stipulations regarding quarterly fulfillment of priority sector targets has pushed banks to look for new customers and strategies in priority sector. The Priority Sector Lending Certificates (PSLC) that are tradeable have come in handy for banks that have limitations in lending directly to small customers. Small loans are being increasingly made in groups through SHGs or JLGs with intermediation of MFIs. Aggregation of demand, risk transfer to intermediary institutions, and separation of lending risks through purchase of PSLCs are the chosen modes of livelihood financing. The small finance banks will hopefully expand lending to small clients in view of their past familiarity with this segment and the high priority sector targets.

Banks and financial institutions follow a fragmented approach to financing livelihoods. There are three possible models (Table 8.13) that seem feasible for banks to reduce risks and reduce costs of lending. A vertically integrated value chain model, a horizontally integrated multiple activity basket at household level, or an aggregation of household credit requirements that

Table 8.13:   Livelihood Financing Models

	Vertically Integrated Value Chain Financing	Horizontally Integrated Household Level Financing	Aggregated Community-based Organization Financing
Preparation required in the financial institution	Understanding the entire value chain—what value is added where and where value gets monetized in the market	Understanding the range of activities in households in given geographies and how the activities contribute to the livelihood incomes	Member requirements and how the aggregation is done at the entity level—governance and financial competence of CBO
Risk mitigation in Banks	Financing gaps and focus on links where value is monetized—Understanding of the market	Risk diversification through appropriate choice of activities—in both farm and nonfarm sectors	Risk diversification through range of activities by different households and risk of individual loans transferred to CBOs
Costs of lending	Financing can be from individual to large marketing and processing entities—hence large average loans reduce costs	Compared to single activity loans, basket of household activities will have larger outlays and hence larger average loans will reduce costs	Aggregated requirements of members result in large loans and lower transaction costs to the banks
Nature and size of exposure	Direct and indirect—small and large loans	Direct—small loans	Indirect—large loans
Examples	Sugarcane and milk	KGFS model	Cooperative societies and FPOs

Source: Authors' own analysis.

diversifies risk across a range of business lines at the community organization level.

A value chain based approach can ensure that producers are able to access markets with certainty. Sugarcane is one such crop where banks finance the farmer, the harvester, sugar mill, and the stockist. Going further, cogeneration units and alcohol distillation units set up by sugar mills are also financed. The result is that the sugarcane farmers are able to get a larger share of customer's money. But sugarcane is an exception. In most other crops (except to some extent—milk), the link between the producer and the final market from a banking viewpoint does not exist. The second alternative is that of comprehensive household level financing for the basket of livelihood activities carried out. Such financing can ensure that the entire cycle of production and consumption is well supported giving the households financial stability. The KGFS model is a case in point. It assesses the financial services needs of the household and overtime tries to respond to all legitimate needs. In so doing it does not separate farm sector activities from that of nonfarm. NABARD had designed a homestead finance product in Kerala, which was given up by banks after a short trial. Such a product offers flexibility to the household, enables deployment of funds in the most profitable lines and ensures that household is able to capture opportunities that arise in the market. With KCC hogging the agricultural finance space, banks have no patience for products where they have to understand multiple activities at the household level. A third possible way is to finance community-based institutions that have the potential to offer support to the range of livelihood activities in different stages in accordance with the aggregated demand from the members of the institutions. Multipurpose

societies were to take care of different needs of members such as for inputs, cropping, consumption requirements, investments, marketing of produce and the like. CBOs can aggregate the requirements of members and provide the farmers goods and services they need. To do the aggregate interventions, the community organizations require credit. However, the cooperative societies and FPOs have not been able to access credit to the extent members of these societies required support. Mr Brij Mohan in his interview lamented the neglect of farmer producer companies, which have a high potential for making value chains work in the interest of farmers. The demand for collateral from the FPOs, knowing fully well the membership holding shares in these companies have thriving livelihood activities and that their landholding and other assets cannot be easily collateralized at the aggregate level.

Currently financing for livelihoods does not follow any philosophy and hence ends up with sporadic loans of different types that do not provide good credit and liquidity solutions to customers. For the borrowing customers, unsuitable products, vexatious sanction processes, high hidden costs, and uncertainty of continuation of credit facilities are becoming a part of the challenges to be faced. With uncertain and unreliable finance flows, it is difficult for people and enterprises to invest in livelihoods and businesses. But, the other side of the story is with the bankers. If farm profitability is not ensured, how can banks fund failing enterprises? Field reports indicate high levels of impaired loans that seem performing assets on account of forbearance of banks. The concepts of lenders' liability and fair practice in dealing with customers should be enforced on banks rather than remaining as advisories.

ANNEXURE 8.1
A Conversation with Shri Brij Mohan,[13] the Veteran Livelihoods and Microfinance Practitioner

Author: How do we define or understand livelihood finance?

Brij Mohan (BM): There is no clear understanding of what is livelihood finance. There is a whole lot of confusion because there is poverty-related finance taking place; there is finance for small and medium industries, and something in between the poverty and small medium industries is also there. It is a way of financing activities of people even while developing an understanding of what people are doing and how it can help them in leading better lives. Among mainstream banks, there is no clear idea as to what is the purpose of lending or the willingness to understand nature of the purpose when it comes to very small loans. To cure the problem of willingness to understand in banks, we seem to have come up with a solution in the form of small finance bank. These transforming entities, having worked with only similar customers knowing what they do and also possibly knowing how they can actually scale up, will be able to finance activities that can be called livelihood. It is still too early to precisely define what livelihood finance is. We should understand it in much better terms of what would be the limits of this, what would be the purpose, what would be the kind of conditions under which one can finance, and then look at what kind of products and processes are best equipped to do this.

One thing more, we have to note is that there must be a line between enterprise finance and livelihood finance. Because, for example, if there is a factory, service unit or shop which is not in the house, I will call it as an enterprise. So, livelihood finance would have to be clearly something that it is lower than enterprise finance and higher than microfinance.

Author: What is special about livelihood finance? How do we attend to the needs of very poor who do not seem to have what we call a livelihood?

BM: Once you start dealing with your people, you will understand the art and science of livelihood lending. For example, in North East, there are many units doing piggery. Once you start financing piggery units, in the name of pig units and not micro finance, then you will know what to do, what not to do while financing a pig farmer. But, the poor require more than finance as we have seen in the "poorest of the poor" projects—like what Bandhan did. Some preloan period support to improve the confidence and skills of the customers is required. May be we require some CSR funding for such efforts by which the really poor customers can be made bankable. If institutions like SIDBI or NABARD help MFIs or SFBs with funds for nonfinancial interventions to improve skills and confidence of very poor, then livelihood finance can truly happen. Today, the very poor are neglected with the branding that they are "not bankable". This attitude should disappear. In such ultrapoor locations, we should realize the need for social investments and try to secure CSR funding to bring the poor to higher levels from which they can seize livelihood opportunities. There are precedents in some projects that have done good work—lifting ultrapoor in to self-employed and tiny enterprises. We need to learn from these successful projects.

Author: What is your view on producer companies? Are they a part of the livelihood finance discourse?

BM: The producer companies are certainly a legitimate part of the livelihood finance discourse. We had the right ideas when introducing this form of institutions, but did not think through the totality of their requirements to take roots, stabilize, and operate successfully. Typically, some support for two or three years of support is available and within this period, the promoting organizations have not done their job of making members realize that the FPO is their organization. Their sustainability is something that we need to work on. If the FPO sells inputs or buys outputs, why can't 5% of surplus be retained in the producer company? If the FPOs are guided in the first three years by a promoter organization, why that 5% saved in the producer company for a 3-year period cannot be used for taking care of their cost

---

[13] Shri Brij Mohan was a former Executive Director of SIDBI, India and has been an active practitioner as part of several institutions, projects, and initiatives in microfinance and livelihoods. He spoke exclusively to the authors on a range of issues in livelihoods finance.

from the fourth year? The members of the FPO should be persuaded to agree to pay those who provide services. While the first two or three years external funding might come from the fourth year onwards, the FPOs should be made ready to pay for costs of hand-holding advice. We have to invest in some form of improving access to finance, access to technology, and access to markets through some collectives. You can create wealth in the hands of poor in rural areas only by aggregation. When agriculture develops, even those who are not directly linked will benefit. FPOs in my view are best suited to serve people in more ways than financing, but finance is a critical tool in FPOs.

ANNEXURE 8.2
SHG Member-wise Loan Details

Name of Member	Start Year	Loan	End Year	Amount	Peak Loan Year	Peak Loan Amount	Total Loan Taken	First Loan to Peak Loan Multiple	Average Loan/Year
Santhamma	1996	500	2006	47,000	2006	45,000	175,450	90	17,545
Sakkamma	1996	500	2006	2,000	2004	40,000	127,495	80	15,937
Kausar Banu	1996	1,000	2006	2,000	2005	58,000	241,075	58	24,108
Nagarathnamma	1997	2,000	2006	2,000	2005	40,000	186,550	20	23,319
Kempamma	1995	1,000	2010	7,000	2007	70,000	575,750	70	47,979
Rathnamma	1996	1,000	2010	74,500	2009	65,000	498,700	65	38,362
H. Girija	1998	3,000	2010	80,000	2007	75,000	572,500	25	63,611
Rathanmma 2	1997	500	2008	2,120	2007	45,000	139,820	90	13,982
Neelamma	1995	500	2009	2,000	2007	65,000	216,320	130	18,027
Chikathayamma	2004	1,000	2009	52,000	2008	50,000	202,060	50	40,412
Kullamma	2004	1,000	2010	32,000	2008	50,000	148,500	50	24,750
Sharadamma	2004	300	2010	33,000	2009	50,000	160,800	167	26,800
Rani	1998	500	2009	80,000	2009	80,000	339,846	160	30,895
Mahadevamma	1998	500	2009	4,000	2008	100,000	257,646	200	25,765
Madevi	1998	500	2009	38,000	2009	33,000	182,546	66	16,595
Muniamma	1998	500	2009	20,000	2007	30,000	147,646	60	13,422
Nagalaxmi	1998	500	2009	60,000	2009	30,000	195,046	60	17,731
Rajamma	1998	800	2009	20,000	2008	56,000	415,446	70	37,768
Halagamma	1998	3,000	2009	80,000	2007	60,000	420,146	20	38,195
Kalpana	1998	500	2009	88,000	2009	60,000	281,196	120	25,563
Rani P.	1998	600	2009	14,000	2007	40,000	219,246	67	19,931
Sumathi	1998	1,000	2009	25,000	2006	40,000	222,096	40	20,191
Dhakshayani	1998	900	2008	77,000	2008	54,000	293,046	60	29,305
Anitha	1998	500	2009	70,000	2009	50,000	265,146	100	24,104
Usha	1998	1,000	2008	73,500	2008	35,000	212,146	35	21,215

The Practitioner Roundtable

The complexities of making livelihoods work in the field are dealt with by practitioners day in day out. While governments, academia and media have their views of what is happening in livelihood space, those closest to it, the practitioners, do not usually get to reveal to others their insights gained from the ringside. This report seeks to rectify this omission in informing readers of the views of practitioners. An exclusive roundtable was organized on July 01, 2016 in Delhi comprising people involved in designing, implementing and funding livelihoods at macro-, meso-, and micro-levels with the support of NABARD. Dr Harsh Bhanwala, Chairman NABARD, Vijay Mahajan of BASIX, Girish Sohani of Bharatiya Agro-Industries Foundation (BAIF), Narendranath of PRADAN, Arindom Datta of Rabo Bank, Meera Mishra of International Fund for Agricultural Development (IFAD), Brigadier Rajiv Williams of Jindal Stainless Ltd, Madhu Sharan of Hand in Hand, Jaydeep Sirvastava of NABARD and Vipin Sharma of Access Development Services deliberated on various issues. Girija Srinivasan and Naasimhan Srinivasan, authors of the report moderated the discussions. The discussions, with some minor edits for language, are carried verbatim in this chapter in a conversational tone.

N. Srinivasan (NS): This space called livelihood is not entirely defined in the local country context. There are some definitions available of what is livelihood. We don't have a Ministry of Livelihoods or Department of Livelihoods. Livelihood is either seen as doing something in agriculture, something in employment, something in social security, something in welfare, may be sometime it's a start up India campaign. Are we able to discern a policy framework for livelihoods? Are you able to glean elements of policy on livelihoods from whatever is available in bits and pieces across institutions, across state governments, and central government departments?

Dr Harsh Bhanwala (HB): I was reading an article yesterday that one unit of GDP used to result in 0.58 units of employment some years back. In recent times this one unit of GDP growth is resulting into much lower unit of employment, at around 0.2, which is a cause of concern. When we try to define livelihoods we try to do it from the perspective of delivering from one platform. Personally I feel a ministry like livelihoods at the central level may not make sense, and we have subjects divided between the center and states; center provides for division of subjects and many of these initiatives come from the involvement of both the governments and within the government farm, non-farm and service sectors. We can take skilling as an example. Government of India has setup a Skilling Ministry, but the parallel initiatives continue. Ministry of Rural development, Urban development, textiles, Labor are all engaged in skilling programs. State governments have their own programs.

We might define livelihood in a very broad sense, but having a separate administration mechanism only for livelihoods in a diverse country like ours and with the large population may not serve much of a purpose. The moment when you try to integrate the grassroots level, these issues of integration will be larger than the livelihoods, and I feel personally a geographical approach, area based approach to livelihoods could be better but it has to ride on digital platform. The moment we decide to digitalize the livelihoods, we can integrate at the supply level, but delivery could be disaggregated in any manner needed. So I would not spend too much time defining it; we all understand what livelihoods are and so many agencies are involved in it. If we can come up with models which are region specific, area based and which are on digital platform it would serve us better.

Narendranath (NN): I am not able to discern policy framework on livelihoods. From a policy framework, we can usually discern the focus on growth, urbanization, industrialization, and so on. When it comes to the livelihoods of the vulnerable poor, what I am able to discern is a kind of palliative effort. Keep people busy with something so that problems and people don't erupt. So you have social security program of NREGS There is lot of talk about using NREGS to dig farm ponds and things like that. But the thinking should be on rural or vulnerable livelihoods in holistic sense and not in sub-components. Similarly is the thinking on livelihoods in relation to forests, rural land, or agriculture. These are the areas where we can actually create livelihoods for the very poor, but these are being sidelined or ignored. So in summary, I am not able to discern a policy framework on livelihoods. If at what is available in terms of program guidance is to be construed as a policy framework, it's not a framework that I really subscribe to.

Girish Sohani (GGS): I go by what Narendranath said, one doesn't probably discern policy framework as such, though there have been lot of different initiatives for livelihoods. But basic to this whole problem is the requirement that we need to understand that there are vertical ways of doing things and there are needs of combining the verticals to create the impact which is interdisciplinary. Livelihoods fall in that second category and the challenge therefore is how to make vertical structures, deliver something which is interdisciplinary and that is probably at the heart of the problem. In health sector, for example, we have ministry of health but that doesn't lead directly to the health because many things which contribute to the health are scattered in fragmented verticals in other ministries. Same happens with livelihoods; there are many other things which get fragmented in the setup we have. Making a different type of structural setup may not be an answer because it will also have requirements of linking all the related verticals. But I think in the transition of society or economy, one passes through phases where sometimes the verticals are more important and sometimes the horizontals become more important. And, probably in case of livelihoods, we are at a stage where we need to give more emphasis on creating those horizontal integrated impacts out of drawing upon the verticals. Some states have created separate structures outside vertical departments to take integrated action. The NRLM efforts were also intended to be different ways of integration, but I don't think it has successfully brought out that type of integration. So, probably the challenge is to create not a framework but operating mechanism for delivering this type of interdisciplinary effort.

Arindom Datta (AD): I think I will just repeat a few things but stress on the few. Yesterday the World Bank President made a statement that 26% of Worlds poor they live in India. That is a huge number. So far as welfare is concerned, as you mention whether it's social security they seems to be some kind of framework, for insurance, financial inclusion and all of that, but if we define livelihood as income generation of increasing income, it's very complex. I don't think they have discernable policy framework because livelihoods is too complex at too many sectors—urban, rural, farm, non-farm, services, manufacturing, and so on. I don't think it's possible also. You can have an overarching principle that inclusive growth which means increasing income and all that but within that what needs to be done has to be done vertically. So, I think you can only come up with a very broad policy that we will have inclusive growth as a base; nothing more specific so far as policy can go.

Madhu Sharan (MS): As Narendra said, as an NGO, we work with the vulnerable groups. I agree with Arindam. We don't need a discernible policy. There is ministry of Rural Development, there is NRLM, and there is NABARD which works very proactively in the area of financial inclusion. All these institutions set some policy on livelihoods. Livelihood is also about access to credit. People have the skills. The Orissa Livelihood Mission is enabling the tribal communities not just with skills, but giving them access to credit at 7% rate of interest on diminishing balance. It is a huge step and so many of women are benefitted. Similarly in Bihar, the Department of Rural Development is proactive. So while it does have to work horizontally to integrate field implementation across agencies, NABARD can take up this responsibility of capacity building in the area of digital literacy.

Meera Mishra (MM): In terms of whether there is a discernable policy, there is not, whether there need to be any, I agree with Arindam and some others that there is no need for this. What I see is a positive development over the last couple of decades. Earlier there was an approach in the country towards poverty alleviation, poverty eradication and in a way the initial schemes of the government like the IRDP and others were from a sort of projected government mindset where the government decided what the poor needed in order to come

out of poverty. Recently from the time of NRLM, I find that there is a thinking that you need to create the environment where the poor have access to finances, access to skill development, and have various platforms and opportunities created in other new areas like tourism or digital India. So, the environment is created, access to finances is improved, enabling platforms have been created, and skill development is being done to enhance the opportunities for the poor. So, in a way, the shift that I see has been from government deciding for the poor to government creating opportunities and filling the gaps so that the poor can access good livelihood opportunities.

Rajiv Williams (RW): Hearing everyone, there is nothing that I can disagree with, but from the corporate perspective, I just feel that a straight jacket framework is just not relevant. It doesn't work. Even if it is there, I don't think people follow it. After government comes up with policies and a framework you realize that there are so many innovative methods that are required. Yesterday we were discussing with the UNDP. Basically we partnered to do skill training for women exclusively in steel sector, in stainless steel. JSW will be giving them not only the opportunity but also jobs. We have said that we would train and absorb. SUCN, an initiative, has nothing to do with any kind of framework which has been created by the government. It's just an initiative that has been taken on, and one million women are going to be trained in next three years. There is nothing happening with the farmers. We must be building capacities and giving them the opportunities wherein they can do multi-cropping systems, avoid the damage of floods, and cope with the storms and cyclones. So there is a lot of work that are starting up. In Gujarat, there is an authority which has been created for CSR in livelihoods. And that is a new model which has been created; I thought it was very encouraging. They shared some of those practices and how we can get engaged into this process. So I would urge and request all of us to be more flexible in our approach. With government policies and framework, it is a number game. That you need to train X number, therefore you partner with us and we will release the funds. Skill development is planned at higher levels, but on the ground nothing is happening. The trained were not employed because there was a huge gap between the trained and the industry needs; the requirement that the industry was not met by what was being churned out. That gap is to be bridged and that will only happen if there is an academia–industry relationship. There is curricular development, and there you start giving them opportunities and absorbing them. I would say please leave the policy framework on livelihoods open. It's a great thing that CSR Section 35 has come up. There are good processes in place and in those listed 13 activities; there is much beyond that we are doing. So don't let us restrict ourselves just some bullet points.

Jaydeep Shrivastava (JS): On the question of policy framework, we have adopted model which is essentially top-down, and the hope that if all function in unison and implementation also takes place the way it is anticipated, we will end up with a situation where people have livelihoods. Therefore the approach has been directed towards farmers, women, and youth. Implementation and coordination are issues, grappling with over so many years. The idea would be to have a bottoms-up approach which would essentially mean that we look at an individual as a person who has to be provided with livelihood, and the opportunities are created around that person or around that area which then develop in a holistic fashion. What is happening currently is that every ministry has a target that does not recognize the individual. Those states where the mechanism is functioning well are able to take advantage of the programs like NRLM. More than 70% of the benefits have gone to the southern states, and the northern states are slow to catch up. What is needed is a concerted approach, if we could move towards a system which is discernable to some extent

with the development process getting slowly shifted towards the state and when it is shifted towards the states, states will have their own priority. Then, looking at that priority, it can allocate funds in a manner which benefits all the section of the society. We have moved towards the digital platform for the transfer of payments to people which will probably remove the bottlenecks in the payments, which is also an important aspect of livelihood promotion. The skill development has to go in tandem. We suddenly ask rural youth to go in for skills; in a sense, it is like we are ignoring agriculture to a certain extent. We need to create a situation where agriculture is given equal opportunity; people who are engaged in agriculture should also be given entrepreneur opportunities in agriculture sector itself so that we arrest the migration to urban areas. So a lot of policy framework is discernible, but a lot has to be done. We have to move towards bottoms-up planning in such a manner that it eventually adds up to mass program. Merely providing skill-development training in a targeted manner to any number of people hoping that they will be absorbed by some industry somewhere will eventually not result in sustainable livelihood opportunities. Then there are certain other variables like climate change which are adding up a whole new dimension to the scenario in livelihood creation especially in the rural areas which have to become a part of policy framework of the government.

NN: When we say that couple of our friends were saying no policy framework may be necessary, my own take is that we need to have a discernable policy framework which actually looks at the vulnerable poor. Obviously the strategies could be different. In such a diverse country, you cannot surely have a centralized strategy for livelihoods promotion but, at least, a policy framework which enunciates the paradigm of the day. There is a lot of focus on urbanization, taking people out of the rural areas and industrialization. Those are the kinds of larger policy frames, which I think are not benefitting the vulnerable community. What we need is to discover the richness of the rural lives. So build those rural areas, as Gandhiji said, "People live in the villages." So the question is—how to bring the people back into the villages, make those villages more exciting and liveable places and build livelihoods around it. The strategies again the people enterpreuner — they will find their own ways and means of doing things. But issue is to create that framework around which much more decentralization, investment on health, education, and the general welfare of the village have to be substantially go up. It cannot be the kind of apology take investment that we have to take. Once you have a framework of that kind then you will see changes of that kind happening.

Vijay Mahajan (VM): I agree that there is no discernable policy framework, although there are several sectoral or programmatic frameworks and if you staple them together, you could probably say there is a framework and inclusive growth has been the more overarching Mantra. But I think, we do need a national policy for livelihoods, for several reasons. With due respect to all of us, whether the NGO sector, the corporate sector, or government sector, we do something and we are so engaged in it that we lose track of the big picture. We are a nation of 1.3 billion people and even a scheme which reaches 50,000, 100,000 or 1,000,000, as Brigadier William just talked about, is just drop in the ocean. Total employment in the country was 474 million as per National Sample survey during 2011–12, and of that 232 million were in agriculture and allied sectors. So, already we had made the transition where India is not an agrarian economy in terms of GDP long ago, but even in terms of employment, we have fallen below 50%. That's a good news; so some structural transformation is happening in the economy. But the bad news is that still 47%–48% are in the agricultural and allied sectors; we first need to worry about them. We need a framework like had China in 1970s; they declared that they will move a 100 million people from

agriculture to non-farm sectors. The slogan at that time was "leave the farm but not the village", and the way they did it was by creating small townships comparable to a block headquarters here. They also created a large number of TVEs—Township and Village Enterprises. The village enterprises were at the erstwhile brigade level; they used to have production teams then brigades and then communes. That was the Maoist era. But then the brigades became villages and communes became townships. By 1989, China had actually moved 100 million people from farm to non-farm but not from the villages to the cities. They continued to live where they were living. No urban rural commuting problem. What we see today of China is phase II, which happened post-1990s when the Eastern China took off. Special Economic Zones and then population movement was allowed, and then you had all the problems of crowding in Beijing, Shanghai, and all that. So phase I is very interesting for us. Now it cannot be replicated in India because we are a democracy and we cannot impose movement restrictions and currency restrictions. But, at least, we can have a unified framework as to what do we do with the fact that millions of people need to move out of agriculture, want to move out of agriculture, if we believe their responses to the NSS survey, and we need to help them get out of agriculture. So what is the framework? And there we can be demographically smart, which is that anyone who is above 35 and still in agriculture, quite honestly, we can let them be. I have a suggestion for them also, not abandoning them but let them be. But anyone who is below 35, with today's life expectancy has another 35 years to live, that person can be helped in economically, financially viable way to move from agriculture to the non-farm sectors. But learning from China, we need to invest in small towns. We have nearly 4,500 census towns and only 450 of them are 100,000 and above. All the others are smaller towns. We need a national policy to invest, so I dislike this smart city emphasis.

What we need is smart towns. Actually, we need smart regional development approach. Our cities are smart enough to corner all the subsidies, all the elites, and everything else, all the power. It's the small town which is suffering. If small towns become growth centers then we could actually have a situation where you continue to live in the village to commute to the nearest town and the quality of life doesn't suffer. You eat your own farm food, you drink your own tube well water and you work in a small town job. What do we do with those who are above 35 in agriculture and an overwhelming number of women even below 35 who may not be able to move out of the villages because of social and other factors. We need a national program for green sector. I define sector as not just agriculture and animal husbandry but activities in renewable energy, waste recycling, eco-tourism, rural tourism and indeed alternate therapy—Yoga and anything which is basically does not use physical material in a very large way to provide goods and services to today's population. And, if you look at that then there are tremendous opportunities which can rise in the green sectors in rural areas, and even for traditional cultivation we can upgrade the skills. So a woman who knows how to do weeding in the field, if she knows paddy transplantation and becomes an expert SRI transplanting person, then she does not only enhance her own farm productivity but of 20 other neighbors. Similarly, youngsters who learn how to do artificial insemination or learn how do tissue culture of banana or something else, acquire a professional identity. Similarly, bio fertilizers and bio pesticides are today's cottage industries. Let's not forget Gandhiji's concept of khadi as cottage industry. Today's cottage industry is solar and bio. It relies on solar energy either through the photosynthesis route or through the photovoltaic route. As a neo-Gandhian, that would be the strategy to really bring energy into economic revival to a scale. So that leaves the question of what is happening to those who are going away from agriculture. Today, actually they join the bottom of the heap as unskilled workers; they come to the cities and wait at those corners to be hired for the day. They become, at best, *chowkidars* (watchmen). They have unsecured jobs. They have awful living conditions. They hardly have additional income compared to additional cost. So it's not really an upward movement. So if we have to improve that then we need to focus on those services sectors and manufacturing sectors where the share of value added is high. So, for example, instead of giving subsidies on backwardness or on certain IT industry, this or that, there should be a single criterion which is very transparent. What is the wage share of value added in your industry? Value added is basically wages, rents, interests, and profits. Wage share is easily discernable from any profit and loss account. Any industry where wage share is above a threshold, it should get a subsidy because it is enhancing employment. And through that, we would create a massive incentive for industry to become more sensible about capital investment in this country. We have automation in India. In a nation where millions of people are unemployed, you have automation for things which are neither hazardous nor particularly cost saving. The reason why that is happening because capital is cheap and labor in the organized sector is expensive. Also, labor as a whole is cheap in the economy. If there was a national policy framework covering all these—let's say between now and 2022 and then from 2022 to 2030, in two steps—we would reduce the percentage of working population in agriculture from 47% to 35% and then from 35% to 25%. For those who will remain in agriculture because the numbers will come down, effectively their wage rate will go up because productivity will up. It is a very interesting way by which we can handle all the three problems. And therefore, we do need a national policy but it has to be stitched together. What Girish said exactly, that multiple verticals will have to be stitched together into a single framework.

RW: Situation in China is very different from the situation in India. And therefore, it is difficult to take the example of China, especially in the case of rural areas with all the issues that we have with politics and democratic system that we follow. Also, if you are talking about quick growth then you have to have short timeframes and not 30 years. Therefore, my take is that moving a certain percentage from farm to non-farm is an option. But the number would be very limited because you don't have the opportunities in non-farm vocations. Even if you create the opportunities with the economic environment as it is today, especially in the core sectors, it is going to take a long time. And therefore, even if you churn out people who are skilled, they may not be employed. If the industry does not offer them that kind of an opportunity, it is going to result in a lot of disparity between the haves and have-nots. This is going to change the balance completely. I think what we need to do for a quick growth is that we must reach out to the communities and let them stay on for the next many years and develop as you rightly said Mr Mahajan about developing the towns instead of smart cities. Do whatever you can and make sure that those establishments and opportunities are available in *N* locations and in *N* geographies. Let the rural youth remain equipped with the new farming technologies, otherwise food security will be a big challenge. So we have to be careful, and I think farm sector needs to be strengthened and only small percentage can be moved out of agriculture to jobs in the urban sector.

NS: The second question deals with the reported good growth. There is a lot of debate about whether we have grown up at the optimum levels in terms of GDP, but generally when we look across the world, the Indian growth has not been that bad. Does growth actually get down to people who are looking forward to growth in a very material sense? Does it actually impact livelihoods of vulnerable people and is it impacting people equitably? Is a good growth rate which corporates and government are happy with also something a common man say in a village is happy with? How do you see this? This round we can have very quick answers because it is another variant of what we have discussed in the first question. Who would like to start?

HB: Nobody denies that we should move people from this sector and what should follow is action plan in 5–6 areas. India is not a totalitarian state as the first point. Second point is that you have subjects divided. The 6–7 action plans would cut across various subjects in the constitution and should take on board people for that purpose. While overall we have a mission statement that we will shift this many people, the action plans have to follow an area-based approach. These plans should be strongly linked to the vulnerability; rural areas and semi-urban areas require widely different approaches to development. So I feel strongly that if the bottoms-up approach, as some of you were talking, has to happen, there may be a policy overall but action plans have to be region specific. So, vulnerability of small sizes, backward regions, small BPL persons, women—there will have to be separate plans for each category. With India, the average size of land holding becoming so small, any intervention in food sector may be limited in impact unless we resolve the basic problem of policy in leasing of land. The value chains will not succeed unless you create FPOs, who aggregate. So we should have general definition that this is to be achieved, action plans needs to be region specific, across sectors, they need to be pointed out and also for each of these actions plans, which require and there are certain legislative changes required, or structural changes required, that also needs to be defined well.

On your second question about whether there is trickledown of the benefits of the economic growth going to the grassroots or to the poorer for livelihood. I am not in a position with data to say that it is or it is not, but I would like to cite example of Sri Lanka. You would recall that when

Jayawardhane was president there, they developed a three pronged strategy for improving their foreign exchange earnings, and the three prong strategy was to export skilled labor overseas because there were not that many job opportunities. To bring in special economic zones, they were the first in the whole of South Asia region to do that and to promote tourism. So my understanding is that economic growth by itself will not necessarily trickledown. It has to be coupled with very strategic and targeted thinking to focus in the areas that will bring benefits to a large number of people and sectors, such as tourism, which have a large footprint. So I think one has to be conscious that just tom-toming the economic growth will not be helpful; it may sound good and some people may quote it but it has to be coupled with right thinking and very strategic and precise kind of focus on those areas that will create jobs for a large number of people.

NN: I think Vijay summarized really very well. I personally have problems with the word trickledown itself; the imagery that comes into my mind is you sitting on a high table, having dinner, and dog sitting on the side waiting for crumbs to fall. There are similar imageries people have created on growth incidentally benefitting the poor. One is "when the tides raise all the boats will rise" but then again I think on… What about the people who don't have a boat? People sitting on the ground or sitting in their houses, they will all get flooded and suffer. The rate of growth, if it is happening 20–30% in cities; it would be less than a percent in the villages in the rural India. Therefore, the trickledown, if at all there are actually trickles, very small trickles and these are not benefitting. Second issue is you know if it's logical, where does it trickle to, who gets these benefits. Somebody has to be there to hold that, to take benefit of it, now as Vijay said the farmers are in distress. If you are doing farming, it should be treated as public service, not a livelihood. If farming is in distress you have tribals universally in distress, the right of their

property, their land, and everything is going away from their hands. Therefore, the earlier point I made just to keep public outbursts from happening, we have palliatives like NAREGA, NRLM which give some little bit of wages, subsidies, or credit, and keeps rural communities below the explosion point. So this kind of growth is not what is in the mind, the desirable growth. Who are the people benefitting the growth. In fact, I was reading Dipankar Gupta's book the other day, he said the growth story of India is written on the shoulders of those millions of rural youth who come to cities, who work at low wage, no security and no place to live, and lead a very bad quality of life. Ask these industries to start paying minimum wages. Ask them to give them proper working and living conditions. Therefore, the point that Vijay made about huge amount of capital infusion in to mechanization is not resulting in employment or wages. So the whole migration story is a very sad story; people come and settle down as *Hamali* and rick-shaw puller, and may be they also get in all kinds of undesirable activities in the cities. We have to find a way in which these people would be able to receive benefits from the growth story. If the prosperity is happening in the cities, are our rural poor, tribal communities like in our WADI program, earning better incomes? If these stories are happening in huge number, then you could say that people are benefitting in the groups. But I believe, as a whole, because it's again such a huge country the numbers are just astronomical, so for poor to benefit you need to have real program, real investment, and a policy thrust.

MM: Coming from like a very rural area in Bihar, I have actually seen this trickledown benefit in the unorganized sector, job opportunities in the hospitality, tourism sector. One person comes to Delhi, he pulls out his nine other relatives from Bihar, migrants going to Punjab, getting good livelihood for four months, and there is actually increase in household incomes which they transfer to their hometowns. So, when we saw a lot of ultra poor, below poverty line family languishing in poverty in Bihar, Jharkhand, Orissa, there is some amount of trickledown of money, and NAREGA has done commendable work. You may call it some kind of a pacifier or something but giving them two months of employment, direct benefit transfer, bank accounts; it has brought some amount of wellbeing because I have seen children now going to school and then tuitions. A households being aspirational is what it means by growth in the villages when a family starts dreaming of putting their children for medicine, so there has been some benefit. But yes, I totally agree it is unorganized and unplanned which is why some people benefit and others don't. We definitely need to have some kind of a planning around this economic growth but in terms of benefits; yes, it has trickled down to make people aspire for greater wellbeing.

MS: Trickledown effect is there, but high growth rates in GDP may not actually reach the poor. The point is that the growth in GDP should have accompanying growth in employment also. Now we need to have good strategies for poor to benefit from high growth rates.

JS: You can create opportunities in rural areas, and you still don't cover all aspects. We have seen toilets were created, bulk toilets created, people don't use them. Opportunity was created. So unless you have geography-related issues, which are region specific, answering some problems of region will not lead to full solutions. We have seen number of rural industrial estates in Haryana lying unused. What Vijay was saying that you create those township facilities and so on. those were created, unused. Houses were created for weaker sections, land was provided, so there is something else which is required for trickledown to emerge and that is basically the investments in these vulnerable people or these distant areas in terms of capacity creation. I was just doing a study on this Bank Sakhi Model, and we are launching it with other banks also after

two pilots. Why Bank Sakhi succeeded? Because discipline was inculcated and they were from that region, they can survive at 3,000 rupees. So any answer to this has to be region specific. Today's policy, mostly, is supply oriented. We need to work on systems for generating demand in rural areas. If you migrate from rural areas, then there is a reduction in demand in rural areas or in the deprived region.

AD: Just a few points, India's GDP is expected to be 2 trillion dollars by the end of 2016, China's will be at 14 trillion. So there is absolutely no comparison. In Europe, if you see, the GDP that we have, they are a population of 10 to 25 million who have similar GDP in absolute terms, are growing in 0% to 2%. So GDP growth is one thing. Second is the way we are calculating the GDP is again very different from the way we did it two years back. I had heard of a study done about five years back and that report was highly contested and then it was not released. They said from independence, they calculated the amount of resources which has been allocated for rural development and anything to do with vulnerable—whether its women, safety nets, employment generation all the schemes put together and they compared it to countries in Latin America as to how much of the resources they require per person to pull them out of poverty. They said India had spent enough resources to pull everyone out of poverty. So the conclusion was—it's not resources, but extremely weak governance that was the cause of continuing poverty. Misplaced priorities and supply side solutions which were not the demand of the poor led to wastage of resources.

GGS: I think, on the theme of GDP itself, some questions which one needs to look into—how much is true wealth creation and how much it is just the size of your tax—whether it is from VAT, whether it is from service taxes, whether it is from excise that adds numbers to growth rates. Though it may have some sort of correlation with how much livelihoods have been created, growth rates are not a good indicator. Now what is happening on the ground is that the labor markets in urban areas are swelling. And those labor markets are in unskilled labor segment. People are just waiting on roadside for jobs for the wage labor opportunity. When we have this swelling condition in the urban side of the labor markets, there is shrinkage of labor availability in the rural areas. There is a huge shortfall because they are not available. Now this also correlates with the NSSO survey finding that employment in agriculture has fallen below 50%. While there is a structural shift, whether that shift has gone into which sector and at what levels is also something which needs to be understood. The incongruence of labor shortage in rural area and a swelling labor supply in urban India needs an explanation. There are sentimental overtones to the 'trickledown' phrase, but I think one needs to understand differently also in terms of what are the multipliers. There has to be a better understanding of the major growth sectors where in the economy, the growth in a particular type of industry, how much it has created a multiplier through the linkage in terms of employment, incomes of the poor, and so on, needs to be studied. I think the multiplier in terms of the employment is probably the most crucial because most of the current growth is without jobs.

NS: I think should I move to the next question. Vijay, I want you to start out with this because you did a bit of this in the first question itself. What is the situation of agriculture-based livelihoods? Niti Aayog brought out a paper in December which talks about some 3–4 critical failures. They are saying that productivity is continuing to be a major issue. The issues in productivity, probably, are reducing the enthusiasm among the farmers. Second, of course, is the question of farmer's share of consumer rupee and remunerative prices. Niti Aayog has said that the MSP doesn't seem to really work in terms of its reach. And the government has recently come up saying we are going to ensure that by 2022,

farmers' income will be doubled. Putting all this together, what do you see happening in agriculture-based livelihoods?

VM: The census told us that between 2001 and 2011 there were 9 million less a first time decline in farmers. NSS 70th round tells us that 15 million hectare of land has vanished from agriculture. I can't believe that all of that has gone to industries or urbanization. Is it a data flaw? But 15 million hectare and 9 million people out of agriculture in structural transformation? This is a good news. Bad news is where are they going? They are going not to better jobs but to unsecured, low end wage employment in urban and construction sectors. On the other hand, who have been left behind have smaller land ownership and their viability is threatened. So we are having the worst of the two sides of structural transformation. If we planned structural transformation, we would have those who are left behind in agriculture, should be better off, and those who leave agriculture should have better livelihoods. Now within agriculture investment in dry land agriculture, improvement is overdue by 30 years. We should have triggered that within 10 years after the green revolution. We have 60 million hectares of dry land; let's do a brown revolution or whatever you want to call it. Even today, on an average, you can treat the watershed for ₹25,000 a hectare. So, for 60 million hectare, we need 30 billion dollar for a 2 trillion economy, its nothing. In a period of five years, it can be done and it can have a multiplier effect—in terms of both output and enhanced income, it would be phenomenal. In terms of technologies, methodologies, experience, institutional frameworks, there is enough. There are a few thousand successful watershed programs we all know we can build on. NABARD itself has so much expertise on it. Why is it that this still is an issue after 30–40 years? Why can't we crack it? Why can't the research system as well as the extension system work intensely on dry lands? The third, which is my favorite, is that we need for every agro economic zone a package—not just a package of practices but package of crops and then a package of practices—which will ensure that with one acre you can make 100,000 rupees of output and, at least, 25,000 rupees of net income. Considering that average farmer does not even own 2 acres, about 50,000 rupees income per year. We need to develop intensively, every agroclimatic zone. NABARD can really help in this. And it can be done through combination of vegetables, crops, cash crops, and so on. If we do that then we systematically propagate that among our millions of small farmers. I think we can make the lives of those continuing in farming a lot better. Last is this business of green skills which is that agriculture still being done in a very traditional way and one major change that is happening in agriculture is that it is getting increasingly feminine. Because men are migrating in large number, women have now to perform those agricultural operations which they were traditionally not performing. The idea which was there behind Mahila Kisan Sashaktikaran Yojana actually needs to be more broadly followed, and women not only need to master agriculture but they need to be given a professional identity. So with these four things, I think we can do a lot better in agriculture. I am not pessimistic; there is space for a lot of hope.

HB: Well said by Vijayji. We don't have micro-level income growth models which are operating in agriculture. Now this responsibility is devolved on certain entities, KVKs. Those who know the functioning of KVKs would not believe in them any longer. Many people think that for research, the huge infrastructure available in agriculture universities is not being used properly. Can we have models of KVKs and research areas which can be outsourced to people who are capable of doing? Now if you want something in animal husbandry, why can't resources be available to say BAIF to expand to newer areas? Second, is dry land agriculture is good? We need to work on more research on extension and carrying it forward, but even in irrigated

areas, irrigation efficiency is not high. We have had a scheme for solar pumping now where the 90% subsidy is available to farmers, why can't we have a scheme which gives 90% subsidy for drip? So irrigation efficiency is going to create number of livelihood opportunities. This is going to lead towards the multiplier effect which Girishji was saying. Investment has to be there in the poly-houses and intensive agriculture too because the kind of production happening there is qualitatively different and weather variations will not affect it much. So we have to shift slowly toward modern agriculture but at a larger scale and money should be available to dry lands. NABARD's focus was entirely on the short-term credits a couple of years back. In last two years, my book size for refinance for term lending has increased to almost ₹90,000 crores, which used to be just half of that. But this quantum is going to be much larger, so that's important for us. Third, equally important is collectivization efforts which includes land as well. Not only the input–output services but we have to deal with land as well. We have to have some mechanism by which leasing of land within village becomes possible. Small and marginal farmers, when allowed to lease-in land of others, can have better livelihoods. Some legislative changes are required for this. Lobbying at the state level to change their laws is needed.

NN: Vijay and Dr Bhanwala really summarized it well. I think the nature of Indian farming is small and rain-fed. But when you go to agriculture ministry or talk to anybody of significance in the ministry or ICAR, the paradigm is totally green revolution. Punjab and Haryana, high intensity, high capital inputs, that is the framework in which all discussions happen. What we today need is a new movement which actually up-fronts the small and rain-fed farmers. Small and rain-fed farmers are creatures totally different in construct from irrigated farmers. Rain-fed farming offers enormous opportunities in terms of variety of crops; we don't need to be dependent on anybody for pulses or oilseeds. All the pulses and oilseeds even today come from rain-fed areas only. Only the cereals and grains come from irrigated areas. Therefore, rain-fed farming offers so many opportunities. The amount of investment, whether it is ₹30 billion or 60 billion, we should find that money and make the investment. This is not a huge amount or unthinkable today. Over a period of 5–10 years, we can really transform the rural rain-fed areas. So at some point of time, you need to have programs around it. So you have to have some program around revitalizing small farmers who own just an acre of land. We have done many experiments with SRI and others; the 1,000 year old paddy variety actually produces 10 tons per hectare. So don't need to get into GM or hybrids. In rainfed areas and tribal areas, they have farming systems, but the people are not just farmers; they also have some livestock; there is a possibility of investing in these farms and livestock development. Adding value in terms of rearing small ruminants, poultry and so on, in these farms, you can actually create farming system there which can return more than ₹100,000 per year income. We have reasonable rural roads today, and it is possible to access markets. Say in Jharkhand, everything comes from outside, so if you will be able to produce lot of vegetables there, local market will spring up. Marketing is not so much of a problem today; Dr Bhanwala talked about land leasing. So some legal framework in which land leasing can happen. One very interesting thing I saw in Kerala is that the Panchayats are very strong. So the decentralization can be a big answer. When the panchayats take responsibility for moving land from one to another, the panchayat say that we take responsibility. So the person giving the land is also happy and he goes away to Gulf or wherever, secure in his belief that he will get the land back on return.. So there are SHG women who are cultivating in small groups. This Joint Liability Group program

of NABARD is really working very well in Kerala, and they are doing really good farming there. So this kind of land leasing is a possibility. And again feminization is really very high and there we need to really work on women, their skills, and their identity. So in many villages where we work, now they have started asking for joint *pattas* and so on because men are not there. Women, how would they get loans if they don't have ownership of the land; so, it is important to look at the structural issue of ownership.

JS: The situation of agriculture-based livelihood is a mixed bag. At some places, people have taken various technological inputs and improved their livelihood, even their income but there are certain factors in general affecting agricultural livelihoods—we can say the four basic factors, one is the climatic factor. If we talk about the climatic factor, because of uncertainty of rain, there have been instances of crop failure which eventually give a sense of hopelessness to farmers and these farmers' distress is directly related to the hopelessness. In addition to climatic factor, there are market related factors. The cost of cultivation has gone up because of various reasons. The input quality is also a suspect; the market prices are not in sync with the cost of cultivation, therefore less income in the hands of the farmers. Then there are policy-related issues like we discussed about agroclimatic zone and no dry land policy, the price spread between the producer and consumer is very high, land leasing is also an issue, all of which need resolution. Then there are social factors which are coming in. With the intrusion of cellphones and the dish television at home, the aspirations of rural area have gone up as high as in urban areas. So therefore, more expenditure on events like marriage, and so on, but the income has not gone up commensurately. Whereas the social transformation of rural areas has been keeping pace with urban areas to some extent, the income of rural people is not rising in the same manner or in the same proportion. I think rural people will be happy staying in villages if there is an opportunity because even ₹3,000 a month is good enough in the villages but it's nothing in urban areas.

Vipin Sharma (VS): Just like we have created industrial areas or industrial zones or can we have agricultural-economic zones? What Vijay and also the Chairman of NABARD mentioned was that micro planning has not been done. In NABARD typically, we will do a potential linked plan but the agroclimatic zones might actually cover 2–3 districts. I feel that we need to look at wage, by which we can reduce the risk of particularly the small and agriculture farmers. You mention climate, you mention high input cost and small and marginal farmers who have less than 2 acres of land but they don't even plough, because they can't take the risk. So we need to see how we can reduce that risk and push them to actually earn more, that's one. The other thing I feel is that we need to concentrate on infrastructure. A comprehensive plan: where there is some storage, some transportation, soil testing, NCDEX, weather bureau, weather station and all the schemes that are available should come into play. Unless we do this at a micro level to strengthen the eco system, these scattered schemes are not going to help small and marginal farmers. We have FPO in Jhalawad, they grow oranges. They get 8 rupees a kg versus Nagpur orange guys getting 16 rupees a kg. If we were to put in infrastructure for sorting, grading, drying, waxing, they would start to get better prices as well. They don't have any capacity to hold, so they will sell at 8 rupees to the trader. We, in access, said we will intervene from our own resources, we put in some money to buy, and we got in a partnership with a fruit company which would take the oranges to Delhi. They were not graded and sorted; some of them were rotten by the time they reached Delhi. We gave the farmers their payment right off, but as an organization we suffered a bit of loss. We need to actually look at what the eco system is, and within that what critical

investments and interventions we need to make. We need to invest in infrastructure and also examine ways in which we can reduce perceived and actual risks that the small and marginal farmers face.

GGS: As far as stimulate in production and looking at vulnerability is concerned, I think what Vijay was saying about farmer earning 100,000 from an acre is definitely possible. The question is how much of it we do with production increase, how much because of nominal price rise. How much profit will come from production increase and how much profit will come from product diversification, are the questions to be tackled. If you add supplementary components into that farming, you can reach much higher level. If you add dairy husbandry, you will find that with 2–3 cows farmers can be taken to very high levels of income—gross and net. With our dairy husbandry program in 80,000 villages, we are having an excellent impact with 3.5 million farmers. Almost 20% of these centers we have taken on to a revenue model, so it is not actually grant based at all. It is all based on service fees. There is still a sort of razor's edge walk all the time, but it is out of the grant mode. What is required is when we talk of scaling up micro models, it is the right combination of funding. We introduced what we call as outbound call center; it is a Samvadini. We have seen it not as a call center in the conventional sense where farmers would call in. It is us calling the farmers and with that type of interaction, we are able to have a stimulate look at their constraints to production and able to take it much higher level with the right advice and the right deliveries, all tuned together. What we are happily surprised about is that not only it is affecting the production system positively it is also creating simultaneously non-farm jobs because we are talking of operating these through rural women. So it is the rural women from farm families who are going to operate these types of call centers which are also stimulating and supporting the agriculture sector productivity. Now with this experience, we are in the process of planning to scale up. This is how we have interpreted digital platforms that Harsh was talking about. I agree with Vijay, I don't see anything dark about the future of agriculture in terms of ability to provide remunerative livelihoods. And the non-farm sector in the villages is where the challenge and immense possibilities coexist. So it may be service provider, it may be these type of ICT-based efforts and so on.

We are sensing that climate change effects are probably bringing about a shift. I think the monsoon or the *Kharif* season is becoming less important than the *Rabi* season in terms of the production and stability in the output of agriculture. But Rabi season is getting different challenges. So you know this shift of importance, one will probably need to study—what is the relative change in contribution in terms of output, in terms of incomes and employment in *Rabi* season even in rain-fed areas because we are still talking of using subsoil moisture that is conserved for later crop. But when we talk of the change of season, there is a great challenge which is becoming reality in many parts of the country and that is wildlife menace. It has nothing to do with agriculture and farming but inflicts a lot of damage

MS: I agree with all the points that have been touched as far as agriculture is concerned. One thing that I am a little particular about is that all of you spoke about women in agriculture; you call it feminization of agriculture. Wherever we go now in rural areas we hardly see men, youth is totally out of it. It is really sad; as all of you have mentioned that men migrate, work for three months in the city; they will come back, will waste eight months sitting in the village but they will not help their mothers in the farms. A lot of issues about skilling, about linkages, about technology, something to do with upgrading, the skills of women, using NSDC to realize the importance of upskilling of women in the various trades that they do to reduce their drudgery need attention. Now a lot of women are involved in agriculture

unless we think about this issue seriously. So somewhere Srinivasan you have to touch upon this issue.

RW: One aspect, which I think has already been referred to, is about the access to finance. It's all on the paper but there are few farmers getting the access to finance in the rural areas. SBI has got a mandate, you got private sector banks, but the reality on the ground is different. This report should present actual happening on the ground that small farmers are not getting the financial support. Jhalawar is one the places I am talking about right now and similar things; you will have problems even in Odisha. The second important thing is infrastructure, especially storage facilities. A lot of private players are coming into this space but the rentals they are asking for, interests they are asking for are pretty steep. The local government needs to work on this infrastructure especially for storage facilities and digital platform.

NS: Let us turn to climate change and its impact on livelihoods. What is the reality and how are we coping with this?

VM: NICRA has put out a lot of district wise data on possible impact and what can be done. For every district in the country, a 40 page document opens. First 20 pages have all the data that you ever want about the district from the point of view of agriculture, land, rainfall, soil types, livestock, and next 20 pages is in the event of various climate contingencies. For example, pre-monsoon did not happen or monsoon set in early, or monsoon set in late, and monsoon set in on time but there is a withdrawal of rain; all these various contingencies. Then it says what are the things to be done, crop-wise which variety to be used, palliative measures to use. The framework is fantastic and through little bit of crowd sourcing, it can be improved.

NN: In PRADAN, we are looking at creating this rain-fed farming system. So across the 12 months what are the various crop and contingency options? Across Rabi, spring, and Kharif, the farmer is planning different things. Today what happens is that farming is not in the top of the mind, farming is a kind of default option. So in that sense, the person is really not applying his mind doing agriculture. So first is that you make agriculture productive and climate smart. Then it becomes glamorous that way, so you will get more people who are interested in farming. Second is to develop systems by which we can side step all these climate aberrations, with some advisory which is again possible. There can be crop-specific measures that can optimize production. What happens now is that farmers get information through SMS—kind of saying whether it will rain in the next three days and in the medium term over next 10–15 days what will happen. When you have a 7–10 days window forecast about what might happens, the person is able to replant, reinvest, or redo something. That is getting more and more accurate over the time. It is not very good today but even 60%–70% is still correct information they are able to provide, provided that the person actually has a 12 months perspective on that farm. Because 2 acres of land that a person has, needs to have a perspective. He should really apply himself to farming sensibly. It is possible to deal with climate change; but in a larger framework, the actual challenge is how to make the small farmers smart.

JS: It actually opens up a new line of thinking as far as farming is concerned. Climate change variables are there to stay and the age old practices of sowing for kharif and seasonality are undergoing changes. Farmers need to be sensitized about the rising temperatures, the unseasonal rains, and flash floods, as also means of coping. Temperature, for example, is going to affect the yield of wheat and paddy crops which are main staple for the Indian population. So if the yield is affected, we need to come up with practices; I mean how to maintain the yield which we currently have. Otherwise, the lower food grain production will open up the problems relating to food security. The animal productivity is likely to be affected—meat production, milk production—because most of the animal energy is going to mitigating the effects of adverse effects of the climate change. Agro forestry, a forestation programs will be adversely affected. Then in a majority of crops, postharvest losses may also increase. Health problems are likely to increase. These are the factors at the ground level already faced by farmers. NABARD has implemented certain climate programs to address climate vulnerability. It is an accredited agency for National Adaption Fund for Climate Change, Adaptation Fund Board of UNFCC, and Green Climate Fund. NABARD has already sanctioned many projects under two of the three facilities. The $10 million fund of UNFCC is fully committed and in the National Fund, ₹236 crore projects have been sanctioned. We are also taking one step in the direction of mainstreaming climate change actions by introducing specific chapter in our Potential Linked Plans. Even the Government of India will have to mainstream the concerns of climate change into their policies. Unless that happens, it's not going to really make an impact. Generally speaking, there is a need for policy intervention from the Government of India.

NS: I have two brief interjections. There are real sector issues apart from financial risk which, in some way, is being looked at. It seems that in hilly states, we have more problems of climate change impacting production, productivity especially fruit crops, plums, peaches, apples, and so on. The fruits are becoming sour, smaller in size, and at times very low production. When fruit crops move to higher altitudes, it means there will be higher costs of cultivation, the logistics how you tie up and how you move produce down. The existing plantations which are affected by temperature rise with a residual life of another say 20 years will cause huge losses to farmers. I don't know what exactly being done on this and who is doing anything.

JS: We also observed, while in Uttarakhand for example, the crops are actually shifting upwards: at around 1,000 meters you get pears, and you go up then you have apricots, plum and at 3,000 meters you get apples but now the pears are being grown at say 1,500 meters and apples are going up and vanishing. Uttarakhand apple crops almost finished, and if you continue to grow at that level where you were growing earlier, then the problem of quality or size of the fruits is coming down. So that's the problem. Most of the hill economy is now being supported by off season vegetables. That is paying them better than the fruit crops, but what about soil erosion?

GGS: But all the states have developed climate change adaptation plans, and some of them are very good. Only thing is how it is being translated into operational policy decisions. That connect may not have happened everywhere and we should make it happen—some of the plans are really very well.

VM: In BASIX, we have a separate organization called C-Tran. So C-Tran has done climate change action plans for seven states—mostly eastern—and also Jammu & Kashmir and Uttarakhand. And it's been more than two years and some places it was released by the Chief Ministers and all that. But these plans are gathering dust for the want of resources to implement. I think as the money start flowing, the states will wake up.

JS: These NEFCC projects which I was referring to earlier, can help with resources. Every state is getting one project at least, but they have a cap of 25 crores because they wanted to cover all these states at least. Because initial allocation was 350 crores, all the 30 states should be covered.

VM: CAMPA afforestation fund of ₹44,000 crore is somewhere in the region. This is an unutilized resource. We had occasion to look at a CAMPA plan for three districts in Odisha and out of ₹800 crore, ₹650 crore was for buildings, roads, bridges, culverts, and those activities are allowed. The money was not directly spent on afforestation, but on activities supposed to support afforestation.

NS: There is a risk of labelling anything that we have been doing normally in NRM or improved agricultural practices as a climate change response. There is a tendency to put environment, green initiative, or some other thing as part of a project and make it look like climate change response. Climate change is a serious enough issue and we have to do things which actually respond to the challenges rather than put a new label on whatever we have been doing earlier.

JS: Every climate change program which is coming to us for processing has to have some link with the vulnerability of the area it is likely to address. Unless it addresses vulnerability, it's a business as usual program; so it has to be based on vulnerability identified in every state. Every state has also identified a nodal department. That nodal department is responsible for preparing, projecting climate vulnerability into projects.

GGS: I think the point is important. Vulnerability have to be addressed and vulnerability in different forms in different locations. In hills, the need is for new investments in higher altitude. In east coast, the vulnerability is more from the disaster management point of view. The different vulnerabilities will require different approaches. But apart from vulnerability response, there is also something more basic that can contribute to mitigation and to food security. And I think it was France that tabled the excellent program idea; their concept was we have to work towards increasing the soil carbon—in steps beyond 0.4% level in soils. So basically soil carbon deterioration is a fact of life all over the world. Soil carbon sequestration in soil probably contributes much higher levels of carbon sequestration than would happen by above ground by afforestation and all that. So, even though afforestation is important, soil carbon sequestration is going to absorb even higher quantities of carbon and at the same time restoring soil health and improving food security. The mechanism of soil carbon enhancement is biotic in nature. We have to find ways of increasing microbial population in soil—so promoting basically restoration of soil. Most of the programs, including soil conservation in watersheds, are generally at the mechanical level, creating soil erosion prevention structures and water percolation structures. Watershed projects do not focus on biological measures. That is an important shift we have to make. This needs to be done in almost 60 million hectares, but then there has to be a shift in the strategy. Beyond just mechanical measures, there have to be vegetative measures and other biological measures. It can be integrated in our watershed projects. It will take care of mitigation as well as food security which is the golden combination.

VM: It is a wonderful opportunity as you say. The microbiological work is not technologically challenging for our farming community. It is doable. The basic disciplines are not very complex.

NS: We will move in a different direction. We can look at some of the government program and schemes focused of poor vulnerable livelihoods. We have this NREGS celebrating 10 years, we have got the NRLM, then there is a Skill India program now brought in. The food security act is doing a much more basic, but important job of reducing vulnerability, ensuring affordable food. What's your take? How do they perform? How effective they are? To what extent we should be supporting these kinds of programs as we go into the future?

MS: NAREGA and NRLM, they have provided livelihood opportunities at the grassroots to some extent. What is actually very important is the financial inclusion space of opening bank accounts and direct benefit transfers because livelihood is closely linked with access to credit and so I feel that these things have worked. Opening bank accounts has been quite revolution in the

villages where women did not have access to credit. However, I just feel that while financial inclusion has been given priority, what is lacking is the training in financial literacy. Some bit of training on skilling on how to build on the capacities of people in the rural areas and the establishing market tie ups. The government schemes are there; there has been a thrust on vulnerable. We have to ensure that they are well targeted.

RW: I will touch upon this skill aspect as Skilling India program was launched with a number of ministries. Unfortunately, there was not even one nodal ministry earlier. Now I think the models that are being worked out need to be revisited. One problem was, as I mentioned earlier also, the number game of high targets. The retention of the students for that period of time in training whether it is six weeks or three months is a challenge. With too much of funds crowding in to skilling, too many players are coming to this space. This prospect of getting easy funds for the project drives many players. That I think disturbs the balance and the thought process of Skilling India. So I feel that from the corporate perspective, the corporate have to engage in skilling in a very major way whether it's going to be in partnership and collaboration with the government or otherwise, but we have to really get into this business of skilling India and taking on onus with responsibility to the youth.

Girija Srinivasan (GS): I have a couple of questions for you. How do you see the performance of NSDC, particularly in funding but more importantly in developing the qualification framework and in ensuring that the skill sets which are developed or as per the job description. How far is it really getting translated into good skill sets among the youth?

RW: Biggest challenge of the National qualification framework the NSQF was that they were made independently and they were not taken into sync with the requirements of the industry. That gap was felt when these people were churned out and they were not being absorbed. Or they were absorbed in menial kind of work. Now one of the guidelines had also mentioned that there should be having minimum of X amount of salary. X amount of salary is not possible for people who have not got adequate qualifications. That kind of salary they were being offered, even if they were employed from remote area to come to an urban environment, they couldn't cope up with that salary and were quitting the jobs within three months. The training partners were getting the money but the trained youth people are still unemployed and many unskilled too, but on papers they were shown to be employed with good salaries. The salary slips are mandatory requirement, these were shown for three months and then people went back. I found this in J&K Himayat Program and Udaan Program. A lot of players have just plug and play skilling courses and not flexible to respond to real work needs and that is unfortunate.

We have a problem with certification. The attraction in certificates is of the government logo which attracts people. If we are going to give them skills training, I think our certification as a corporate is much higher in value than the government certification. That certification piece of the course is important, but at the same time do not over do it. And for the government jobs, may be the government certificate is required. If there is a corporate who is in a particular industry space, their certificate should have much more weight. NSDC has outsourced a number of agencies to certify and that was an absolute muddle. Nothing useful has happened, there is no accountability and a lot money been wasted.

GS: NSDC works with one set of institutions. Ministry of Rural Development has a large program for skilling. Do you find common norms getting implemented now? Is policy framework basically of upgrading whatever systems were in place being implemented? Now there is a cabinet decision on how much funding would happen and then norms for placement. How far do

you really find the common norms getting implemented?

RW: I think the thrust is now with the ministry of skills coming up, and they are working towards this kind of the norms. And that could make a change hopefully. It's not been seen yet, but hopefully they have taken on that responsibility; it should make an impact.

VM: We should distinguish NSDC from NSDA. NSDC is actually an implementing agency. It also attracts a lot of attention but the policy framework is to be made by National Skill Development Authority, and Mr. Ramadurai is Chairman of both. NSDA ambit goes well-beyond NSDC. Suppose to cut across other ministries. National Skill Development Authority was created basically for policy making and financing mechanism. NSDC's proper name should have been National Skill Development and Finance Corporation and that's why it's under the ministry of Finance and not under the labor or other ministry. The sector skills council, 60 of them now were created as industry associations to lay out the quality framework and to engage in certification of skill providers. In theory, it looks very good. But the way it got practiced in NSDC leaves a lot to be desired.

MS: We, Hand in Hand, are now partnering with NSDC to skill about 500,000 women across six states. We are building skills in green chili and coriander cultivation. We have five sectors and in the agriculture sectors, all the courses have to be certified by NSDC, and it is a very cumbersome process. Ours is only skilling women. We have actually fought a long battle with NSDC saying that once we skill, we'll also give them loans if we have to lead to employment generation. We will give them livelihood component loan and that will be like a microfinance operation because we have to sustain. But we are actually facing a challenge because they are very particular about all the courses getting passed by their sector skills council, and they are returning back to us that "in your green chilly plantation, you have not given the adequate combination of theoretical and practical inputs." We are, in a way, happy that there is some amount of standardization in the curriculum, real time monitoring, and data collection. In the last one year, they have really tried to standardize; they are training us as partners that this is how you should monitor, this is how you should use your digitization. They have built our capacities also. We got a loan on a three year moratorium, and we also got a grant of 20%, and then we are getting money to do micro finance. With the startup kit for trained women, we are going to provide loans of ₹25,000 with a two years repayment term. Our targets are women above 45 who will not be taken up by any industry. If we have to create employment of 350,000 women, it can't be by just skill building, which is why we wanted to bundle a livelihood loan.

NS: I just wanted to take this slightly further somehow. Any talk about skill development is always about the urban skills, the normal trades; what is popular in the entire NSDA/NSDC framework are computer skills, beautician, nursing, security guards, and retailing—they take about more than 60%. But where are the agricultural, rural skills in this?

NN: This skills piece in MORD is not done well. All kinds of training institutions got into it and they have back offices where they create identity, certificates, and all kinds of things happen but the skill delivery in front office is very weak. NREGS is a good program. If NREGS is to be converted into livelihood generating opportunity, then much more resources need to be allocated, not just ₹34,000 crores and so on, which is the highest this year since last 10 years. But it is lower compared to what was last year in real terms. Investment in the rural areas in terms of building rural infrastructure in watershed development and in terms of any other facilitating factors requires to go up. NRLM currently has no livelihood perspective; it remains a SHG promotion program despite the livelihood tag. Microfinance and

credit facilitated by NRLM takes a person to a certain level but doesn't actually kick start the person's household economy; it needs investments and that investment have to come from public sources. So why do we expect market to come and invest in rural areas, they will not unless it is profitable. We have NAREGA which never talks to NRLM, NRLM never talks to other ministry, and within the ministries they don't converge. If you had a framework then things could converge. Resource is not a problem; huge amount of money is available in the system. The need is to bring it together, converge it. We have done it in micro planning in villages, it works. But unless there is a political will to design a common framework, it will be difficult to bring this convergence. There is much more convergence happening in Kerala compared to other places because decentralization is so strong.

GGS: There is need for focus on skills which are relevant in rural areas, whether it is in agriculture or in non-farm sectors. It is about the green skills, it is about ICT applied for agriculture. I think that focus is very necessary to be brought in because today it is not there. Basically, whatever skilling is done is non-farm is urban oriented. Whether this is apathy out of ignorance or apathy out of design I am not sure. Because if you combine this present status of skilling with what happening in NREGS, there are huge allocations, hardly any meaningful utilization—except for few states where there is a slightly better effort. The situation is dismal. So, that brings this question to the mind whether there is a design involved. But let us remember the fact that this situation in NREGS skills training—and other skilling in NRLM is all oriented toward urban skills. It would be worthwhile to put forth the tremendous possibilities that exist in the rural sector for the green skills not just green skills ICT applied to the rural agricultural development. We have to bring to center stage the rural agri-oriented skilling and create those types of opportunities; then I think there will be a correction to what is wrong with the present situation. About 30–35% of the population ultimately will have to be absorbed in good quality agriculture, even though their aspirations may not be there. Any policy on skilling and agriculture should have this kind of focus.

JS: The idea actually is to create work force for industry and services sector if we are focused on increasing GDP numbers. If we are serious about rapid growth then the only option is to focus on services and industry because agriculture growth is anyways very low due to whatever issues. Put a lot of inputs, it will increase may be up to 4%. Therefore, all the skilling is geared towards creating labor force for industry and services sectors. Meanwhile, some agricultural training programs will also be provided. But the major focus remains on industries and services.

VS: This is a design fault. Agriculture should become glamorous. Look at 15 years of what happened to grapes in Nashik. I think there is a story to be told how much capital formation takes place locally, how much value addition takes place locally, and within the value chain how your strategies will help accrual of greater benefit to farmers. Then I think agriculture can become glamorous. So you see what is the next thing which can be done by the local farmers or their households or in the village. I think that's the missing trick in skills and where the green skilling becomes relevant.

NN: And even for the investor, Arindam just told me in the beginning of the session that one of the largest loans of 10 crore is given to the producer company of chicken. But the energy it took to take chicken production from whatever it was in 1985 to the current level required huge amounts of investments, lot of NABARD's money, lot of grant money from the government and so on has gone into it. Now any bank can come in and make huge loans. The production is growing, people are setting up more farms, expanding farms, and more and more new farmers are getting added, they are buying

land all through commercial funds. But without the initial foundation all this would not have been possible.

JS: The expenditure pattern in rural areas is actually undergoing a change, and the expenditure pattern now requires regular flow of income say on a monthly basis or weekly basis so as to meet the bills for mobile recharges or cable TV. Agriculture gives income after certain period of time, therefore wage employment will always have the choice of the youth and wage employment is provided by industries and service sector other than agriculture. So therefore, their skilling has to take care of aspirations of the youth which is towards wage employment, towards regular income flow. Agriculture, as such, is uncertain in nature. You never know how much you are going to earn. In remote areas the production has to be consumed in the local areas only, otherwise transportation cost will make prohibitive unless you go the collectivization or FPO route which will make sense for a small farmer.

GGS: It is a very important insightful point that changes in consumption patterns, is matched by income flow in farm sector. We might find youth not favoring agricultural skills. It points to the need for a move towards agricultural development which makes regular income possible. In the dairy sector, it is almost a daily income. If you take vegetables, it may not be daily but it is almost weekly. They're are possible, but I think that it is an important design element to be brought in. But what I feel is in making agriculture glamorous, there are things other than income involved. And one of that is drudgery and there has to be drudgery reduction in agriculture. What it points to is efforts on simple mechanization: farm mechanization in India. It is probably not directed towards addressing this requirement, considering that we have small farms. India, it so happens, is sitting on the borderline geographically of two different types of farm mechanization: the western types of farm mechanization, larger scale operations, and so on. But the East of India, the entire south-East Asia farm mechanization has gone about in machinery which is suitable for small farms. There is a very interesting study by IFPRI on this farm mechanization. What probably is required in India to bring in that eastern farm mechanization, more which will make it worthwhile from the labor point of view, for the small farmers to engage? So, making money is one aspect of the glamorization, reducing drudgery is second aspect, and there is also a third aspect—the sophistication of agriculture by introducing gadgets. Gadgets play a role, and they can add to productivity; they can add to better economics. Take a small dairy farm. The efficient functioning of the dairy farm depends on lot of things relating to whether animal has been fed in time, whether it is having proper growth, it comes into heat at the right age, whether its daily productivity is tracked. The farmer will know whether its potential is higher and because of poorer management it is not yielding enough. All that is required is to have an animal-wise record that is kept in a tab, it can be a small app or a small program which can analyze for the farmer and give him guidance. The data entry is something farmer can do today, young farmer can very much do. We have to bring in that type of system for small farms. The app-based farming will glamorize agriculture and add to earnings. So, I think glamorization is very necessary if the younger generation has to be more interested in green skills and rural activities.

MS: Also, research and documentation should be given importance. There are value chains across the country, which have worked at micro level like grapes in Nashik. We know that there is a lot of work happening in this value chain space of dairy or mushrooms or soybeans but we don't know of models. We have to replicate, but we don't know where to go first. There is a lack of documentation in agriculture space.

NS: I think, to wind up this particular part on skills, even some of the normal requirements like you want good quality seeds, you want to know how to do systemic cultivation of any particular crop, or how you maintain your drip system. One can go for some external service provider or a program design where an NGO does it over the period of three years but not really institutionalizing the knowledge they bring in. Whatever people pick up casually will improve their farming system with that variant. Actually can we convert this tendency to provide it through a program, into something more generic across a large number of people in specific skills addressed at a significant percentage of youth locally? To whatever extent we can glamorize, make it look much better. We should try to look at issues of how there can be a steady income throughout the period, through green skill development. Now I will shift to another question. What is the nature of private sector contribution to livelihood security in whatever they do? Not that many of them are actually involved in the rural areas, and vulnerable peoples livelihoods, but to the extent they are involved, are they making livelihoods secure?

RW: I don't think private sector is doing enough in this space. There's so much that we can do, there is so much that we have to do. Extractive industries and manufacturing sector should bring in more resources. Now there is a lot of sensitization in the corporate sector. From the CSR perspective, we are now going forward in reaching out to rural people. The FIICI have come out with agri-committees and skill development committees, focusing on skills and livelihoods. But there has to be a lot more on this kind of industry platform.

VS: I think we need to look at private sector in two slices: one is of course what you do is CSR and other is out of emanating more out of corporate strategy for the BOP. The sense I get is that the corporates are focused mostly on urban areas and less on rural areas except for extractive industries. Other is within urban areas, the greater focus for whatever reason is on skilling following the model of how the government wants to do it. I think you have that kind of flexibility to actually look at generating true and tangible outcome out of your investments as a corporate. The other is that since so many corporates now have a statutory obligation to contribute through their CSR for identified sectors and areas, is there any kind of way or through CII/FICCI where 10 large corporates get together to say "ok let's have a big vision to impact on this one sector"? Is there a large vision in a specific sector that can be implemented with a lot of focus by joint effects of committed corporates?

JS: We in NABARD are also now partnering with many CSR foundations. So far we have partnered with about 20 foundations, entered into MoU with them, trying to leverage funds for integrated developments of watershed and tribal areas. So, like two models we are following either share the expenses on whatever agreed term—60:40 or 50:50 or 30:70—or we fund the infrastructure part and you fund the social part. Both the models are working in the field, we have leveraged close to ₹200 crore and we are working in 8 states. Last year we have introduced a vertical within farm sector department by the name of Nabsamarthya. It will actually be a NABARD Foundation in a year's time. At the moment, Nabsamarthya is involved in setting up 25 rural enterprise promotion centers in a tie-up with Skill India Mission or something of that nature. Nabsamarthya will take up other activities also, like value chain promotion and whole lot of activities. May be this could become a model of collective CSR projects. We can leverage more CSR funds in future once we get registered.

NN: Actually the private sector is not present in the areas where we work—deep tribal areas. The only private sector you see there are the money lenders, the traders, and local private sectors. In terms of doing business in the village, we don't see corporates unless it is the seed sellers, small machineries, fertilizer companies and so on. Even these

go normally to places where the farming is little more prosperous. So where we have now managed to make investments in terms of public funds, we have trained up lot of farmers, so there is a thriving agriculture happening. Lots of private sector people have come and set up shops and they give credit for their seeds, fertilizers; so a lot of cooperation is happening in that sense. The transport *walas*, the market players are coming into the villages to buy the fruits and vegetables. So the private sector will follow but not lead investment. They won't normally immediately come; they don't risk their money in starting totally something new in the villages. As for CSR, some are interested in villages—especially sensitive corporates.

VM: Well, quoting Friedman, "the business of business is business." Why do you even expect them to invest in small livelihoods? CSR regulations have just come in; corporates are just beginning to get their act together. A lot of good things are beginning to happen; a lot of not so good things are also happening. Let us, first, in the next five years improve CSR implementation and maximize collaborations between CSR foundations and entities like NABARD on the one hand and actually grassroots implementing agencies like BAIF or BASIX or PRADAN. Once that happens, some positive experience of working together builds we need to enhance that. No preaching either side—let us get on with our roles.

RW: One interesting thing is happening now is the linking of business with human rights. How western corporates base their public outreach initiatives on human rights? Corporates are trying to respond to challenges and answer positively on issues relating to human rights.

VM: In a recent Time Magazine, a month ago, there was an article on breakdown of capitalism. In that article, one of the things they talk about is when 2008 crisis happened in the US, the treasury consulted like 500 people to design what to do. Out of that came out several strategies. In a review, it has been found that 90% of the people that they talked to came from the financial sector or were academics studying the financial sector. When a senior treasury official was asked, "Should they have consulted others? He countered, "Who else? Who else would know about finance? One of the problems about CSR today, having sat on the CIA committee for two years, is that corporations still suffer from the belief that because we know business, we also know development.

MS: With Vodafone Foundation, Hand in Hand entered into a CSR project. So we have the largest base of women at Tamil Nadu who are very literate and tech savvy. They are using a mobile app to get 10,000 women over the next three years to use a digital app and 3,000 to have a portal like Myntra or Flipkart in three years. It is doing well over the initial 7–8 months, and Vodafone does very strong monitoring. So we see a lot of benefits. We benefited a lot because our women farmer producer companies set up portals for marketing of products and began to use mobile apps for getting information in and out. Vodafone has done a very interesting project with SEVA also along similar lines. So these are very good CSR initiatives, where there is a lot of benefit in rural sector, women empowerment, digitization, and market access also.

NS: I will now come to the last question. In the next five years, if you look at say something like 2020–21, what do you think are priorities that we have got to take care of inclusively? What are your three priorities which make livelihoods much more sustainable, enjoyable?

RW: Skills is number one. The second piece is the work on markets—how to link the markets which has a number of areas. The third is to join these multiple threads in different places together.

MS: For me the biggest priority would be access to affordable finance; by easy I

mean at their doorstep. Second would be to mainstream women's rights and issues. And by mainstreaming, I mean it would require skilling women, getting women to the markets, in digitization, and skills in the technology space. Third would be to have an overarching policy guideline to protect the interest of the ultra poor to see that their livelihood continues to be lucrative and glamorous.

GGS: My number one priority is facilitated structural transformation for rural people. Taking people out of agriculture and getting them into remunerative rural–non-agriculture livelihoods. The second thing is that of technological change in farming geared towards productivity and incomes. The third thing is skills provision.

JS: I would say promotion of agri-enterprises should be one of the priorities which would include relevant skill set promotion and a conducive policy environment for agri-enterprises. The second priority is availability of finance coupled with financial literacy. The third is amalgamation of vulnerability into planning process of the country, if possible right at the micro level. That paradigm shift in the planning process which includes various climate related vulnerability and social exclusion vulnerability into focus.

NN: First is to focus on rain-fed small farming systems with women focus. The second is focusing on self-employment for the rural areas. If they want to come out of agriculture into something more productive or more lucrative, it is not possible for them because their current skills sets and knowledge itself is so limited. So focusing on human capital in the rural areas in terms of health, education and skill building; I think the whole package of things and along with that goes decentralization, much more power to the panchayat, much more power to the local body and peoples' organizations to think and act what they want to do with their resources. The third is a larger policy framework which allows convergence—policy convergence and resource convergence. We should facilitate converging resources from multiple departments all over the place and each with small, sub-optimal and ineffective plans. Putting it all together and having a policy framework of doing benefits for the rural areas and the small farmers is the third priority.

VM: Livelihoods, Livelihoods and Livelihoods. How do you translate that? First is because the largest numbers of people are still in agriculture. I agree with Naren that we need to maximize livelihood potential and most of it will now come from the rainfed areas. Second, self employment which is a combination of three things—skills, access to finance, and access to markets. Pure self employment is like asking somebody to jump into the sea. A better alternative is wage employment, but there are not enough jobs. In between these two, there is something called micro franchisee. Every large company needs to distribute its products and the old style of doing it was through their own channel—the employee—and that's too costly. Increasingly both products and services need to be distributed through network of micro franchisees, who are all self-employed, who are all entrepreneurs, and who all earn in proportion to what their producers sell. They have the advantage of brand name, customer footfall, quality control, and assured supply chain and all that. The third one is small towns. I can tell you that there will be no "Make in India", if Make in India is going to be in the metros. Our metros are too expensive; land costs are comparable to New York City. Even our IT-cost advantage is now really falling off; when we started we used to be 1/5th of the international cost. Now down to 1/3rd. So today Bongaigaon can do to Bangalore what Bangalore did earlier to Boston. So we need to decentralize those services particularly which can be offered using telecom. And my favorite destination for this is North-East because of high quality education, high English knowledge, and remoteness. You should just wire up entire North-East with gigabytes of bandwidth and they would just be sitting in their beautiful little houses and doing high-tech programming for Silicon Valley.

NS: It has been absolutely useful to me and Girija. The wealth of information, number of pointers on what probably we could look at for further areas of investigation. I am sure that the readers of the report will benefit from your sharing. Our heart-felt thanks for your taking time off and contributing magnanimously!

Conclusion: Continuing Concerns and a Wish List

The livelihood scenario is beginning to show promise at least for the near future. A favorable monsoon, announcement of a number of new programs aimed at the small and the vulnerable people, key reforms in the economic and real sector, and an improved customer and business sentiment in general leads us to believe that there could be an accelerated growth with positive effects on the entire economy. However, as pointed out at the beginning of the report, the situation in agriculture-based livelihoods needs to be watched carefully. Water is a key resource that deserves attention, not just in policy but also at the farm level. The distress in rainfed and dryland areas has been aggravated by extreme climate events tending to substantiate the claims relating to the adverse effects of climate change. In a large agrarian economy (in terms of number of people engaged), like India, climate change can impact vulnerable livelihoods to a disproportionately large extent compared to others. Water is the emerging key issue in not just agriculture but in other aspects of life too. The continuing problems between states over sharing of water are a pointer to the threat faced by livelihoods in these states (the Cauvery water dispute between Tamil Nadu and Karnataka has taken an ugly turn with violations of legal, ethical, and human rights obligations). Water should be recognized as a valuable natural resource that ought to be safely exploited, conservatively used, and equitably shared among different uses and users. The traditional attitude of water being a freely available resource should be replaced by the reality that it is a valuable resource carrying a significant real cost counted in terms of loss of livelihoods. The ongoing government attempts in improving irrigation facilities, upgrading quality of irrigation, and improving productivity of water will improve water availability for agriculture as per the need. At the same time, the move toward regulating the use of water and creating of a national legal framework is a timely and laudable step. But equitable sharing of water alone does not provide complete solutions to parched lands in several parts of the country. Agricultural research for long has concentrated on irrigated farming assuming that all inputs are available endlessly and the role of research is to find the best combination of "abundant inputs" to produce best productivity levels. However, the reality of India is that vast parts of the country (68% of net sown area) are rain dependent and lack irrigation. Research should focus on finding mainstream solutions for cultivation under the conditions of water scarcity. Millions of livelihoods in dryland regions can be stabilized only through agronomic practices and risk-adjusted crop planning where research plays a key role. Both funding and institutional mandates have to be turned toward looking at farming as a livelihood issue and not as a scientific challenge in raising productivity without examining the natural resource cost of the same.

Profitability of agriculture, despite the MSP interventions, is marginal in many crops and negative in some. Markets and prices for agriculture are caught in policy and regulatory quagmire, from which the government is trying to extricate the farmers. The slant in policy thinking toward consumers' interest places the burden of affordable food and industrial raw material on farming community. When produce prices tend to increase, trade policy and essential commodities regulations are used to effectively block higher price realizations by the farmer. When market prices of produce fall, MSP does not protect the farmers. Risk mitigation arrangements provide nominal relief and have limited outreach. But for the fact that rural incomes rely less on agriculture, the suffering of farm households would have been greater. The smaller farms, however, depend more on agricultural incomes than larger farmers and are affected by continuing low profitability of agriculture.

A third major area of concern is in relation to employment. The demographic dividend that India can reap with its large predominantly young labor force can also become a potential problem, if employment opportunities are not available. There is a huge mismatch between incremental employment created and the accretion to the labor force with each passing year. The assumption that employment is merely a function of skills upgradation has to be challenged. Even assuming that all the addition to the labor market can be provided with skill training, there are not many jobs in sight. The millions that pass out of schools and colleges do not desire to engage in skill-based livelihoods, whether wage employment or self-employment. Attitudinal change is needed in the society on the nature of skill-based livelihoods. A school-level national campaign should be launched to convince

adolescents that skill-based livelihoods can be as dignified and fulfilling as white-collar jobs. The manufacturing and services activities do not have the potential to create such a large number of jobs. Already there have been discussions on the need to take labor out of agriculture in order to ensure viability of farming. In addition to the already high rates of migration from agriculture to non-agriculture and from rural to urban areas, the imminent exodus of people from agriculture places a heavy load on the secondary and tertiary sectors for employment. Skill development for millions might create an army of skilled people with nowhere to go. Viable solutions to meet the demand for jobs have to be found.

It is in this context that one has to look more carefully into the operation of welfare schemes and social safety nets. There is an increasing emphasis on reducing subsidy expenditure in government and improving targeted delivery of the same through digitization and authentication of recipients of government benefits. While digitization and biometric authentication of beneficiaries of government program are a highly welcome step, this needs to be inclusive and it should be ensured that all those with legitimate needs and rights are included. The way the current programs such as FSA operate seem to indicate that a number of eligible people stand excluded both voluntarily and involuntarily as they failed to come up with the required documents for digitization. While the outgo from the government's resources becomes less on account of such exclusion, this is also produced as evidence of improved targeting and reduction of leakages. Legitimate savings through plugging of leakages is an objective that cannot be disputed. But savings achieved through excluding families that deserve the safety net on technical grounds cause distress and cannot be claimed as a success. The framework for operating the government's social and welfare safety nets should become truly inclusive.

In the livelihoods landscape, there are continuing conflicts between different interest groups and segments. While the commitment to safeguard livelihoods and ensure betterment of the vulnerable are well articulated, the practice in the field does not carry the sensitivity required to protect the vulnerable and uphold their rights. The ongoing problems of recovery of dues on credit sales from larger entities by the smaller and microenterprises are a case in point. The relationship between agricultural producer and the traders has always remained unfair and heavily weighted in favor of the traders. The dealings between landlords and the agricultural tenants have worked to the detriment of tenants who have an uncertain existence even as they put in their best labor to produce results. Even in the organized sector, employers tend to employ labor through informal mechanisms and contracts that deny the rights to the laborers that would have been available had they been taken on formal employment. Religious pressures intruded into the livelihoods of flayers and leather workers forcing some of them to move out of the vocation that was traditionally practiced by them for generations. Gender disparity continues to exist in all spheres of economy, in terms of jobs, wage rates, and attitude toward dealing with women at work. If the country has to protect livelihoods of the vulnerable and ensure equitable incomes to these sections of society, these conflicts and unfair relationships need to be resolved not merely through law but through reflection by the concerned segments. The exploitative relationships must be brought to an end. This cannot be brought about just by law and its enforcement, but needs a social campaign to make people at different walks of life sensitive to the impact they create on other's livelihoods. Another "Swachh Bharat Abhiyan" to clean up exploitative relationships is badly needed.

Financial sector has shown signs of becoming more friendlier to the poorer sections of people. Institutional and product innovations have ensured that there would be greater attention to the requirements of vulnerable people. However, specific forms of organizations brought in to protect farmers' interest and offer them a superior quality of service have not been successful. In particular, the producer collectives and farmer producer organization have not found adequate support from the banking system and even other policy establishments. This needs to change as farmers collectives have the potential to buttress agricultural livelihoods through aggregation of inputs, outputs, and services through lower delivery costs and sharing of profits with members.

A number of new schemes have been launched targeting the small, tiny, and vulnerable. Most of these have a skill development or financing element. The proposed outreach of these schemes is quite high. More thoughtful implementation of these schemes is needed to secure the desired impacts. Today the emphasis is on outreach and reporting completion of targets of outreach. But the impact-related measurements, monitoring, and reporting are deprioritized. Unless the new initiatives focus on impacts and adjust design and strategies toward securing the desired results, viable livelihood opportunities will continue to be elusive for vulnerable sections of people. The skills courses can invest in higher skill levels and combine enterprise skills to direct trained people toward self-employment or microenterprises. The smart cities campaign can focus on smaller towns to create a demand for services that can absorb more people nearer to their villages and generate better livelihoods with a higher quality of life than possible in larger cities. The reporting on skills schemes can focus only on employment and enterprises created and the cost of creating them rather than on number of people trained.

The rush of new policies and schemes dares us to dream. The livelihood wish list for the year ahead comprises (a) incremental changes to policies (both markets and pricing) focusing on farm incomes, (b) reorienting research to find cropping solutions for water-deficient areas, (c) relook at impact of skill programs and increase livelihood opportunities, (d) launch of campaigns to reduce unfairness and exploitation in relationships between buyers and sellers at different levels, and (e) strengthening safety nets to become fully inclusive. The litmus test of equitable growth would be whether those at the bottom of the pyramid grow equitably at least at the same growth rates as those at the top of the pyramid.

References

A. Venkateswaran. "A Socio Economic Conditions of Handloom Weaving In Kallidaikurichi of Tirunelveli District." *International Journal of Social Science and Humanities Research* 2, no. 2 (April 2014–June 2014): 38–49.

Aashish, Kumar. *Impact Assessment of Marketing Assistance Schemes of MSMEs: With Special Reference to Vaishali, Bihar.* Gandhinagar: Entrepreneurship Development Institute of India.

All India Co-ordinated Research Project on Agrometeorology. *Annual Report 2014–15.* Available at: http://www.nicra-icar.in/nicrarevised/images/publications/NICRA_APR_2014-15.pdf (accessed on October 21, 2016)

Ansari, Shah Nawaz. "Socio-economic Aspect of Artisans in India in 20th Century." *International Journal of Humanities and Religion* 3, no. 1, (February 2014): 020–024.

Appadurai, Arivudai Nambi, Moushumi Chaudhury, Ayesha Dinshaw, Namrata Ginoya, Heather Mcgray, Lubaina Rangwala, and Shreyas Srivatsa. *Scaling Success: Lessons From Adaptation Pilots in the Rain-fed Regions of India.* Washington, D.C.: World Resources Institute, 2015.

Ashok, M. V., Gyanendra Mani, and D. K. Panwar. *Financing Value Chains: Challenges and Opportunities—Monograph.* Mumbai: NABARD, 2015.

BAIF. *Annual Report 2013–14, 2014–15.* BAIF, Pune.

Bhagavatuls, Suresh. *The Working of Entrepreneurs in a Competitive Low Technology Industry: The Case of Master Weavers in the Handloom Industry.* Bengaluru: IIM Bangalore, 2010.

BIRD. *Study Report on Impact of Interest Subvention Scheme (ISS) for Crop Loans on Cooperative Banks.* Lucknow: Bankers Institute of Rural Development, 2015.

Centre for Budget and Governance Accountability. *Connecting the Dots—An Analysis of the Union Budget 2016–17.* Centre for Budget and Governance Accountability, March 2016.

Centre for Budget and Governance Accountability. *Of Bold Strokes and Fineprints—An Analysis of the Union Budget 2015–16.* Centre for Budget and Governance Accountability, March 2015.

Chandrasekhar, S., and Nirupam Mehrotra. "Doubling of Farmer's Income by 2022—What Would It Take?" *Economic and Political Weekly*, 51, no. 18 (April 30, 2016).

Chatterjee, Ashoke. "India's Handloom Challenge Anatomy of a Crisis." *Economic and Political Weekly* l, no. 32 (August 8, 2015).

Chopra, Deepta. *"They Don't Want to Work" Versus "They Don't Want to Provide Work": Seeking Explanations for the Decline of MGNREGA in Rajasthan.* Manchester: Effective States and Inclusive Development Research Centre (ESID), 2014.

Climate Change and Agriculture: Moving towards Resilience for Small Holder Producers. Policy Brief No. 3. Pune: WOTR, 2015. (Project on Promotion of Climate Change Adaptation in Semi-arid and Rain-fed regions of Maharashtra, Madhya Pradesh and Andhra Pradesh.)

Datta, Pooja, Rinku Murgai, Martin Ravallion, and Dominique van de Walle. *Right to Work? Assessing India's Employment Guarantee Scheme in Bihar.* Washington, D.C.: The World Bank, 2014.

Desai, Sonalde, Prem Vashishtha, and Omkar Joshi. *Mahatma Gandhi National Rural Employment Guarantee Act A Catalyst for Rural Transformation.* New Delhi: National Council for Applied Economic Research, 2015.

Dhanya, V. "Implications of MGNREGS on Labour Market, Wages and Consumption Expenditure in Kerala." *RBI Working Paper Series.* Mumbai: Department of Economic and Policy Research, Reserve Bank of India, 2016.

Economics of Climate Adaptation Working Group. *Shaping Climate Resilient Development: A Framework for Decision-making.* USA: Mckinsey, 2009.

FAO. *Andhra Pradesh Farmer Managed Groundwater Systems Project:* GCP/IND/175/NET—*Terminal Report.* Rome: Food and Agriculture Organization of the United Nations, 2010.

Food and Agricultural Organization. *Climate-smart Agriculture: Policies, Practices and Financing for Food Security, Adaptation and Mitigation.* Rome: Food and Agricultural Organization, 2010.

GGRC. *Micro Irrigation in Gujarat: A Case Study of State Effectiveness.* Vadodara: Gujarat Green Revolution Company Limited, 2015.

Global Insights. "Employment Guarantee as Social Protection: Lessons from Tamil Nadu, India." *Global Insights Policy Brief No.* 6. Brighton: Institute of Development Studies, University of Sussex. July, 2013.

Government of India. "Evaluation Report on Efficacy of MSP on Farmers." *PEO Report No.* 231. New Delhi: NITI Aayog, January 2016.

Government of India. "Raising Agricultural Productivity and Making Farming Remunerative for Farmers." *Occasional Paper.* New Delhi: NITI Aayog, December, 2015.

Government of India. *Agricultural Statistics at a Glance 2014*. Ministry of Agriculture. New Delhi: Oxford University Press.

Government of India. *All India Report of Sixth Economic Census 2014*. New Delhi: Ministry of Statistics and Programme Implementation, March, 2016.

Government of India. *Bharat Microfinance Report 2016*. New Delhi: Sa-Dhan.

Government of India. *Climate Change and India: A 4X4 Assessment—A Sectoral and Regional Analysis for 2030s*. New Delhi: Ministry of Environment and Forests, 2010.

Government of India. *Draft Consultation Paper on Handlooms*. New Delhi: Planning Commission Government of India, October, 2014.

Government of India. *Education, Skill Development and Labour Force 2013–14*. Vol. 3. Chandigarh: Labour Bureau, Government Of India Ministry Of Labour Employment, 2014.

Government of India. *Evaluation Study of Targeted Public Distribution System in Selected States*. Sponsored by Ministry of Food and Consumer Affairs, National Council of Applied Economic Research, New Delhi, September, 2015.

Government of India. *India's Initial National Communication to the United Nations Framework Convention on Climate Change*. New Delhi: Ministry of Environment and Forests, 2004.

Government of India. *India's Intended Nationally Determined Contribution: Working Towards Climate Justice*, 2015. Available at: http://www4. unfccc.int/submissions/INDC/Published%20 Documents/India/1/INDIA%20INDC%20 TO%20UNFCCC.pdf (accessed on October 21, 2016).

Government of India. *India—Second National Communication to the United Nations Framework Convention on Climate Change*. New Delhi: Ministry of Environment and Forests, Government of India, 2012.

Government of India. Minutes of the Empowered Committee Held on 22nd June, 2015. Ministry of Rural Development, GOI, 2015. Available at: http://ddugky.gov.in/ddugky/ (accessed on 1 August 2016).

Government of India. Minutes of the Meeting to Review Implementation of Projects under Roshini Project under DDU-GKY, July 21, 2015. Available at: http://ddugky.gov.in/ (accessed on 1 August 2016).

Government of India. *National Policy for Skill Development and Entrepreneurship 2015*. New Delhi: Ministry of Skill Development and Entrepreneurship, 2015.

Government of India. *Note on Handloom Sector*. New Delhi: Development Commissioner Handlooms, December 31, 2015.

Government of India. *Prayas: A Compilation of Success Stories of Handloom Clusters*. New Delhi: Ministry of Textiles, 2016.

Government of India. *Price Policy for Kharif Crops: Marketing Season 2016–17*. New Delhi: Commission on Agricultural Costs and Prices, Ministry of Agriculture, March, 2016.

Government of India. *Quarterly Report on Changes in Employment in Selected Sectors (Oct, 2014 to Dec, 2014)*. New Delhi: Ministry of Labour and Employment, 2015. Available at: http://labour. gov.in/content/reports/QES_24th_final.pdf

Government of India. Report of the Department Related Parliamentary Standing Committee on Science and Technology, Environment and Forests. Placed in the parliament on 26 February 2016.

Government of India. *Revised Draft Report on "Evolving a National Statistical Reporting Mechanism for Social Progress in the Country."* New Delhi: Social Statistics Division, Central Statistics Office, Ministry of Statistics and Programme Implementation, 2015.

Gulati, Ashok, Surbhi Jain, and Nidhi Satija. "Rising Farm Wages in India The 'Pull' and 'Push' Factors." *Discussion Paper* 5, New Delhi: Commission for Agricultural Costs and Prices, Department of Agriculture and Cooperation, Ministry of Agriculture, Government of India, April, 2013.

Holmes, R., S. Rath, and N. Sadana. "An Opportunity for Change? Gender Analysis of the Mahatma Gandhi National Rural Employment Guarantee Act." *Project Briefing* 53. London: Overseas Development Institute, 2011.

IFMR LEAD. *Mission Brief* prepared as part of the study: *Implementation of the National Action Plan on Climate Change (NAPCC): Progress and Evaluation*. Chennai/New Delhi: IFMR LEAD, 2015.

IFMR LEAD. *Why Small Farmers in Tamil Nadu Borrow Money at 60 times Interest*. Chennai/ New Delhi: IFMR LEAD, 2016. Available at: Indiaspend.org.

Independent Evaluation Group. Adapting to Climate Change: Assessing the World Bank Group Experience (Advance Edition). Phase III. Washington, D.C.: World Bank, 2013.

Institute for Policy Research. *Annual Policy Review April 2015–March 2016*. PRS Legislative Research, Institute for Policy Research Studies, 2016.

International Chamber for Service Industry. "Potential of Service Sector Catering to Domestic and International Demand—Presentation in *Advantage North East Conference*, International Chamber for Service Industry, New Delhi, February 2016.

International Labour Organisation. *India Labour Market Update July 2016*. New Delhi: International Labour Organisation, India Country Office, 2016.

KPMG and FICCI. *North East India: Economically and Socially Inclusive Development*. Mumbai: KPMG and FICCI, November, 2015.

Labour Bureau. *Quarterly Report on Changes in Employment in Selected Sectors (October, 2015 to December, 2015)*. Shimla: Labour Bureau.

Leitch, Helen. *Producer Companies in India: Potential to Support Productivity Profitability of Poor Smallholder Farmers*, World Bank, 2014.

Mahajan, Vijay. *State of India's Livelihoods Report 2014*. Chapter No. 5. Farmer producer Companies. New Delhi: SAGE Publications, 2014.

Mathew, Hans Verghese. "Flaws in the UIDAI Process." *Economic and Political Weekly* 51, no. 9 (February 27, 2016).

Mehrotra, Santosh, Ankita Gandhi, and Bimal Sahoo. "Estimating the Skill Gap on a Realistic Basis for 2022." *IAMR Occasional Paper No. 1/2013*. Institute of Applied Manpower Research, Planning Commission, Government of India, February, 2013.

Mehrotra, Santosh. "The Private Sector's Commitment to the National Skill Development Programme is Shaky." The Wire. Available at http://thewire.in (accessed on May 31, 2016).

Meky, Muna Salih. *Skills Development Programs in India: Labor Market Impacts and Effectiveness Findings of an Evaluation Study*. Washington, D.C.: World Bank, 2015.

Ministry of Agriculture, Government of India. *Annual Report 2013–14, 2014–15, 2015–16*. Ministry of Agriculture.

Ministry of Agriculture, Government of India. Annual Report, 2014–15, Department of Animal Husbandry, Dairying & Fisheries Ministry of Agriculture, Government of India.

Ministry of Agriculture, Government of India. *Outcome Budget 2014–15, 2015–15*. Ministry of Agriculture.

Ministry of Agriculture, Government of India. *Pocket Book on Agricultural Statistics 2016*. Ministry of Agriculture.

Ministry of Finance, Government of India. *Annual Report 2013–14, 2014–15, 2015–16*. Ministry of Finance.

Ministry of Finance, Government of India. *Economic Survey 2013–14, 14–15, 14–16*. Ministry of Finance, Government of India, July 2014.

Ministry of Finance, Government of India. *Outcome Budget 2014–15, 2015–16*. Ministry of Finance.

Ministry of Finance, Government of India. *Union Budget February 2012, 2013, 2014, 2015, 2016*. Ministry of Finance, Government of India.

Ministry of Housing & Urban Poverty Alleviation, Government of India. *Annual Report 2014–15, 2015–16*. Ministry of Housing & Urban Poverty Alleviation.

Ministry of Labour and Employment, Government of India. *Annual Report 2013–14, 2014–15, 2015–16*. Ministry of Labour and Employment.

Ministry of Labour and Employment, Government of India. *Outcome Budget 2014–15, 2015–16*. Ministry of Labour and Employment.

Ministry of Medium Small and Micro Enterprises Government of India. *Annual Report 2013–14, 2014–15, 2015–16*. Ministry of Medium Small and Micro Enterprises, GoI.

Ministry of Medium Small and Micro Enterprises, Government of India. *Outcome Budget 2014–15, 2015–16*. Ministry of Medium Small and Micro Enterprises.

Ministry of Rural Development, Government of India. *Annual Report 2013–14, 2014–15, 2015–16*. Ministry of Rural Development.

Ministry of Rural Development, Government of India. *Presentation to Performance Review Committee*. DDU-GKY, MORD, GOI, July, 2016, Available at: http://ddugky.gov.in/ddugky/DocumentsForDownload/PRC_9_July_2016.pdf (accessed on 1 August 2016).

Ministry of Rural Development, Government of India. *Programme Guidelines*. DDU-GKY, Ministry of Rural Development, Government of India, 2015.

Ministry of Statistics and Programme Implementation, Government of India. *Key Indicators of Land and Livestock Holdings in India*. NSS 70th Round, NSSO, Ministry of Statistics and Programme Implementation, GOI. December 2014.

Ministry of Statistics and Programme Implementation, Government of India. *Key Indicators of Situation of Agricultural Households in India*. NSSO Survey 70th Round, NSSO, Ministry of Statistics and Programme Implementation, GOI, December 2014.

Ministry of Statistics and Programme Implementation, Government of India. *Key Indicators of Situation of Agricultural Households in India*. NSSO Survey 59th Round, NSSO, Ministry of Statistics and Programme Implementation, GOI, December 2004.

Ministry of Statistics and Programme Implementation, Government of India. *Key Indicators of Debt and Investment in India*. NSS Survey 70th Round, NSSO, Ministry of Statistics and Programme Implementation, GOI, December 2014.

Ministry of Statistics and Programme Implementation, Government of India. *Informal Sector and Conditions of Employment in India*. NSS 68th Round, Ministry of Statistics and Programme Implementation, GOI, July 2014.

Ministry of Statistics and Programme Implementation, Government of India *Key Indicators of Urban Slums in India*. NSS 68th Round, Ministry of Statistics and Programme Implementation, GOI, 2015.

Ministry of Textiles, Government of India. *Annual Report 2014–15, 2015–16*. Ministry of Textiles.

Ministry of Textiles, Government of India. *Outcome Budget 2014–15*. Ministry of Textiles.

MUDRA Bank. *Review of Performance of Pradhan Mantri Mudra Yojana*. MUDRA Bank 2016. Available at: http://www.mudra.org.in/

Muraleedharan, Sarada. MGNREGS and Kerala: The Untold Story. UNDP, ftp://ftp.solutionexchange-un.net.in/public/gen/cr/res22031301.pdf,

N. Srinivasan. *State of Rural Finance in India*. New Delhi: Oxford University Press, 2016.

NABARD. *Guidelines for Preparation of Detailed Project Reports by Project Facilitating Agencies for Climate Proofing*. Mumbai: NABARD, 2016.

NABARD. *Status of Microfinance in India 2015–16*. Mumbai: NABARD.

NABARD. *The System of Crop Intensification*. Mumbai: Department of Economic Analysis and Research, NABARD Head Office, 2016.

Narayanan, N. C., and Nitin Lokhande. "Designed to Falter: MGNREGA Implementation in Maharashtra." *Economic and Political Weekly* 48, no. 26–27 (June 29, 2013).

Narayanan, Sudha, and Upasak Das. "Women Participation and Rationing in the Employment Gurantee Scheme." *Economic and Political Weekly* 49, no. 46 (November 15, 2014).

National Bank for Agriculture and Rural Development, Government of India. *Annual Report 2013–14, 2014–15, 2015–16*. National Bank for Agriculture and Rural Development.

National Institution for Transforming India (NITI) "Union Budget 2015–16: Central Plan." *NITI Brief No.* 2. National Institution for Transforming India (NITI), 2015.

Nayak, Amar K. J. R. All India Baseline Study on Producer Companies & Contract Farming Practices, 2014.

NHDC. *Report on Market Research for Promotion of India Handloom Brand*. New Delhi: NHDC, 2016.

Panda, Bhagirathi. "National Rural Employment Guarantee Scheme Development Practice at the Crossroads." *Economic and Political Weekly* l, no. 23 (June 6, 2015).

Punj, Shweta, and M. G. Arun. "Where Are the Jobs." *India Today*, April 20, 2016.

Rabo Bank. "Joining Both Ends of the Supply Chain." Rabo Bank Industry Note No. 500. Rabo bank, July 2015.

Ranaware, Krushna, Upasak Das, Ashwini Kulkarni, and Sudha Narayanan. "MGNREGA Works and their Impacts: A Study of Maharashtra." *Economic and Political Weekly* 50, no. 13 (March 28, 2015).

Rangarajan, C., and S. Mahendra Dev. "How Deep is Indian Poverty." *Indian Express*, December 15, 2015.

RBI (Reserve Bank of India). *Annual Report 2013–14, 2014–15, 2015–16* Reserve Bank of India.

RBI. *Report of the Committee on Medium-term Path on November 2015 Financial Inclusion*. RBI Website.

Reddy, V. R., M. S. Reddy, and S. K. Rout. "Groundwater Governance: A Tale of Three Participatory Models in Andhra Pradesh." *Water Alternatives* 7, no. 2 (2014): 275–297.

Saha, Debabrata, and R. C. Sundriyal. "Perspectives of Tribal Communities on NTFP Resource Use in a Global Hotspot: Implications for Adaptive Management." *Journal of Natural Sciences Research* 3, no.4 (2013).

Sen, Kunal. *Success and Failure in MGNREGA Implementation in India*. Manchester: Effective States and Inclusive Development, 2014.

Shah, Mihir, Neelakshi Mann, and Varad Pande, ed. and comp. *MGNREGA Sameeksha: An Anthology of Research Studies on the Mahatma Gandhi National Rural Employment Guarantee Act, 2005 2006–2012*. New Delhi: Orient BlackSwan, 2012.

Shah, Tushaar, and Avinash Kishore. *Solar-powered Pump Irrigation and India's Groundwater Economy: A Preliminary Discussion of Opportunities and Threats*. Colombo: IWMI, 2012.

Sharma, Vipin. State of India's Livelihoods—Access Development Services—2012. New Delhi: SAGE Publications, 2012.

Singh, Sukhpal and Tarunvir Singh. Producer Companies in India: A Study of Organization and Performance, Centre for Management in Agriculture, Indian Institute Management, Ahmedabad, 2013.

Srinivasan, Girija, and N.Srinivasan. *State of Livelihoods India Report 2015*. Access Development Services. New Delhi: SAGE Publications, 2015.

State of India's Livelihoods—Access Development Services—2013. New Delhi: SAGE Publications, 2013.

State of India's Livelihoods—Access Development Services—2014. New Delhi: SAGE Publications, 2014.

Swantini. Skill Development in India–Present Status and Recent Developments. Available at: www.swantini.in.

Tanusree, Shaw. "A Study of the Present Situation of the Traditional Handloom Weavers of

Tashina Esteves, K. V. Rao, Bhaskar Sinha, S. S. Roy, Bhaskar Rao, Shashidharkumar Jha, Ajay Bhan Singh, et al. "Agricultural and Livelihood Vulnerability Reduction through the MGNREGA." *Economic and Political Weekly* 48, no. 52 (December 28, 2013).

The Hindu. "Aadhaar-based Biometric Authentication: Dark Clouds over the PDS." *The Hindu*, September 10, 2016.

Third Bi-monthly Monetary Policy Statement. August 10, 2016. Mumbai: RBI.

Varanasi." *International Research Journal of Social Sciences* 4, no. 3 (March, 2015): 48–53.

Venkateswarlu, B., Shalander Kumar, Sreenath Dixit, Ch. Srinivasa Rao, K. D. Kokate, and A. K. Singh. *Demonstration of Climate Resilient Technologies on Farmers' Fields: Action Plan for 100 Vulnerable Districts*. Hyderabad: Central Research Institute for Dry land Agriculture, 2012.

Verma, Shilp, Sunderrajan Krishnan, Ankith Reddy V., and K. Rajendra Reddy. *Andhra Pradesh Farmer Managed Groundwater Systems (APFAMGS): A Reality Check*. Colombo: IWMI, 2012.

Vijay Shankar, P. S., Himanshu Kulkarni, and Sunderrajan Krishnan. "India's Groundwater Challenge and the Way Forward." *Economic and Political Weekly* 46, no. 2 (January 8, 2011): 37.

Viswanathan, Brinda. "Enumeration of Crafts Persons in India." *Monograph* 24/2-13. Chennai: Madras School of Economics, February 2013.

Vittal, K. P. R., H. P. Singh, K. V. Rao, K. L. Sharma, U. S. Victor, G. R. Chary, G. R. M. Sankar, J. S. Samra, and Gurbachan Singh. *Guidelines on Drought Coping Plans for Rain-fed Production Systems.* Hyderabad: Central Research Institute for Dry-land Agriculture, 2003.

Vyas, Mahesh. "264 Million is India's Demographic Dividend." Centre for Monitoring Indian Economy (CMIE) website.

Wheebox. *India Skills Report 2016.* In partnership with PeopleStrong, CII, LinkedIn and Association of Indian Universities.

World Bank. "Climate Change Impacts in Drought and Flood Affected Areas: Case Studies in India." *Report No.* 43946-IN. Washington, D.C.: The World Bank, June, 2008.

World Bank. *Deep Wells and Prudence: Towards Pragmatic Action for Addressing Groundwater Overexploitation in India.* Washington, D.C.: World Bank, 2010.

World Economic Forum. "The Future of Jobs: Employment, Skills and Workforce Strategy for the Fourth Industrial Revolution." *Global Challenge Insight Report.* Cologny: World Economic Forum, January, 2016.

WOTR. *System of Crop Intensification—A Step Towards Climate Resilience.* WOTR, 2015.

About the Sponsors

National Bank for Agriculture and Rural Development

MISSION
Promotion of sustainable and equitable agriculture and rural development through effective credit support, related services, institution development and other innovative initiatives.

Major Activities

- Credit Functions: Refinance for production credit (Short Term) and investment credit (Medium and Long Term) to eligible banks and financing institutions
- Development Functions: To reinforce the credit functions and make credit more productive, development activities are being undertaken through:

  - ✓ Research and Development Fund
  - ✓ Financial Inclusion Fund (FIF)
  - ✓ Financial Inclusion Technology Fund (FITF)
  - ✓ Farm Innovation and Promotion Fund (FIPF)
  - ✓ Farmers' Technology Transfer Fund (FTTF)
  - ✓ Watershed Development Fund (WDF)
  - ✓ Rural Infrastructure Development Fund (RIDF)
  - ✓ Tribal Development Fund (TDF)
  - ✓ Cooperative Development Fund (CDF)
  - ✓ Rural Innovation Fund

- Supervisory Functions: NABARD shares with RBI certain regulatory and supervisory functions in respect of Cooperative Banks and RRBs.
- Provides consultancy services relating to Agriculture & Rural Development (nabcons@vsnl.net)

NABARD Head Office
Plot No. C-24, G-Block, Bandra Kurla Complex, Post Box No – 8121, Bandra (E), Mumbai – 400051
Visit us at: www.nabard.org

Rabobank Group

Rabobank Group ("Rabobank") is an international full-range financial services provider founded on co-operative principles more than 110 years ago. Headquartered in the Netherlands, the Group's operations include banking, asset management, leasing, insurance and real estate services, serving over 8 million clients in 40 countries. Internationally the Group's focus is providing financial solutions to food and agribusiness companies and commodity traders. In the Netherlands, Rabobank is a market leader in financial services, catering to all sectors.

In terms of core Tier-1 capital (the core measure of a bank's financial strength from a regulator's point of view), Rabobank is among the world's 30 largest financial institutions and is consistently awarded a high rating by all rating agencies. As per December 31, 2015, Rabobank had EUR 670 billion in assets, with a net profit of EUR 2.2 billion and core Tier-1 ratio of 16.4%.

The Rabobank Foundation was established in 1973 as an independent foundation. The organization is funded by local member Rabobanks and Rabobank Nederland, which donate a small percentage of their profits to the Rabobank Foundation. The Rabobank Foundation helps underprivileged and disadvantaged people to become economically active and independent. The support provided by the Rabobank Foundation reflects Rabobank's unique history and roots and is consequently focused first and foremost on enabling the development of small co-operatives located in rural regions. This support is provided through donations, loans, trade financing and technical assistance. In line with Rabobank's own co-operative background, the Rabobank Foundation especially focuses on establishing and promoting co-operative savings and loan systems.

About the Authors

Girija Srinivasan is an expert in development finance and rural livelihoods with extensive international experience of consulting, technical assistance, and studies. She had been a development banker for 12 years. She has authored documents and books on community based approaches in finance livelihoods and microfinance. She has authored the Social Performance Report in Microfinance for four years from 2011 to 2014. She had authored the SOIL Report 2015 jointly with N. Srinivasan.

N. Srinivasan has been pursuing his personal interests in financial inclusion, rural finance, and livelihoods after three decades in RBI and NABARD. He is currently active as an expert adviser and international consultant for different principals. He had authored the well-known publication on microfinance—*State of the Sector Report on Microfinance in India* for four years. He has also authored a book on Rural Finance and the 2015 edition of SOIL Report jointly with Girija Srinivasan. He also serves on several industry forums on the themes of financial inclusion, microfinance, and responsible finance.